Understanding Scientific Understanding

OXFORD STUDIES IN PHILOSOPHY OF SCIENCE

General Editor:
   Paul Humphreys, University of Virginia

Advisory Board
   Anouk Barberousse (European Editor)
   Robert W. Batterman
   Jeremy Butterfield
   Peter Galison
   Philip Kitcher
   Margaret Morrison
   James Woodward

Understanding Scientific Understanding

HENK W. DE REGT

OXFORD
UNIVERSITY PRESS

Oxford University Press is a department of the University of Oxford. It furthers
the University's objective of excellence in research, scholarship, and education
by publishing worldwide. Oxford is a registered trade mark of Oxford University
Press in the UK and certain other countries.

Published in the United States of America by Oxford University Press
198 Madison Avenue, New York, NY 10016, United States of America.

CIP data is on file at the Library of Congress
ISBN 978–0–19–065291–3

For Pieter and Daan

Contents

Preface

THIS BOOK HAS been long in the making. I started writing in the academic
year 2009–2010, when I had the privilege to spend a year as a Lorentz Fellow
at the Netherlands Institute for Advanced Study (NIAS) in Wassenaar. But it
incorporates results that have been achieved over an even longer period of
time. In fact, I started thinking about scientific understanding already during my PhD research at the Vrije Universiteit Amsterdam in the early 1990s,
when I studied the work of Erwin Schrödinger, especially his views on visualizability as a condition for scientific theories. A few years later, after having
completed my PhD thesis, Dennis Dieks encouraged me to generalize my
previous work on Schrödinger and to make it the starting point of a research
project on the intelligibility of theories in modern physics. This research
was carried out at Utrecht University, during a three-year postdoctoral project funded by the Netherlands Organization for Scientific Research (NWO).
Subsequently, I broadened the scope of my research even more in the five-year
research program "Understanding Scientific Understanding," also funded by
NWO and carried out at the Vrije Universiteit Amsterdam in the years 2001–
2006. The aim of this program was to develop a theory of scientific understanding, a topic that had been neglected by philosophers of science. The
two PhD students in this research program, Sabina Leonelli and Kai Eigner,
helped to broaden the perspective by including projects on understanding in
biology and psychology. This book presents my share in that program, and its
case studies focus on physics. As a result of a research program that started in
2001, it is the fruit of at least fifteen years of research in philosophy of science.

The book presents the philosophical theory of scientific understanding
that I have developed in the course of these years, plus some detailed historical case studies in support of this theory. My motivation for constructing
it was that no such theory existed in philosophy of science. Of course, I was
not the first philosopher who observed that understanding is a central aim
of science, but earlier discussions of understanding turned out to be rather

superficial, in the sense that they did not really address the notion of under-standing itself but focused on the related notion of explanation. For example, in the preface to his seminal 1984 book *Scientific Explanation and the Causal Structure of the World*, Wesley Salmon writes that the purpose of his book is to get clear on what scientific understanding is: "Our aim is to understand scientific understanding" (p. ix). However, he immediately adds: "We secure scientific understanding by providing scientific explanations; thus our main concern will be with the nature of explanation." This is typical of the way in which scientific understanding has been treated in philosophy of science until recently. The importance of understanding was acknowledged, but its nature and structure remained unanalyzed. It has been my main goal over the last fifteen years to rectify this situation by developing a philosophical theory of scientific understanding on the basis of a thorough investigation of its role in scientific practice. I am glad to have discovered that I am not on my own but part of a more general trend, as the situation has changed in recent years, with understanding having become a focus of attention both in philosophy of science and in epistemology.

Acknowledgments

MANY PEOPLE HAVE helped and supported me over the years. First and foremost, I would like to thank my mentors and former supervisors Dennis Dieks, Hans Radder, and Peter Kirschenmann, from whom I have learned so much and who have encouraged and inspired me during various stages of my career and my research on understanding. The 2005 paper "A Contextual Theory of Scientific Understanding," in which an earlier version of my theory of understanding is presented and which forms the basis of chapter 4 of this book, was co-authored with Dennis. I owe him a great debt of gratitude for his part in the development of the contextual theory of understanding. Ever since they supervised my PhD research, Hans and Peter have had a strong influence on my thinking about science. Our countless discussions on a great variety issues in philosophy of science, and their feedback on my papers and draft chapters, have been very useful to me and I am enormously grateful to them for this. Thanks are also due to my PhD students Sabina Leonelli and Kai Eigner, who participated in my research program and have contributed to its success in important ways. Over the years, versions of chapters have been presented and discussed in our departmental research group Philosophy of Science and Technology. I thank its members—in particular Edwin Koster, Huib Looren de Jong, David Ludwig, Gerben Meynen, and Jeroen de Ridder—for their continuous interest in and feedback on my work.

I am grateful to the many colleagues with whom I have exchanged ideas about scientific understanding and related philosophical topics. I cannot mention them all but they include (in alphabetical order): Christoph Baumberger, Hein van den Berg, Soazig le Bihan, Mieke Boon, Marcel Boumans, Jeremy Butterfield, Hasok Chang, Heather Douglas, Igor Douven, Steffen Ducheyne, Dingmar van Eck, Kate Elgin, Jan Faye, Victor Gijsbers, Stephen Grimm, Sebastian de Haro, Frank Hindriks, Kareem Khalifa, Maarten Kleinhans, Theo Kuipers, Janneke van Lith, Frans van Lunteren, Caterina Marchionni, James McAllister, F. A. Muller, Wendy Parker, Arthur Petersen, Sabine Roeser,

Samuel Schindler, Michael Strevens, Mauricio Suárez, Paul Teller, Jos Uffink, Erik Weber, Daniel Wilkenfeld, and René van Woudenberg.

The actual realization of the book manuscript has been made possible through the support of a number of institutions and individuals, to whom I am very grateful. First of all, the Netherlands Institute for Advanced Study (NIAS) provided an ideal environment for scholars who want to devote their time to researching and writing a book. I thank the NIAS staff and fellows of the academic year 2009–2010, and in particular Kees Ruys, who has since then become a dear friend. I am also indebted to the Netherlands Organization for Scientific Research (NWO), which provided the financial support for a large part of the research on which this book is based, and to Paul Humphreys and Peter Ohlin, Oxford University Press, for their encouragement to submit my manuscript to OUP and for their continuing support over the years. With the support of a grant from the Varieties of Understanding Project at Fordham University and the John Templeton Foundation, I was able to complete the manuscript. I thank Bas Jongeling for correcting my English, Joost van Ommen for his help with the illustrations, Paul van Acker for supplying the cover image, Andrew Ward for his assistance during the production process, Lynn Childress for editing the manuscript, and two anonymous reviewers for comments on previous versions of the text.

Finally, my warmest thanks go to those who are closest and most important to me, and who encouraged and supported me unfailingly in the long process of writing this book: my sons Pieter and Daan, and above all my wife and companion in life Martien Rienstra.

THIS BOOK DRAWS in part on material that has been published in the following journal articles: "Visualization as a tool for understanding," *Perspectives on Science* 22 (2014): 377–396; "The epistemic value of understanding," *Philosophy of Science* 76 (2009): 585–597; "Wesley Salmon's complementarity thesis: Causalism and unificationism reconciled?" *International Studies in the Philosophy of Science* 20 (2006): 129–147; "A contextual approach to scientific understanding," *Synthese* 144 (2005): 137–170 (with Dennis Dieks); "Discussion note: Making sense of understanding," *Philosophy of Science* 71 (2004): 98–109; "Space-time visualisation and the intelligibility of physical theories," *Studies in History and Philosophy of Modern Physics* 32B (2001): 243–265; "Ludwig Boltzmann's *Bildtheorie* and scientific understanding," *Synthese* 119 (1999): 113–134; "Erwin Schrödinger, *Anschaulichkeit*, and quantum theory," *Studies in History and Philosophy of Modern Physics* 28B (1997): 461–481; "Philosophy and the kinetic theory of gases," *British Journal for the Philosophy of Science* 47 (1996): 31–62.

Understanding Scientific Understanding

1

Introduction

THE DESIRE TO UNDERSTAND

The act of understanding is at the heart of all scientific activity; without it any ostensibly scientific activity is as sterile as that of a high school student substituting numbers into a formula.

—P. W. BRIDGMAN, *Reflections of a Physicist* (1950, 72)

IT MIGHT SEEM a commonplace to say that the aim of science is to provide understanding of the world around us. Scientists and laypeople alike will typically regard understanding as one of the most important and highly valued products of scientific research and teaching. Indeed, science appears to be quite successful in achieving this aim: Who would doubt that science has given us understanding of such diverse phenomena as the motions of the heavenly bodies, the tides, the weather, earthquakes, the formation of rocks and fossils, electricity and magnetism, and the evolution of species? Climate scientists, who strive to understand the process of global warming and other climate changes, provide a contemporary example of the centrality of understanding as an aim of science. The main task of the Intergovernmental Panel on Climate Change (IPCC) is to assess progress in scientific understanding of the climate system and climate change, as can be gleaned from its 2007 report. In the one-page introduction of the technical summary of *Climate Change 2007: The Physical Science Basis* (IPCC 2012), the terms "understand" or "understanding" are used nine times. Here is a typical passage:

> While this report provides new and important policy-relevant information on the *scientific understanding* of climate change, the complexity of the climate system and the multiple interactions that determine its behaviour impose limitations on our ability to *understand* fully the

future course of Earth's global climate. There is still an incomplete *physical understanding* of many components of the climate system and their role in climate change. (IPCC 2012; italics added)

But what does it mean to seek or to achieve such understanding? What exactly is scientific understanding? This is the question that this book aspires to answer. It is first and foremost a philosophical question, and one that has indeed been addressed by philosophers of science in the context of the long-standing debate about scientific explanation. Wesley Salmon, one of the key figures in this debate, spent the greater part of his career developing a philosophical account of scientific explanation. As he emphasized in his essay "The importance of scientific understanding" (1998, 79–91), the principal goal of scientific explanation is the production of understanding of events and phenomena. Salmon's own theory, which will be discussed in detail in chapter 3, focuses on causal explanations, highlighting the fact that understanding is often achieved by uncovering the causes of phenomena. While there are alternative philosophical views of how scientific understanding is attained through scientific explanations, most philosophers agree on the idea that understanding—whatever its precise nature—is a central aim of science.[1]

The question of the nature of scientific understanding is also a historical question: to answer it we can do no better than look at how scientific research has actually produced understanding in the course of its historical development. Indeed, science as a historical phenomenon may be defined with reference to the notion of understanding: it is traditionally presumed that science was born in ancient Greece, when Ionian philosophers of nature—in particular Thales of Miletus and his school—first adopted what may be called a naturalistic approach to explaining natural phenomena: they abandoned the idea that nature is subject to the capricious will of supernatural gods and thereby beyond human comprehension, and instead assumed that observed phenomena can be understood in terms of natural causes and laws. This important change in the attitude toward nature has been emphasized, for instance, by the physicist Erwin Schrödinger. In his 1948 Shearman Lectures, delivered at University College, London, which were later published under the title *Nature and the Greeks*, he stated:

---

1. Note that the term "understanding" can be used in various ways, both in and outside science. I am specifically concerned with *explanatory understanding*: the understanding of why a phenomenon occurs that results from a scientific explanation of that phenomenon. Other types of understanding, such as objectual understanding, understanding-how and understanding-that, will not be discussed in this book. See Baumberger et al. (2017) for an overview of notions of understanding in epistemology and philosophy of science.

> The grand idea that informed these men was that the world around them was something *that could* be *understood*, if one only took the trouble to observe it properly. . . . They saw the world as a rather complicated mechanism, acting according to eternal innate laws, which they were curious to find out. This is, of course, the fundamental attitude of science up to this day. (Schrödinger [1954] 1996, 57)

The prospect of understanding forms the basis of most—if not all—Greek natural philosophy since Thales. It is, for example, fundamental to Aristotle's philosophical work. "All men by nature desire to know," reads the famous opening sentence of his *Metaphysics* in the well-known translation by W. D. Ross. In his introduction to Aristotle's philosophy, however, Jonathan Lear argues that Aristotle's words are better interpreted as referring to a desire to understand: "To have *epistēmē* one must not only know a thing, one must also grasp its cause or explanation. This is to understand it: to know in a deep sense what it is and how it has come to be" (Lear 1988, 6). It was therefore the idea that humans can understand nature that sparked the development of science.

1.1 Scientific understanding: diversity and disagreement

My aim in this book is to investigate and explicate the nature of the understanding that science can provide. A first question that may be asked in this context is: Are there universal, timeless criteria for scientific understanding? Even a cursory look at the history of science suggests that the answer is: no. As a first illustration, I will sketch an episode from the history of physics in which discussions about understanding played a crucial role: the genesis of quantum mechanics in the 1920s, which involved heated debates about the intelligibility of this theory and the related question of whether it can provide understanding of the phenomena in the domain of atomic physics. This case shows that scientists' standards of intelligibility and understanding vary strongly—not only diachronically but also synchronically. (The episode will be analyzed in detail in chapter 7; more historical evidence for the thesis that criteria for understanding vary will be given in chapters 5 and 6).

The first quantum theory of atomic structure was developed by Niels Bohr, who presented it in his famous papers of 1913 and 1918. It included an atomic model that was problematic in various respects—both empirically and conceptually—and in the early 1920s many physicists attempted to improve Bohr's theory. After a number of years when not much progress was made, two new, rival quantum theories of the atom appeared on the scene: in July 1925 Werner Heisenberg submitted a paper which contained the foundations of matrix mechanics, and in early 1926 Erwin Schrödinger published a series of papers in which he presented wave mechanics as an alternative to matrix mechanics. Heisenberg's theory was intended to describe only relations between observable quantities, such as the frequencies and intensities of spectral lines emitted by atoms; it did not provide a concrete picture or model of the internal structure of atoms. Thus, it was a highly abstract theory which, moreover, was based on a type of mathematics—matrix theory—that most physicists were unfamiliar with at the time. Schrödinger's wave mechanics, by contrast, suggested the possibility of a visualizing atomic structure: his theory described the atom in terms of wave phenomena. Also, the mathematics of his theory was simpler and more familiar to physicists than that of matrix mechanics: it was based on wave equations, which were part and parcel of university physics teaching.

Immediately, proponents of the two theories engaged in intense, sometimes even emotional discussions on the question of which theory was superior. It was Schrödinger who brought the notions of understanding and intelligibility to the center of the debate, claiming that his wave mechanics was much better in providing true understanding of the phenomena, over and above mere description and prediction. Schrödinger expressed a strong commitment to the view that visualization is a necessary condition for scientific understanding: "We cannot really alter our manner of thinking in space and time, and what we cannot comprehend within it we cannot understand at all" (Schrödinger 1928, 27). Accordingly, he argued, only theories that are visualizable in space and time are intelligible and can give us understanding of phenomena. Schrödinger was not alone in this respect: many physicists supported the idea that understanding requires visualization and space-time description. Therefore, according to Schrödinger, visualizability is a necessary condition for the intelligibility of a scientific theory. Wave mechanics is visualizable (or so Schrödinger suggested) and thereby intelligible; matrix mechanics, by contrast, is not visualizable, and accordingly unintelligible. This was not merely a philosophical point: Schrödinger also argued that visualizable, intelligible theories are more fruitful. Because of its visualizability and its mathematical structure, wave mechanics was more easily applicable to a great variety of physical problem situations. It was therefore more favorably received and—at least initially—empirically more successful than matrix mechanics.

The advocates of matrix mechanics maintained, however, that their theory could yield understanding as well, and they tried to refute Schrödinger's line of reasoning by arguing that intelligibility is not necessarily associated with visualizability. Wolfgang Pauli, who like Heisenberg was a member of Bohr's group, admitted that matrix mechanics was an unusual theory that might indeed appear less intelligible than wave mechanics. However, he claimed that understanding it was a question of becoming familiar with the new conceptual system of the theory. Pauli admitted that the demand for intelligibility is legitimate, but he stated: "It should never count in physics as an argument for the retention of fixed conceptual systems. Once the new conceptual systems are settled, they will also be intelligible" (Pauli 1979, 188). In other words, when future generations of physicists are used to quantum mechanics, they will find it intelligible even though it is not visualizable.

The competition between the two theories ultimately led to their synthesis. On the one hand, Schrödinger's hope for a visualizable interpretation of quantum mechanics was not fulfilled: his atomic model turned out not to be completely visualizable due to specific technical problems (see section 7.3). Heisenberg, on the other hand, abandoned his radically abstract approach and reintroduced visualizable notions, such as position and momentum of electrons, at the atomic level. The combination of matrix and wave mechanics led to quantum mechanics as it is accepted and taught today. With hindsight, it is clear that Schrödinger's thesis that visualizability is a necessary condition for intelligibility must be rejected—there is no a priori relation between understanding and visualization. Still, it does not follow that his ideas were completely misguided and worthless. History only shows that standards of intelligibility and understanding may vary and change. Moreover, as will be argued in more detail in chapter 7, the history of quantum mechanics shows that debates about understanding and intelligibility often stimulate scientific development.

Almost every physicist will agree that understanding is a key aim of science, but there appears to be strong variation in views about what is required for such understanding. The case of quantum theory illustrates this nicely. Even today physicists and philosophers debate the question of whether—and if so, how—quantum mechanics can provide understanding (the many different interpretations of the theory can be seen in this light). Of course, one might think that quantum theory is an exceptional case, being an esoteric, counterintuitive theory that applies to a remote domain of reality. Thus, Richard Feynman famously stated that nobody understands quantum mechanics. Of atomic behavior he said: "Even the experts do not understand it the way they would like to, and it is perfectly reasonable that they should not, because all of direct, human experience and of human intuition applies to large objects" (Feynman et al. 1963–1965, 3:1 –1). While quantum theory surely is a strange theory, the fact that scientists disagree about its intelligibility is not exceptional: as the other case studies in this book will show, the history of physics abounds with debates about the intelligibility of theories and criteria for scientific understanding.

1.2 Integrating history and philosophy of scientific understanding

It was the observation of historical controversies such as the one sketched in section 1.1, and the failure of existing philosophical theories of explanation and understanding to deal with them, that inspired the study that has resulted in this book. The problem appears to be that traditional philosophical accounts of explanation are typically uninformed by historical and empirical studies of science. The debate about explanation in the philosophy of science is—notwithstanding the rejection of Carl Hempel's covering law model—still very much in line with the logical empiricist tradition, with the consequence that (1) philosophical analyses of scientific explanation ignore the variation among (past and present) scientists' views of how explanatory understanding is achieved; and (2) while paying lip service to the idea that good scientific explanations produce understanding, they regard the notions of understanding and intelligibility as philosophically irrelevant and accordingly neglect debates about understanding in actual scientific practice (see chapters 2 and 3).

This book presents a philosophical theory of scientific understanding that sheds light on episodes like the one I have sketched. It is a philosophical study but it also contains detailed historical case studies of scientific practice. In contrast to existing philosophical studies of the topic, it takes into account scientists' own views about explanation and understanding and analyzes their role in scientific debate and development. The aim of the book is to develop and defend a theory of understanding that describes criteria for understanding actually employed in scientific practice and explains their function and historical variation.

The way in which this study approaches its subject differs fundamentally from mainstream philosophical discussions of explanatory understanding (which are scarcely informed by historical and empirical studies of science). Combining systematic philosophical analysis with historical case studies, the book stands in the tradition of history and philosophy of science (HPS). The HPS tradition has its roots in the early 1960s, when scholars like Norwood Russell Hanson, Stephen Toulmin, Paul Feyerabend, and Thomas Kuhn based their philosophical analyses of science on serious study of the history of science. Despite the enormous impact of Kuhn's work, the idea of combining historical and philosophical study of science into a single discipline, HPS, was not without difficulties, and from the 1980s onward it appeared that historians and philosophers were parting ways again. In recent years, however, the ideal of HPS has been revived and currently new attempts are being made to flesh it out and develop it into truly integrated history and philosophy of science.[2]

A serious problem for the HPS approach was, and still is, the question of how historical studies of science can be used to bolster a philosophical claim about science. This problem has been pinpointed by Joseph Pitt as "the dilemma of case studies":

> What do appeals to case studies accomplish? Consider the dilemma: On the one hand, if the case is selected because it exemplifies the philosophical point, then it is not clear that the historical data hasn't been manipulated to fit the point. On the other hand, if one starts with a case study, it is not clear where to go from there—for it is unreasonable to generalize from one case or even two or three. (Pitt 2001, 373)

In other words, the philosopher who uses case studies is either guilty of "cherry-picking" or of overgeneralization. A skeptical reader might think that my study of scientific understanding cannot but fall prey to this dilemma, since this book presents a philosophical theory of scientific understanding plus a number of historical case studies, suggesting that the theory has been developed on the basis of the historical material and that the case studies exemplify the theory.

This worry is unfounded, however, because Pitt's dilemma rests on a misguided view of the relation between philosophy and history of science. It assumes what Jutta Schickore (2011) calls the "confrontational model of HPS," on which philosophical theories of science have to be confronted with historical data. Much scholarly work in the HPS tradition (such as that of Imre Lakatos and his followers, and that of Larry Laudan) was based on this model, and this is understandable, because a key motivation for starting HPS was the idea that at the time philosophy of science (in particular, logical empiricism) was out of touch with real science. The idea was to "test" philosophical theories of science against the historical record. While there is nothing wrong

---

2. Since 2007 international conferences on integrated history and philosophy of science are being organized under the acronym & HPS. See Schickore (2011) and Mauskopf and Schmaltz (2012) for reviews of the long-standing debate about integrating history and philosophy of science, and for assessments of the current state of the art in HPS.

with this motivation—indeed, I believe that philosophy of science should take account of the actual practices of past and present science—there are serious difficulties with the simple confrontational model. The main source of problems is that the model conceives the relation between philosophy and history of science in terms of the relation between theory and data, comparable to the theory-data relation in the sciences themselves. It assumes that philosophers want to/can/should make general claims about the nature of science, while historians merely want to/can/should describe specific historical episodes.

This simple view of philosophical and historical study of science is untenable because, on the one hand, universal philosophical theories of science are bound to fail, and, on the other hand, purely theory-neutral descriptions of historical episodes are impossible.[3] The former point follows from the fact that science, as a historical entity, is subject to change: not only is our current scientific knowledge different from that of, say, one or two centuries ago, our idea of what science is, what its methods are, and so on has also altered in the course of the centuries. Thus, a universal (static) philosophical account of the nature of science for all times is a chimera.[4] The latter point follows from the fact that it is impossible to write history of science without at least some philosophical conceptions about the nature of science. Any historical study of an episode in the history of science must assume, first of all, some idea of what science is in order to select relevant historical data, and furthermore, employ more specific philosophical notions (e.g., regarding the nature of scientific theory, observation, experiment, explanation, etc.) in order to interpret the data and construct a coherent narrative out of them.

These observations suggest that a different model of HPS is needed, one that truly integrates history and philosophy instead of merely confronting them. If it is acknowledged that philosophical analysis and historical study of science have to be inextricably intertwined, an integrated HPS will emerge that results in the dissolution of Pitt's dilemma. This study of scientific understanding aspires to exemplify such an integrated approach.

Several scholars have attempted to formulate an integrated HPS approach that transcends the confrontational model. Schickore argues that the study of

---

3. These problems echo problems at the level of science itself, in particular, problems of induction and theory-ladenness of observation. But they are even more troublesome at the meta-level because every historical case is unique and historical study always involves interpretation.

4. This would also apply to a universal philosophical theory of science that ignores differences between scientific disciplines. Just as the nature of science varies throughout history, it varies across disciplines.

science (for which she uses the term "metascientific analysis") should adopt a hermeneutic approach: "Initial case judgments—judgments that identify portions of the historical record as noteworthy—and provisional analytic concepts are gradually reconciled until they are brought into equilibrium" (Schickore 2011, 471). Thus, philosophical analysis and historical research should continuously and mutually interact. Applied to the topic of this book, this approach implies starting with a particular historical episode selected on the basis of our initial view of scientific understanding, and then investigating this case using our preliminary philosophical conceptions of understanding, explanation, intelligibility, etc., as tools for analysis and interpretation. The attempt to construct a coherent narrative may require articulation or modification of the employed philosophical concepts, which can subsequently be applied in other historical case studies. While it is not to be expected that this process converges on a universally valid philosophical conception of scientific understanding, it will most likely generate conceptual tools that are useful for analyzing and interpreting a range of cases of (past and present) scientific practice.

Although he does not use the term "hermeneutic," a comparable approach is defended by Chang (2012), who proposes the following "mode of history-philosophy interaction" as a possible method for integrated HPS:

Existing philosophical framework
- Historiographical puzzle: an episode that is difficult to understand
- Search for a new philosophical framework
- Better understanding of the episode, in the new philosophical framework
- Further development of the new philosophical framework
- Application of the new framework to other episodes

(Chang 2012, 121)[5]

Note that where Schickore designates philosophical concepts as "tools," Chang uses the term "framework," which suggests that philosophy is more than just a resource for writing history of science. I agree with the latter view: philosophy of science can make substantive claims about science that transcend the particular, without immediately lapsing into universalism. This important aim of philosophy has been aptly characterized by Hans Radder (1997, 649) as "exposing and examining structural features that *explain or make sense of non-local patterns* in the development of science." The philosophical theory

---

5. Alternatively, one may start from existing historiography and a philosophical puzzle; see Chang (2012, 122).

of scientific understanding presented in this book should be regarded as a framework that elucidates such non-local patterns.

The research on which my theory is based has roughly followed Chang's procedure, and accordingly also exemplifies the hermeneutic approach advocated by Schickore. I started with the historical episode summarized section 1.1: the genesis of quantum mechanics in the 1920s (in which I had become interested for different reasons). The observation that physicists like Schrödinger, Pauli, and Heisenberg debated whether the various proposed quantum theories were intelligible, what the criteria for intelligibility were, and in what sense, if any, quantum mechanics could provide understanding of the phenomena, was hard to interpret in terms of the framework of traditional philosophy of science, which deemed these issues uninteresting and even irrelevant from an epistemological perspective. Standard philosophical models of scientific explanation largely ignore historical studies of science. But a look at the history of quantum mechanics reveals a "historiographical puzzle for the existing philosophical framework": philosophical questions about explanatory understanding that the historical actors considered highly important and that affected the development of atomic physics in the 1920s, were invisible from the perspective of the traditional philosophy of scientific explanation.

A detailed analysis of the historical episode inspired me to develop a new interpretation of the concept of "intelligibility," which helped me to better understand the historical case (for my first attempt at analyzing the case with the notion of intelligibility, see De Regt 2001). Through an iterative process of further developing the philosophical tools, and applying them to other examples from the practice and history of science, I have developed—in collaboration with Dennis Dieks—a contextual theory of understanding (De Regt and Dieks 2005). Additional historical case studies and systematic inquiry led to further articulation and refinement, but also to substantial modifications, of this theory. This book is the end result of this process, presenting a philosophical framework for the analysis of scientific understanding and a number of case studies using this framework. For the sake of clarity, the philosophical theory is presented first (in chapters 2–4) and the historical case studies are described next (in chapters 5–7). Obviously, this order does not follow the way the study was carried out, and neither does it reflect the justificatory relation between the historical and philosophical aspects. Moreover, chapters 2–4 do present historical examples as well, and chapters 5–7 contain further discussion and articulation of the philosophical framework.

My theory of scientific understanding is a contextual theory because historical studies show that there are no universally valid, timeless standards of explanatory understanding. Nonetheless, the theory does specify a general characterization and criteria for achieving scientific understanding, so that one might ask whether this is consistent with the thesis that conceptions of understanding vary throughout history (and across disciplines). However, there is no contradiction. As long as the general characterization and criteria for understanding include elements that allow for historical and disciplinary variation, it is perfectly well possible to formulate an account that transcends the purely local context (see chapter 4 for further elucidation of the contextuality). It is plausible that, in addition to historical variation, there is also disciplinary variation in concepts and criteria of understanding. The present study focuses on the physical sciences, and the case studies in chapters 5–7 deal with the history of physics only. I submit, however, that the proposed account of understanding may be applicable to the natural sciences more generally, and I present some examples from other sciences to illustrate this claim. But further research should reveal to what extent the theory possesses a wider validity.

Although the empirical evidence on which my philosophical theory is based is first and foremost historical, I will also refer to results from cognitive science and psychology in support of my arguments. Thus, my approach may be regarded as "naturalistic" in the sense that it is based on the idea that philosophy of science should take into account results of empirical studies of science, of which history of science is but one example: sociology and psychology of science may be relevant as well.[6] While I consider empirical findings like these highly relevant for developing a sound philosophical account of explanation, I do not endorse a thoroughly naturalistic position in the spirit of Quine, who championed a complete reduction of philosophy to empirical science. In my view, there should be room for conceptual analysis. Moreover, if the naturalistic approach is conceived as the idea that "the study of science must itself be a science" (Giere 1999, 173), I agree only if it is kept in mind that it is a human science, not a natural science. Accordingly, its methods may differ from those of natural science, as the hermeneutic approach for HPS outlined by Schickore (2011) illustrates.[7]

---

6. For instance, a recent experimental study into the way in which scientists and laypeople classify various cases of explanations confirms the central thesis of this book: intelligibility is crucial for scientific explanation (Waskan et al. 2014).

7. Cf. Radder (1997), who acknowledges that historical study is an important resource for the philosophy of science, but criticizes fully naturalistic approaches and instead promotes the idea that philosophy cannot do without interpretation, normative assessment, and reflexivity.

1.3 Overview

The book begins with an argument against the traditional view—due to Hempel—that understanding is merely a psychological and subjective by-product of explanation, and therefore irrelevant for philosophical analyses of science. In chapter 2, I argue that, by contrast, achieving understanding of phenomena is a central epistemic aim of science. I introduce the notion of intelligibility, defined as the value that scientists attribute to the cluster of qualities that facilitate the use of the theory, and show that it is essential for achieving understanding. Note that on this definition the epithet "intelligible" applies to theories, not to phenomena.[8] Intelligibility is a pragmatic value, but I argue that this does not undermine the objectivity of scientific explanation and understanding. Chapter 3 investigates what existing theories of explanation—such as causal and unificationist models—assert or imply about the nature of understanding. On the basis of a discussion of the merits and problems of these models, I conclude that we have to accept a plurality of types of explanation, and that an overarching theory is needed that explains how each type generates understanding. Wesley Salmon has suggested that causal and unificationist models can be reconciled as complementary ways of achieving understanding, but a critical analysis of his proposal shows that this attempt fails. Instead, a more radically pluralist approach is required. In chapter 4, a contextual theory of scientific understanding is presented, which answers this demand: it accommodates the diversity of types of explanation by showing how various explanatory strategies function as alternative tools to achieve the goal of understanding. It is based on the idea that understanding of phenomena requires intelligible theories, and that scientists need conceptual tools and associated skills to use a particular theory in order to achieve understanding of the phenomena. The availability and acceptability of conceptual tools can change with the historical, social, or disciplinary context. The chapter closes with a discussion of the implications of the theory for the issues of reductionism and scientific realism.

   The second half of the book offers historical case studies that highlight various aspects of the issue of understanding. Chapter 5 focuses on the relation

---

8. Accordingly, to avoid confusion, I will use the terms "intelligibility" and "intelligible" only in connection with the understanding of theories (in quotations, however, these terms sometimes apply to phenomena). The relation between understanding theories and understanding phenomena is crucial to my account of scientific understanding (see section 2.1).

between metaphysical worldviews and scientific understanding. It examines the seventeenth-century debate about the intelligibility of Newton's theory of universal gravitation, and the subsequent development of physicists' views on contact action versus action at a distance in the eighteenth and nineteenth centuries. This case nicely illustrates how criteria for understanding may change in time. Initially, Newton's theory was criticized because it failed to conform to the Cartesian intelligibility ideal of contact action; the idea of forces acting at a distance was unacceptable to most seventeenth-century physicists. But between 1700 and 1850 action at a distance rather than contact action and causal chains dominated the scientific scene, and attempts to formulate theories of gravitation based on contact action were ignored. Only in the second half of the nineteenth century did contact action again become an acceptable explanatory resource. I analyze this episode with the help of a distinction between metaphysical and scientific intelligibility. Chapter 6 examines how mechanical models can provide understanding, by means of a detailed study of the period when mechanical modeling was most prominent in physical science: the nineteenth century. I survey the work and ideas of key representatives of the mechanical approach in physics: William Thomson (Lord Kelvin), James Clerk Maxwell, and Ludwig Boltzmann. These physicists advanced explicit views of the function and status of mechanical models, in particular of their role in providing understanding. Thus, Kelvin famously wrote: "I never satisfy myself until I can make a mechanical model of a thing. If I can make a mechanical model I can understand it" (Kargon and Achinstein 1987, 206). I investigate how such views affected scientific practice, in particular, via a case study of attempts to explain the so-called specific heat anomaly with the help of the kinetic theory of gases. Finally, I examine Boltzmann's mature views on the status and value of mechanical models, specifically his "picture theory" (*Bildtheorie*), which involves a pragmatic conception of understanding that accords with the contextual theory of scientific understanding defended in this book. Chapter 7 discusses the relation between visualizability and intelligibility by means of an in-depth study of the episode that I have briefly discussed: the transition from classical physics to quantum physics in the first quarter of the twentieth century. Focusing on the views and contributions of Niels Bohr, Wolfgang Pauli, Werner Heisenberg, and Erwin Schrödinger, I analyze the debate on the intelligibility of matrix mechanics and wave mechanics. The relation between visualization and understanding is further illustrated by an account of the discovery of electron spin in 1926, and by an exploration of the role of visualization in postwar quantum physics, focusing on the introduction of Feynman diagrams. I conclude that visualiz-ability is but one out of many possible tools for understanding, albeit one that has proved to be very effective in science. Chapter 8 concludes the book with a discussion of the scope of my contextual theory and a reflection on the issues of relativism and normativity.

2

Understanding and the Aims of Science

IN *NATURE AND THE GREEKS,* Schrödinger argues that science is "something special": it is a Greek invention, based on the Greek way of thinking, and it is accordingly, "not the only possible way of thinking about Nature." Subsequently, he asks himself: "What are the peculiar, special traits of our scientific world-picture?" and immediately answers this question as follows:

> About one of these fundamental features there can be no doubt. It is the hypothesis that *the display of Nature can be understood.* . . . It is the non-spiritistic, the non-superstitious, the non-magical outlook. A lot more could be said about it. One would in this context have to discuss the questions: what does comprehensibility really mean, and in what sense, if any, does science give explanations? (Schrödinger [1954] 1996, 90–91)

Schrödinger then observes that philosophers from Hume to Mach to the logical positivists failed to give positive answers to these questions. On the contrary, they argued that scientific theories are merely economical descriptions of observable facts, which do not supply explanations. This view, which was endorsed by most of Schrödinger's physicist colleagues, seems to lead to a strange tension: the basic hypothesis of science, that Nature is understandable, does not seem to have any positive content—it consists merely in a denial of supernatural, nonscientific worldviews.

However, this situation would change very soon: with hindsight, one can say that the year when Schrödinger presented his ideas in his lectures at University College, London, was a turning point in the philosophical attitude toward explanation in science. For it was in 1948 that Carl Hempel and

Paul Oppenheim put the topic of explanation on the philosophical agenda, with their pioneering paper "Studies in the Logic of Scientific Explanation" (reprinted in Hempel 1965). But Hempel, whose covering law model of explanation was to dominate the debate for the next two decades, was still reluctant to talk about understanding. The reason was, as he explained in his 1965 essay "Aspects of Scientific Explanation," that "such expressions as 'realm of understanding' and 'comprehensible' do not belong to the vocabulary of logic, for they refer to the psychological and pragmatic aspects of explanation" (Hempel 1965, 413). In Hempel's logical-empiricist view, the aim of philosophy of science is to give an account of the objective nature of science by means of logical analysis of its concepts. Its psychological and pragmatic aspects may be of interest to historians, sociologists, and psychologists of science (in short, to those who study the phenomenon of science empirically) but should be ignored by philosophers. Since Hempel, philosophers of science have gradually become more willing to discuss the topic of scientific understanding, but it has remained outside the focus of philosophical attention until quite recently.

In this chapter, I will argue—against the traditional view of Hempel and others—that understanding is not merely a psychological byproduct of explanation but in itself a central epistemic aim of science. First, in section 2.1, I investigate in more detail why the notion of understanding has long been neglected by philosophers of science, and I discuss philosophical views that deny an epistemic role to understanding in science. Subsequently, in section 2.2, I challenge these views by arguing that understanding is indeed pragmatic but nonetheless crucial for achieving the epistemic aim of scientific explanation. This thesis is further elaborated in section 2.3, where I analyze pragmatic understanding in terms of the notion of intelligibility and examine the implications for the objectivity of scientific explanation and understanding. Finally, in section 2.4, I argue that understanding is both a means to, and an end of, explanation.

2.1 The neglect of understanding

Why was the theme of scientific understanding ignored by philosophers of science, while the period since World War II witnessed ample discussion of scientific explanation? The debate about explanation started in the logical empiricist tradition, which regarded logical analysis and reconstruction of the finished products of scientific activity as the chief task of philosophy of science. The aim of such reconstructions was to assess the validity of scientific claims to knowledge, and the central logical-empiricist thesis was that only empirical evidence and logic are relevant to the justification of knowledge. Logical empiricism came under serious attack in the early 1960s, but whereas it lost the battle in the domain of scientific methodology (under the influence of Popper and Kuhn and their followers) it has remained dominant in the area of scientific explanation. Although many philosophers of explanation criticized Hempel's covering law model in the 1960s and 1970s, most analyses did not depart radically from the logical-empiricist viewpoint but continued in the same spirit. One aspect of the logical-empiricist philosophy of explanation, voiced explicitly by Hempel, is that understanding and related notions such as intelligibility and comprehensibility lie outside its domain. To be sure, Hempel recognized that there is a relation between explanation and understanding, but he argued that philosophers may—or rather should—ignore the latter because these notions are not logical but psychological and pragmatic. Hempel (1965, 425–433) claimed that understanding belongs to the pragmatic dimension of science, which is irrelevant to the philosophical analysis of science. To begin with, he observed that there exists a pragmatic interpretation of explanation, which surfaces if one conceives of explanation as an activity that has understanding as its goal:

> Very broadly speaking, to explain something to a person is to make it plain and intelligible to him, to make him understand it. Thus construed, the word "explanation" and its cognates are pragmatic terms: their use requires reference to the persons involved in the process of explaining. In a pragmatic context we might say, for example, that a given account A explains fact X to person P_1. We will then have to bear in mind that the same account may well not constitute an explanation of X for another person P_2, who might not even regard X as requiring an explanation, or who might find the account A unintelligible or unilluminating, or irrelevant to what puzzles him about X. Explanation in this pragmatic sense is thus a relative notion: something can be significantly said to constitute an explanation in this sense only for this or that individual. (Hempel 1965, 425–426)

The notions of understanding and intelligibility are pragmatic because they refer to human subjects: the persons (e.g., scientists) who offer or receive the explanatory account. According to Hempel, a pragmatic conception of explanation which includes these notions may perhaps be of interest to empirical scientists, such as psychologists or historians of science, but it is irrelevant to the philosophy of science. In line with logical-empiricist tenets, he held that philosophers of science should occupy themselves only with analysis and assessment of scientific statements (e.g., theories) and their relation to the empirical evidence. The hallmark of scientific knowledge is, in Hempel's view, its objectivity: "proper scientific inquiry and its results may be said to be objective in the sense of being independent of idiosyncratic beliefs and attitudes on the part of the scientific investigators" (Hempel [1983] 2001, 374). Accordingly, philosophical analyses and evaluations of science—for example, of scientific explanation—should uncover the objective relations between theory and evidence, and should therefore abstract from pragmatic issues:

> For scientific research seeks to account for empirical phenomena by means of laws and theories which are objective in the sense that their empirical implications and their evidential support are independent of what particular individuals happen to test or to apply them; and the explanations, as well as the predictions, based upon such laws and theories are meant to be objective in an analogous sense. This ideal intent suggests the problem of constructing a non-pragmatic concept of scientific explanation. (Hempel 1965, 426)

An objectivist account of scientific explanation should avoid pragmatic aspects, such as understanding and intelligibility because these are relative and subjective: whether or not a proposed explanation is intelligible and provides understanding may vary from person to person and has no implications for its objective validity, or so Hempel argues.[1] It should be noted that sometimes Hempel refers to understanding in a positive way, but then he gives a very different interpretation of the term. When he refers to "scientific understanding" or "theoretical understanding," he means an objective feature associated with scientific explanation in the nomological sense. For example, Hempel (1965, 488) writes that the understanding conveyed by scientific explanation "lies rather in the insight that the explanandum fits into, or can be subsumed under, a system of uniformities represented by empirical laws or theoretical principles," and that "all scientific explanation ... seeks to provide a systematic understanding of empirical phenomena by showing that they fit into a nomic nexus" (see section 3.1 for further discussion). In sum, Hempel's insistence on excluding pragmatic aspects—among which are considerations regarding understanding and intelligibility—from a philosophical theory of scientific explanation was motivated by his fear that they would

---

1. Cf. Hempel's (1966, 41) insistence on an objective criterion of simplicity, which does not refer to "intuitive appeal or ease with which a hypothesis or theory can be understood or remembered."

introduce a subjective, relativistic element into the conception of explanation, which would undermine its objectivity.

Hempel was right that the notion of understanding is pragmatic in the sense that it concerns a three-term relation between explanation, phenomenon, and the person who uses the explanation to achieve understanding of the phenomenon. One can use the term "understanding" only with—implicit or explicit—reference to human agents: scientist S understands phenomenon P by means of explanation E.[2] That understanding is pragmatic in this sense implies the possibility of disagreement and variation based on contextual differences. For example, as described in chapter 1, in 1926 some physicists believed that atomic phenomena could be understood on the basis of matrix mechanics, while most physicists disagreed. Such differences can be traced back to different scientific, philosophical, or social backgrounds (see chapter 7 for an extensive analysis of this case).

Hempel was wrong, however, when he concluded that this entails that understanding is purely subjective and that a philosophical account of scientific explanation that refers to understanding and intelligibility—or indeed to any other pragmatic aspect of explanation—necessarily contradicts the alleged objectivity of science. This conclusion follows only if one interprets objectivity in an extremely strong way. As Heather Douglas (2004, 2009b) has shown, objectivity is a complex notion with various aspects that may be understood in different ways. The strongest sense of objectivity—which is the sense in which it has traditionally been understood—is "value-free objectivity": the idea that individual thought processes should be objective in the sense that all values should be banned from the reasoning process (Douglas 2009b, 122–123). Douglas argues convincingly that this kind of objectivity is unattainable and undesirable, even as an ideal. Rejecting value-free objectivity does not mean giving up the idea of objectivity altogether: science can be objective in other senses and aspects, so that relativism and subjectivism can be avoided. In section 2.3, I will argue that understanding and intelligibility can be related to contextual values without threatening objectivity. In section 2.2, I will argue that understanding, albeit pragmatic, is essential for achieving the epistemic aims of science and that, accordingly, philosophers of science are mistaken if they ignore the pragmatic dimension of science.

Today, the Hempelian view that understanding should be banned from philosophical discourse is defended by J. D. Trout (2002, 2007), who focuses

---

2. One might, of course, claim that explanation itself is pragmatic in this sense and that one can only say that theory T explains P for scientist S (this is van Fraassen's view; see section 4.4.3). However, this deviates from standard usage of the term "explanation."

on the idea that a good explanation produces a feeling or sense of understanding. Such feelings, often referred to as *Eureka* or *Aha!* experiences, have been experienced and reported by many a scientist. Archimedes is, of course, the classic example, but Trout also mentions Galen, Ptolemy, Kekulé, Darwin, Avogadro, and Perrin. According to Trout (2002, 214), this sense of understanding "may be conveyed by a psychological impression that the explanatory mechanisms are transparent and coherent, or that the explanation seems plausible, and so should be confidently accepted." However, such a subjective feeling is neither a necessary nor a sufficient condition for a good explanation. Moreover, it is not a reliable indicator of the truth of a theory or explanation: in many of the cases cited, the scientists who relied on the feeling of being right were dead wrong. Trout claims that instead of being the direct result of our knowledge of true theories or explanations, the sense of understanding is partly a product of two well-known biases in cognitive psychology. The first of these, the hindsight bias, is the effect, demonstrated in many psychological experiments, that people systematically overestimate their predictive power in after-the-fact contexts: they remember their earlier predictions as having been more accurate than they actually were (the "I-knew-it-all-along" effect). This bias is operative in explanatory accounts: with hindsight one often has the mistaken feeling of understanding precisely why a particular event occurred. The second effect that results in counterfeit understanding is the overconfidence bias: people are "systematically prone to believing that they are right when they are not" (Trout 2002, 226). This effect also applies in the case of answers to explanatory why-questions: anyone—layperson or scientist—will experience biased (unjustified) feelings of understanding when giving an explanatory account to answer a why-question.[3]

Trout (2002, 213) concludes that the feeling of understanding is "just a kind of confidence, abetted by hindsight, of intellectual satisfaction that the question has been adequately answered." Such feelings can be dangerous and misleading and should not be allowed to play a role in the evaluation of explanations. Consequently, Trout claims, we should not try to justify our theories of explanation by referring to alleged understanding-providing features. The fact that a particular explanation of a phenomenon gives us a feeling of understanding is not a reliable cue to it being a correct or accurate

---

3. A related bias has been dubbed the "illusion of explanatory depth": experimental evidence suggests that people overestimate their understanding of how things work or why particular phenomena exist (Keil 2006, 242). Petri Ylikoski (2009) argues that there is no reason to assume that scientists are less prone to the illusion of explanatory depth than ordinary people and that scientific understanding may be equally biased.

explanation. On the contrary: the feeling of understanding will induce us to stop looking for better explanations, but wrongly so, because it is a product of the above-mentioned biases. In sum, Trout conceives of understanding as a subjective experience that may be induced by explanations, and concludes that understanding is at best irrelevant and possibly even detrimental to achieving the epistemic aims of science, and that philosophical accounts of explanation should therefore ignore it.

Like Hempel, Trout (2002, 217) endorses a strongly objectivist approach to scientific explanation: "What makes an explanation good concerns a property that it has independent of the psychology of the explainers; it concerns features of external objects, independent of particular minds." To be sure, in his response to my discussion of his views (De Regt 2004a), Trout (2005, 199) claims that he does not want to eliminate talk of understanding completely: it is only allusions to the psychological sense of understanding that he criticizes. He allows for "understanding proper" in contrast to "the mere sense of understanding," and for "genuine understanding" in contrast to "counterfeit understanding." Trout (2007, 585–586) characterizes genuine scientific understanding as "the state produced, and only produced, by grasping a true explanation," where "one might, for example, treat grasping as a kind of knowing." However, he does not say what scientific understanding is a state of, or what kind of knowing "grasping" exactly is. Trout's conception of "genuine" scientific understanding is simply defined in terms of explanation, which can allegedly be analyzed in a fully objective manner. Thus, it appears to be in line with Hempel's objective conception of "scientific" or "theoretical understanding," and does not add anything of philosophical interest that is not already covered by the term "explanation."

I agree with Trout that purely subjective feelings of understanding can be misleading and should not be regarded as necessary or sufficient conditions for scientific understanding.[4] However, there is more to *Eureka* experiences than just feeling and emotion. Archimedes experienced a sudden flash of insight which, as legend has it, was accompanied by such strong emotions

---

4. By contrast, Peter Lipton (2009) and Stephen Grimm (2009) maintain that the sense of understanding can fulfil a positive epistemic function. Drawing on Alison Gopnik's "Explanation as Orgasm" (2000), Lipton (2009, 57–60) argues that feelings may be motivating the search for understanding: "Just as orgasm is nature's way of encouraging reproduction, the feeling of understanding is nature's way of encouraging cognitive activities that generate understanding." This does not imply, however, that the feeling of understanding cannot be separated from the understanding itself, and that the latter cannot be objective. But, Lipton argues, the subjectivity of the feeling does not rule out that it may be a reliable guide to inferring the best explanation. Grimm elaborates on this point by arguing that the feeling of understanding is conditionally reliable.

that he forgot to put on his clothes before running out into the street and shouting *Eureka!* ("I have found it!"). But the flash of insight is not the same as the emotion. Experiments by Jung-Beeman et al. (2004) have revealed an essential difference between problem-solving via a flash of insight and problem-solving via straightforward following of methods or rules. The two routes to problem solutions involve different cognitive and neural processes in different hemispheres. This suggests that the *Eureka* experience comprises a special kind of understanding over and above the phenomenology (the feeling of understanding) associated with it.[5]

The possible meanings of understanding are not exhausted by the two extremes of either purely subjective feeling or fully objective, non-pragmatic explanation. This was first hinted at by Michael Friedman, who in his groundbreaking paper "Explanation and Scientific Understanding" (1974) argued that a philosophical theory of scientific explanation should make it clear how explanations provide us with understanding.[6] While he agrees with Hempel that a satisfactory conception of understanding should be objective, in the sense that it "doesn't vary capriciously from individual to individual," he suggests that this does not entail that understanding cannot be pragmatic. According to Friedman (1974, 7–8), Hempel wrongly identifies "pragmatic as psychological" with "pragmatic as subjective." By contrast, he claims, understanding can be "pragmatic as psychological" without also being subjective. Friedman's point is that understanding has to do with the thoughts, beliefs, and attitudes of persons, and is thereby pragmatic in the sense of psychological. However, this does not preclude that understanding can be objective in the sense that it is "constant for a relatively large class of people," instead of individually varying (Friedman 1974, 8). Friedman's insight is very important, and my analysis in the next sections will be based on this idea. However, there is a flaw in his discussion due to the fact that he adopts a monolithic conception of objectivity. He equates objectivity in the sense of independence of the beliefs and attitudes of people with objectivity in the sense of being "constant for a relatively large class of people." The former is absolute, the latter is relative. Friedman's "pragmatic as psychological" notion of understanding

---

5. See sections 2.2 and 4.3 for further discussion of the difference between these two modes of understanding.

6. Since Friedman's pioneering paper philosophers of science have been less reluctant to discuss the notion of understanding, and, as we will see in chapter 3, particular models of explanation are often defended by pointing to the understanding-providing power of the favored type of explanation. Friedman himself defends an account of explanatory understanding based on the idea of unification; see section 3.1.

still allows for large-scale variation (e.g., between scientific communities or paradigms), whereas Hempel's objectivist notion of understanding does not. The more sophisticated account of objectivity developed by Douglas (2009b) distinguishes between the two ideas that Friedman identifies; in section 2.3, I will employ her insight to develop a consistent analysis of the pragmatic nature and objectivity of scientific understanding.

I conclude that understanding has long been ignored by philosophers of science because of its supposedly subjective nature. Thus, Hempel and Trout endorse a strongly objectivist approach in which scientific understanding is legitimate only if it is interpreted as non-pragmatic. However, their interpretation de facto identifies understanding with explanation, and thereby makes it redundant.[7] Friedman has paved the way for a pragmatic conception of understanding that avoids subjectivity. In the next section, I will argue, in the spirit of Friedman and contra Hempel and Trout, that there is more to understanding than either purely objective explanations or purely subjective feelings. In between these two extremes a pragmatic (though not subjective and arbitrary) kind of understanding exists which has a crucial epistemic function, and which needs to be taken into account in a philosophical analysis of scientific explanation. This pragmatic understanding is not a product of scientific explanation. Accordingly, there are three different ways in which the term understanding is used in connection with scientific explanation, which should be clearly distinguished:

PU: phenomenology of understanding = the feeling of understanding that may accompany an explanation (e.g., an *Aha!* experience)
UT: understanding a theory = being able to use the theory
UP: understanding a phenomenon = having an adequate explanation of the phenomenon

UP is generally regarded as an epistemic aim of science. It is not at odds with the traditional Hempelian view; it corresponds to what Hempel calls scientific understanding. UP can be accompanied by PU: explanations may produce a sense of understanding, but this is not necessarily the case.

---

7. Khalifa (2012) defends a similar position, which he terms EMU: the Explanatory Model of Understanding. EMU states: "Any philosophically relevant ideas about scientific understanding can be captured by philosophical ideas about the epistemology of scientific explanation without loss" (17). Crucial to Khalifa's argument is his claim that the skills needed for pragmatic understanding "can be replaced by propositional knowledge concerning explanatory details" (26). In section 2.2, I will counter this claim by arguing that skills are based on tacit knowledge that cannot be made explicit.

Accordingly, as Trout rightly claims, it is epistemically irrelevant whether or not UP is accompanied by PU. So far I agree with Hempel and Trout. However, contra their objectivist view, I submit that UP necessarily requires UT: the (pragmatic) understanding of the theory that is used in the explanation. In the next sections, I will substantiate my thesis that UT is essential for achieving UP.

2.2 Understanding as an epistemic skill

Few people—be they scientists, philosophers, or laypeople—will deny that explanation is one of the principal aims of science. According to many, it is the central epistemic aim. Thus, Kitcher (2001, 66–68) discusses four traditional proposals for articulating the epistemic aims of science of which he considers this the most promising: "The (epistemic) aim of science is to achieve objective understanding through the provision of explanations." This proposal is in line with the view of Hempel and Trout, which simply identifies objective understanding with explanation. As such, this view effectively renders the notion of understanding redundant, and its proponents have rejected other, non-redundant, pragmatic conceptions of understanding as epistemically irrelevant. Is this traditional account of explanatory understanding as the epistemic aim of science tenable? In the present section, I will argue that it is not, and my analysis will show that the epistemic aim of explanation (and ipso facto of objective understanding) can be reached only by means of a pragmatic type of understanding.[8]

To prove my thesis, I will employ a generic conception of scientific explanation that accords with the various more specific theories of explanation proposed in the literature. Accordingly, even adherents of the traditional view of explanatory understanding should be able to agree with my presuppositions and cannot reject my thesis out of hand. My basic assumption is that all explanations are, in a broad sense, arguments.[9] An explanation is an attempt to

---

8. Kitcher (2001, 73–76) also criticizes the traditional attempt to formulate the epistemic aim of science in terms of objective understanding and explanation in a context-independent way. His analysis differs from mine but appears to be compatible with it.

9. This may seem similar to what Salmon (1984) has dubbed the "epistemic conception of explanation," which would imply that adherents of the alternative "ontic conception" (including Salmon himself) would disagree. However, Salmon's distinction is misleading: explanations, including Salmon's causal-mechanical ones, are always epistemic and not ontic, in the sense that they are items of knowledge (cf. Bechtel and Abrahamsen 2005, 424–425). I submit that any explanation is a structured epistemic item (and not merely a list of disconnected facts) and can therefore be regarded as an argument in the broad sense.

answer the question of why a particular phenomenon occurs or a situation obtains, that is, an attempt to provide understanding of the phenomenon or the situation by presenting a systematic line of reasoning that connects it with other accepted items of knowledge (e.g., theories, background knowledge). Explanations are arguments in a broad sense in that they are not necessarily linguistic items; they need not be sets of statements. Phenomena can also be explained, for example, by means of pictorial representations—these may count as arguments as well. Thus, explanations can take on a variety of forms. The classic model of explanation that Hempel defended, the deductive-nomological (D-N) model, is but one way of articulating the idea that explanations are arguments. It consists in a "narrow" interpretation of arguments as sets of statements in which the conclusion follows deductively from the premises. But explanatory arguments may alternatively fit the phenomenon to be explained into an accepted epistemic framework by representing it in a model, for instance a mechanistic one, and such representations are not always linguistic (see chapter 3 for an overview of the various conceptions of scientific explanation). Starting from this generic conception I will argue that all explanations involve a kind of understanding that is pragmatic and thereby incompatible with the strongly objectivist, non-pragmatic conception of understanding defended by Hempel and Trout. This pragmatic understanding is an essential ingredient of the epistemic aims of science; without it the epistemic aim of explanation will remain out of reach.

While my analysis assumes the broad conception of explanation already sketched, I will first show that even on the narrow Hempelian view of explanation pragmatic understanding is required for explanation. According to Hempel, an explanation fits an explanandum phenomenon into a broader theoretical framework by deducing it from covering laws plus boundary conditions. For example, one can explain the fact that jets fly by deducing it from Bernoulli's principle and the relevant background conditions (borrowing an example from Trout 2002, 202). Note, however, that merely knowing Bernoulli's principle and the background conditions is not equal to having an explanation: in addition, one should be able to use this knowledge in the right way to derive the explanandum. Thus, a student may have memorized Bernoulli's principle and have all background conditions available but may still be unable to use this knowledge to account for the fact that jets can fly. The extra ingredient needed to construct the explanation is a skill: the ability to construct deductive arguments from the available knowledge.[10]

---

10. Hempel never acknowledged the importance of skills for achieving understanding. Yet even his objectivist view of understanding cannot do without skills, as is revealed by this

Wittgenstein's discussion of understanding a mathematical series nicely illustrates this point. Wittgenstein (1953, sections 151–155) considers a situation in which somebody (A) writes down a series of numbers: 1, 5, 11, 19, 29, while someone else (B) watches and tries to figure out how the sequence should be continued. Wittgenstein: "If he succeeds he exclaims: 'Now I can go on!'—So this capacity, this understanding, is something that makes its appearance in a moment" (1953, section 151). But what is it that appears so suddenly? In this case there are several possibilities: perhaps B has found the formula $a_n = n^2 + n - 1$, or he has not tried to find a formula but has asked himself what the series of differences between succeeding numbers is (4, 6, 8, 10, and so on), or B simply says "I know *that* series" and continues it. Wittgenstein:

> But are the processes which I have described here *understanding*? 'B understands the principle of the series' surely doesn't mean simply: the formula '$a_n = \ldots$' occurs to B. For it is perfectly imaginable that the formula occurs to him and that he should nevertheless not understand. 'He understands' must have more in it than: the formula occurs to him. And equally, more than any of those more or less characteristic *accompaniments* or manifestations of understanding. (Wittgenstein 1953, section 152)

Understanding involves more than mere knowledge of the relevant formula (or in the scientific case: theories, laws, and background conditions), but this "more" should not be sought in any of the subjective experiences that may accompany the appearance of understanding. Wittgenstein (1953, section 154): "If there has to be anything 'behind the utterance of the formula' it is *particular circumstances*, which justify me in saying that I can go on—when the formula occurs to me." According to Wittgenstein, when we say that someone not only knows a formula but also understands it, we do not refer to a special experience (*Aha!* feeling) or mental state of this person, but to a context ("particular circumstances") in which she is able to apply the formula and continue the series. Understanding is not merely knowing the formula, but in addition being able to use the formula in the case at hand. Wittgenstein's insight is important: even without fully endorsing his philosophical behaviorism, we can conclude that understanding involves abilities, and that it is thereby pragmatic and context-dependent.

---

statement: "The understanding [a scientific explanation] conveys lies rather in the *insight* that the explanandum fits into, or can be subsumed under, a system of uniformities represented by empirical laws or theoretical principles" (Hempel 1965, 488; italics added). The insight that the explanandum fits into a deductive system transcends mere knowledge and requires deductive reasoning skills.

It might be objected that these abilities can easily be explicated as knowledge of rules that must be applied, and so do not require additional pragmatic understanding. Applying a formula, or constructing a deductive argument in which the explanandum (the statement describing the phenomenon to be explained) is derived from the explanans (the premises: theories, laws, and boundary conditions), simply consists in following particular rules of logic, or so it is argued. However, following a rule presupposes rules for its application (e.g., a rule for deciding whether the right circumstances for application of the rule obtain), and so on, leading to a regress that can only be stopped by an appeal to a "tacit" understanding that the rule is used correctly. This understanding is a form of tacit knowledge, which can only be acquired in a social context, by participating in the shared practices of a social group, for example, a scientific community. It is an example of what Collins (2010, 119–138) calls "collective tacit knowledge," a type of knowledge that one can obtain only when immersed in a society and that cannot be made fully explicit.

Additional support for the thesis that deductive explanation requires abilities, or skills, is provided by Harold Brown's analysis of the comparable case of deductive proofs in formal logic. Brown (2000, 195) argues, in a Wittgensteinian vein, that although each step in such a proof is justified by appeal to an explicit rule, "the process of constructing a proof—that is, the process of deciding which rule to apply at each stage—is not governed by any comparable set of rules" (cf. Brown 1988, 169ff.). This implies that one cannot learn to construct proofs by first learning explicit rules and subsequently applying them. Instead, one needs to develop a skill by practicing, perhaps guided by someone who possesses this skill. Here the social basis of the relevant tacit knowledge comes to the fore: it is only within a community of practitioners that the skill can be acquired. Brown characterizes this skill as a type of judgment, which he defines as "the ability to evaluate a situation, assess evidence, and come to a reasonable decision without following rules" (Brown 1988, 137). The case of proofs in mathematics and logic is analogous to (deductive) explanation in science, as was already recognized by Hempel (1965, 426). But while Hempel invoked the analogy with proofs in support of his thesis that explanation is non-pragmatic, it now turns out that even mathematical and logical proofs are inextricably linked to pragmatic skills and judgment (cf. Avigad 2008).

One might object that judgment is only relevant in the context of discovery, in which one tries to find new proofs. However, Brown (1988, 170–171) observes that logicians typically rely on judgment in the evaluation of given proofs as well: "explicit following of rules is characteristic of an unskilled, rather than of a skilled, performance." While the novice consciously follows rules, the expert immediately recognizes which steps are valid and which ones

are not: this "leaps to the mind." Moreover, the fact that understanding transcends mere knowledge suggests that the skill of judgment is relevant to the
context of justification. For example, as Avigad (2008, 319) observes, it is common practice that different proofs of the same theorem are published and
regarded as important contributions. Although additional proofs do not add
knowledge with respect to the correctness of the theorem, they do enhance our
understanding of it. This understanding, which Avigad analyzes in terms of
abilities, is apparently considered to be an epistemic aim in itself. Elgin (1996,
122–124) also argues that understanding is an epistemic achievement, which
is more comprehensive than knowledge and includes abilities and capacities.
In sum, understanding in the sense of skill and judgment is not merely an
instrumental tool that figures in the context of discovery but pertains to the
context of justification as well.

The fact that deductive reasoning—and accordingly deductive-
nomological explanation—involves skill and judgment has two important
implications. First, as intimated above, skills cannot be acquired from textbooks but only in practice because they cannot be exhaustively translated
into explicit rules (Brown 1988, 164–165; Collins 2010, 138). Accordingly, to
possess a skill is to have implicit, tacit knowledge. This idea is supported by
experimental studies of children's cognitive development, which reveal that
children can learn to perform specific cognitive tasks without being able to
state explicitly what they are doing and why they do it (Clements and Perner
1994; Clements, Rustin, and McCallum 2000).[11] What is the nature of the
tacit knowledge exemplified by cognitive skills? Collins (2010) distinguishes
three types of tacit knowledge: relational, somatic, and collective tacit knowledge, of which only the latter two are interesting for our purposes.[12] The
classic examples of tacit knowledge, such as the skill to ride a bicycle, to
play the piano, or to drive a car, are cases of somatic tacit knowledge. These

---

11. Against this conclusion, it has been argued, most notably by Reber (1993), that tacit
knowledge involves implicit learning, that is, the unconscious and unintentional adoption of rule-following procedures. However, Reber's thesis is questionable. In a review of
the literature, Shanks (2005, 208–210) observes that although some grammar learning
experiments *prima facie* suggest that people do achieve unconscious knowledge of rules,
the results are equally well explained without recourse to such implicit learning. Moreover,
other experiments support the idea that grammaticality decisions are not based on adopted
implicit rules but on accumulated information that generates a feeling of familiarity. Shanks
(2005, 216) concludes that "it has yet to be proved beyond doubt that there exists a form of
learning that proceeds both unintentionally and unconsciously."

12. Relational tacit knowledge is "knowledge that is tacit for reasons that are not philosophically profound but have to do with the relations between people that arise out of the nature
of social life" (Collins 2010, 11). An example is knowledge that is deliberately kept secret.

skills comprise tacit knowledge because of the way they are "inscribed in the material of body and brain"; such abilities are "established in our neural pathways and muscles in ways that we cannot speak about" (Collins 2010, 11, 99ff.). Collins (2010, 117) argues that somatic tacit knowledge is often implicit but can in principle be made explicit because it is rooted in "causal sequences" that may ultimately be explained and understood scientifically. This does not hold for collective tacit knowledge, however, which is knowledge that is located in a society and that can only be acquired by participating in that society. A prime example is the skill to apply the right rule in the correct way in the appropriate circumstances. Since rules and their application are sensitive to the social context, which is itself continuously changing, collective tacit knowledge can only be obtained by taking part in that social context and cannot be explicated, for example, by means of a scientific description or explanation that could be used to build a machine that mimics human behavior. As the brief discussion of the jet example suggests, and as will be demonstrated in more detail later, the skills needed to construct scientific explanations involve tacit knowledge of rules, which is accordingly of the collective kind.[13]

Second, the fact that particular skills of the scientist are crucial for constructing and evaluating explanations and for achieving understanding entails that the epistemic aim of science has an inherently pragmatic aspect. Many philosophers of science hold that the pragmatic and the epistemic dimension of science can and should be kept separate. As we saw in section 2.1, Hempel was one of them: he believed that philosophy of science should ignore the pragmatic aspects of scientific explanation. A contemporary exponent of this view is Bas van Fraassen, who explicitly contrasts an epistemic and a pragmatic dimension of theory acceptance (van Fraassen 1980, 4, 88). The epistemic dimension contains the relevant beliefs concerning the relation between a theory and the world, while the pragmatic dimension contains reasons scientists may have for accepting a theory independently of their beliefs about its relation to the world; these reasons typically pertain to the use and usefulness of the theory. In contrast to Hempel, van Fraassen (1980, 97–157)

---

13. Interestingly, Trout (2002, 221–223) also emphasizes the role of skills and implicit knowledge. He argues that this proves that the psychological feeling of understanding is epistemically irrelevant: if explanatory knowledge can be implicit, a conscious feeling cannot be required for it. However, although Trout is surely right that a feeling of understanding is neither necessary nor sufficient for explanatory understanding whereas (implicit) skills are crucially important, it does not follow that the process of achieving explanatory understanding can be captured in an account based on internalization of rule-following procedures, as Trout suggests.

argues that explanation is not an epistemic aim of science but belongs to the pragmatic dimension of theory acceptance. Both Hempel and van Fraassen see the epistemic and the pragmatic as separate domains. In their view, the pragmatic dimension pertains to the relation between the theory and its users, that is, to the dimension that seems to be excluded from the epistemic dimension by definition.

The thesis that the epistemic and the pragmatic can and should be kept separate presupposes that the epistemic status of a theory depends exclusively on a direct evidential relation with the phenomena it purports to describe or explain. On this presupposition, pragmatic elements such as the virtues of a theory that facilitate its use by scientists are indeed epistemically irrelevant: they do not carry any additional justificatory weight. However, as our discussion of the role of skills in deductive reasoning has made clear, this presupposition is false. Skills and judgment are required for establishing and evaluating relations between theories and phenomena, as embodied in, for example, deductive-nomological explanations. It can be concluded that although it may be possible and useful to distinguish analytically between the epistemic and the pragmatic, the two are inextricably intertwined in scientific practice: epistemic activities and evaluations (such as the production and assessment of knowledge claims) are possible only if particular pragmatic conditions are fulfilled.

That it is impossible to separate the pragmatic and epistemic dimensions of explanation is the case with deductive-nomological explanations but even more so with scientific explanations that do not conform to the deductive-nomological ideal. And the latter are the rule rather than the exception in scientific practice: usually there is no simple deductive relation between explanans and explanandum. Instead, as Cartwright (1983), Giere (1999, 2004, 2006), Morgan and Morrison (1999), and others have shown, the connection between theory and phenomena is usually made through models. To analyze the role of models in achieving explanatory understanding, we first need to clarify the relation between models, theory, and empirical data. An influential view that has resulted from extensive and detailed investigations of the use of models in scientific practice asserts that scientific models function as "mediators" between theory and the world.[14] The core idea of the "models-as-mediators" account is that models—being representations of the object or system that one wants to understand scientifically[15]—are not simply derived

---

14. The *locus classicus* for this view is the volume edited by Morgan and Morrison (1999). See Suárez (1999, 168–172) for a concise presentation, and Morrison (2015) for further discussion and application to concrete cases.

15. Note, however, that there are widely different accounts of representation, and that the target systems of models may be real, fictional, or ideal (Knuuttila 2005). For my purposes

from theories, but neither are they based on empirical data alone. Since models are thus partially independent of theory as well as of the world, Morgan and Morrison (1999, 10–11) identify them as "autonomous agents." According to Morrison (1999, 63–64), such autonomous models are crucial for achieving the explanatory aim of science, because they exhibit detailed structural dependencies of the target systems in ways that abstract theory cannot achieve.

Since models typically contain both theoretical and empirical information, there is a spectrum of types of models, ranging from highly concrete data models (such as a graph that is considered the best fit of a number of data points) to highly abstract theoretical models (such as the representation of a gas in terms of a collection of molecules). This implies that there is no sharp distinction between theories and models. Consider, for example, the kinetic theory of gases, which represents real gases as aggregates of particles in motion obeying the laws of Newtonian mechanics. In a sense, the bare kinetic theory provides a very general model of gases. But more specific models (which include descriptions of the structure of the particles, for example) have to be constructed if one wants to explain particular gas phenomena on the basis of the kinetic theory.[16] Notwithstanding the vague boundary between theories and models, it would be a mistake to think that model-based explanation does not need theories at all (cf. Morrison 2007). It remains useful to draw a distinction between theory and model in specific cases and to analyze the nature and function of theories in relation to model-based explanation.[17]

A clear and insightful account of "model-based understanding of scientific theories," which fits scientific practice very well, is offered by Giere (2006, 59–69); in my analysis of the way model-based explanations produce scientific understanding I will use his view.[18] Giere characterizes scientific theories

---

these differences may be ignored, since I am concerned not so much with the representational aspects of models but rather with their explanatory power.

16. Alternatively, it might be claimed that the kinetic theory consists only of the laws of Newtonian mechanics (and some additional statistical laws and assumptions), and accordingly does not contain a model of gases. However, this makes it difficult to view the kinetic theory as a distinct theory and as being a theory of gases. Thus, it appears that the particle model of gases forms an essential part of the kinetic theory.

17. This holds, in particular, for the physical sciences, which more often feature explicitly articulated theories (compared with the life sciences and social sciences). As this book focuses mainly on physics, it is appropriate and relatively unproblematic to make the theory-model distinction in concrete cases.

18. A similar view of the relation between theories and models is defended by van Fraassen (2008, 309–311). One might think that my approach would benefit from adopting the more pragmatic theory-conception of Cartwright, Shomar, and Suárez (1995), who advocate "an instrumentalist view of theory: a good theory is not primarily a collection of models (nor of claims) that cover the phenomena in its domain. When it comes to models of the

as (collections of) principles which provide the basis for the construction of more specific models of parts (or aspects) of the real world. Scientific knowledge of the relevant parts of the world is provided by empirical data, gathered from observation and experimentation. These data are represented in data models; it is these stylized representations of empirical data that constitute the "phenomena," for which scientists want to find explanations that provide understanding. A model-based explanation of a phenomenon is obtained by constructing a specific model (in Giere's terminology, a "representational model") that represents the target system (the phenomenon) in such a way that theoretical principles can be applied to it. If a phenomenon is successfully embedded in a theory by means of such an explanation, we have gained scientific understanding of it (UP).

As an illustration, consider again the kinetic theory of gases. On the basis of this theory one may try to explain particular gas phenomena, described by phenomenological laws or data models. An example of such a phenomenological law is the combination of the basic experimental gas laws of Boyle, Charles, and Gay-Lussac, which yields a relation between pressure, volume, and temperature:

$$\frac{PV}{T} = constant. \tag{2.1}$$

This combined gas law can be explained with the kinetic theory, but this requires the construction of a specific representational model. The kinetic theory provides only a generic model of a gas as a collection of tiny particles in motion (obeying Newton's laws of motion). To derive specific conclusions about the behavior of a gas, we need to add further assumptions regarding the nature of these particles, their interactions, and so on. A simple representational model that allows for such conclusions is the so-called ideal-gas model. This model specifies the properties of the gas particles as follows: gas particles

phenomena, theory is rather a tool for their construction" (Suárez and Cartwright 2008, 62–63). However, as van Fraassen observes, this "toolbox view" is not necessarily incompatible with a semantic conception of theories: while the latter focuses on the structural relations between *products* (models and theories), the toolbox view concentrates on the *processes* of constructing models. Now, on the one hand, I do not deny that theories may serve representational purposes (see also section 4.5.1), but, on the other hand, my analysis of scientific understanding highlights the role of theories in the construction of model-based explanations. Hence, I do not adopt a view on which theories are merely instrumental, but prefer Giere's theory-conception, which emphasizes the pragmatic dimension but still allows for representational success (for an illuminating account of the model-based view of theories, see Frisch 2005, 9–12).

are smooth, hard elastic spheres, whose dimensions are negligible compared to the dimensions of the container (therefore, they may be conceived of as point masses); the particles do not interact except via collisions; the influence of gravity on the particles is negligible; and collisions with other particles and with the walls of the container are perfectly elastic. Given these (idealizing) assumptions, and invoking some additional statistical considerations, the following relation between pressure and volume can be derived:

$$PV = \frac{2}{3} N \left\langle \frac{1}{2} mv^2 \right\rangle, \tag{2.2}$$

where N is the number of particles, m their mass, and v their velocity.[19] To derive formula (2.2), which represents the Boyle-Charles law $PV = constant$, the macroscopic pressure is identified with (modeled as) the force exerted by the particles on a unit area of the wall of the container. In order to derive the combined gas law, one has to invoke an additional modeling assumption regarding temperature. The kinetic theory identifies heat with kinetic energy, and this makes it possible to define the temperature of the gas in terms of the average kinetic energy of the particles:

$$\frac{3}{2} kT = \left\langle \frac{1}{2} mv^2 \right\rangle, \tag{2.3}$$

where k is the so-called Boltzmann constant. Substituting (2.3) in (2.2) yields:

$$PV = NkT. \tag{2.4}$$

This is the ideal-gas law, which adequately represents the phenomenological combined gas law of Boyle-Charles-Gay-Lussac (formula 2.1). The latter is a data model, while the former is a consequence of the representational ideal-gas model. The agreement between (2.1) and (2.4) is an explanatory success of the kinetic theory: we understand some basic gas phenomena through a model-based explanation using kinetic theory. This example nicely illustrates the relation between theory, models, and phenomena: the theory supplies the principles (e.g., the laws of Newtonian mechanics and the identification of heat with kinetic energy) and presents a generic model of gases, which must be articulated in order to construct explanations of phenomena. Even elementary gas laws such as Boyle's law can be explained only if specific

---

19. See, for example, Feynman et al. (1963–1965, 1: ch. 39), for a clear exposition.

representational models are developed (in this case, the ideal-gas model).[20] Such models do not follow deductively from the bare kinetic theory, however. Rather, model-building is an art that requires particular skills.

To substantiate this claim, let us have a closer look at the process of model construction. The function of a model is to represent the target system in such a way that the theory can be applied to it. In other words, models replace the bridge principles that on the traditional, Hempelian account relate a theory to empirical phenomena. In the terminology of Morgan and Morrison (1999), models "mediate" between theory and phenomena. In contrast to bridge principles, which establish a strict deductive relation between theory (explanans) and phenomenon (explanandum), mediating models connect the two in a looser way. A detailed analysis of how this connection is established has been provided by Cartwright (1983). Her so-called simulacrum account of explanation asserts that "to explain a phenomenon is to construct a model that fits the phenomenon into a theory" (Cartwright 1983, 17). In the modeling stage, the target system is presented in such a way that the theory can be applied to it: we decide to describe system S as if it is an M (where M is a model of which the behavior is governed by the principles of the theory). The construction of models is not a matter of deduction but a complex process involving approximations and idealizations. There are no algorithms or formal principles that tell us how to get from the description of a real system to a suitable model: "There are just rules of thumb, good sense, and, ultimately, the requirement that the equation we end up with must do the job" (Cartwright 1983, 133). This implies that the construction of a model, and accordingly the construction of an explanation, is a process in which scientists have to make pragmatic decisions and must accordingly rely on skills and judgment.

Again, modeling gases on the basis of the kinetic theory serves as an example. To arrive at the above-sketched (model-based) explanation of the combined gas law, one needs to construct a suitable model of the gas by making appropriate idealizations (e.g., modeling the particles as point particles without internal structure). There are no strict rules for deciding which idealizations to make: it is a matter of skill and judgment, involving the ability to use the kinetic theory effectively. Once these pragmatic decisions have been made and the ideal-gas model has been built, the explanation can be derived by applying the theoretical principles to the model. This derivation produces the ideal-gas law (2.4). However, real gases obey the ideal-gas law only approximately, so another pragmatic decision must be made, namely whether or

---

20. In sections 4.2 and 6.2, modeling practices on the basis of the kinetic theory of gases will be discussed in more detail.

not the data model (the phenomenon) fits the ideal-gas model well enough. While this might appear uncontroversial in the present case, it is not a trivial issue. Moreover, it turns out that an acceptable fit occurs only in particular circumstances. At extreme values of pressure and temperature, for example, the behavior of real gases diverges strongly from the ideal-gas law. This observation led J. D. van der Waals to refine the ideal-gas model: he developed a model of particle systems in which the particle size and the interaction between particles cannot be ignored. Application of the kinetic theory to his model yields the so-called Van der Waals equation, which holds in domains where the ideal-gas law fails, namely liquids and gases above the critical temperature. As in the case of the ideal-gas model, the construction of the Van der Waals model is based on pragmatic decisions about which idealizing assumptions to retain and which to relax.

In sum, model-building necessarily involves idealization and approximation, and this requires skills and judgment. An early defense of this thesis was given by Hilary Putnam in 1978:

> What the theory [in physics] actually describes is typically an idealized "closed system." The theory of this "closed system" can be as precise as you want. And it is within this idealization that one gets the familiar examples of the "scientific method." But the application of physics depends on the fact that we can produce in the laboratory, or find in the world, open systems which approximate to the idealized system sufficiently well to yield very accurate predictions. The decision that conditions have been approximated well in a given case—that it is even worthwhile to apply the idealized model to this case—typically depends on unformalized practical knowledge. (Putnam 1978, 72)

Putnam (1978, 71) explicitly identifies such "unformalized practical knowledge" with skills. His analysis implies that skills and judgment play a role not only in the context of discovery (the construction of the model) but also in the context of justification: assessing whether or not the model is a good (or good-enough) representation of the system involves pragmatic decisions as well. This is supported by work on models as representations of reality (Bailer-Jones 2003; Giere 2004; Suárez 2004; Frisch 2014), which assigns an essential role to "model users" in determining the representational force of a particular model. Both the construction and the evaluation of model-based explanations is a pragmatic and contextual affair.

I conclude that explanation—an acknowledged epistemic aim of science—can only be achieved with the help of a pragmatic kind of understanding.

This is the case for deductive-nomological explanations, and even more so for model-based explanations that are typically not deductive. In order to construct and evaluate scientific explanations merely possessing knowledge is not enough: in addition particular skills are needed to use and apply this knowledge. Thus, achieving this epistemic aim unavoidably has a pragmatic dimension in which skills and judgment play crucial roles. The epistemic value of a theory cannot be determined in isolation from its use, and successful use of a theory requires pragmatic understanding.

2.3 Intelligibility, values, and objectivity

What exactly is pragmatic understanding? When do scientists possess it? In the previous section, it was described somewhat loosely as the ability to use the relevant theory, and as being based on skills and judgment. I will now give a more precise analysis of the nature of and conditions for pragmatic understanding. Scientists seek explanations that fit the phenomenon to be explained into a theoretical framework and connect it with relevant background knowledge. The connection between the phenomenon and theoretical and background knowledge is typically made through models. The construction and evaluation of such model-based explanations involves making suitable idealizations and approximations, and this requires pragmatic understanding: scientists need to make the right judgments regarding idealization and approximation, and possess the right skills to build a model on this basis. But what are the right skills? This depends on the characteristics of the theory that the scientists are dealing with. Take simplicity, for instance, which is often regarded as a theoretical virtue: it may seem obvious that a simple theory is easier to work with than a complex theory. However, simplicity can come in a variety of ways, for example: ontological simplicity, if a theory assumes few basic entities; logical simplicity, if a theory is based on few independent postulates; mathematical simplicity, if its equations are simple. In the words of McAllister (1996, 112–113), these are different forms of simplicity and there are many more. Some scientists will prefer mathematical simplicity while others prefer logical simplicity because they are more skilled to work with theories of that particular form. Another example is visualizability: most scientists will appreciate visualizable theories because they are more tractable than abstract ones. However, as we shall see in chapter 7, some scientists prefer abstract theories over visualizable ones. It appears that particular theoretical qualities are valued by scientists because they facilitate the use of the theory in constructing models. But, as is clear from the examples, not all scientists value the same qualities: their preferences are related to their skills, which are acquired by training and experience. Scientists from different disciplines or research communities, and from different historical periods, will possess different skills because factors such as the accepted background knowledge and the characteristics of entrenched theories will have a crucial influence on what skills are learned. In other words, it is the context that determines what skills scientists possess and what theoretical qualities they value.

There is a long-standing debate in philosophy of science about the theoretical qualities that play a role in the construction and evaluation of scientific theories. Since Kuhn (1977), philosophers have used the notion of values to characterize these qualities, and they have listed and discussed what they believe are the most important values in science. Kuhn suggests that there are five values that are desiderata for any scientific theory: accuracy, consistency, scope, simplicity, and fruitfulness.[21] His main point, which departs from traditional analyses of theory choice, is that these desiderata "function not as rules, which determine choice, but as values, which influence it" (Kuhn 1977, 331). This is because the desiderata may conflict in specific situations, they may pull in different directions, and different scientists may end up with different choices, depending on how they rank the desiderata in the case at hand. Moreover, scientists may apply the desiderata in different ways (as was shown for the case of simplicity). There is no universally shared algorithmic decision procedure to apply the criteria, and accordingly judgment plays a crucial role. Later philosophers, among them Ernan McMullin (1983), Helen Longino (1990), Hugh Lacey (1999), and Heather Douglas (2009b), have developed elaborate and sophisticated accounts of the role of values in science, which extend, refine, and revise Kuhn's analysis but remain faithful to its basic idea. A main bone of contention is the distinction between values that are central to science and values that influence scientific decision-making but are not essential to it. The former category has been termed "epistemic" (McMullin), "constitutive" (Longino), or "cognitive" (Lacey), and philosophers disagree about which values fall into this category, and even about whether the distinction is viable at all.

I will not discuss these debates in detail, but conclude that there seems to be a fair degree of consensus about two basic values in science: an empirical and a logical one. Scientific theories (and explanations for that matter) should conform to the observable world; a desideratum that in its minimal form can

---

21. Kuhn proposed this list in the context of his response to critics who had argued that his theory of science was unacceptably relativistic. He replied that his view does not deny that general standards for good science exist and that his list constitutes "*the* shared basis for theory choice" (Kuhn 1977, 322).

be called empirical adequacy. Moreover, theories should not contain contradictory elements—they should be internally consistent. Douglas (2009b, 93–94) sets these two desiderata apart as necessary conditions for all science and suggests that they function not as values but as strict criteria (she employs a distinction between "cognitive values" and "epistemic criteria" to mark this difference). While I agree that empirical adequacy and internal consistency are the two basic requirements in science, I submit that they are nonetheless values in Kuhn's sense, and henceforth I will call them the *basic scientific values*. Every scientist should have empirical adequacy and internal consistency high on her list of values, but there may still be variation in how these values are ranked and applied in specific cases. Empirical adequacy is far from straightforwardly and unambiguously applicable as a criterion: the usual situation in scientific practice is that theories or models fit the empirical evidence only partially and that a choice between different theories or models involves value judgments about which evidence is considered most important. For example, when in 1876 Ludwig Boltzmann proposed a particular molecular model that solved an empirical anomaly for the kinetic theory of gases, James Clerk Maxwell rejected this solution because it appeared to contradict other empirical evidence. Neither physicist was irrational or unscientific—they only valued the empirical adequacy of the model differently (see section 6.2 for a detailed account of this case). Moreover, scientists sometimes temporarily prefer less empirically adequate theories if they comply better with other values.

At first glance, internal consistency may seem an uncontroversial desideratum, and less complicated than empirical adequacy. But even consistency appears to be a value that may at times be waived. A closer look at scientific practice reveals that many actual scientific theories and models have been internally inconsistent. For example, Frisch (2005) shows that classical electrodynamics is an inconsistent theory that can nevertheless be used to describe and explain phenomena in the classical domain involving charged particles. Moreover, in this domain classical electrodynamics is to be preferred over a quantum treatment, even though the latter approach would (theoretically) lead to more accurate results. The reason is that a quantum treatment of classical phenomena would be enormously complex while the gain in accuracy will in practice be negligible. A classical treatment, by contrast, is much simpler and yields results that are for all practical purposes accurate enough. This is a clear illustration of Kuhn's thesis that values may be applied and ranked differently in different context: in this specific context a substantial gain in simplicity is valued higher than a slight gain in accuracy (Frisch 2005, 17).[22]

---

22. See De Regt and Gijsbers (2017) for an analogous account of why Newtonian gravitational theory is in most contexts preferable to Einstein's theory of general relativity.

Incidentally, Frisch (2005, 9–12), argues that the fact that inconsistent theories do play a legitimate role in scientific practice is an important argument in favor of a model-based conception of theories à la Morgan and Morrison, Cartwright, and Giere (this conception is discussed in section 2.2 and is a basic ingredient of my account of understanding). Traditional syntactic and semantic theory conceptions have difficulty accommodating this fact, since they assume that models and explanations follow deductively from theories. Since one can derive any arbitrary sentence from a contradiction, an inconsistent theory would produce logical anarchy and would have no empirical content. On the model-based view, by contrast, theories are merely provide the basis for the construction of specific models for the explanation of particular phenomena, but these autonomous models do not follow deductively from the theory. The construction of such models is a pragmatic affair in which there is a crucial role for the users of the theory, the scientists. Frisch (2014, 3036) argues that there are "additional context-dependent constraints that users of a theory employ in constructing representations with the help of a set of basic equations, and that the existence of such constraints allows even for formally inconsistent sets of equations to play a useful role in science."[23]

Historical studies have revealed that the construction and evaluation of theories is not only guided by the values of empirical adequacy and internal consistency, but that scientists employ other values as well. In addition to general values such as simplicity, scope, and consistency with accepted background knowledge, scientists in various disciplines and historical periods have promoted other, more specific theoretical values, such as visualizability, causality, continuity, or locality (see chapters 5, 6, and 7 for examples). These values are not simply additional in the sense that they fill gaps that remain after the two basic scientific values have been applied. Instead, there can be fruitful interaction and trade-off between the two basic values and other values.[24] As I have argued, scientists' preferences for particular values other than the two basic ones can be related to their skills. Scientists prefer theories with properties that facilitate the construction of models for explaining phenomena, and that is the case if their skills are attuned to these properties. If such

---

23. See Meheus (2002) and Colyvan (2008, 116–117) for further discussion and additional examples of inconsistent theories and models. Vickers (2013) presents critical analyses of cases of alleged inconsistency in science.

24. Thus, the production of empirically adequate theories is more often stimulated than hindered by reliance on other theoretical values. As McAllister (1996) argues on the basis of historical evidence, scientists usually rely on established aesthetic canons (containing accepted aesthetic criteria for theory choice) and this conservatism is conducive to empirical progress.

an appropriate combination of a scientist's skills and theoretical properties occurs, the scientist has pragmatic understanding of the theory. I suggest rephrasing this idea of pragmatic understanding with the help of the notion of *intelligibility*. If scientists understand a theory, the theory is intelligible to them. I define the intelligibility of a theory (for particular scientists) as follows:

Intelligibility: the value that scientists attribute to the cluster of qualities of a theory (in one or more of its representations)[25] that facilitate the use of the theory.

It is important to note that intelligibility, thus defined, is not an intrinsic property of a theory but an extrinsic, relational property because it depends not only on the qualities of the theory but also on the skills of the scientists who work with it. Theories are not intrinsically intelligible or unintelligible, but intelligible or unintelligible to a particular scientist or group of scientists. In other words, intelligibility is a context-dependent value. I have endorsed Kuhn's view that preferred theoretical qualities function as values, and that scientists make value judgments when constructing or choosing theories. The notion of intelligibility is to be regarded as the aggregate value of all qualities that are relevant to the use of the theory in scientific practice. I submit that this is an important—arguably the most important—reason for valuing particular qualities in theories (there may be other reasons as well, for example, metaphysical ones).

Intelligibility is a measure of the fruitfulness of a theory, but it is a contextual measure: a theory can be fruitful for scientists in one context and less so for scientists in other contexts.[26] Thus, which theories are deemed intelligible can vary through time, across disciplines, or even within a particular discipline. For example, as noted in chapter 1, around 1926 Schrödinger's wave mechanics was far more popular in the general physics community than Heisenberg's matrix mechanics because it was visualizable and mathematically less intricate. As Beller (1999, 36) observes, it "was successfully applied to a great variety of problems unamenable to matrix treatment." For mainstream physicists in the 1920s, wave mechanics was more intelligible than matrix mechanics.

---

25. It often happens that a theory can be represented in different ways (think of the various formulations of classical mechanics), and each of these representations may have its own specific qualities, which may be relevant to the intelligibility of the theory.

26. There may be a discrepancy between scientists' perception of the fruitfulness of a theory and its actual fruitfulness for these scientists. Such errors of judgment will hamper their work. I assume that they are the exception rather than the rule.

Its theoretical qualities, especially its visualizability and mathematical simplicity, allowed physicists to construct models to explain specific phenomena.
The proponents of matrix mechanics, by contrast, rejected visualizability as a
condition for intelligibility. Heisenberg, for example, was able to develop the
foundations of matrix mechanics precisely by abandoning the search for a
visualizable model of atomic structure (see chapter 7 for a detailed analysis of
this case). Scientists prefer a more intelligible theory to a less intelligible one,
not because it gives them a feeling of understanding but rather because they
have to be able to use the theory in practice.

It might be objected that my thesis that pragmatic understanding and
the (contextual) value of intelligibility are inextricable elements of science
threatens the time-honored objectivity of science. However, as I have already
hinted at in section 2.1, this complaint is based upon a misguided conception of objectivity. In the traditional view, objectivity is interpreted in the
sense of exclusion of any kind of values from the reasoning process. Thus,
in the words of Hempel ([1983] 2001, 374), science should be objective "in
the sense of being independent of idiosyncratic beliefs and attitudes on the
part of the scientific investigators." However, as Longino (1990) and Douglas
(2009b) have argued, this strong interpretation of objectivity is unattainable
and unfruitful as a condition for (evaluating) science. They have developed
and defended alternative conceptions of objectivity that are more realistic and
allow for a role of values in science. I will apply their analyses to the issue of
scientific understanding and show that its pragmatic and value-laden nature
does not bar the possibility of objective understanding.

To begin with, it is worth noting that the fact that understanding is pragmatic (in the sense that it is human subjects who understand) does not entail
subjectivity. As in the case of knowledge, it may well be possible that there are
objective procedures to obtain and assess understanding.[27] What procedures
could guarantee the objectivity of scientific understanding? In her account of
scientific objectivity, Douglas (2009b, 115–132) lists a number of ways in which
objective knowledge claims can be produced. While she focuses on the objectivity of knowledge, her analysis can also be used to illuminate how scientific
understanding can be objective. According to Douglas (2009b, 117), asserting that a knowledge claim is objective means asserting that it is trustworthy
given the processes that produced it. She distinguishes between three types of

---

27. This point was brought home to me by Catherine Elgin (2010), in her review of our book
Scientific Understanding: Philosophical Perspectives (De Regt, Leonelli, and Eigner 2009).
Incidentally, the suggestion that the pragmatic nature of explanatory understanding is consistent with the possibility of objective tests of understanding can already be found in the
work of Michael Scriven (1959, 452; 1962, 225).

processes that are relevant to the production of knowledge claims: (1) human interactions with the world; (2) individual thought processes; (3) social processes. There are various ways in which the objectivity of these processes can be secured: Douglas lists eight interpretations of objectivity, of which she regards seven as normatively acceptable. I will discuss only those types of objectivity that are relevant to the achievement of scientific understanding. Human interactions with the world can produce objective empirical claims if they are obtained by repeated interventions (manipulable objectivity) or via multiple avenues (convergent objectivity). In these ways scientists can collect objective evidence. For our purposes, it is important to discover how scientists subsequently achieve objective understanding of such evidence, and here the other two types of processes are relevant.

First, the thought processes of individual scientists who construct and evaluate theories, models, and explanations should conform to a condition that secures the objectivity of their conclusions. Traditionally, this condition was formulated in terms of the "value-free ideal": only if all values are banned from the reasoning process, the results may be regarded as objective. However, as the philosophical debate about values in science has made clear, this ideal is highly problematic: values do play a role in science and value-free objectivity is an unrealistic goal.[28] According to Douglas (2009b, 123), aspiring to this ideal is actually detrimental to science, and she therefore rejects it and replaces it by "detached objectivity": while values inevitably enter the reasoning process, one should not rely on values instead of on empirical evidence. For example, one should not ignore particular evidence because it does not comply with one's values. However, in cases where the evidence does not speak unambiguously in favor of one theory, one has to weigh the relevant empirical findings and it is unavoidable that this involves value judgments (cf. the case of Maxwell versus Boltzmann). Thus, the fact that explanation requires the value of intelligibility (which in turn depends on contextual skills and values) does not necessarily preclude objectivity: as long as individual scientists comply with the requirement of detached objectivity, their explanations may be regarded as objective (trustworthy), even if value judgments have played a part in the process of construction and assessment.

Second, there are several ways in which the social processes that produce a generally accepted scientific explanation can ensure that the

---

28. In his later years, even Hempel ([1983] 2001) accepted Kuhn's analysis of values in science and acknowledged that the role of values does not necessarily undermine the objectivity of science (see esp. 388ff.).

understanding produced by this explanation is objective. Of the three types that Douglas distinguishes, two are significant for the achievement of scientific understanding. "Concordant objectivity" is accomplished if the individual judgments of people agree. If a community of scientists agrees about particular results, for example, observations or explanations, one can regard these results as objective in this sense. In a situation where there is initial disagreement one can strive for "interactive objectivity," which is realized if the consensus is achieved via a critical discussion of the results in question. While concordant objectivity merely looks at the state of a scientific community (consensus), interactive objectivity focuses on the procedure by which this state is reached. The latter idea is elaborated by Longino (1990, 64–66). Both types of objectivity in the sense of characteristics of a social community can be regarded as articulations of the well-known idea of intersubjectivity.

The process of achieving explanatory understanding is a combination of individual thought processes and social processes. In the simplest case, an individual scientist first develops an explanation of a phenomenon on the basis of an intelligible theory, and subsequently a community of scientists accepts this explanation (concordant objectivity). Usually, the situation is more complicated: the accepted explanation results from the combined contributions of a number of scientists and critical discussion in the scientific community (interactive objectivity). Whether or not the understanding that is produced may be considered objective depends on whether the individual and social processes conform to the given conditions for objectivity. However, objectivity is not absolute but can come in degrees (Douglas 2009b, 117). Thus, in cases where individual thought processes are objective to a certain extent (but biasing values still play some role), social processes can further strengthen the objectivity of understanding by balancing (or filtering) out these biasing influences. The fact that explanation and understanding are crucially based on skills does not entail that it is subjective and idiosyncratic either. On the contrary, acquisition of required skills, attuned to preferred theoretical values, is relative to scientific communities rather than individuals, a point that is implicitly made in Kuhn's *The Structure of Scientific Revolutions* (1970).[29] As argued in section 2.2, being involved in the shared practices of a social group such as a scientific community is essential for gaining the collective tacit knowledge that forms the basis of a skill. However, social objectivity does not

---

29. See Rouse (2003) for an analysis of Kuhn's view in which the role of skills is made explicit: "Accepting a paradigm is more like acquiring and using a set of skills than it is like understanding and believing a statement" (107).

guarantee that scientific explanations are value-free at the community level; there can be a shared bias toward particular values in the community. The historical and disciplinary variation of intelligibility criteria, illustrated by the case studies in this book, are clear evidence of this fact, which is unavoidable but unproblematic—the value-free ideal is unattainable and scientific progress is possible without it.[30]

Finally, it can be concluded that the pragmatic kind of understanding associated with intelligibility differs essentially from the subjective, highly individual sense of understanding that Trout criticizes. Achieving understanding of phenomena (UP) may or may not be accompanied by an *Aha!* experience (PU), which is indeed a subjective feeling. But UP requires pragmatic understanding (UT), which is independent of such a feeling of understanding. UT is present when the skills of scientists are appropriately geared toward the qualities of the relevant theories. This implies that the cognitive biases that Trout discusses turn out to be irrelevant. Both the hindsight bias and the overconfidence bias occur only in situations in which people have to assess their own cognitive powers and beliefs. They can indeed affect the subjective feelings of understanding (PU) that people may experience when receiving an explanation, and hamper an objective estimation of their (past or present) cognitive situation. But such feelings cannot have an influence on the pragmatic understanding that is required for the construction of model-based explanations. Pragmatic understanding does not involve an assessment of cognitive powers or any other kind of subjective feeling; on the contrary, it can be present in the form of tacit knowledge that scientists aren't even consciously aware of.

2.4 Understanding: a means and an end

We value understanding, and we value science because it provides us with understanding of the world. Indeed, the understanding that comes with scientific explanation is regarded as one of the central epistemic aims of science. In this chapter, I have argued that in order to achieve understanding of phenomena (UP), we need to understand the scientific theories on which we base our explanations—these theories have to be intelligible (UT). Moreover, I have interpreted scientists' understanding of theories in terms of abilities: scientists understand a theory if they have the skills

---

30. In line with this, it should be noted that objectivity does not guarantee truth. But it ensures that explanatory understanding is the result of reliable processes. In section 4.5, the relation between understanding and truth will be discussed in more detail.

to use the theory in a fruitful way. For example, the kinetic theory of gases is intelligible to those physicists who are able to use the theory in the construction of models for particular phenomena, which involves the skills to make the approximations and idealizations necessary to achieve a fit between the data model and the constructed model that obeys the theoretical principles. It might seem confusing and risky to use the same term—understanding—for two quite different notions: the understanding of phenomena (UP) which is the aim and product of scientific explanations, and the understanding of theories (UT) which is the means to achieve this end. Should we not be careful to distinguish the two and has my discussion so far perhaps already conflated them and created unnecessary confusion? After all, it's all too easy to slip from the one into the other mode. When Richard Feynman ([1965] 1992, 129) famously remarked, "I think I can safely say that nobody understands quantum mechanics," of course, he did not mean that nobody—not even experts in the field—understands the theory itself (like first-year physics students who do not understand quantum mechanics and hence fail their exam on the subject).[31] Rather, he plausibly meant that even those who are familiar with the theory have trouble in seeing how one can understand the world if quantum mechanics is true.

For the sake of conceptual clarity, it is indeed important to distinguish UP and UT. (For that reason, I will always use the terms "intelligibility" or "intelligible" when referring to UT, and never use "understand" or "understanding." For example, the phrase "*T* is intelligible to *S*" will be used instead of "*S* understands *T*.") However, there is also an important correspondence between the UP and UT, which justifies the use of the same term "understanding" in both cases (this correspondence is in fact suggested by the Feynman quote). At the end of section 2.1, I defined UP as "having an adequate explanation of the phenomenon," which was subsequently elaborated in terms of deductive-nomological and model-based explanation. Thus, it was simply stated by definition that scientific explanations, such as D-N- and model-based explanations, provide understanding of phenomena, and it was not further specified what understanding viewed as a product of explanation consists in. This will surely not satisfy everyone. So what more can be said about understanding as a product of explanation? In section 2.2, I argued that an explanation provides understanding of a phenomenon by presenting a systematic line of reasoning

---

31. A similar remark attributed to Feynman is: "If you think you understand quantum mechanics, you don't understand it." I have been unable to find the source of this remark, however.

that connects it with accepted empirical and theoretical knowledge. The established connection between the phenomenon and the rest of our theoretical and empirical knowledge allows us to further apply, extend, and refine our knowledge, and this is the sense in which the explanation provides understanding of the phenomenon.[32]

This can be illustrated once again with the example of the kinetic theory of gases. Elementary phenomenological gas laws can be explained on the basis of the kinetic theory by constructing the ideal-gas model, as we saw in section 2.2. The intelligibility of the kinetic theory is a precondition for constructing the model-based explanation of the phenomenological law. But in what sense does this explanation provide understanding? The answer is: by connecting our empirical knowledge of gaseous behavior with accepted theoretical knowledge (in this case, e.g., with Newtonian mechanics) the explanation allows us to make inferences about the behavior of gases in novel situations, and to extend, apply, and refine our knowledge. For example, proceeding from the kinetic explanation of the combined gas law, J. D. van der Waals developed an equation for the state of particle systems in which the particle size and the interaction between particles cannot be ignored. This Van der Waals equation applies to domains where the ideal-gas law fails, namely to liquids and to gases above the critical temperature.

The crucial point is that the skills that are required for constructing and evaluating an explanation are the same as those required for using and extending it. And, as I have argued, it is precisely the possible use and extension of an explanation that embodies the understanding that comes with it. In other words, understanding of the theories on which the explanation is based (UT) corresponds in a fundamental way with the understanding generated by the explanation (UP). This might seem hopelessly circular. However, while there is indeed a circular aspect to it, this is not a vicious but a virtuous circularity. First, scientists employ their initial understanding of theories to construct explanations, which may or may not be successful. If they are, their success does not depend only on the intelligibility of the theories in question; it also depends on the extent to which the explanations conform to the basic scientific values of empirical adequacy and internal consistency. Only if the explanations are successful may the scientists consider their understanding as vindicated, as being understanding of the phenomena. In that case, further

---

32. Douglas (2009a) offers an account of the relation between explanation and prediction that is in line with the analysis I provide here.

application, extension and refinement of their knowledge of the target systems may be achieved using the same skills that were needed to construct the original explanations. In sum, the interaction between UT and UP constitutes a feedback mechanism between constructing and using explanations that—if successful—produces new scientific knowledge and is the motor of scientific development.

3

Explanatory Understanding

A PLURALITY OF MODELS

IN THE PREVIOUS chapter I have argued, contra philosophers like Hempel, van Fraassen, and Trout, that understanding is an epistemic aim of science. I do not want to suggest, however, that I am the first to claim this. Nowadays many philosophers of science assert that explanations provide us with understanding, and defend a particular model of explanation by appealing to its alleged understanding-providing virtues. This has been common practice since Michael Friedman rehabilitated understanding in his paper "Explanation and Scientific Understanding" (1974). Wesley Salmon, who developed his very influential causal-mechanical model of explanation in the 1980s, also emphasized that good explanations should give us understanding (Salmon 1984, 259; 1998, 79ff.). In the wake of Friedman and Salmon, many later philosophers of science have endorsed the thesis that understanding is the product of scientific explanations and an epistemic aim of science. However, there is no agreement on what the criteria for scientific understanding are. Several competing accounts of scientific explanation have been proposed, which present different characterizations of the nature of the understanding that is produced by explanations. Two prime examples are Salmon's causal-mechanical conception, which is based on the idea that science gives understanding of the world by uncovering its causal structure, and the unificationist conception defended by Friedman and Philip Kitcher (1989), which asserts that scientific theories provide understanding by unifying the phenomena. On their views, it is the causal nature, respectively the unifying power, of a theory that qualifies as the pre-eminent understanding-providing virtue.

In this chapter, I will analyze the implications of the most important current views of explanation for the nature of scientific understanding. I will investigate the arguments of philosophers for their claims that their favored type of explanation is the preferred (or unique) way to achieve understanding of the phenomena. After sixty years of debate about scientific explanation, there is currently no consensus favoring one model but rather a plethora of different models of scientific explanation, and of associated conceptions of understanding. The models that I will review can be divided into two classes: nomological and unificationist models (section 3.1) and causal and mechanistic models (section 3.2). I discuss the merits and the problems of these conceptions, and argue—on the basis of examples from historical and contemporary scientific practice—that none of them fully succeeds in capturing the nature of scientific understanding. A plurality of types of explanation will have to be accepted; and what is needed is an overarching theory that explains how each type generates understanding. In section 3.3, I examine Salmon's attempt to reconcile causal-mechanical and unificationist explanation. On the basis of a critical analysis of this proposal, I conclude that it fails and that we need a more radically pluralist approach (section 3.4).

3.1 From covering law explanation to unificatory understanding

The modern history of the philosophy of scientific explanation starts with Hempel's covering law model, according to which scientists explain phenomena by showing that they are consequences of general laws.[1] The criterion for explanation is "nomic expectability": by citing laws we give grounds for expecting the occurrence of the phenomenon, given particular initial and background conditions. As we saw in chapter 2, Hempel claimed that the notion of understanding is pragmatic and subjective, and he therefore deemed it irrelevant, if not dangerous, for philosophy of science. However, he did have some things to say about the nature of scientific understanding. On the one hand, he made a suggestion about the way scientific explanations can induce understanding in people: "the [deductive-nomological] argument shows that, given the particular circumstances and the laws in question, the occurrence of the phenomenon *was to be expected*; and it is in this sense that the explanation enables us to *understand why* the phenomenon occurred" (Hempel 1965, 337, original italics). In other words, if we feel that we understand a phenomenon after it has been explained scientifically, this is because

---

1. Hempel distinguished three types of covering law explanations: deductive-nomological, deductive-statistical, and inductive-statistical explanations (see Hempel 1965). For our purposes, the differences between these three types are not important, so I will restrict my discussion the deductive-nomological variant.

we are no longer surprised (indeed, we expect) that this phenomenon occurs. As far as subjective understanding is concerned, Hempel thus reduces it to "rational expectation." On the other hand, as was mentioned in section 2.1, Hempel sometimes alludes to a different conception of understanding, which he calls "scientific" or "theoretical understanding" and which he claims is the only kind of objective understanding that one may legitimately speak about. When Hempel refers to understanding of this kind, it is often to contrast it with views of understanding that he rejects, such as, first, the idea of empathic understanding that is supposed to be essential for explanation in history, and second, the understanding that is allegedly generated by teleological explana- tions, which explain phenomena in terms of purposes (Hempel 1965, 240, resp. 256). In both cases, Hempel suggests, the underlying belief is that understanding is achieved because the phenomenon is explained in terms of concepts or processes with which we are familiar. However, such an anthro- pomorphic view of understanding as reduction to the familiar is untenable, according to Hempel.[2]

From a philosophical perspective, Hempel and Oppenheim argued in their 1948 paper, the only legitimate form of scientific understanding is "understanding in the theoretical, or cognitive, sense of exhibiting the phenomenon to be explained as a special case of some general regularity" (Hempel 1965, 257).[3] This objective kind of understanding is, of course, nothing else than explanation of phenomena by subsuming them under covering laws. In his 1966 book *Philosophy of Natural Science*, Hempel for- mulated the opposition between subjective and objective understanding in a slightly different way: "What scientific explanation, especially theo- retical explanation, aims at is not this intuitive and highly subjective kind of understanding [familiarity, HdR], but an objective kind of insight that is achieved by a systematic unification, by exhibiting the phenomena as manifestations of common underlying structures and processes that con- form to specific, testable, basic principles" (Hempel 1966, 83). Here we see that the covering law model of explanation can be related to a conception of

---

2. See section 4.4.1 for further discussion of the "familiarity view of understanding" and its problems.

3. Cf. Hempel in his 1942 paper on historical explanation: Empathic understanding (*Verstehen*) "must clearly be separated from scientific understanding. In history as anywhere else in empirical science, the explanation of a phenomenon consists in subsuming it under general empirical laws" (Hempel 1965, 240). And in his 1959 paper on functional explana- tion: "A class of phenomena has been scientifically understood to the extent that they can be fitted into a testable, and adequately confirmed, theory or a system of laws" (Hempel 1965, 329).

understanding based on *unification*: a scientific explanation of a phenomenon provides understanding because it allows us to see the phenomenon as an instance of a general pattern, rather than as merely an isolated event. The intuition that understanding consists in seeing how things fit into a greater scheme is quite common and basic (cf. the terms "comprehension" and "comprehensive").[4] Erwin Schrödinger, for example, asked in his *Nature and the Greeks* ([1954] 1996, 90–91): "What does comprehensibility really mean, and in what sense, if any, does science give explanations?" Observing that contemporary philosophers of science (read: logical positivists and empiricists) regard only description and prediction as true aims of science, Schrödinger suggests that there is still room for understanding in this modest picture of science: "There are factual relations between our findings in the various, widely distant domains of knowledge ... relations so striking and interesting, that for our eventual grasping and registering them, the term 'understanding' seems very appropriate" (Schrödinger [1954] 1996, 91–92). Additional evidence for regarding understanding via unification as the basic idea behind Hempel's covering law model is provided by his discussion of the problem of explaining laws. While the standard formulation of deductive-nomological explanation is concerned with the explanation of particular events, Hempel suggested that general regularities or laws can be explained in a similar manner, namely by subsuming them under more general laws (Hempel 1965, 247).[5] Explanation of Boyle's law by kinetic theory, for example, invokes the more general laws of Newtonian mechanics plus particular assumptions about the nature of gases. Accordingly, Philip Kitcher (1981, 508) is quite correct when he suggests that behind the logical empiricists' "official" view of nomological explanation one can discern an "unofficial view" of explanation as unification.

The first "official" model of explanation by unification was developed by Michael Friedman (1974). His motivation for doing so was his belief that a

---

4. Cf. Scriven (1962, 225): "Understanding is, roughly, organized knowledge, i.e., knowledge of the relations between various facts and/or laws. These relations are of many kinds—deductive, inductive, analogical, etc. (Understanding is deeper, more thorough, the greater the span of this relational knowledge.)"

5. There is a problem with such explanations, however, which was already observed by Hempel and Oppenheim in a famous footnote to their 1948 paper (Hempel 1965, 273): it will always be possible to deduce a law (L_1) from the conjunction of it with another law ($L_1 \cap L_2$), which qualifies as a more general law. But such a derivation surely does not constitute an acceptable explanation. Hempel never succeeded in solving this problem, which hinges on the problem of giving an adequate criterion for the generality of laws. Kitcher's alternative characterization of laws provides a solution of this problem (Kitcher 1989, 447).

philosophical theory of explanation should clarify how explanations provide understanding, and his observation that Hempel's model failed in this respect. As mentioned, Hempel suggested that science provides understanding in the sense of rational expectation. But, as Friedman (1974, 8) observed, well-known counterexamples, like the barometer prediction of a storm, show that rational expectation is insufficient for understanding: we do not understand the occurrence of a storm by merely referring to the barometer's indication. Remarkably, Friedman ignored the fact that Hempel also recognized an objective conception of understanding, namely the "theoretical" or "scientific" understanding associated with subsumption and unification. However, his own alternative is exactly in this spirit: he proposes an objectivist account of scientific understanding and explanation based on the idea of unification. Friedman (1974, 15) argues that "science increases our understanding of the world by reducing the total number of independent phenomena that we have to accept as ultimate or given." In his paper, he attempts to elaborate this intuition into a precise account of explanatory unification: explanations would have to be unifying in the sense that they reduce the number of independently accepted phenomena by subsuming them under a more general law. Friedman's approach proved to be untenable, however.[6]

To avoid these problems, Philip Kitcher (1981, 1989) presented an alternative model of explanatory understanding, on which unification is achieved by deriving descriptions of different phenomena using the same "argument patterns":

> Understanding the phenomena is not simply a matter of reducing the "fundamental incomprehensibilities" but of seeing connections, common patterns, in what initially appeared to be different situations.... Science advances our understanding of nature by showing us how to derive descriptions of many phenomena, using the same patterns of derivation again and again, and, in demonstrating this, it teaches us how to reduce the number of types of facts we have to accept as ultimate (or brute). (Kitcher 1989, 432)

This idea is explicated as follows: a successful explanation must belong to the so-called explanatory store $E(K)$, where K is the set of statements endorsed by the scientific community, and $E(K)$ is the maximally unifying systematization of K, that is, the set of derivations that employs fewer argument patterns than

---

6. See Salmon (1998, 70) for a summary of the problems for Friedman's approach.

any other systematization of *K*. A formal elaboration of this idea is provided by Kitcher (1989, 432–435). First, he defines the notion of a "general argument pattern." Any candidate explanation is a derivation of a specific conclusion from a set of premises, which can be viewed as an instantiation of some general argument pattern. Second, he defines the notion of "stringency of patterns," on the basis of which the degree of systematization of any particular set of derivations can be determined. On the basis of these notions it is possible to determine whether a particular derivation belongs to the maximally unifying set *E(K)* and can accordingly be regarded as explanatory. It follows that the value of a candidate explanation cannot be assessed in isolation but only by seeing how it "forms part of a systematic picture of the order of nature" (Kitcher 1989, 430).[7]

As mentioned, Kitcher regarded his model of explanatory unification as an explication and elaboration of what he believed to be the "unofficial Hempelian view" of explanation, based on the idea that unification provides an objective kind of scientific understanding. A close look at Kitcher's model reveals that it can indeed be seen as an improved version of Hempel's account in a number of ways. First, as in the deductive-nomological model, the basic assumption is that an explanation is always a (deductive) argument. Second, Kitcher suggests a solution to the notorious problem that Hempel's model faces, namely the problem of characterizing what a law is (see note 5 in this chapter). His approach introduces a new perspective on laws: they can be characterized as "the universal premises that occur in explanatory patterns" (Kitcher 1989, 447). Third, the unificationist model allows for the explanation of laws in terms of more comprehensive laws, while it evades Hempel's problem of finding a criterion for generality. In sum, Kitcher's unificationist model turns out to be a sophisticated version of Hempel's deductive-nomological model, preserving the basic features of deductive argument and subsumption under laws but avoiding the problematic aspects of its predecessor.

Kitcher did not see a tension between the alleged subjectivity of understanding and an objectivist approach to scientific explanation. On the contrary, he argued that, precisely because achieving understanding is a universal aim of science, a universally valid, objective account of explanation should be possible. To be sure, there can be strong variation in the nature of actual explanations (e.g., in the topics of explanation, in what counts as a legitimate answer, etc.), but it is still worthwhile to search for an underlying ideal that

---

7. See section 3.3 for further discussion of the "global" nature of unifying explanations.

is common to all explanations. According to Kitcher, this common ideal is attainment of scientific understanding:

> The search for understanding is, on many accounts of science a fundamental goal of the enterprise. That quest may take different forms in different historical and disciplinary contexts, but it is tempting to think that there is something that underlies the various local endeavors, something that makes each of them properly be seen as a striving after the same goal. The Hempelian conception proposes that there is an abstract conception of human understanding, that it is important to the development of science, and that it is common to the variety of ways in which understanding is sought and gained. Scientific explanations are intended to provide objective understanding of nature. The task of characterizing the ideal notions of explanation, why-question, and relevance is thus one of bringing into focus one of the basic aims of science. (Kitcher 1989, 419)

The unificationist conception of explanatory understanding has obvious merits. Its basic idea squares with the fact that many successful scientific theories are unifying: for example, Newtonian mechanics, Maxwell's electrodynamics, chemical atomic theory, and molecular genetics. An important advantage of the unificationist model is that its applicability is very general, since it does not require that theories are of a specific form. This implies that no theory is in principle incapable of providing understanding. No matter what its specific features are, if a theory turns out to be the maximally unifying systematization of a particular body of knowledge, it provides genuine explanations and understanding. In this respect, unificationism differs from causal and mechanical conceptions of understanding (to be discussed in section 3.2), which do pose restrictions on the form of theories. In contrast to these conceptions, unificationist models thus allow for the possibility that quantum mechanics provides understanding, a feature recognized as a major advantage by Friedman (1974, 18) and Salmon (1998, 76).

Since Kitcher's landmark essay of 1989, further work on unification has been done by others and alternative proposals have been offered, for example, by Erik Weber (1996, 1999) and Todd Jones (1997). Of special interest is the model of Gerhard Schurz and Karel Lambert (1994), which has been further developed in Schurz (1999). Schurz and Lambert focus explicitly on understanding: their aim is to provide a detailed analysis of how unification leads to understanding independently of a particular view of scientific explanation. In fact, however, this is not essentially different from the approach of Friedman and Kitcher, who analyze unification while simply assuming that unification provides understanding and is thereby explanatory. Schurz and Lambert also seek to develop an objective theory of scientific understanding that does not relate understanding to the psychology of individuals. Their basic assumption is: "To *understand* a phenomenon P is to know how P fits into one's background knowledge" (Schurz and Lambert 1994, 66). Fitting a phenomenon P into a "cognitive corpus" C requires giving an argument that connects P to the other elements of C in such a way that the resulting corpus is more unified. Schurz and Lambert (1994, 78–81) provide specific guidelines for comparing the unification of cognitive corpora. Their model differs from Kitcher's in that unification can be achieved via many different types of connections, not only deductive systematization.

Notwithstanding the merits and attractiveness of unificationism, and its advantages over Hempel's covering law model, critics have questioned the basic assumptions of the unificationist conception of scientific understanding. Eric Barnes (1992) argues that Friedman and Kitcher, when distinguishing between derived (understood) and underived (mysterious) phenomena, presuppose (without any justification) an account of understanding according to which individual phenomena can be rendered understood. James Woodward (2003b, 359–373) and Carl Craver (2007, 42–49) claim that not all unifications provide explanatory understanding (think, for example, of taxonomy) and argue that Kitcher's model cannot distinguish between explanatory and non-explanatory unification. In the same vein, Victor Gijsbers (2007) submits that unification, in both Kitcher's and Schurz and Lambert's sense, is neither a necessary condition nor a sufficient condition for explanation. The reason it is not sufficient is that it cannot account for the role of causality and laws in explanation: the unificationist conception is unable to deal satisfactorily with cases in which there exists an explanatory asymmetry (e.g., the example of the flagpole and the shadow; see section 3.2), and it does not discriminate between explanatory unifications on the basis of laws and non-explanatory unifications on the basis of accidental generalizations. Moreover, Gijsbers (2007, 495–498) argues, unification is not a necessary condition because there exist legitimate explanations in which the explanatory premises are no less in need of explanation than the explanandum. On Kitcher's and Schurz and Lambert's models, however, such arguments would be disunifying and accordingly not explanatory. [8] The upshot of these criticisms is that although unification clearly is a valuable achievement, it does not always

---

8. See Humphreys (1993) and Halonen and Hintikka (1999) for related criticisms.

increase our understanding of the phenomena. There are situations in which the explanation that provides the best understanding is not the most unifying one. Consequently, unification cannot be the single universal criterion for scientific understanding. While unification may provide understanding in some cases, in other cases understanding is achieved by other means.[9]

It cannot be doubted that the quest for unification has played an important role in the history of science. In physics, for example, it inspired the development of Maxwell's theory of electromagnetism and of present-day theories such as the Standard Model (Weinberg 1993; Wayne 1996; Cat 1998; Morrison 2000). However, it is not clear that the pursuit of unification was always motivated by a desire for understanding (for arguments against a historical connection between unification and understanding, see Barnes 1992, 7; Morrison 2000, 106). Moreover, even if this were the motivation in particular cases, this would not yet entail that unifying power is the quintessence of scientific understanding. For drawing this conclusion would ignore the historical variation in scientists' intelligibility standards, of which the debate between Schrödinger and Heisenberg discussed in chapter 1 is but one example (more will follow in subsequent chapters). In addition to unification, other theoretical virtues such as causality and visualizability have been deemed essential for achieving understanding at some points in history or by some members of the scientific community. What is more, it often happens that newly proposed scientific theories are regarded by the contemporary scientific community as supplying no understanding at all, notwithstanding their potential for unification; for example, Bohr's 1913 atomic theory or Newtonian gravitational theory (see chapter 5 for a discussion of the latter case). The scientists who rejected these theories as non-explanatory did not refer to an alleged lack of unifying power but to the lack of other qualities such as visualizability, continuity, or to the fact that the theory conflicted with accepted metaphysics.

In response to this objection, unificationists may argue that one can give (rational) reconstructions of actual history in which explanation by unification is the underlying driving force. Schurz and Lambert (1994, 103–107), for example, reconstruct the development of atomic theories from the late-nineteenth century up to 1925 in terms of increasing unification. They

---

9. Mäki (2001, 502–504) claims that unification is important in economics, and that objections to unificationism apply to the derivational variant and not to the ontological variant that he favors. He suggests, however, that unification is not explanatory in itself: "Increased understanding may not as such amount to increased unification, but increased unification may provide grounds for increased reliance on the capacity of a theory to provide understanding. Explanatory understanding is a matter of revealing the way the world works, without presupposing a priori that the world itself is maximally unified to any particular degree."

interpret the conceptual problems associated with Bohr's 1913 model (e.g., the stability postulate, implying discontinuous electron orbits and "quantum jumps") and with the new quantum mechanics of the 1920s (the EPR paradox; see section 3.2 for discussion) as "dissimilated elements" which contribute to a decrease of unification. Accordingly, while there is a general trend toward unification, there are sometimes unification-decreasing shifts, and these explain why scientists think some models or theories do not provide understanding (Bohr's 1913 model of the atom would be a case in point). This approach implies that the strong commitments scientists typically have about particular understanding-providing virtues are examples of "false consciousness." Kelvin's famous remarks on the indispensability of mechanical models for scientific understanding, cited in chapter 1, would be a case in point. On this view, Kelvin's belief was ultimately rooted in the unifying power of mechanics and not in any particular understanding-generating property of such models themselves. Kitcher (1989, 436) employs this "false consciousness" idea, when he argues that the concept of causal dependence is a derivative of unification, but that this does not imply that all individuals are aware of this (instead "our everyday causal knowledge is gained by absorbing the lore of our community" and is thus only indirectly linked to unifying power). However, if one favors a philosophical theory of explanation and understanding based on the actual practice and history of science, in line with a naturalistic approach to the philosophy of science, one should not distort history and appeal to false consciousness. When scientists explicitly base their judgments about theories on particular criteria, this should be taken seriously unless it can be proved that in fact other criteria are at work.[10]

It may be concluded that unification is a "tool" for achieving understanding, but only one among a variety of tools. Interestingly, this conclusion can be also drawn from Kitcher's analysis of the role of argument patterns. In order to support his claim that unification is essential for scientific understanding, Kitcher (1989, 437–438) presents an argument that is similar to the line of reasoning developed in section 2.2. Citing Kuhn, he suggests that "scientific knowledge involves more than knowing the statements" (of a theory). In addition, in order to apply the theory successfully to concrete situations, one needs to understand it, and this requires an "extra cognitive ingredient." According to Kitcher, this extra ingredient is the set of argument patterns associated with the theory: internalization of these argument patterns is a prerequisite for

---

10. See Woodward (2003b, 369–371) and Gijsbers (2007, 489–491) for further criticism of Kitcher's attempts to reconstruct causal arguments in terms of unificationism.

producing scientific knowledge. In other words, Kitcher acknowledges the crucial role of skills. He is right, but it is a *non sequitur* to conclude from this that unification (in Kitcher's sense of reducing the number of argument patterns) is the only way to produce increasingly more scientific understanding. Obviously unification can be an effective tool to achieve this goal: seeing analogies between theories in the form of similar argument patterns is a way of extending the range of a particular skill. But understanding can equally well be increased by internalizing two or more different argument patterns instead of one unified argument pattern. The former scenario may even be preferable, in cases where scientists are better equipped to employ the separate argument patterns than the unified one. Finally, note that Kitcher's argument is based on the idea that understanding the theory is a condition for generating scientific knowledge, that is, for producing scientific understanding of nature. In chapter 2, my analysis of understanding as an inextricable element of the aims of science led to the same conclusion. I will elaborate this idea in the next chapter, where I present a general theory of scientific understanding that explains the role of various intelligibility standards, such as causality and unification, in achieving understanding.

3.2 Causal conceptions of explanatory understanding

The main rival of unificationism is the causal conception of scientific understanding. Whereas unificationism is the natural successor of Hempel's covering law model, the causal approach to explanation and understanding is rooted in fundamental criticism of that model. Already in the late 1950s, some philosophers argued that Hempel's model failed to capture the intuition that scientists often explain and understand phenomena by uncovering their causes. Contra Hempel (1965, 349), who claimed that "causal explanation is, at least implicitly, deductive-nomological," Michael Scriven (1959, 456) suggested that causal stories can be explanatory in themselves. His classic example is that of explaining the stain on the carpet by telling a story of how one's knee hit the table, which caused an ink bottle to turn over, so that the ink ran over the edge; an explanation that does not refer to laws.[11] Other famous counterexamples to the covering law model also suggest that causality may be

---

11. Hempel responded that this causal story is merely an "explanatory sketch," which deserves articulation into a complete covering law explanation. Woodward (2003b, 157–160 and 175–181) rightly criticizes this response, which he calls the "hidden structure strategy"; see section 3.3 for further discussion.

crucial for achieving understanding. Thus, in the barometer case one deduces the future occurrence of a storm from a barometer reading plus the law that whenever the barometer drops, a storm will occur. While this deduction is a valid explanation according to the Hempel's model, it does not provide understanding of why the storm occurs. Instead, explanatory understanding can be acquired by discovering the common cause of the two nomologically correlated events, namely the very low air pressure. Similarly, in the well-known case of the flagpole and the shadow a causal analysis provides understanding, whereas a covering law explanation does not, or so it is argued. In this case, the length of the shadow of a flagpole is explained by citing the height of the flagpole, relevant circumstances such as the position of the sun, plus the general laws of geometrical optics. On the deductive-nomological model, however, one may equally well deduce the height of the flagpole from the length of the shadow. While both arguments conform to Hempel's criteria, on most people's intuitions only the former provides understanding. While we may be able to predict the length of the flagpole on the basis of the length of its shadow, few people would argue that this argument helps us to understand why the flagpole is, say, 15 feet long. This asymmetry is not captured by the deductive-nomological model but can be accounted for by invoking causality: causes explain effects, effects do not explain causes. For this reason, many authors claim, if we want to understand the phenomena, we should look for their causes.

One of the most prominent advocates of the causal conception of understanding, Wesley Salmon, states that "underlying causal mechanisms hold the key to our understanding of the world" (Salmon 1984, 260). This is because "causal processes, causal interactions, and causal laws provide the mechanisms by which the world works; to understand why certain things happen, we need to see how they are produced by these mechanisms" (Salmon 1984, 132). In his later work, he emphasized the importance of scientific understanding even more strongly (Salmon 1998, 3, 79–91). Salmon categorized his conception of scientific explanation as an "ontic" one: in contrast to "epistemic" conceptions, such as Hempel's and Kitcher's, which regard explanations as arguments, ontic conceptions assert that "events are explained by showing how they fit into the physical patterns found in the world" (Salmon 1998, 64). Thus, on the causal-mechanical conception, scientific explanation consists in giving a description of the causal network of processes and interactions that lead up to the event-to-be-explained.

In order to give this idea more substance one needs an adequate analysis of causality. In his seminal book *Scientific Explanation and the Causal Structure of the World*, Salmon (1984, 135–183) presents a detailed theory of causality. In his later years he further refined and elaborated it in discussion with others, but his approach remained essentially the same.[12] The two basic elements of Salmon's theory are causal processes and causal interactions. Processes are the basic entities of Salmon's ontology, and a causal process is a process that is able to transmit a "mark" (consisting in a persistent change in its structure). Causal processes are the means by which causal influence is transmitted. If two or more causal processes intersect and the result is a persistent change of (at least one of) the processes, this is called a causal interaction. In other words, causal interactions generate and modify causal structure. Salmon's claim is that only if we can describe the world in terms of such causal processes and interactions do we possess scientific understanding of it (Salmon 1998, 60).

Salmon intends his theory to be generally applicable. In all cases where a causal theory is available or possible, such a theory allegedly provides the best way to generate scientific understanding of phenomena. It should be noted that Salmon does not claim that causal-mechanistic explanation is an a priori condition for scientific understanding. Like most present-day philosophers he rejects apriorism and acknowledges the logical possibility that his favorite type of explanation may not be applicable in all situations (Salmon 1998, 313; 1984, 239–240). Still, Salmon assigns a superior status to causal-mechanical explanation by claiming that if an explanation of that form is possible, then that is the best explanation. Therefore, his position is not pluralistic: he remains committed to the view that causal analysis is the privileged road to scientific understanding.

It seems, however, that even if Salmon's qualifications are taken into account, present-day scientific developments cast severe doubt on the alleged privileged status of his model of causal explanation as the way to scientific understanding: not only are there domains of reality where causal-mechanical explanation fails, but in addition, scientists sometimes do not use it in situations where it is in principle applicable.

---

12. For a summary of his original theory, see Salmon (1998, ch. 8). For his refinements of this theory in the light of criticisms by Phil Dowe and Philip Kitcher, see Salmon 1998, ch. 16). The main objection relates to the question of whether an account of causation requires counterfactuals. Salmon's original theory of causality refers to counterfactuals (esp. in his criterion for mark transmission, which is the basis for distinguishing between causal processes and pseudo-processes). Salmon was unhappy with this and accepted an alternative way to characterize causal processes and interactions proposed by Phil Dowe (1992, 2000). Dowe invokes the notion of conserved quantities (quantities that obey conservation laws; e.g., momentum, energy, charge). In his theory of causation, a causal process is a world-line of an object that possesses a conserved quantity, and a causal interaction is an intersection of world-lines that involves an exchange of conserved quantities.

At the deepest levels of physical reality Salmon's concept of causality is highly problematic. The main obstacle is the failure of the notion of a causal chain; causal connections of this type (i.e., continuous space-time trajectories along which energy and momentum are transported) do not exist according to the standard interpretation of quantum theory. The best known example in which quantum physics and Salmon's analysis of causality conflict is the Einstein-Podolsky-Rosen (EPR) situation. A central thesis of Salmon's theory is that every empirical correlation requires a causal explanation, either in terms of a direct causal connection or in terms of a common cause. In the EPR case, however, a direct causal connection is impossible because the two correlated events are too far apart in space and too close in time for a signal to connect them; and the violation of Bell's inequality entails that an explanation of EPR correlations in terms of a common cause is impossible as well.[13] Accordingly, Salmon has problems in applying his model of explanation to contemporary fundamental physics, which induces him to add disclaimers such as: "If quantum mechanics requires non-causal mechanisms, they also explain what goes on" (Salmon 1984, 133).[14] His dilemma is that he wants to remain faithful to modern science and to quantum mechanics as it is usually interpreted by scientists (e.g., he wants to leave room for indeterminism), while his analysis of causality is not a natural part of modern physics.

That quantum theory presents fundamental difficulties for a causal analysis is well known, but sometimes not considered as decisive because of the interpretational problems surrounding the theory. However, we need not restrict our attention to quantum theory. Physics is full of examples that show that causal-mechanical explanation is not always the actually preferred manner of achieving understanding. Consider, for instance, the way the special relativistic Lorentz contraction is usually understood. This example is particularly interesting because here a causal-mechanistic account is possible: such an explanation was given by Lorentz himself in his electron theory, and the same explanation is possible within the framework of special relativity. In this

---

13. See, e.g., van Fraassen (1991, 81–89). It might be thought that EPR correlations can be explained by means of common cause analysis in terms of an interactive fork (instead of the conjunctive fork); see Salmon (1984, 168–172). However, the problem is that the particle trajectories do not count as causal processes at all, according to Salmon's criteria. So retreating to the (weaker) interactive fork does not help in the EPR situation. Hofer-Szabó et al. (1999) argue that on a more general interpretation of the common cause principle the Bell inequalities do not rule out the existence of common causes in an EPR situation. However, Hofer-Szabó et al. abandon a crucial assumption of standard common cause explanation (viz., that there should be a single common cause for all correlated pairs).

14. Cf. Salmon (1984, 258; 1998, 76, 325).

account the changes in the intermolecular forces that occur if a body is set into motion are identified as the mechanism that makes the length contractions understandable. However, this explanation is not the standard one and is not found in textbooks on the theory of relativity. The usual way of making the contractions intelligible is by connecting them deductively to the basic postulates of special relativity (the relativity postulate and the light postulate): length contractions must necessarily occur if these postulates both apply to physical reality—this is a matter of logic. Causal reasoning is not involved.[15]

To be sure, there are areas of contemporary science where causal-mechanistic explanation is prevalent, for example, in the biological sciences, where mechanistic approaches are currently quite popular (these will be discussed in more detail later). But, as Ruth Berger (1998) shows by means of a case study in population biology, even in biology causal analysis is not always the preferred explanatory strategy. Biologists construct macro-level mathematical models to explain population dynamics and consider micro-level causal description—which is in principle possible– as irrelevant for understanding the phenomena.[16] In sum, Salmon's model fails to apply to the most fundamental physical theories, and in some other cases it is not used even when it can be applied. (Note that even quantum theory can be regarded as an example of the latter type because a causal version of it is available, Bohm's theory, which, however, is largely ignored by the general physics community). These facts are sufficient to cast doubt on the core idea that causality has a special status as the fundamental, privileged standard of intelligibility.

A proposal for a specific intelligibility standard such as Salmon's always faces the danger of being superseded by science. Historically minded readers will observe that the preference for causal mechanisms can plausibly be related to the success of this concept within nineteenth-century science.[17] But even in pre-twentieth-century physics causal-mechanical explanation was not always the norm. It is true that Newton's theory of gravitation was criticized because it failed to conform to the Cartesian intelligibility ideal of contact

---

15. See Dieks (2009), who compares the "bottom-up" account of Lorentz with the "top-down" account of Einstein and concludes that they are equally viable ways of explaining relativistic effects. The decision to use either the former or the latter is a matter of pragmatics.

16. Berger's case study is discussed in more detail in section 3.3. See Morrison (2009) for a related analysis of the way in which mathematical abstractions can provide understanding in population biology.

17. Salmon himself is at pains to avoid this impression. Cf. his plea for "causal-mechanical understanding (but not the nineteenth-century English version satirized by Duhem)" (Salmon 1998, 87).

action; its implication of *actio in distans* was unacceptable to most seventeenth-century physicists. But between 1700 and 1850 action at a distance rather than contact action and causal chains dominated the scientific scene (van Lunteren 1991, 126). It was only after 1850, with the advent of ether theories, that contact action and causal mechanisms again came to be regarded as standards of intelligibility (in chapter 5, I will investigate this case in more detail).

Salmon's causal-mechanical model of explanatory understanding is clearly inspired by the physical sciences. It may be questioned, however, whether it is a satisfactory model for all scientific disciplines. Because the model is so closely tied to physical science, it does not seem to fit the explanatory practices of the life sciences, let alone the social sciences. This has induced philosophers to develop alternative causal models of explanation that are better suited for these purposes. First, models based on alternative analyses of causality. Second, models based on a different conception of mechanism, which apply especially to the life sciences. In the remaining part of this section, I will discuss representatives of these alternative approaches. Among the former are the manipulationist theory developed by James Woodward (2003b), which is particularly well-suited to explanation in the social and biomedical sciences, and the so-called kairetic account of Michael Strevens (2008).

Woodward's theory of causal explanation is based on a conception of causation in which intervention and manipulation are central. According to Woodward, a causal relation is a relation between variables X and Y, and "X causes Y" holds if and only if the value of Y would change under some intervention on X. The idea of intervention is crucial in this "manipulability theory" of causation because interventions allow us to change X while holding other variables constant, thus determining its contributing effect on Y.[18] A typical example from scientific practice is the case of determining the relation between administration of a particular drug to a patient and his recovery from a particular disease. Medical scientists have a standard method for finding this out: the double blind testing procedure. One group of patients is given the drug, while another (control) group is supplied with a placebo, holding all other circumstances equal (as far as possible), and it is observed whether or not a statistically significant difference in recovery results between the two groups of patients. In this experiment, the experimenter intervenes

---

18. Although Woodward's theory is motivated by the intuition that the use of the concept of causation is rooted in the practical values of manipulation and control, he defines the notion of intervention without reference to free human action, and thereby evades anthropomorphism. In contrast to existing agency theories of causation, he defends an objective theory of causation. As regards explanation, his aims are objectivist as well (Woodward 2003b, 184).

by manipulating the cause (changing the intervention variable, which has two values: treated/untreated) and observing whether an effect results (change of the two-valued variable recovery/nonrecovery).[19] Woodward asserts that a good (causal) explanation exhibits patterns of counterfactual dependence that describe the outcomes of interventions. Explanations thereby allow us to answer "what-if-things-had-been-different questions." For example, explaining the recovery of the patient by citing the drug administration amounts to answering the question of what would have happened in case the patient would not have taken the drug: he would (probably) not have recovered. A double blind experiment devised to support this explanatory claim can be seen as an attempt to establishing such a counterfactual dependency relation. An important advantage of Woodward's approach lies in its general applicability. Since it does not make specific assumptions about causal mechanisms or require laws of nature, it not only applies to physics but to biomedical and social sciences as well (where mechanisms and laws are harder to find). Because he does not pose unrealistic demands on explanations, Woodward is able to accommodate a wide range of explanatory practices across the various sciences.

What are the implications of Woodward's theory of explanation for the nature of scientific understanding? Although he does not present a detailed analysis of understanding, he considers it an essential product of explanations: "It is a plausible constraint on what an explanation is that it must be something that provides understanding" (2003b, 179).[20] His views on what understanding consists in become clear from his discussion of a possible objection to the manipulability theory (Woodward 2003b, 221–223). One might argue that there seem to be cases in which one may have knowledge of counterfactual dependence relations (and, accordingly, answers to what-if-things-had-been-different questions), while such alleged explanations do not provide real understanding. An example would be the explanation of the fact that the pressure of a gas increases with its temperature on the basis of the ideal-gas law $PV = nRT$. It is widely assumed, for example, by Salmon and his followers, that this law provides no understanding and that we need an

---

19. Although Woodward's analysis of causation in terms of intervention and manipulation is intuitively plausible, critics have objected that it is prone to vicious circularity (De Regt 2004b) or infinite regress (Baumgartner 2009).

20. Woodward (2003b, 179) argues that this poses an epistemic constraint on explanatory information: "Such information must be accessible to those who use the explanation." In section 3.3, we will see that he uses this constraint to argue against the so-called hidden structure strategy of Hempel and Peter Railton.

account in terms of underlying mechanisms, which is in this case provided by the kinetic theory and statistical mechanics. Contrary to this view, however, Woodward argues that the ideal-gas law does provide understanding, albeit of a rather shallow kind. A statistical-mechanical explanation furnishes deeper understanding in the sense that it allows us to answer a wider range of what-if-things-had-been-different questions about the phenomenon. But there is no essential difference between the shallow and the deeper explanation: the latter just gives us more information relevant to the manipulation and control of the phenomenon. Thus, Woodward's causal theory of explanation does not qualify as an "ontic" conception, like Salmon's.[21] Understanding is not a question of getting the ontology right, but of knowing how systems behave under a range of interventions. This idea is quite compatible to the view of understanding that I will develop in the next chapter.

We saw that Salmon assigns a privileged status to causal explanations, although he allows for the possibility that in some domains causal explanations are impossible. Woodward's approach is different: rejecting the goal of a universally valid theory of all scientific explanation, he tries to develop and defend a theory of causal explanation that applies as broadly and wide-ranging as possible (Woodward 2003b, 4–6). Unfortunately, he does not elaborate on the problems with causation and explanation in quantum mechanics, exemplified by the Einstein-Podolsky-Rosen (EPR) correlations. As mentioned, these correlations cannot be explained by means of direct causal influence or by referring to a common cause. Accordingly, a causal explanation in terms of the manipulability theory is impossible because one cannot manipulate the outcomes on one wing of the experiment by intervening on the other wing (and neither by intervening on the source). Woodward (2003b, 92) calls EPR a "recherché case" and does not discuss the question of whether or not his theory would be able to deal with it, in contrast to Salmon, who acknowledged the failure of his theory in the quantum-mechanical domain but did not abandon the search for a way in which quantum-mechanical phenomena can be understood.

Michael Strevens (2008) has presented a model of scientific explanation that he dubs the "kairetic" account. While agreeing with Salmon and Woodward that phenomena are explained by describing how they are causally produced, Strevens (2008, 27–35) does not commit himself to a particular metaphysical theory of causation but instead has an "ecumenical"

---

21. Woodward (2003b, 223–224) explicitly argues against associating explanatory power with a realistic interpretation of theories. See section 4.5.1 for further discussion of the relation between scientific realism and explanatory understanding.

view: (almost) all existing theories of causation are compatible with the kairetic account. Its starting point is the idea that of the many different causal influences on a phenomenon only some are relevant to its occurrence. For example, when a car accident happens, both the icy road and the gravitational effect of Mars causally influence the event, but only the former is causally relevant. This is because the ice makes a difference to the occurrence of the event while Mars's gravitational effect does not. The core of the kairetic theory is the so-called optimizing procedure to identify the difference makers for events-to-be-explained (Strevens 2008, 86–110). This procedure involves eliminating irrelevant influences and abstracting the remaining influences in such a way that irrelevant details are removed (e.g., not the exact structure of the ice but only the fact that the icy layer was, say, at least 1 mm thick is relevant). The optimizing procedure leads to a "stand-alone explanation," which is complete and sufficient for scientific understanding of the event. There can be many standalone explanations of one particular event, which can all be satisfactory and sufficient for understanding.[22] However, Strevens (2008, 123–137) argues that some may be better than others and that in particular "deepening" explanations, which give a lower-level account of why higher-level causal laws obtain, are superior from an explanatory point of view.

Strevens' book is entitled *Depth*, and "science is said to be deep just when it provides understanding" (Strevens 2008, 136). Thus, understanding is a central aim of science. But exactly what is it? Strevens (2008, 3) asserts that scientific understanding is "that state produced, and only produced, by grasping a true explanation."[23] He distinguishes three grades of understanding: partial or qualified understanding, full understanding, and exhaustive understanding. If we have a standalone explanation that contains black boxes as placeholders for causal mechanisms, we have merely partial (qualified) understanding (Strevens 2008, 153–154). Full understanding is achieved if we have a mechanistic account of all relevant (difference-making) influences. Exhaustive understanding, finally, is the complete (possibly infinite) account of all causal influences on the event-to-be-explained. Strevens (2008, 154): "Exhaustive understanding is a kind of ideal, but an ideal to which those interested in

---

22. Strevens (2008, 117) states that "science understands a phenomenon just in case it can provide a standalone explanation of the phenomenon," and while there may be many different standalone explanations for one phenomenon, "knowledge of any is sufficient for scientific understanding of the event's occurrence."

23. This formulation is identical to Trout's (2007, 585–586); see section 2.1 for discussion of Trout's conception of understanding.

only full understanding need not take the trouble to aspire." The underlying idea is that full understanding requires knowledge of the relevant causal mechanisms in fundamental physical terms (130–131). It follows that Strevens adheres to what Salmon calls an "ontic" conception of explanation and understanding (cf. 6). Moreover, his ambitions may be classified as universalistic and objectivist. He assumes that "there is an underlying set of principles that has always determined what does and does not count as a good explanation for us" (38), and his aim is to describe these principles. For this reason, he rejects relativist theories of explanation, according to which "the nature of the explanatory relation changes according to preferences, cultural traditions, knowledge, conversation context, or some other observer-dependent factor" (22).

Salmon's causal-mechanical account of explanation is modeled on explanatory practices in the physical sciences. An important type of explanation that seems to fall outside the scope of Salmon's theory is functional explanation, which is quite common in the life sciences, psychology, and the social sciences. These sciences are concerned with complex organized systems of which the components contribute to keeping the system (organisms, human minds, societies) in working order. A functional explanation typically accounts for the role or presence of a component item by citing its function in the system. The standard example in philosophy of science is the heart: humans have a heart because it has the function of pumping blood, and pumping blood is required to stay alive.

Since the turn of the millennium, many philosophers of science have devoted their efforts to developing mechanistic models of explanation that are tailored to the practices of contemporary life sciences. Inspired by groundbreaking ideas of Robert Cummins (1975) and William Wimsatt (1976), they argue that, at least in the life sciences and neuroscience, functional explanation and causal explanation may be integrated by analyzing functions in terms of mechanisms. The core of their alternative approach is a new analysis of what constitutes a mechanism. In contrast to Salmon, who identifies a mechanism as a network of causal processes and interactions, the "new mechanists" state that a mechanism is an organized whole that by virtue of the interaction of its component parts produces specific behavior or performs a particular function. Important differences with Salmon's view notwithstanding, most new mechanists place themselves in the tradition of causal-mechanical explanation, and regard their proposals as complementing rather than replacing Salmon's account. They regard the differences as a natural consequence of the fact that new scientific developments give rise to new types of mechanisms. As Craver (2007, 3–4) suggests, it is only natural that a single correct definition of what a mechanism is does not exist: the history of science has witnessed a great variety of mechanisms and mechanistic explanations.

In their influential paper "Thinking about Mechanisms," which may be regarded as the beginning of the "new mechanist" movement, Peter Machamer, Lindley Darden, and Carl Craver (2000) characterize mechanisms as entities and activities organized such that they produce the phenomenon-to-be-explained. Their account is further developed in subsequent publications (see, e.g., Craver 2007; Darden 2008). Different characterizations of mechanisms have been proposed by Glennan (2002, S344) and Bechtel and Abrahamsen (2005, 423), for example, but all agree on the essential elements: biological mechanisms exhibit complex organization and by virtue of the organized interaction of their parts produce specific functional behavior. Thus, key terms are: productivity, complexity, and functionality. Mechanistic explanation of phenomena is achieved by providing a model, or representation, that describes the mechanisms that produce them (Machamer, Darden, and Craver 2000, 3; Glennan 2002, S347; Bechtel and Abrahamsen 2005, 425).[24]

As an example, consider the circulatory system. This is a complex, organized system that produces life-sustaining behavior. Every element (the heart, lungs, kidneys, veins, etc.) has a specific function that contributes to keeping the system in working order: the interaction of all functioning elements guarantees the survival of the organism. The function of the system as a whole, namely its contribution to the survival of the organism, is explained by providing a mechanistic description of it in terms of component parts and their interaction, for example, by representing it as in figure 3.1. Every component part has a function of its own, which can be further analyzed and explained in a mechanistic fashion.

The new mechanists strongly emphasize the intelligible, understanding-providing nature of mechanistic explanations. Thus, Machamer, Darden, and Craver (2000, 21) state that "the contemporary mechanical worldview ... is a conviction about how phenomena are to be understood." They suggest that mechanistic explanations possess special features by which they furnish understanding, which can be characterized in terms of *intelligibility* and which may be traced back to our *familiarity* with them through our sensory experience:

---

24. Some authors suggest that the mechanistic approach can also be applied to domains outside biology, e.g., chemistry and cognitive psychology (Bechtel 2008; Darden 2008; Ramsey 2008).

HUMAN CIRCULATORY SYSTEM

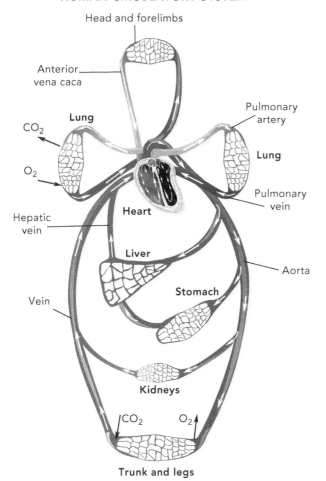

FIGURE 3.1 A mechanistic account of the human circulatory system. Courtesy of Shutterstock.

Intelligibility, at least in molecular biology and neurobiology, is provided by descriptions of mechanisms, that is, through the elaboration of constituent entities and activities that, by an extension of sensory experience with ways of working, provide an understanding of how some phenomenon is produced. (Machamer, Darden, and Craver 2000, 22)[25]

25. Incidentally, Carl Craver has abandoned the views regarding understanding and intelligibility expressed in the 2000 paper with Machamer and Darden. In his 2007 book *Explaining*

One of these features is obviously causality (or, in the new mechanists' terminology: productivity). Another one, according to Machamer, Darden, and
Craver (2000, 3), is continuity: "Productive continuities are what make the
connections between stages intelligible."[26] In addition, the visualizability of
mechanistic explanations is a feature that contributes to their aptness for providing understanding. As Bechtel and Abrahamsen (2005, 427–430) observe,
mechanistic explanations are typically not purely linguistic but contain diagrammatic representations. Scientists often prefer diagrams to linguistic representations because the former can directly convey the spatial organization
of mechanisms (and temporal change can be represented visually as well),
which allows them to grasp their structure directly and fully. The representation of the circulatory system in figure 3.1 provides a case in point. The
structural relations between the various component parts are immediately
clear, and the interaction and productive relations are visually depicted. The
arrows, for example, represent flow of blood and the transportation of oxygen, CO_2, nutrients, and waste products. Different shadings are used to indicate blood with low and high oxygen content (light and dark, respectively).
Diagrammatic representations of complex mechanisms are far more tractable
than linguistic representations. Moreover, reasoning about diagrams can be
facilitated by simulation tools such as scale models or computer models. For
these reasons, mechanistic explanations are highly effective in producing scientific understanding.[27]

The fact that the new mechanists consider the amenability of mechanistic
explanations to visual and diagrammatic representation a crucial advantage
with respect to the provision of understanding suggests that they acknowledge
that understanding is, at least partly, a matter of pragmatics. Whether or not
an explanation furnishes understanding depends on the skills, the interests,
and the background knowledge of the person who receives the explanation
and these may vary with the context. Craver (2001, 71) argues that mechanistic

---

the Brain, he rejects the idea that (psychological) accounts of human understanding can be
relevant for a philosophical (esp. normative) theory of scientific explanation. Thus, in line
with Trout's argumentation discussed in section 2.1, Craver (2007, ix, 21) states that feelings
of understanding can be misleading and should not be used as indicators for the quality
of an explanation. Moreover, there can be explanation without (individual) understanding,
for example, in cases where the system is too complex and/or understanding is distributed
among many scientists (Craver 2007, 28–34).

26. Cf. Machamer et al. (2000, 12): "In a complete description of the mechanism there are
no gaps that leave specific steps unintelligible; the whole process is rendered intelligible in
terms of entities and activities that are acceptable to a field at a time."

27. See Machamer et al. (2000, 8–9) for a different example.

explanations of functions are always contextual and "ineliminably perspec-tival," since they are given in the context of a particular explanatory framework chosen on the basis of our interests. He suggests that this contextual aspect of (functional) explanation can complement Salmon's view (1984, 275), which recognizes only etiological and constitutive aspects to causal-mechanical explanation.

The causal conception of explanatory understanding is a valuable alter-native to the unificationist conception. Despite the common emphasis on causality, however, a closer look at the various models of explanation dis-cussed above reveals important differences regarding the associated claims about scientific understanding. While Salmon and Strevens defend an ontic view, identifying the search for understanding with uncovering the causal structure of the world, Woodward takes a different approach when he inter-prets understanding as knowing how systems behave under interventions and accordingly being able to manipulate and control them. The new mech-anists emphasize not only causality but also visualizability and continuity as the understanding-providing features (intelligibility standards) of mech-anistic explanations.

Notwithstanding its popularity and wide applicability, causality cannot be regarded as the universal standard of intelligibility, as has become clear from its failure in the quantum domain and the de facto application of alter-native standards in other scientific fields and disciplines. Although it is evi-dent that certain intelligibility standards play a dominant role in particular scientific fields and domains, they do not possess a privileged status in an absolute sense: their importance and function can vary in history and across fields or disciplines. In sum: like unification, causality is an important tool for achieving scientific understanding, applicable in many but not in all situ-ations. The idea of "tools for understanding" will be further developed in chapter 4.

3.3 Are causal and unificatory understanding complementary?

The fact that there is no universal standard of intelligibility, and that scien-tific understanding can be achieved in different ways, leads to the question of how these various routes to understanding are related. What does the road map for understanding look like? Do different intelligibility standards merely lead us along different roads to the same destination: the State of Understanding. Or do they take us to different states in one country, the United States of Understanding? For example, does the understanding that is the product of causal explanation differ from that of explanation by unification, and if so, how are these different products—causal and unificatory understanding—related?

An answer to this question has been suggested by Wesley Salmon, who, in his later work, attempted to reconcile his own causal-mechanical model of explanation with the unificationist model. When he became convinced that both were viable models of explanation, he hoped for "a new consensus" among philosophers of science which would lead to a "peaceful coexistence" of the two models (Salmon 1990, 184–185). More specifically, he argued that causal explanation and explanation by unification are "complementary" (Salmon 1998, 10, 73, 90, 170, 362). In the present section, I will analyze the precise meaning and the prospects of this "complementarity thesis."[28]

First of all, the term "complementary" implies that causal-mechanical explanation and explanation by unification are not merely two different enterprises which by coincidence are both called "explanation," but two parts or aspects of a greater whole. What is this greater whole? One might be inclined simply to say that both are types of explanation and thus explanation is the overarching notion. However, this does not answer the question in a satisfactory manner. The complementarity thesis entails that explanation can no longer be defined in either causal or unificationist terms, but that an independent characterization should be found of what it means to explain something scientifically. Such an independent characterization may be achieved by focusing on the notion of understanding, and this was indeed the strategy that Salmon followed. In line with the analysis presented in chapter 2, scientific explanation can be regarded as an activity with understanding of the phenomena (UP) as its product or aim: a satisfactory explanation by definition provides understanding. According to Salmon (1998, 76), "one of the chief aims and accomplishments of science is to enhance our understanding of the world we live in," and this understanding has two aspects, associated with the two conceptions of explanation. Salmon suggested that both explanation by unification and causal explanation produce understanding, but of different (complementary) types. Together the two complementary types of understanding add up to the greater whole: complete scientific understanding. To avoid confusion, I will call such complete understanding *superunderstanding*,

---

28. Marchionni (2008) defends an analogous complementarity thesis for the social sciences, arguing that micro-level explanations (in terms of individuals and their interactions) and macro-level explanations (in terms of social structures) are "strongly complementary," which implies that a better explanation results when both are integrated.

while the complementary aspects of superunderstanding will simply be called understanding (of course, one still has to specify the nature of superunderstanding). With these definitions, the complementarity thesis can be formulated as follows:

Complementarity Thesis: Causal-mechanical explanation and explanation by unification produce complementary types of understanding that are mutually exclusive and jointly exhaustive components of complete understanding (superunderstanding).[29]

Salmon first advanced and elaborated his complementarity thesis in the 1990 essay "Scientific Explanation: Causation *and* Unification" (Salmon 1998, 68–78). A clear statement can be found in the introduction to his 1998 collection of essays. After having reviewed the connection between causality and explanation, he writes:

> Nevertheless, I do not claim that all scientific explanation is causal; instead I distinguish two general types of scientific explanation—one depending on causal and/or mechanical factors, the other emphasizing theoretical unification. Although many philosophers see a conflict between these two conceptions, I find them mutually compatible and complementary. One and the same phenomenon can often be explained in both ways, each providing a different sort of understanding. (Salmon 1998, 9–10)

Salmon drew inspiration from the enlightening ways in which unificationists Friedman and Kitcher described their disagreement with the causalists, namely in terms of distinctions between "global" and "local," or "top-down" and explanation. Friedman (1974, 19) concluded his defense of unificationism with the claim that "the kind of understanding that science provides is global rather than local": the aim of science is not to understand individual facts (i.e., local understanding) but to understand many facts by relating them to each other (i.e., global understanding). Causalism appears to be local, while unificationism is global. Kitcher (1985, 638) characterized

---

29. It should be noted that this is my explication of Salmon's position. To be sure, Salmon himself did not provide an explicit formulation of his complementarity thesis, and it is therefore not certain that he would have endorsed the interpretation I have given. However, I will argue that if one does not want to render the complementarity thesis vacuous, a characterization of this form is needed.

Salmon's causal approach as bottom-up because "explanation of individual occurrences is fundamental." Having offered various objections to this approach, he concluded that scientific understanding should instead be achieved in a top-down manner: theoretical explanation by means of unification of regularities is prior to (causal) explanation of individual events: the latter kind of explanation draws on the former (Kitcher 1985, 639; 1989, 436).

Salmon (1985, 651–653) replied that the source of controversy lies not in an opposition between unificationism and causalism but in one between derivational and causal-mechanical conceptions of explanation. He suggested that both derivational and causal-mechanical explanatory accounts employ general laws, and thereby unifications. Salmon (1985, 653) concluded his response with the remark that "Kitcher's provocative distinction between 'bottom up' and 'top down' approaches requires further clarification." Attempts at such further clarification led him to believe that both approaches are valid, namely as ways to achieve complementary types of understanding, which together add up to what I have called "superunderstanding."

Crucial to the clarification was the notion of "ideal explanatory text," introduced by Peter Railton in the context of a defense of his deductive-nomological-probabilistic (D-N-P) model of explanation. According to this model, the fact that $e = G$ at some time t_0 is explained by an account of the following form (Railton 1981, 236):

(a)   A theoretical derivation of a probabilistic law of the form (b)

(b) $\forall x \, \forall t \, [F_{x,t} \rightarrow \text{Probability} \, (G)_{x,t} = r]$ (probabilistic law)

(c) F_{e,t_0} (initial condition)

(d) $\text{Probability} \, (G)_{e,t_0} = r$

(e) $(G)_{e,t_0}$ (parenthetic addendum)

Railton (1978) had introduced this model as an improvement on Hempel's D-N model, which he regarded as incomplete because it does not include "an account of the mechanism" that brings about the phenomenon to be explained (Railton 1978, 208). Hempel's model needs such an additional account in order to deal with counterexamples such as the well-known barometer case. In the above schema, (b-c-d) represents a Hempelian deductive schema, while the added premise (a) represents the mechanistic underpinning of the explanation. (The parenthetic addendum (e) represents the fact that event e actually happened.) It is premise (a) that is most interesting from the perspective of our discussion, particularly because Railton explicates it in terms of causal mechanisms. In his 1981 paper on the D-N-P model he expands on the nature of the theoretical derivations figuring in the schema:

> The place to look for guidance is plainly scientific practice itself. If one inspects the best-developed explanations in physics or chemistry text-books and monographs, one will observe that these accounts typically include not only derivations of lower-level laws and generalizations from higher-level laws, but also attempts to *elucidate the mechanisms at work*. (Railton 1981, 242)

Railton (1981, 242) admitted that he did "not have anything very definite to say about what would count as 'elucidating the mechanisms at work,'" but as a concrete example he mentioned the "tunnelling" mechanism that is part of the explanation of alpha-decay. Not surprisingly, Salmon (1990, 156) was very sympathetic toward this view, and he classified Railton's approach as "strongly mechanistic."

Railton observed that it would be too strong a requirement if we would ask of every scientific explanation that it gives a full-fledged D-N-P account of the form presented in the schema. The schema provides the *ideal explanatory text*. In practice, scientists almost never attempt to specify this complete ideal text: in most cases this is impossible or inappropriate. Usually they search for *explanatory information*, defined as follows (Railton 1981, 240): statement S provides explanatory information concerning *p* iff S enables us to answer questions about the ideal D-N-P text (for the explanation of *p*) in such a way as to eliminate some degree of uncertainty about what is contained in the text. On Railton's view, there exists a "continuum of explanatoriness" (240): from the ideal explanatory text, on the one hand, to statements completely devoid of explanatory information, on the other. These considerations led Railton (1981, 244) to a definition of scientific understanding: "we understand why a given ... phenomenon occurred to the extent that we are able, at least in principle, to produce the relevant ideal D-N-P text or texts." This entails that any statement S provides a degree of understanding proportional to the amount of explanatory information it contains, and only the ideal explanatory text provides complete scientific understanding.

Railton's conception of understanding can be invoked to flesh out the complementarity thesis. I argued that the notion of complementarity presupposes the existence of a greater whole, and I suggested that one might give an independent characterization of this greater whole in terms of understanding. This was indeed the strategy pursued by Salmon, who developed his complementarity thesis along these lines: he claimed that causal-mechanical explanation and explanation by unification produce complementary types of understanding. This claim implies that both types are aspects or components of a greater superunderstanding. The exact nature of superunderstanding was left unspecified for the time being. With the notion of the ideal explanatory text, we can now give an exact specification of superunderstanding, the key concept in the complementarity thesis: one possesses superunderstanding (complete understanding) of a phenomenon p if and only if one is able to formulate the ideal explanatory text relevant to the occurrence of p.

The ideal explanatory text contains (1) arguments that subsume phenomena under laws; and (2) theoretical derivations of these laws. Any information that contributes to our knowledge of the ideal text is explanatory information that enhances our understanding of the phenomenon p. If we identify superunderstanding with the ideal explanatory text, the complementarity thesis can be interpreted as stating that the two complementary types of explanation (explanation by unification and causal-mechanical explanation) roughly correspond to the elements (1) and (2) of the ideal text. As described in section 3.1, Kitcher's model presents explanation by unification as a deductive argument from general laws, where laws are characterized as "the universal premises that occur in explanatory patterns." In other words, unification supplies information that contributes to our knowledge of how the phenomenon can be subsumed under general laws (argument b-c-d in the schema). Causal-mechanical explanation, by contrast, provides information about the underlying causal mechanisms that bring about the phenomenon, and thereby partly covers premise (a) in the schema: the theoretical derivations of the laws. Railton emphasized that in addition to derivation from higher-level laws this involved "elucidating the mechanisms at work," but he did not present an analysis of what a mechanism is. However, such an analysis is needed if the model is to have any content. To fill this lacuna Salmon invoked his own theory of causality, described in section 3.2, which gives a precise account of what it means to exhibit the underlying causal network of processes and interactions.

Consequently, any information that contributes to our knowledge of the ideal explanatory text is either knowledge about how phenomena can be subsumed under unifying laws or about the underlying causal mechanisms. In other words, it is either explanatory information of a global, top-down type or of a local, bottom-up type. The sum of these two complementary types of information is the total amount of explanatory information that is in principle available: the ideal explanatory text. To possess it means to have superunderstanding.

Salmon (1998, 73) illustrated the complementarity thesis with an example concerning the motion of a helium balloon in an airplane. If you release a helium-filled balloon in an accelerating plane, it will (perhaps to your surprise) move forward. Salmon argued that two highly different explanations of this phenomenon can be given. First, a causal-mechanical account in terms of the behavior of molecules: the acceleration leads to an increase of pressure in the back of the plane, which in turn induces the balloon to be pushed in the forward direction. The second explanation invokes Einstein's principle of equivalence, known from general relativity: the effects of the acceleration are equivalent to those of a gravitational field in the backward direction, which entails that the balloon moves in the opposite direction. Salmon claimed that the latter explanation is of the unifying kind because it appeals to a general principle. He concluded that both explanations are correct and give understanding: they are "not antithetical but, rather, complementary" (Salmon 1998, 74).

It is instructive to have a closer look at this case. First, note that in the causal-mechanical account of the motion of the balloon general (read: unifying) principles appear to play a role as well, in the form of the laws of mechanics. This illustrates the general problem of whether it is possible to give a causal-mechanical account without explicitly or implicitly referring to laws. Initially, Salmon (1985, 651) believed that this is impossible, but he did not see it as a problem for his theory of explanation. It seems to pose a problem for the complementarity thesis, however, because local and global understanding are defined as mutually exclusive and jointly exhaustive components of superunderstanding. If causal-mechanical explanation without laws is impossible, we cannot have purely local, bottom-up understanding, and we do not have mutually exclusive types of understanding.

It has been argued, however, that causal explanation can be achieved on a purely local level, without reliance on laws. For example, Railton (1981, 249) claimed: "Many proffered explanations succeed in doing some genuine explaining *without* either using laws explicitly or (somehow) tacitly asserting their existence." Proponents of this view have to present an analysis of causation that allows for singular causal relations. Salmon's theory of causality, in which causal processes and interactions are ontologically basic, is congenial to this view but Salmon's original characterizations of causal processes and interactions turned out not to be independent of laws and counterfactuals. In his later work Salmon modified his definitions, with the help of the conserved quantity theory of causation proposed by Phil Dowe (1992), in order to solve this problem.[30] It remains controversial, however, whether the conserved quantity approach really is a solution and can do without laws or counterfactuals.[31]

In sum, the example reveals that there are problems with making a strict distinction between causal-mechanical and unificationist explanation as being mutually exclusive. However, even if singular causal explanation turns out to be impossible, one may distinguish between explanations that—albeit not purely local—do concentrate on the "nitty-gritty details of causal processes and interactions" (Salmon 1998, 74), in contrast to global explanations that focus on general, unifying principles. In this sense causalism and unificationism can still be regarded as complementary: while they are not mutually exclusive, they remain jointly exhaustive. In other words, even in that case we can still adhere to a weaker version of the complementarity thesis.

Let us turn to the second explanation of the helium balloon case, which Salmon presented as an example of the global, top-down unificationist type because it is based on the equivalence principle. Salmon suggested that this top-down explanation provides a different way of reading the ideal explanatory text: "We can think in terms of reading the ideal explanatory text either from the bottom-up or from the top-down" (1998, 77).[32] Both explanatory strategies can be legitimate and illuminating, and the choice for one of them may be determined by pragmatic considerations and may vary with the context. In this case, Salmon suggested, the top-down explanation is attractive to physicists while the bottom-up explanation will appeal to laypeople. A closer look at the example reveals, however, that the equivalence principle does nothing more than translate the case to be explained into another case which is supposedly already understood, namely the situation in which a helium balloon is released on the earth's surface. In order to explain and understand the latter situation one needs to refer to a different ideal explanatory text. Consequently, the helium balloon example does not appear to be a case in which there is one ideal explanatory text which can be read in two different ways (top-down vs. bottom-up) giving rise to complementary explanations. Rather, the example refers (implicitly) to two ideal explanatory texts. This objection is peculiar to this specific case and does not apply to the other examples of complementarity provided by Salmon (1998, 73–74).

---

30. See Salmon (1998, 248–260). Cf. section 3.2, esp. n. 12.

31. See Psillos (2002, 121–127) for critical discussion. An alternative account of singular causal explanation is given by Woodward (2003b, 209–220).

32. Cf. Salmon (1990, 185).

With the complementarity thesis Salmon (1998, 11) hoped to achieve a "rapprochement between two dominant traditions regarding scientific explanation that have generally been seen as mutually incompatible." He believed that "progress in the development of both approaches has eradicated many—perhaps all—of the grounds for conflict between them" (11), and stated that with Railton's conception of explanatory information and the ideal explanatory text, "much of the longstanding battle ... can be resolved" and a "new consensus" might be achieved" (Salmon 1990, 162). It is worth noting, in addition, that the complementarity thesis provides a (partial) solution to Salmon's problem that the causal-mechanical conception of explanation implied that one of the most successful scientific theories ever—quantum mechanics—is devoid of explanatory power. The unificationist conception, by contrast, is perfectly able to account for the explanatory power of quantum mechanics. Consequently, the complementarity thesis allowed Salmon to acknowledge that quantum mechanics can provide understanding, without having to give up causalism altogether (Salmon 1998, 75–76).

The "new consensus" that Salmon hoped for has not emerged. To be sure, some authors explicitly endorse Salmon's complementarity thesis and distinguish between two irreducible aspects of superunderstanding, corresponding to the unificationist conception and the causal conception (e.g., Cordero 1992, 188–189; Weber 1996, 1). But many others who at first sight seem to agree with Salmon's diagnosis are actually merely paying lip service to it, and ultimately regard one of the two aspects as truly fundamental. Schurz and Lambert (1994, 72–75), for example, acknowledge that both causality and unification are important, but they hold that the former can be reduced to the latter. Moreover, they employ a very general notion of causality that is hard to reconcile with Salmon's specific causal-mechanical view. Although they state that they agree with Salmon that "causality is important in the explication of scientific understanding," they immediately add that causality is a theory-relative notion, assuming that "every scientific corpus C contains some general principles about causality, that is, about the structural features of the real connections between real phenomena" (Schurz and Lambert 1994, 74). As discussed in section 3.1, Kitcher (1989, 436) also suggests that while causality plays an important role in explanatory practice, unification is more fundamental. He claims that causal modes of explanation result from, and are justified by, their success in unifying our beliefs.[33] By contrast, others have proposed accounts of explanation that at first sight seem to reconcile unificationism and causalism, but on closer inspection assume causal-mechanical explanation to be

---

33. See section 3.1 and Woodward (2003b, 369–371) for criticisms of Kitcher's thesis.

more fundamental. Rob Skipper (1999, S204), for example, argues that unification is achieved by "delineating pervasive causal mechanisms." Michael Strevens, in his paper "The Causal and Unification Approaches to Explanation Unified—Causally," argues that explanation is essentially the specification of causes; unification is merely required "to solve a problem faced by the causal account, namely, the problem of determining which parts of the causal network are explanatorily relevant" (Strevens 2004, 154).

The fact that as yet no consensus has been achieved is not in itself a strong argument against Salmon's complementarity thesis. In addition, however, I submit that there are two objections to the thesis that cast doubt on the underlying conception of scientific understanding. The first objection pertains to the implication that causal-mechanical explanation and explanation by unification are complementary in the sense of: jointly exhaustive.[34] The complementarity thesis implies that there are two—and only two—modes of explanation. In particular, Salmon's elaboration of the thesis in terms of the opposition between global and local (or top-down vs. bottom-up) approaches, and of Railton's ideal explanatory text, confirms this reading. The ideal text contains all explanatory information, both of a very global and of a very local kind, and we may choose to focus either on global or on local aspects. To be sure, there are "intermediate stages between the two extremes—there are degrees of coarse- or finegrainedness" (Salmon 1998, 77). But such differences in degree still presuppose two extremes and leave no room for a fundamentally different third aspect. This reading entails that a local (bottom-up) explanation will always be possible—because in every ideal explanatory text there will be local details to focus on. Salmon's claim is that this kind of explanation must be causal: it must refer to basic causal processes and interactions (e.g., between individual molecules or organisms).

However, explanatory scientific practice often does without causal explanation altogether; sometimes causal reasoning is not even part of the ideal explanatory text, as becomes clear when we look again at the examples discussed in section 3.2. First, the notorious case of quantum mechanics: despite Salmon's hope to the contrary, the complementarity thesis does not render harmless the quantum-mechanical examples in which causal-mechanical explanation is problematic. The reason is that the thesis implies that in

---

34. To be sure, Salmon refused to commit himself explicitly to this implication. He stated that there are "*at least* two major aspects" (Salmon 1998, 76, italics added) and that "perhaps there are other [explanatory] virtues that I have not discussed" (1998, 78). However, it remains unclear what other aspects or virtues he hinted at—and how these relate to the global/local opposition. Moreover, in the same text Salmon (1998, 77) referred to an "explanatory duality," which implies the existence of two, and only two, approaches.

every situation there should be the possibility of a local, bottom-up explanation. But this is not the case in quantum mechanics, where continuous space-time trajectories do not exist.[35] Therefore, Salmon (1998, 76) stated, the answer to the question "Can quantum mechanics explain?" "must be, for the time being at least: In a sense 'yes', but in another sense 'no.'" On his view, the ideal quantum-mechanical explanatory text is as yet out of reach because some phenomena defy causal explanation; but his view implies that such an ideal text remains desirable. The practice of science belies this view, however: most physicists are content without causal-mechanical explanations of some quantum phenomena. Causal alternatives to quantum theory, such as Bohm's theory, have been ignored by the general physics community (Cushing 1994, 144–162). Moreover, quantum mechanics is no exceptional case: physicists' understanding of the special relativistic Lorentz contraction is another example that contradicts the causal-mechanical explanatory ideal. In this case a causal-mechanical account is possible, but physicists do not consider Lorentz's causal bottom-up account as providing additional explanatory information that brings us closer to a complete understanding of the phenomenon of length contraction. In biology causal accounts do not always contribute to scientific understanding either. Ruth Berger (1998) argues that this is true of so-called dynamical explanations, which are based on nonlinear dynamical modeling and employed to account for complex phenomena of which causal descriptions are possible in principle but useless in practice. Dynamical explanations have gained importance in many scientific disciplines such as geology, medicine, psychology, ecology, and biology. Berger analyzes a specific case from population biology: the attempts at explaining the erratic population cycles of Dungeness crabs, which inhabit the North American Pacific Coastline. The strong fluctuation in crab harvests has been studied for decades by biologists, who strive for "a complete understanding of the cycles in catch in the northern California Dungeness crab fishery" (Botsford quoted by Berger 1998, 314). Biologists have advanced (purely mathematical) nonlinear dynamical modeling explanations of this phenomenon. Causal histories (of individual crabs, or populations), although in principle traceable, are completely irrelevant for understanding the phenomenon; they would not be included in the ideal explanatory text by these scientists. In these

---

35. Incidentally, Railton's view of causal mechanisms is more liberal, but also more vague, than Salmon's. Railton designates the quantum-mechanical tunnelling mechanism as a causal mechanism, but admits that he is unable to provide a precise definition of what a mechanism is. Thus, he runs the risk of rendering the notion vacuous. Salmon, by contrast, does provide an exact definition (in terms of causal processes and interactions), which however leads to problems with respect to quantum mechanics.

examples a bottom-up, causal account (the local aspect of the ideal explanatory text) is either nonexistent (quantum mechanics in its standard interpretation), or rejected (Lorentz contraction), or considered irrelevant (population biology). But the complementarity thesis implies that in all cases an explanatorily relevant causal account that adds to our understanding must exist.[36]

My second objection to Salmon's complementarity thesis, as elaborated in terms of Railton's notions, relates to the objective character of the ideal explanatory text. Railton emphasizes that the content of the ideal text, and thereby the question of whether or not a purported explanation does in fact contain explanatory information, is independent of our epistemic condition. According to Railton (1981, 243), "a proffered explanation supplies explanatory information (whether we recognize it as such or not) to the extent that it does in fact (whether we know it or not) correctly answer questions about the ideal explanatory text." Salmon endorsed an objective view of explanation, and had no quarrels with this implication of Railton's analysis. This view implies that criteria for scientific understanding are objective and universal, and not amenable to change. But this is in conflict with the actual variation in scientists' criteria for understanding that is exhibited by the history of science. A viable philosophical account of scientific understanding should accommodate this variation, and the associated complementarity thesis cannot be based on a notion of superunderstanding that is insensitive to such contextual variation. The examples given above serve as illustrations: in these cases contemporary

---

36. Of course one might question whether Salmon would actually have endorsed this implication. Perhaps he would have said that we should aspire to achieve as much understanding as possible; but that in cases where either causal explanations or unifications are unavailable, we just have to be content with as much understanding as we can possibly get. For example, imagine that the biological world were so complex that only individual causal chains could be described, while unification would be out of reach. One might claim that Salmon would identify superunderstanding with the amount of understanding that we can possibly achieve. I believe that this interpretation is untenable, however. The reason is that it renders the notion of ideal explanatory text, and accordingly that of superunderstanding, vacuous: it allows us to regard as ideal any incomplete text which we believe (for whatever reasons) to be the best we can get. Another way in which proponents of the complementarity thesis might try to counter my objection is by arguing that complete scientific understanding (superunderstanding) does not require the actual production of the ideal explanatory text but merely the in principle ability to produce this text. Indeed, Railton (1981, 247) explicitly states that "the actual ideal is not to produce such texts, but to have the ability (in principle) to produce arbitrary parts of them." But this counterargument is effective only in the population biology case because only here can one legitimately claim that causal histories of individual crabs are in principle traceable, so that one is in principle able to produce an ideal explanatory text that includes them. In the examples from quantum mechanics and relativity the causal accounts are excluded from the ideal text: in the former case there is an in principle impossibility to produce them but this does not bother scientists, in the latter case causal accounts are available but rejected by the scientific community.

scientists prefer non-causal explanations over causal ones and appear to have no problem with the absence or irrelevance of causal accounts of the phenomena in question. But surely this has not always been the situation: Lorentz's proposal, for example, reflected a causal ideal that was dominant in classical physics. The history of gravitational theory, cited in section 3.2 and more extensively analyzed in chapter 5, is another example of how attitudes toward causal-mechanical explanation can change in time. If we do not want to brush away the opinions of scientists (past or present) as irrelevant, we should acknowledge contextual variation in criteria for understanding, and, accordingly, in the ideal explanatory text. Indeed, Railton's objective interpretation of the ideal text appears to be inconsistent with his claim that the scientists themselves dictate what should be in the text.[37]

Salmon's complementarity thesis presupposes a duality of two explanatory approaches: a global (or top-down) approach, and a local (or bottom-up) approach. These two approaches are complementary in the sense that they produce different types of understanding that together amount to super-understanding (described by the ideal explanatory text). Global understanding is of the unifying type, and local understanding is of the causal-mechanical type. I have argued that this thesis is problematic with respect to the aspect of local understanding: there are cases in scientific practice where local, causal-mechanical explanation (even if available) is ignored by scientists. In those cases scientists prefer other strategies to achieve understanding (mathematical modeling or symmetry arguments, for example). One might reply that such strategies are of a global kind and that scientists have pragmatic reasons for preferring them. However, proponents of the complementarity thesis are committed to the assumption that available causal-mechanical accounts always add to the amount of understanding (finally resulting in superunderstanding). But this is not confirmed by the practice of science: sometimes scientists do not ascribe any explanatory value at all to the local aspect.

These conclusions cast doubt on the status of a central element of the complementarity thesis: the idea of superunderstanding, which is fleshed out in terms of the ideal explanatory text. Apparently, scientists do not consider superunderstanding better or more complete than "ordinary" understanding. Superunderstanding is not regarded as an aim of science, not even as an

---

37. To be sure, Railton (1981, 243) acknowledges that, when we ask scientists which models ought to be part of the ideal explanatory text, "we should be prepared to accept indefiniteness and even disagreement in the answers we receive." However, this refers to possible controversy about which models counts as realistic descriptions, and not to a fundamentally contextual variation in criteria for explanation.

ideal. Admittedly, Salmon and Railton intended the ideal explanatory text to be "ideal" in the sense of "perfect" and not in the sense of an "ultimate aim." But the examples presented refute that interpretation as well: scientists do not regard as perfect only the sum of local and global understanding; understanding can be perfect even without local, causal-mechanical understanding.[38] When superunderstanding is abandoned, the notion of complementarity becomes meaningless, since it presupposes that the complementary aspects add up to a greater whole (superunderstanding). With the rejection of superunderstanding the distinction between global and local understanding disappears as well (at least, when interpreted as complementary ways of reading the ideal explanatory text). In sum, Salmon's complementarity thesis has dissolved.

3.4 Unifying the plurality of modes of explanation

The rejection of the complementarity thesis does not imply that the idea that different types of explanation have a common aim is misguided. It remains plausible that the various ways in which scientists explain phenomena have understanding as an aim or product. Both explanation by unification and causal explanation are important ways in which understanding may be achieved. However, as was concluded in the previous sections, they cannot be regarded as embodying a universal standard of intelligibility, nor can they be viewed as complementing each other in the sense that together they provide superunderstanding, that is, the complete understanding given by an ideal explanatory text.

What is more, the fact that the various types of explanation produce understanding can be invoked in an argument against the thesis that explanations refer to underlying ideal texts. Understanding, as Woodward (2003b, 179–181) convincingly argues, requires epistemic accessibility. As was observed in section 2.1, understanding, in contrast to explanation, necessarily involves a subject. Thus, if information is considered as contributing to understanding, it must be in principle accessible to the understanding subjects; persons who use the explanation must be able to know or grasp the information. But this is not the case for ideal explanatory texts containing laws unknown, and perhaps

---

38. Cf. Strevens (2008, 124), whose notion of "exhaustive understanding" is identical to superunderstanding. Strevens suggests that although exhaustive understanding might be an ideal, it is not a true aim of science; full understanding, which is based on knowledge of relevant factors, suffices.

unknowable, to the users of the explanation. Ideal explanatory texts (or "hidden structures," as Woodward calls them) do not provide understanding. Instead, Woodward (2003b, 181) concludes, to understand how actual explanations work, "we need to see them as explanatory structures in their own right and not merely as vehicles for conveying information about underlying explanations of a quite different form."

When they are regarded as "explanatory structures in their own right," there is no need to suppose that there exist only two complementary types of explanation. Instead, as the examples suggest, there is a variety, even a plurality, of explanatory strategies to attain the aim of understanding. Scientists choose from a host of available strategies whatever suits them best in a particular case to achieve this aim. The history and practice of science shows that there is a variation in preferred tools for attaining understanding. We have encountered some examples previously (causal-mechanical reasoning, visualization, and mathematical abstraction) and more will be given in the following chapters. The importance of such tools can vary in the course of history and across fields or disciplines.

But this brings us back to the question of the nature of scientific understanding. Since Railton's definition of understanding in terms of the ideal explanatory text has been rejected, an alternative characterization is needed. What exactly is scientific understanding? My review of the various models of explanation has yielded a wide variety of views of the nature of scientific understanding. Many philosophers defend their favorite theory of explanation by referring to its alleged understanding-providing power, but they neglect to provide an account of what understanding consists in and to show how it is produced by scientific explanations. Typically, authors merely state, without any justification, that their favorite type of explanation furnishes understanding. They simply define understanding in terms of the proposed model of explanation. Barnes (1992), for example, rightly criticizes unificationists for this reason, but typically fails to provide substantial arguments for the causal view he adopts.

Moreover, when arguments for or against particular conceptions of explanatory understanding are provided, they are often based on our alleged intuitions regarding understanding. The cases of the barometer and of the flagpole and the shadow, for example, appeal to intuitions as to whether or not explanatory understanding is provided by the arguments at issue. This is, of course, a legitimate strategy to find out more about the nature of understanding, but an important additional question is what the source of our intuitions is. We should not remain content with simply relying on intuitions. If we want to discover the true nature of understanding, we should first ask ourselves why we have the particular intuitions that we have about explanatory understanding; and second, not treat our intuitions as incontrovertible but be prepared to adjust or relativize them if necessary. For example, if it turns out that scientists from different disciplines or in different historical periods have different intuitions regarding which kind of explanations provide understanding and which ones do not, we should accept this as further evidence and search for a theory of understanding that accounts for these differences. (The role and status of our intuitions concerning explanatory understanding will be further analyzed in section 4.4).

In sum, we need a general theory of scientific understanding that is independent of a specific model of explanation but that allows for the possibility that understanding can be achieved via markedly different explanatory strategies and that incorporates intuitions about understanding. I submit that a satisfactory overarching theory of understanding can be formulated on the basis of the assumption that understanding is pragmatic. In chapter 2, it was argued that the fact that understanding is a pragmatic notion does not preclude regarding it as a universal epistemic aim of science. The analysis hinged on a distinction between understanding a phenomenon (UP), the product of explanations, and understanding a theory (UT), a pragmatic condition for achieving UP. Since UP and UT appear inextricably connected, understanding in the pragmatic sense (UT) is crucial for achieving the epistemic aims of science (among them UP). The fact that there is a pragmatic dimension to explanation implies that explanation is contextual: it can have different forms in different contexts. The various models of explanation discussed in the present chapter function as tools for understanding in different (historical or disciplinary) contexts. I conclude that understanding is a universal aim of science that can be achieved by contextually varying modes of explanation. In the next chapter I will develop my contextual theory of scientific understanding in full detail.

4

A Contextual Theory of Scientific Understanding

EXPLANATORY UNDERSTANDING CAN be achieved in many different ways. In chapter 1, we saw that in the 1920s physicists followed different approaches in their quest for understanding quantum phenomena: Heisenberg and Pauli favored the abstract theory of matrix mechanics, while Schrödinger preferred a very different strategy, which led him to develop the visualizable theory of wave mechanics. Both approaches were valid routes to understanding: in principle, basic quantum phenomena, such as the spectrum of hydrogen, could be explained by either theory.[1] Although the differences between wave mechanics and matrix mechanics were later resolved and the two theories were combined in the formalism of quantum mechanics, even today there are different ways of understanding quantum phenomena. The standard interpretation of quantum mechanics is acausal and standard explanations typically take the form of nomological or unificatory explanation. Causal explanations are not impossible, however: Bohm's theory is a viable alternative to the standard interpretation, which allows for a causal, spatiotemporal description of particle trajectories. While the Bohm theory is not favored by most physicists (which shows that causal explanation is not always the norm or the ideal to which scientists aspire), there are no scientific arguments for ruling out this approach as a way to achieve understanding (see Cushing 1994).

This example from the history and practice of physics supports the conclusion of chapter 3, namely that the various models of explanation proposed in the philosophical literature should not be regarded as rival theories of explanation but instead provide us with a variety of available strategies to achieve

---

1. See section 7.3 for detailed discussion.

understanding. If, as was suggested in section 3.4, we want to construct a general theory of scientific understanding that allows for the possibility that understanding is achieved via such highly different explanatory strategies, it should be pluralistic and independent of any specific model of explanation. In the present chapter, I will present a theory of scientific understanding that is able to accommodate this diversity by acknowledging the pragmatic, and accordingly context-dependent, nature of understanding, while at the same time retaining the idea of understanding as a universal epistemic aim of science. The basic idea of the theory is the thesis that explanatory understanding of phenomena requires intelligible theories, as argued for in chapter 2, where intelligibility has been defined as the value that scientists attribute to the cluster of qualities that facilitate the use of a theory.

In this chapter, the notion of intelligibility will be further explicated and used as the basis for a theory of scientific understanding, according to which scientists need conceptual tools and associated skills to use a particular theory in order to achieve understanding of the phenomena. The availability and acceptability of conceptual tools can change with the historical, social, or disciplinary context. In this way, the theory accounts for the variety of ways in which understanding may be achieved in scientific practice. The outline of the chapter is as follows. Section 4.1 articulates and defends the basic idea of the contextual theory of understanding, encapsulated in a Criterion for the Understanding of Phenomena, in which intelligibility is the key concept. Section 4.2 proposes a Criterion for the Intelligibility of Theories, which captures its pragmatic and contextual nature, and presents illustrations from scientific practice. In section 4.3, the role of conceptual tools in understanding is analyzed and supported by empirical evidence from cognitive psychology and concrete cases from physics. Section 4.4 elaborates on various aspects of the contextuality of scientific understanding: its historical dynamics, the role of intuitions, and the relation of my contextual theory to existing pragmatic theories of explanation. Section 4.5 discusses the implications of the theory for the issues of reductionism and scientific realism. The final section briefly discusses to what extent my contextual theory of understanding implies relativism.

4.1 Understanding phenomena with intelligible theories

The assumption that achieving explanatory understanding is one of the main aims of science, perhaps even its most important epistemic aim, lies at the basis of this book and has been the leading idea of my initial investigation into the nature of understanding in chapter 2. As long as we refrain from a specification of what precisely understanding consists in, this thesis will be denied by few scientists and philosophers. Even Hempel agrees, as we saw in section 2.1, if understanding is defined as the product of covering law explanation. Another leading philosopher of science in the analytic tradition, W. V. O. Quine, writes in *The Pursuit of Truth* (1992, 20) that "nowadays the overwhelming purposes of the science game are technology and understanding" (as opposed to prediction).[2]

However, is it possible and useful to speak in such general terms of science and to ascribe universal aims to it? Or is the notion of understanding, if conceived as a universal aim of science, merely a blanket term, devoid of specific content? It could be argued that the idea that science has universal aims is futile and misguided, and that different scientific disciplines, and different scientists in different periods of history, simply have different aims. Indeed, a close look at the history of science reveals a wide variety of aims of scientists in different periods of history, and some historically minded philosophers have concluded from this that science does not have any universal aims at all.[3] Laudan (1984, 138), for example, claims that it is impossible to state what the central cognitive aims and methods of science are or should be because "we have seen time and again that the aims of science vary, and quite appropriately so, from one epoch to another, from one scientific field to another, and sometimes among researchers in the same field."[4] Two decades earlier, a similar observation was made by Toulmin (1963, 21), who argued that "the intellectual and practical activities of scientists ... have a great range and variety of purposes, which can only misleadingly be summed up in a nutshell definition."

While I agree with Toulmin and Laudan that philosophers of science should take the history and practice of science seriously, and should acknowledge the actual variation in the aims of scientists, I submit that a general characterization of the aims of science can be given that is not vacuous or

---

2. By using the term "science game," Quine, of course, refers to the Wittgensteinian notion of a language game, of which he deems science an example.

3. Even Karl Popper acknowledges this: chapter 5 of *Objective Knowledge*, entitled "The Aim of Science," starts with the disclaimer "To speak of 'the aim' of scientific activity may perhaps sound a little naïve; for clearly, different scientists have different aims and science itself (whatever that may mean) has no aims. I admit all this" (Popper 1972, 191). However, he subsequently suggests that "it is the aim of science to find *satisfactory explanations*, of whatever strikes us as being in need of explanation".

4. Cf. Laudan (1990, 47–54) and Longino (1990, 17–19).

meaningless. The apparent contradiction can be resolved by distinguishing between three levels on which scientific activity may be analyzed:

- *macro-level*: science as a whole
- *meso-level*: scientific communities
- *micro-level*: individual scientists

This distinction allows us to assert that on the macro-level science has a particular aim, which on the meso- or micro-level can be articulated in different ways. For example, all scientists will agree that they aim to produce knowledge that is supported by experience; this is a macro-level aim of science (in accordance with the general empiricist idea on which modern science is based). However, when it comes to the question of exactly how, and how strongly, scientific knowledge has to be supported by experience, the answers given by scientists from different communities, and sometimes even by scientists within the same community, will differ; these are meso- or micro-level differences (associated with a variety of possible empiricist methodologies and epistemologies).

Thus, the three-level distinction can reconcile the existence of universal aims of science with the existence of variation in the precise specification and/ or application of these general aims. The macro-level characterization of aims must necessarily be general in order to accommodate meso- and micro-level differences, but it may still provide us with significant information about science. The examples and case studies presented in this book support the thesis that achieving understanding is among the general (macro-level) aims of science. But this leaves open the possibility that scientists in different historical periods or in different communities have quite different specific views about how precisely scientific understanding is to be achieved, which is indeed suggested by the examples and case studies. An important question is whether this variation of the way in which the macro-level aim is articulated appears at the meso- or at the micro-level: Are the observed differences characteristic of communities or is there (also) individual variation? This question can only be answered by empirical investigation, that is, by historical or sociological study of scientific practice. I will present historical case studies that attempt to shed light on this issue in chapters 5, 6, and 7. In the present chapter, I will develop a theory of understanding that allows for both possibilities: it focuses on the way in which individual scientists achieve understanding, and accordingly it allows for the possibility that there is individual variation. However, as the case studies in the next chapters will show, while individual scientists may have different preferred ways to achieve explanatory understanding, the most important variations appear at the meso-level. Within a particular research community standards of intelligibility and strategies to obtain understanding are usually shared. This should not surprise us because scientific understanding is closely related to communication: scientists who construct explanations are not merely interested in enhancing their own understanding of phenomena, but they typically want to share their insights with others. Scientific understanding is a community achievement and success in achieving understanding requires communication between scientists. When a scientist tries to communicate his or her understanding of a phenomenon to someone else (be it another scientist, a student, or a layperson), there must be shared standards of intelligibility.

How precisely can the idea of scientific understanding as a universal, macro-level epistemic aim of science be reconciled with the existence of meso- and micro-level variation in scientists' views about strategies for achieving understanding, and, what is more, with variation in ideas about when understanding has been achieved? First, recall the distinction, introduced in chapter 2, between:

UP: understanding a phenomenon = having an adequate explanation of the phenomenon (relating the phenomenon to accepted items of knowledge)
UT: understanding a theory = being able to use the theory (pragmatic understanding)

Understanding in the sense of UP is a universal epistemic aim of science. In other words, it is a macro-level aim. However, as I argued in chapter 2, UP necessarily requires UT, which was articulated with the help of the pragmatic notion of intelligibility. Because UT is pragmatic, it is contextual, and accordingly it allows for meso- and micro-level variation in the way in which it is specified and applied in concrete situations. I will now analyze the relation between UP and UT in more detail and develop a theory of scientific understanding that accounts for the existing variation in explanatory strategies.

The basic idea of the theory is the thesis, argued for in chapter 2, that scientists need intelligible theories in order to achieve scientific understanding of phenomena. The historical examples given so far support this idea. The early history of quantum theory, briefly described in chapter 1 and more extensively analyzed in chapter 7, is a case in point: the fact that the theory of matrix mechanics appeared unintelligible to many physicists hampered the construction of explanations to understand phenomena by means of this theory. Not only Schrödinger and most mainstream physicists, but even Bohr, Heisenberg, and Pauli had difficulties using matrix theory to explain and understand concrete phenomena in the domain of atomic physics. By contrast, the more intelligible theory of wave mechanics yielded explanatory understanding of a wide variety of phenomena in a relatively straightforward manner. (Because of its initial unintelligibility—and the fact that it remains a counterintuitive theory that is difficult to master—many physicists adopted the positivist idea that quantum mechanics can furnish only description and prediction but no understanding of phenomena. This is a mistake, however.)

Another example can be found in the history of psychology: in the period between the two world wars psychology was dominated by neo-behaviorists, who took a radically positivist stance and claimed that the aim of science is merely prediction and control, and not understanding of phenomena. However, their goal of developing mathematical theories of relations between independent and dependent variables (stimulus and response, respectively) turned out to be unattainable without at least some understanding (intelligibility) of the theoretical structure: in order to manage the functional relations between dependent and independent variables, they introduced so-called intervening variables. Only on the basis of particular interpretations and understanding (surplus meaning) of these intervening variables were psychologists able to explain and predict concrete phenomena. An example was Edward Tolman's account of the behavior of rats in a maze (see Eigner 2009). Because of their unintelligibility, the abstract theories of the behaviorists were unfruitful: explanation, and indeed even prediction and description, of behavior, requires intelligible theories. The positivist idea of abandoning understanding and intelligibility was sterile.

Only intelligible theories allow scientists to construct models through which they can derive explanations of phenomena on the basis of the relevant theory.[5] In other words, understanding scientific theories is a prerequisite for understanding phenomena scientifically. This can be stated in more precise form as the Criterion for Understanding Phenomena:

CUP: A phenomenon P is understood scientifically if and only if there is an explanation of P that is based on an intelligible theory T and conforms to the basic epistemic values of empirical adequacy and internal consistency.

CUP is the basis of the theory of scientific understanding defended in this book. Note that CUP is implicitly pragmatic, since the notion of intelligibility is included in the criterion. Intelligibility is a pragmatic (and accordingly

---

5. To be sure, the distinction between theory and model is not a clear-cut one. However, as has been argued in section 2.2, this does not render the distinction useless nor invalidate an analysis of the role of theories in model-based explanation.

context-dependent) notion because a theory's intelligibility depends not only on the qualities of the theory but also on the scientists involved: whether or not scientists deem a theory intelligible is related, for example, to their skills and background knowledge. More generally, CUP implies that whether or not a phenomenon is understandable in principle is determined by the epistemic framework accepted by the scientific community. Since there may be large-scale historical and disciplinary variation in accepted theoretical frameworks (Toulmin 1963; Kuhn 1970), the understandability of phenomena is context-dependent at the meso-level.

It is important to note that, according to CUP, having an intelligible theory *T* is only a necessary condition for scientifically understanding *P*. Obviously, mere intelligibility is not sufficient for success in achieving explanatory understanding of phenomena: in addition we need to use *T* to actually construct the explanation that relates *P* to other accepted items of knowledge. Therefore, CUP also contains a requirement about the actual explanation: it should conform to the two basic scientific values of empirical adequacy and internal consistency. As argued in section 2.3, empirical adequacy and internal consistency are generally accepted basic requirements for scientific theories and explanations, but it should be noted that they function as values rather than as rigid constraints on theorizing and explanation, implying that there may be contextual variation in application and trade-offs between these and other values. Nonetheless, a reasonable degree of empirical adequacy appears to be a necessary condition for an explanation in order to produce understanding of phenomenon. Thus, CUP does not entail that, for example, astrologers understand particular personality traits of people if they have an intelligible astrological theory of these traits. Many astrologers will claim that their theories are perfectly intelligible to them, and they might indeed be right: if they have developed a facility in working with their theory that allows them to "model" the character and behavior of their subjects, their astrological theory is intelligible to them. However, in order to provide genuine understanding of the phenomena, the explanations based on astrological theories must also conform—at least to a sufficient degree—to the basic scientific values of empirical adequacy and internal consistency. The candidate explanations of the astrologers typically fail in this respect: astrological models of character traits and human behavior are descriptively and predictively inadequate.

A more interesting example is the theory of intelligent design (ID), which is defended by its proponents as a superior alternative to the Darwinian theory of evolution, specifically to the idea of natural selection. Adherents of ID sometimes suggest that their theory is more intelligible than the theory of evolution. Thus, William Dembski (2004, 45) states: "The fundamental claim of intelligent design is straightforward and easily intelligible: namely, there are natural systems that cannot be adequately explained in terms of undirected natural forces and that exhibit features which in any other circumstances we would attribute to intelligence." The suggestion is that it is very difficult to understand how complex functional features of organisms can emerge as an outcome of a process of "blind" variation and selection. The classic example is the eye: while the eye has an obvious function and clearly contributes to fitness in most environments, it appears—at least prima facie—inconceivable how the eye has developed via an evolutionary process in which all intermediate stages also had the advantage of increased fitness.[6] Trading on the alleged inconceivability of a Darwinian account, ID is presented as an alternative theory of the emergence of complex functional features of organisms, which provides understanding of this process by postulating an intelligent agent who has brought these features into existence.

Critics have objected that ID does not qualify as a scientific theory but is a religious doctrine. However, this response is problematic, as Kitcher (2007, 8–14) argues, because it rests on the dubious assumption that there are sharp and straightforwardly applicable demarcation criteria for science. First, there are well-known obstacles to formulating such criteria (think of the Duhem-Quine problem in relation to the testability criterion). Second, the history of science shows that metaphysical ideas (e.g., ideas implied by religious doctrines) can positively contribute to scientific research and development. Isaac Newton, whose theological views interacted with his scientific work, is a case in point (see chapter 5). Accordingly, it is more sensible to regard ID as a scientific research program, in line with what its proponents claim. The question is then whether ID provides theoretical principles that can be used to construct (model) explanations of specific phenomena. Kitcher observes that it does not. At least two kinds of principles are needed to make the theory of ID into a theory that can advance scientific understanding:

> First there have to be principles that specify when Intelligence swings into action. Perhaps they will tell us that Intelligence operates when there are potentially advantageous complex traits that can't evolve by natural section. Second, there must be principles that explain what Intelligence does when it acts. Perhaps these will identify the sorts of genetic changes Intelligence can arrange, or the ways in which it can inhibit the normal operation of selection. (Kitcher 2007, 105–106)

---

6. The case of the eye was discussed by Darwin himself, who recognized the problem and advanced a possible scenario (see Kitcher 2007, 83–85).

The problem with current ID proposals is that such principles are absent. Thus, while the general idea of ID may appear intuitively intelligible, this idea is not fleshed out in terms of theoretical principles that are intelligible in the sense of my definition (section 2.3): principles that can be used to construct specific, empirically adequate explanations of concrete phenomena. As yet, ID has not yielded scientific understanding in the sense of CUP.

In short, scientific understanding requires intelligible theories. In addition, in order to provide genuine understanding, an explanation must not only be based on an intelligible theory but also conform to the two basic scientific values. The combination of these necessary conditions provides a necessary and sufficient condition for scientific understanding.

At this point, some readers may worry that CUP fails as a necessary condition for scientific understanding because it implies that phenomena can be understood only by means of theories, a conclusion that seems to be at odds with current views that de-emphasize the centrality of theories and theorizing in science. Rejecting the "theory-dominant" approach of earlier philosophy of science, philosophers have drawn attention to aspects of scientific practice that are equally important as theorizing and may be independent of it. First, since the 1980s, philosophers of science have studied the nature and function of experimentation in science, arguing that experimenting is a scientific practice with "a life of its own" (Hacking 1983; cf. Radder 2003a). Rejecting the thesis that all observation is theory-laden, Hacking and other "new experimentalists" claim that experimentation can be theory-independent. If this is correct, it would suggest that scientists can achieve understanding without theories: Who would want to deny that scientific experiments provide us with understanding of the phenomena under investigation? A second argument against theory-dominant philosophy of science is the observation that in many scientific fields and disciplines theories appear to be relatively unimportant or even completely absent; think, for example, of more descriptive branches of biology, geology, or the social sciences. The thesis that theories are essential for achieving scientific understanding seems to entail that these fields and disciplines cannot deliver understanding at all, which obviously would be an unacceptable conclusion. Surely we do not want a return to the logical positivists' idea that theoretical physics is an ideal for all science. Does CUP imply a return to such a narrow-minded view of science? Third, recent philosophy of science has witnessed a shift of focus from theories to models. In fact, as we have seen in section 2.2, the idea that models "mediate" between theory and phenomena is an important element of my analysis of scientific understanding, leading to the thesis that intelligibility of theories is a necessary requirement for the production of understanding. However, taking the idea that models are "autonomous agents" to the extreme, some authors seem to suggest that model construction may happen in a way that is completely theory-independent. If this is so, and if such models provide scientific understanding, my claim that intelligible theories are required for understanding would be falsified.

In sum, there are some prima facie reasons to doubt the universal validity of CUP. Its basic idea—the thesis that understanding of phenomena requires intelligible theories—seems to ignore non-theoretical dimensions of scientific practice, or at least to deny that these may produce understanding. Is this indeed the case? Does CUP involve a return to the misguided theory-dominant philosophy of science of the old days? This would be too hasty a conclusion. I will argue that my account of scientific understanding, and in particular CUP, is not at odds with current developments in philosophy of science. To begin with, let me stress once again that the philosophical theory presented in this book is concerned with explanatory understanding, that is, the understanding produced by scientific explanations. A scientific explanation is an answer to the question of why a particular phenomenon occurs, and a successful explanation makes us understand why the phenomenon occurs. As has been made clear in previous chapters, this type of understanding is a central aim of science, and it is this type of understanding that this book is about. I do not deny that other types of understanding play a role in science too. Thus, in addition to understanding-why, scientists will often want to understand that or understand how a phenomenon occurs. Exploratory research, for example, does not aim at understanding-why but merely at understanding-that or understanding-how. Obviously, these types of understanding precede explanatory understanding: understanding why P assumes that one understands that P. Similarly, phenomenological laws can be seen as providing understanding that a phenomenon occurs or understanding how a system behaves. My account of explanatory understanding does not deny but rather presupposes the importance of these other types of understanding.[7] As described in section 2.2, my analysis employs a generic account of explanation according to which an explanation is an attempt to answer the question of why a particular phenomenon occurs, that is, an attempt to provide understanding of the phenomenon by presenting a systematic line of reasoning that connects it with other accepted items of

---

7. An inquiry into the nature of these other types of understanding is beyond the scope of this book, however. For my purposes understanding-that and understanding-how may simply be regarded as types of knowledge. See Baumberger et al. (2017) for an overview of different types of understanding.

knowledge. The central idea of CUP is that theories are essential for achieving such explanatory understanding.

But does this limitation suffice to counter the objection that my account ignores the possibility of achieving explanatory understanding without theories? Isn't it plausible that, for example, theory-free experiments or theory-independent models can also provide us with such understanding? A closer look at the alleged counterexamples reveals that this is not the case: either they involve theory or they don't provide explanatory understanding. The crucial point is that theory is far more pervasive than the objection suggests. Of course, science can be practiced in the absence of full-fledged, explicitly articulated theories, and there is no a priori reason to assume that this cannot lead to (explanatory) understanding. But, as I have argued in chapter 2, in order to account for scientific practice traditional syntactic and semantic theory-conceptions need to be replaced by a more liberal view, such as Giere's conception of theories as (collections of) principles that provide the basis for the construction of specific models of the real world. On such a view, it appears that theory plays a far more important role than is sometimes suggested. Thus, while explicitly articulated theories may be less common in certain areas of geology, biology, psychology, and sociology, scientific activity will still be guided by more loosely circumscribed theoretical principles.

The same applies to experimentation: although experimentation is not subordinate to theorizing, scientific experiments are always conducted in a theoretical context and require theoretical interpretation. Thus, while Newton's optical experiments and Boyle's air-pump experiments are sometimes regarded as theory-free, Radder (2003b, 161–172) shows that they depend fundamentally on theoretical interpretation. In the case of Newton's famous prism experiments, for example, "the theoretical model of light as consisting of rays . . . structured the way in which Newton performed and understood his experiments on the dispersion of light" (Radder 2003b, 166). Obviously, some aspects of experimental practice do not involve theoretical interpretation (e.g., the material realization of an experiment can sometimes be described in a non-theoretical way, by using ordinary language), but these are insufficient for explanatory purposes. Consequently, it appears implausible that theory-free experimentation—if it exists at all—can produce scientific understanding of the explanatory kind.

For model-building, a similar conclusion holds. In the spirit of the "models as mediators" approach (described in section 2.2), it has been suggested that models may be constructed in a way that is fully independent of theory. If this is true, and if such models provide explanatory understanding, my account has been falsified. A possible example is the London model of superconductivity, analyzed by Nancy Cartwright, Towfic Shomar, and Mauricio Suárez. They argue that this is a case of phenomenological model-building that is not driven by theory and yet "increased radically our understanding of superconductivity" (1995, 142). A closer look at their argument, and especially at their response to criticisms (Suárez and Cartwright 2008), shows however that their claim of theory-independence is not as radical as it appears to be at first sight. For they don't claim that theory plays no role at all, but rather that theories function as tools for the construction of models.[8] What they oppose is a strong "theory-driven view," on which models simply follow from theories by procedures of de-idealization. While they use the London model to argue against the theory-driven view of models, they deny (in response to criticism) that "theory plays no role whatsoever in model building" (Suárez and Cartwright 2008, 66)—which is already obvious from the fact that the London model employs classical electromagnetic theory (Suárez and Cartwright 2008, 65–66). In sum, while models are "autonomous agents" that do not follow deductively from theory, they are almost never completely theory-free. Perhaps it is possible to devise a purely phenomenological model of a phenomenon, which does not relate to any theories at all, but such a model would merely have a descriptive and perhaps predictive value but yield no explanatory understanding.

Another counterexample against my thesis that theories are necessary for achieving understanding example has been suggested by Erik Weber. According to Weber (2012a), we can explain and understand why one pendulum has a longer period than another by invoking the pendulum law, which allegedly does not involve any theory. But, as Kuhn (1970, 118–120) has shown, the pendulum law is not a phenomenological law that can be straightforwardly derived from empirical observations. On the contrary, it derives from an idealized model that is based upon a specific theory of motion. It is only by virtue of being embedded in, or constructed on the basis of, more general theories that prima facie phenomenological laws and models may provide explanatory understanding. This distinguishes them from cases like the barometer example, in which there is prediction but no understanding (see section 4.4.2 for further discussion of this case).

All in all, I conclude that CUP does not impose a serious limitation on the scope of my account of scientific understanding. Theories are essential for achieving genuine explanatory understanding. To be sure, these theories can be low- or high-level ones, and they may be implicit or explicit, but

---

8. This view of theories is in fact compatible with my approach; see section 2.2.

without any theory it is impossible to construct models that fulfill an explanatory function. A similar conclusion is drawn by Morrison (2007), one of the founders of the models-as-mediators approach. While regarding models as autonomous agents, she rejects the idea that model-building is completely theory-independent. Morrison (2007, 198) argues that although theory does not determine model construction, "the way we model phenomena is typically constrained by theoretical laws or principles that are part of the larger scientific context." CUP should be interpreted along these lines: its claim that explanations should be "based on an intelligible theory" does not imply that they must be derived from theory—it only means that the construction of explanations requires an intelligible theoretical context.[9]

Additional support for the plausibility of CUP—in particular, for its basic idea that understanding (UP) and intelligibility (UT) are intrinsically related—can be gained from the fact that the advancement of scientific understanding crucially depends on communication. Scientific research is a community enterprise, which involves collaboration of, and communication between, scientists. Full-fledged scientific explanations are almost never the work of individuals but the outcome of the interaction between (groups of) scientists. Accordingly, the understanding provided by scientific explanations is a concrete cognitive achievement shared by the members of the scientific community (an achievement which is ideally also understood—at least to some extent—by the general public). Such shared understanding of phenomena can be produced only if scientists are able to exchange their results and understand each other's claims, theories, and models. In short, scientists need to interact and communicate, and intelligibility is an obvious precondition for fruitful communication.

An insightful and fruitful perspective on the relation between understanding and communication is offered by Paul Humphreys (2000), who introduces a distinction between primary and secondary understanding. Primary understanding is gained when an individual or group of scientists

---

9. Incidentally, other types of understanding that are not explanatory and do not involve theories, yet do play a role in science, have been identified by Sabina Leonelli and Peter Lipton. On the basis of a case study in biology, Leonelli (2009, 203–206) distinguishes between theoretical and embodied understanding, where the latter is, at least to a large extent, independent of theorizing and does not have an explanatory goal. Lipton (2009) argues that we should not identify understanding with having an explanation, but rather with the cognitive benefits that explanations provide (e.g., knowledge of causes or necessity). He argues that there are ways to gain these benefits—and thus understanding—without actually having an explanation. An example would be Galileo's famous thought experiment demonstrating that gravitational acceleration is independent of mass. See De Regt (2013) for an overview of the debate concerning the possibility of understanding without explanation.

discovers a new explanation for some phenomenon; secondary understanding is achieved "when one individual or group is provided by another individual or group with all the items of knowledge that the first needs in order
to arrive at some (improved) level of understanding. . . . Secondary understanding thus involves a method of instruction" (Humphreys 2000, 269).
Humphreys argues that secondary understanding is impossible without primary understanding, but that the two types do not have to be achieved in
the same way. Traditionally, philosophers of explanation have focused on the
production of secondary understanding in explanatory dialogues, in which
one individual communicates an answer to an explanation-seeking question
to another individual. Success in achieving secondary understanding evi-
dently requires intelligible communication between the persons involved.
But what precisely are the conditions for intelligibility in such a situation,
we might ask. This is a question that Humphreys does not address (he does
not refer to the notion of intelligibility). I submit that these conditions can
be specified on the basis of the definition of intelligibility provided in section 2.3. Suppose primary understanding of a phenomenon is gained by
scientist Angelina on the basis of theory T. As was argued in chapter 2, the
ability to use the relevant theories (UT) is a necessary requirement for constructing the explanation that produces primary understanding. Angelina is
able to come up with the explanation because T is intelligible to her, where
intelligibility is the value that she attributes to the qualities of T that facilitate her use of it. Now, suppose that Angelina wants to communicate her
achievement to Brad, so that Brad also obtains (at least some level of) understanding of the phenomenon. In this case, Brad does not have to construct
the explanation from scratch. However, he should be able to follow the steps
that led Angelina to the construction of the explanation, since an explanation presents "a systematic line of reasoning that connects it with other
accepted items of knowledge" (see section 2.2), and he should reproduce
this line of reasoning to acquire understanding.[10] In short, the intelligibility
that lies at the basis of primary understanding appears to be a requirement
for achieving secondary understanding as well.[11]

---

10. Of course, the level of detail in which he reproduces the explanation may vary, and this
will correspond with a variation in the level of understanding that is achieved. Understanding
clearly is a matter of degree (e.g., there will be differences between the level of understanding of expert scientists, science students, and laypeople). I submit that these differences in
degree of understanding correspond with different degrees of intelligibility. This idea is a
topic for further research, however.

11. In other words, intelligibility provides the link between primary and secondary understanding. This is an interesting result given Humphreys's remark that an important but

4.2 Criteria for intelligibility

I have formulated a criterion for understanding phenomena that refers to the notion of intelligibility. The crucial question is now: How do we decide whether a scientific theory is intelligible? Are there criteria for assessing the intelligibility of theories? Intelligibility has been defined as the value that scientists attribute to the cluster of qualities of a theory that facilitate the use of the theory. At first sight, it may therefore seem that only these scientists themselves can decide whether a particular theory is intelligible to them, and moreover, that this involves a purely subjective value judgment. Fortunately, this is not the case—more objective ways of assessing intelligibility do exist. Since intelligibility is not an intrinsic property of theories but a context-dependent value ascribed to theories, it is not possible to specify a universally valid standard of intelligibility (such as, for example, "only causal-mechanical theories are intelligible"). But this does not entail that intelligibility is merely a matter of taste and that no criteria can be formulated at all. Since intelligibility can be regarded as a measure of how fruitful a theory is for the construction of models by scientists in a particular context, it is possible to determine this measure by means of a criterion or test. There may be different ways to test whether a theory is intelligible for scientists, and not all of them may be applicable in all cases or for all disciplines. In this section, I will propose one specific criterion that appears to be particularly well-suited to test the intelligibility of theories in the physical sciences. Accordingly, this criterion will apply to most of the examples and case studies presented in this book.

As a first step toward the formulation of a criterion for intelligibility, compare a successful scientific theory with a hypothetical oracle whose pronouncements always prove true. In the latter case, empirical adequacy would be ensured, but we would not speak of a great scientific success (and perhaps not even of science *tout court*) because there is no understanding of how the perfect predictions were brought about.[12] An oracle is nothing but a black box that produces seemingly arbitrary predictions. Scientists want more than this: in addition they want insight, and therefore they need to open the black box and consider the workings of the theory that generates

---

as yet unanswered question is how primary and secondary understanding are related (2000, 270).

12. The historiography of science supports this idea. Toulmin (1963, 27–30), for example, stresses the generally acknowledged point that Ionian astronomers were as scientific as their Babylonian contemporaries. The Babylonians "acquired great *forecasting-power*, but they conspicuously lacked *understanding*." By contrast, while its predictive power was meager, Ionian philosophy of nature is traditionally considered as the beginning of natural science.

the predictions. Whatever this theory looks like, it should not be merely another black box producing the empirically adequate descriptions and predictions (on pain of infinite regress). In contrast to an oracle, a scientific theory should be intelligible: the theory itself should be understood. The opacity of an oracle entails that the way in which its predictions are generated is unclear. The intelligibility of scientific theory, by contrast, implies that it should be possible to grasp how its predictions are generated. A sign that such a grasp has been achieved is the fact that one has developed a "feeling" for the consequences of the theory in concrete situations (where "feeling" does not refer to an emotion or an immediate intuition, but corresponds to having a rough, general idea). It suggests that it is possible to understand how a theory works without being able to use it for making precise calculations. To be sure, this demand for a general outline of how the theory works is still vague. But it can be given more substance by making use of an observation by Werner Heisenberg about what understanding in physics amounts to in actual practice.[13] Inspired by Heisenberg, I propose the following Criterion for the Intelligibility of Theories CIT_1 as one way of objectively testing the intelligibility of scientific theories:

CIT_1: A scientific theory T (in one or more of its representations)[14] is intelligible for scientists (in context C) if they can recognize qualitatively characteristic consequences of T without performing exact calculations.[15]

---

13. In Heisenberg's famous 1927 uncertainty paper; see section 7.3 for a detailed discussion. Richard Feynman endorses essentially the same view as the early Heisenberg and attributes it to Dirac. Feynman et al. (1963–1965, 2:2-1) associate physical understanding of the behavior of a system with having "some feel for the character of the solution in different circumstances." Feynman adds: "What it really means to understand an equation—that is, in more than a strictly mathematical sense—was described by Dirac. He said: 'I understand what an equation means if I have a way of figuring out the characteristics of its solution without actually solving it'. So if we have a way of knowing what should happen in given circumstances without actually solving the equations, then we 'understand' the equation, as applied to these circumstances. A physical understanding is a completely unmathematical, imprecise, and inexact thing, but absolutely necessary for a physicist."

14. See section 2.3 for an elucidation of this clause.

15. Criterion CIT_1 applies specifically to theories formulated in mathematical terms, as is usual in the physical sciences. For theories in other disciplines, especially non-mathematical ones, other criteria may apply. Moreover, there may be other ways to determine intelligibility of theories in the physical sciences as well. CIT_1 is a sufficient condition for intelligibility, not a necessary one; there may be alternative criteria CIT_2, CIT_3, etc. A possible way to apply CIT_1 to non-mathematical, qualitative theories is to replace "exact calculation" by "fully explicit logical argumentation." Intelligibility of such theories then implies the ability to recognize consequences without following all the steps the "formalism" of the theory requires.

Note that CIT_1 captures the pragmatic and contextual nature of intelligibility (and thereby of UP: understanding phenomena). CIT_1 explicitly refers to the scientists who use the theory, and to the particular context C in which they operate. Whether theory T is intelligible depends not only on the qualities of T itself but also on such contextual factors as the capacities, background knowledge and background beliefs of the scientists in C. Accordingly, CIT_1 allows for the possibility that a scientific theory considered unintelligible by some (in one scientific community, at one time) will be regarded as intelligible by others (in another community or at another time). Thus, CIT_1 can accommodate the variety of ways in which understanding is achieved in scientific practice. Qualitative insight into the consequences of a theory can be gained in many ways and therefore the criterion does not favor one particular skill or theoretical quality. Its fulfillment requires an appropriate combination of skills and qualities. The preferred theoretical qualities, to which skills have to be attuned, can provide "tools" for achieving understanding. Visualizability is an example of such a quality: visualizations are widely used as tools to construct models of phenomena. However, while visualizability is valued by many scientists, it is not a necessary condition for understanding; there are scientists who prefer abstract theories to visualizable ones (examples will be given in chapter 7). Moreover, a look at scientific practice shows that the intelligibility standards that have been proposed by philosophers of explanation as conditions for scientific understanding (for instance, causality and unification) have indeed played a role at various times and in various situations. However, while they are certainly relevant to the analysis of scientific understanding, they do not have the status of exclusiveness and immutability that is sometimes ascribed to them: their importance and content depend on the context and are subject to change or development.

Let me illustrate criteria CUP and CIT_1 by applying them to the concrete case that was discussed in section 2.2: the explanation of the combined gas law by the kinetic theory of gases. This example is generally regarded as a paradigm case of an explanation that increases our understanding and has often been invoked to promote a particular, allegedly universal, intelligibility standard, such as causality (Salmon 1984, 227; Barnes 1992, 8), visualizability (Cushing 1994, 14), or unifying power (Friedman 1974, 14–15). I submit, however, that a superior account of how the kinetic theory provides understanding of gas phenomena, such as described by the combined gas law, can be given on the basis of CUP and CIT_1.

As we saw in section 2.2, the kinetic explanation of the combined gas law involves the construction of a model (the ideal-gas model) that represents the target system in such a way that a theoretical prediction of the relationship between pressure, volume, and temperature can be derived (the ideal-gas law), which fits the combined gas law. The ideal-gas model does not follow deductively from either the kinetic theory or the description of the phenomena, but is constructed in a process that involves idealizations and approximations. Skills and judgment are needed to make the right steps, and it is the intelligibility of the kinetic theory (to scientists who possess these skills) that allows for the construction of a model that fits the phenomena (and thereby provides explanatory understanding). In a word, understanding is achieved only if CUP applies.

That the kinetic theory is intelligible to scientists is indicated by the fact that they are able to reason with it in a qualitative way, recognizing characteristic consequences of it (in accordance with CIT_1). Such qualitative understanding of the theory provides the basis for detailed calculations that yield understanding of specific phenomena. Examples of such qualitative reasoning abound in textbooks that introduce the theory. Consider, for example, the way Ludwig Boltzmann—one of the founders of the kinetic theory of gases—introduces it in his *Lectures on Gas Theory*. He presents the molecular-kinetic picture as a "mechanical analogy" that can be used to explain the observable properties of matter (Boltzmann 1964, 26). He argues that, for solid and fluid bodies, "the appearance of a continuum is more clearly understood by assuming the presence of a large number of adjacent discrete particles, assumed to obey the laws of mechanics" and the "further assumption that heat is a permanent motion of the molecules" (1964, 28). Subsequently, a purely qualitative discussion leads him to conclude that a gas can be pictured as a collection of freely moving molecules in a container, which is described as follows:

> If no external forces act on the molecules, these move most of the time like bullets shot from guns in straight lines with constant velocity. Only when a molecule passes very near to another one, or to the wall of the vessel, does it deviate from its rectilinear path. The pressure of the gas is interpreted as the action of these molecules against the wall of the container. (Boltzmann 1964, 32)

In a quite straightforward way, this molecular-kinetic picture can give us a qualitative "feeling" for the behavior of macroscopic properties of gases. A lucid account of such reasoning is given by Richard Feynman, in the very first chapter of his famous *Lectures on Physics* (Feynman et al. 1963–1965, 1:1–2ff). Like Boltzmann, Feynman takes the atomistic view of matter as the starting point of his reasoning (in contrast to Boltzmann, however, he adopts an unabashedly realist interpretation of it). On the basis of a simple, idealized picture of a gas in a container, Feynman derives some qualitative results concerning the relations between pressure, temperature, and volume. First of all, the molecular-kinetic picture gives a qualitative account of the fact that a gas exerts pressure on the walls of its container. If a gas molecule collides with a wall of the container, it gives it a little push. The total effect of the pushing of the molecules produces the pressure. In more formal terms: molecules exert forces on the wall and the total force of all molecules on a unit area equals the macroscopic pressure. Subsequently, the relation between pressure and temperature can be determined qualitatively, given the basic principle of the kinetic theory that heat is molecular motion. This principle implies that adding heat to a gas in a container of constant volume will lead to an increase of the velocities of the molecules, so that they will hit the walls of the container more often and with greater force. Accordingly, the pressure of the gas will increase. In a similar manner, Feynman argues that if one decreases the volume of the container slowly (i.e., under constant pressure), the temperature of the gas will increase. When these conclusions are combined, one obtains a qualitative expression of the ideal-gas law.

This reasoning does not involve any calculations; it is based on general characteristics of the theoretical description of the gas. Its purpose is to give us the understanding that is needed to construct specific models of target systems; the understanding that we need before we embark on detailed calculations. Such calculations are subsequently motivated, and given direction, by the understanding we already possess.[16] Incidentally, it should be emphasized that my account does not intend to downplay the value of exact calculation. I do not want to suggest that exact calculation should be replaced with some kind of intuitive understanding, or that understanding is superior to explanation in the natural sciences (compare the *Verstehen–Erklären* debate in the social and human sciences). Exact mathematical techniques and logical rigor in argumentation are obviously essential in modern science. My aim is to clarify the nature of understanding as an epistemic aim of science (which is inherently connected with explanation, as CUP states), and I argue that that intelligibility of theories is essential for achieving this aim. Qualitative reasoning can play an important role in the process of constructing model-based, understanding-producing explanations, and this is why CIT_1 is an indicator of intelligibility.

---

16. See Boltzmann (1964, 62–68) and Feynman et al. (1963–1965, 1:39-6ff.) for quantitative calculations of the relations between pressure, volume, and temperature (ideal-gas law) on the basis of the kinetic theory.

The example of the kinetic explanation of the combined gas law illustrates how scientific understanding of a phenomenon is based on the ability to recognize qualitative consequences of the theory without performing exact calculation (criterion CIT_1). The general picture of moving gas particles allows us to make qualitative predictions of macroscopic properties of gases in particular situations. The kinetic theory has qualities that provide tools which can be employed by physicists who possess the relevant skills in order to gain understanding of the behavior of phenomena in its domain. One might ask why this account is superior to a causal-mechanical account, or even whether there really is a difference. After all, the story just told does employ causal reasoning. The answer is that my account explains how in this case understanding can be achieved by means of causal arguments; it does more than merely affirming that causality supplies understanding. Causal reasoning is used to generate qualitative predictions; it is an instrument that helps us to get a feeling for the behavior of gases. In section 3.4, I observed that although many philosophers defend their favorite theory of explanation by claiming that it furnishes understanding, they typically neglect to show how such understanding is produced and merely assert that their favored type of explanation yields understanding. By contrast, my account clarifies the way in which the kinetic explanation provides understanding. The example shows that causal concepts function as tools for achieving understanding. However, this does not imply that causal reasoning is a necessary condition: the possibility of gaining understanding by other means is left open.

As a second example, consider meteorology, a science concerned with highly complex systems. Weather predictions are obtained by means of computer calculations in which the Navier-Stokes equations are solved for very large systems, using many auxiliary theories to incorporate small-scale effects. If meteorologists were merely occupied with making correct predictions in this manner, they would fail to understand the weather. But this is not the case: meteorologists are concerned not only with "brute force" computer calculations but also with formulating intelligible meteorological theories and models. An example is "PV thinking," based on Ertel's equation of potential vorticity (see Ambaum 1997, 3–10). The goal of PV-thinking is to provide qualitative understanding, in the sense of facilitating the recognition of qualitative consequences of applying the Navier-Stokes equations to the atmosphere by means of a relatively simple picture. For example, in 1951 Ernst Kleinschmidt applied PV thinking in order to gain a qualitative understanding of the behavior of cyclones, adding that a representation of cyclones in terms of potential vorticity should be regarded as merely "an illustrative picture" [*anschauliches*

Bild] (quoted in Ambaum 1997, 4). Even though the PV picture cannot be interpreted realistically, it is a useful tool for understanding cyclones (and atmospheric evolution in general). Therefore, there is more to meteorology than brute force calculation: meteorologists also aim at scientific understanding in the sense of criteria CUP and CIT_1.[17]

The criteria for understanding and intelligibility presented in this and the previous section form the basis of an account of scientific understanding in which explanation, understanding, and prediction are interrelated epistemic goals of science. Earlier I introduced the case of an oracle producing perfect predictions as a contrast to science, which aims at more than merely correct predictions. However, not only is mere prediction without understanding insufficient for science, prediction turns out to be impossible without understanding, as the cases of behaviorist psychology and quantum physics illustrate. Our hypothetical oracle is just a figment of the imagination: in reality one can only make successful predictions if one understands the relevant theories. Conversely, the ability to predict—the recognition of qualitative consequences of the theory (CIT_1)—shows that scientists have such understanding, or in other words, that the theory is intelligible to them. The inherent connection between prediction and explanatory understanding is nicely captured by Douglas (2009a, 454), when she observes that "the relation between explanation and prediction is a tight, functional one: explanations provide the cognitive path to predictions, which then serve to test and refine the explanations." She refers to earlier formulations of CUP and CIT_1 (presented in De Regt and Dieks 2005) to support her case for reintroducing prediction to explanation. Although she does not mention the term "intelligibility" and ignores the difference between UT and UP, Douglas's general assessment of the relation between explanation, understanding, and prediction is fully

---

17. A comparable situation occurs in cognitive science, where connectionist models in terms of neural networks are used to represent cognitive phenomena such as face and word recognition. Although such connectionist models can achieve high empirical accuracy, they are regarded as unintelligible by cognitive scientists, as Eigner (2010, 54–55) observes. Eigner quotes cognitive scientist Derek Partridge (1991, 72): "Why a certain model is doing what it is observed to be doing, and what would be needed to make it do something differently, are both extremely difficult questions to answer." Partridge explicitly compares the problem to the situation in meteorology. Just as brute force calculations of weather prediction do not provide understanding and a qualitative model is needed, Eigner states that "the behavior of a neural network can only be understood if it can be explained 'in psychologically meaningful terms, rather than in terms of the implementation structures.' He [Partridge] argues that it is incomprehensible how neural networks perform their tasks because they do not allow for 'reasoning by analogy with one's own supposed thought processes.' " (Eigner 2010, 55; quoting Partridge 1991, 17).

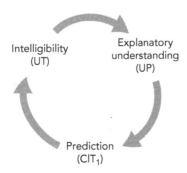

Intelligibility
(UT)

Explanatory
understanding
(UP)

Prediction
(CIT$_1$)

FIGURE 4.1 The relations between understanding, explanation, and prediction.

compatible with my analysis. This relation is pictured, in a simplified way, in figure 4.1.

4.3 Conceptual tools for understanding

In section 2.2, I argued that the skills and judgments involved in achieving understanding cannot be reduced to rule-following procedures. Criterion CIT$_1$ can be regarded as an objective test of such implicit, "tacit" skills. But what skills are needed obviously depends on the features of the theory (in a particular representation). Explaining a phenomenon, for example, by constructing a model of it on the basis of a theory, requires skills that are appropriately geared to the properties of the theory in question. These theoretical properties provide the "tools for understanding" and the scientist should be suitably skilled to use these tools. Just as a carpenter needs tools and the skills to use them for doing his job, a scientist needs tools and associated skills for understanding phenomena. By applying criterion CIT$_1$, one can check whether a scientist's skills are attuned to the theory's properties. Because qualitative insight into the consequences of a theory can be gained in many ways, CIT$_1$ can accommodate the variety of ways in which understanding is achieved in scientific practice. Visualizability has already been mentioned as an example of a theoretical quality that may enhance intelligibility. As the case studies in chapter 7 will illustrate, visualizable theories are often regarded as more intelligible than abstract ones, because many scientists prefer visual reasoning in the construction of explanations of phenomena, using pictorial representations or diagrams as tools. Indeed, visualization skills are widely shared among scientists and humans in general. But empirical studies have shown that spatial-visual skills vary across the population and can be improved by education (Mathewson 1999; Titus and Horsman 2009). Accordingly, some people may have a stronger preference for visual reasoning than others, and some scientists may even prefer abstract theories over visualizable ones. The same holds for causal reasoning. Causal structure is a quality that is often regarded as enhancing the intelligibility of theories, and causal concepts (e.g., process, interaction, collision, energy, or momentum transfer) are widely used as tools for understanding. Yet, as will be illustrated, even causal tools are not irreplaceable.

How precisely do conceptual tools function in the attainment of scientific understanding? Although criterion CIT_1 is but one way of assessing intelligibility, it does reveal important aspects of the process of understanding. First, note that in order to recognize consequences of a theory without calculation and to be able to argue about them, a conceptual framework is required in terms of which one can argue qualitatively. Here an instructive analogy is to be noticed with problem-solving methods, in which heuristic strategies often play an important role. Heuristics can guide the search for solutions in a variety of ways, not only "by drastically restricting the number of possible roads" but also "by positively suggesting which general directions to take in the searching process" (Radder 1991, 196). Analogous to problem-solving heuristics, the "intuitive" recognition of theoretical consequences requires conceptual tools. With the help of these tools one can circumvent the calculating stage and reason toward a qualitative conclusion in a different, more intuitive manner (in extreme cases, the conclusion may seem to appear in a flash of insight).[18]

My use of the term "intuitive" in the previous paragraph might worry philosophical readers who associate this with a mysterious source of knowledge that lies outside the bounds of rational thinking and sensory experience, or with some kind of supernatural faculty (a "sixth sense"). But this is definitely not what I mean here. Rather, the notion of "intuition" refers to a factor in human reasoning and decision-making, which has been extensively studied and discussed by psychologists such as Gerd Gigerenzer (2007) and Daniel Kahneman (2011). While Gigerenzer and Kahneman disagree about the reliability of intuitions, they both acknowledge their existence and their role in decision-making processes. Gigerenzer (2007, 16) defines intuition (or "gut feeling") as "a judgment (1) that appears quickly in consciousness, (2) whose

---

18. As was mentioned in chapter 2, experiments by Jung-Beeman et al. (2004) show that problem-solving via a "flash of insight" differs crucially from problem-solving via a straightforward application of methods or rules: the two routes to problem solutions involve different cognitive and neural processes in different hemispheres. This supports the idea that a special, more intuitive kind of understanding exists.

underlying reasons we are not fully aware of, and (3) is strong enough to act upon." He argues that such intuitive judgments are not mysterious but produced by heuristics that typically have been developed in an evolutionary process of adaptation to our environment (2007, 47–49). An example is the "gaze heuristic," which helps baseball players to catch a ball that is high up in the air: "Fix your gaze on the ball, start running, and adjust your running speed so that the angle of the gaze remains constant" (2007, 10). Baseball players do not subconsciously carry out detailed mathematical calculations of trajectories—they use a simple heuristic that quickly produces a reliable result. According to Gigerenzer (2007, 58–64), the human mind can be regarded as an "adaptive toolbox," consisting of a great number of heuristic tools based on our evolved capacities. These evolved capacities, of which language, emotion, and object tracking are but a few examples, are acquired via natural selection or cultural transmission, and "are always functions of both our genes and our learning environment. They evolved in tandem with the environment in which our ancestors lived and are shaped by the environment in which a child grows up" (Gigerenzer 2007, 59). While Gigerenzer focuses on decision processes in everyday life and professional contexts, it seems plausible that similar mechanisms are at work in scientific practice. This would support my thesis that skill and intuitive judgment play a central role in the process of achieving scientific understanding. If a theory is intelligible to scientists because its theoretical qualities match their skills, they can reason "intuitively" with it. Like our everyday intuitive skills, scientists' skills are the outcome of a complex learning process in which their evolved cognitive capacities interact with the environment in which they find themselves (that is, the historical and disciplinary context of their science).

   Kahneman is more critical of intuitions than Gigerenzer, highlighting their adverse effects in decision-making, but he does not deny their usefulness in everyday life. Like Gigerenzer, Kahneman stresses that there is nothing mysterious or magical about intuitive judgments: they are produced by a part of our cognitive system that he dubs System 1, which he contrasts with System 2:

- *System 1* operates automatically and quickly, with little or no effort and no sense of voluntary control.
- *System 2* allocates attention to the effortful mental activities that demand it, including complex computations.

(Kahneman 2011, 20–21)

System 1 includes skills and capabilities that may be innate (acquired through evolution) or learned (acquired through education or practice). Kahneman emphasizes that System 1, which cannot be switched off, regularly fails, especially in situations that are novel or complex. He cites many experiments (partly conducted by himself and his long-time collaborator Amos Tversky) in which subjects appear to be prone to various kinds of biases and to flawed reasoning (e.g., the hindsight and overconfidence biases cited in section 2.1, and the well-known case of Linda the feminist bank teller).[19] In such cases, System 1 leads us astray, and System 2 has to intervene if we want to achieve reliable results. According to Kahneman, our intuitive skills are acquired by learning and ultimately rooted in memory and recognition.[20] He approvingly quotes Herbert Simon, who described the working of expert intuition as follows: "The situation has provided a cue; this cue gives the expert access to information stored in memory, and the information provides the answer. Intuition is nothing more and nothing less than recognition" (Simon quoted by Kahneman 2011, 11, 237). In his later work, and as a result of his discussion with Gary Klein, Kahneman has abandoned his skeptical view of intuition for a more nuanced position. In their joint paper "Conditions for Intuitive Expertise: A Failure to Disagree," Kahneman and Klein (2009) argue that while purely subjective confidence is not to be trusted, it is possible to acquire intuitive skills that lead to accurate judgment if the following two conditions apply:

- An environment that is sufficiently regular to be predictable
- An opportunity to learn these regularities through prolonged practice

(Kahneman 2011, 240; Kahneman and Klein 2009)

Scientists are usually working in contexts where these conditions hold; that is, contexts that resemble Kuhnian normal science. Of course, situations may occur in which their acquired skills fail to apply (e.g., in time of crisis and revolution) and a need for re-schooling arises—but this is the exception rather than the rule.

---

19. Kahneman (2011, passim); see esp. chapter 19 for the hindsight bias and chapter 15 for the Linda problem. Interestingly, Gigerenzer (2007, 93–97) argues that the allegedly mistaken answer that most people give in the Linda case is not based on a reasoning fallacy but on "an intelligent conversational intuition."

20. Kahneman rejects Gigerenzer's claim that intuitive heuristics is "frugal," in the sense that it uses the principle "less is more." By contrast, Kahneman (2011, 458) argues that "skill is more often an ability to deal with large amounts of information quickly and efficiently."

Scientists use their expert skills to construct models of the object or system they want to understand scientifically. As has been argued in section 2.2, model construction is partly a matter of making the right approximations and idealizations, which requires skillful use of the available conceptual tools. Consider, for example, the way in which visualization is used for achieving understanding in physics. The important role of visualization in scientific practice has been emphasized by many physicists: Faraday, Maxwell, Schrödinger, and Feynman are well-known examples. Indeed, Feynman's preference for visualization shines from almost every page of his famous lectures on physics. A simple illustration is the use of "field lines" in electrostatics (Feynman et al. 1963–1965, 2:4–11). Although intuitive application of this concept is possible only in simple situations, it is quite useful to get a feeling of how electrostatic systems behave. And this, according to Feynman (2–1), is precisely what it means to have physical understanding of the situation in question: "If we have a way of knowing what should happen in given circumstances without actually solving the equations, then we 'understand' the equations, as applied to these circumstances." (2–1; note that this is in full agreement with criterion CIT_1.)

To see how visualization can be a tool for understanding, let us have a close look at the way in which so-called bag models are employed for dealing with quark confinement. An example is the MIT bag model, which was put forward in the context of quantum chromodynamics (QCD), the fundamental theory describing hadron structure (see Hartmann 1999). The problem with QCD is that reliable tests are possible only by means of "black box" numerical techniques, using the so-called lattice QCD approach. Although QCD equations of motion can be solved numerically with the lattice approach, it does not supply understanding; it does not make QCD intelligible. But like every other scientist, hadron physicists strive for explanatory understanding—which is after all an epistemic aim of science—and therefore they construct models, of which the MIT bag model is an example. This model was proposed in order to achieve understanding of quark confinement: quarks supposedly exist only in pairs or triplets, confined to a very small spatial volume. The existence of quark confinement is empirically supported by the fact that no single quarks have been observed, and moreover, it appears (but has not been proven rigorously) to be a consequence of QCD. The MIT bag model represents hadrons as elastic "bags" in which (two or three) quarks are spatially confined, forced by external pressure (similar to nucleons in the nuclear shell model). With the help of boundary conditions and suitable approximations, the single model parameter (bag pressure) can be adjusted to fit hadronic observables (e.g., mass and charge). Hartmann (1999, 336) observes that the predictions of the model only modestly agree with empirical data, and asks: Why do physicists retain the model, despite its shortcomings? His answer is that this and similar models provide "plausible stories." Hartmann (1999, 344) suggests that the significance of such qualitative stories lies in their ability to provide understanding, but he adds that it is "very difficult to explicate how a model and its story exactly provide understanding." My theory of understanding makes it clear how the MIT bag model, and the story that goes with it, provides scientific understanding. The model is constructed by means of a visualization of hadrons that allows physicists to make qualitative predictions about their structure without carrying out calculations by means of lattice QCD. As such, in contrast to the lattice approach, visual models of hadron structure render the theory of QCD intelligible. A simple visualization provides the basis for developing the MIT bag model in mathematical detail, thereby advancing our understanding of the phenomena in the domain of QCD. Accordingly, my analysis substantiates the observation of particle physicist Thomas Cohen (quoted by Hartmann 1999, 330): "Models of the hadrons are essential in developing intuition into how QCD functions in the low energy domain."

Visualization is an important tool, but it would be a mistake to conclude that it is essential for achieving understanding. Scientists have recourse to a variety of conceptual tools that facilitate model-building. For example, many theoretical physicists have developed a familiarity with, and intuition for, the general behavior of the solutions of the mathematical equations they use. This enables them to acquire a feeling for the qualitative behavior of the described systems without invoking visualizable physical mechanisms. For instance, it is possible to get an intuitive feeling for how quantum-mechanical systems in two-slit-like situations behave, by familiarity with the linear character of the Schrödinger equation. There is no reason to reject the claims these physicists often make, namely that the theory they are working with is intelligible to them in a purely mathematical way, and that it allows them to achieve understanding of the phenomena in its domain. On my account of scientific understanding, such different tools as visualization and mathematical abstraction can both be employed to obtain scientific understanding.

Another instructive example is the deflection of light by matter predicted by general relativity. There are at least three well-known ways of understanding this phenomenon. All strategies use general relativity, but employ different conceptual tools for bringing out the consequences of the theory. The first approach focuses on the variation of the velocity of light in a gravitational field; this is a consequence of general relativity that can be grasped intuitively by the use of the equivalence principle. The deflection of light can subsequently be understood by means of an analogy with the propagation of light in a medium with a variable refractive index. No specific causal mechanisms are invoked (the light signal itself can be considered a causal chain, but we are talking about the explanation of the deflection, and no mechanism in the ordinary sense is specified for that). The second approach is more abstract. It does not mention the variation in the velocity of light, but invokes the non-Euclidean character of the spatial geometry to explain the non-Newtonian curvature of the light rays.[21] Finally, one can describe the light rays as null-geodesics in the four-dimensional metrical field. This can be done in an abstract mathematical way, but the procedure is often made visualizable via analogies with two-dimensional curved surfaces. It is noteworthy that these different ways of obtaining a feeling for how light propagates according to general relativity can be used alongside each other. Depending on the kind of problem to which one wishes to apply the analysis, on the calculational techniques one favors, or on other preferences, one or the other can be chosen.

None of the three approaches employs causality as a tool for understanding: no causal chains are identified that are responsible for the deflection of the light. However, a causal way of obtaining understanding is also available. Popular expositions of general relativity, but also informal arguments among scientists, often make use of conceptual tools that have proved their understanding-providing value in Newtonian gravitational theory and are therefore "imported" into relativity theory. This leads to accounts according to which masses pull and "attract" light. It is difficult to give this notion of an attractive gravitational force a definite meaning within the formal framework of general relativity, and a realistic interpretation therefore appears problematic. However, the Newtonian causal mechanisms can still fulfill the role of conceptual tools providing understanding. There are many more examples in which the causal-mechanistic worldview makes itself felt in the terminology used in obtaining understanding, but has lost most of its substance and cannot be taken literally. Many so-called mechanisms in physics are not mechanisms in the ordinary sense of the word at all. An interesting case is the "mechanism" adduced in quantum field theory to explain how particles acquire mass (the so-called Higgs mechanism). This mechanism consists in the introduction into the Hamiltonian of an additional field, with a potential that has a ground state energy that is less than zero. Mathematical considerations involving spontaneous symmetry breaking,

---

21. See Eddington (1920, ch. 6) for a clear exposition of these different ways of understanding the deflection of light.

and the introduction of new fields, which are shifted with respect to the old ones, lead to a rewritten Hamiltonian that can be interpreted as describing massive particles. The whole reasoning is based on the form of the equations and analogies, and certainly no classical causal mechanism, transporting mass to particles that were massless before, is involved. Moreover, the quantum fields do not correspond to particles in the classical sense and the same problems with the notion of a causal chain arise as in the EPR case. The Higgs mechanism might be considered an example of the "noncausal mechanisms" that Salmon (1984, 133) alludes to. But it is unclear how such a "mechanism" would fit into Salmon's theory of explanation. By contrast, my approach has no problem in accounting for the explanatory power of this kind of argument.

In sum, scientific theories can be rendered intelligible with the help of a variety of conceptual tools, of which visualization, mathematical abstraction, and causality are prime examples. This idea was anticipated in chapter 3, which reviewed existing models of scientific explanation and associated conceptions of understanding. I concluded that these models of explanation can "peacefully co-exist" if one does not conceive of them as rival proposals for absolute, universal conditions for understanding, but instead as supplying tools that may be used for achieving understanding in different (historical or disciplinary) contexts: they allow skilled scientists to recognize the consequences of a scientific theory and thereby facilitate model-building. This offers a new perspective on the status and function of models of explanation. Causal reasoning, for example, does not lead to understanding because it reveals the underlying structure of the world, but because it enhances our ability to predict how the systems that we study will behave under particular conditions. This view of the nature and purpose of causal explanation is more in line with the spirit of Woodward's manipulationist theory of causation and explanation than with that of Salmon's "ontic" theory. Woodward (2003a, 114; 2003b, 221–224) emphasizes that scientific understanding can be achieved at different levels—it is not a matter of getting the ontology right but rather of being instrumentally successful in answering questions about the behavior of the systems under study. This view of causal explanation is clearly congenial to my account of scientific understanding.[22]

---

22. A theoretical quality that has not figured prominently in the examples is unifying power (it was mentioned only in the context of the kinetic explanation of the combined gas law). Can unification be used as a tool to render theories intelligible? Yes, but only in an indirect way: as argued in section 3.1, the understanding-providing feature of unification (in Kitcher's sense) is the fact that it allows us to see analogies between theories in the form of similar argument patterns, which extends the range of a particular skill.

4.4 The context dependence of understanding

In the previous sections, I have emphasized repeatedly that scientific understanding is contextual. Intelligibility—the *sine qua non* of UT—is defined explicitly as a contextual value. The reason is that whether or not a theory is intelligible to scientists depends on their skills and preferences for particular theoretical qualities and is accordingly determined by the context. So far, however, I have not yet investigated how precisely understanding depends on the context and how contextual variation of intelligibility comes about. In section 4.3, we saw that scientific practice displays a variety of conceptual tools and associated skills for achieving understanding. It is the historical, social, or disciplinary context that determines what tools are available and deemed suitable for explanatory purposes. There is no universal tool for understanding, but a variety of "toolkits," containing particular tools for particular situations. What tools scientists have at their disposal, and whether they possess the relevant skills to use these tools, depends on the context in which they find themselves.[23] In the present section, I will examine the context dependence of understanding in more detail and discuss some of its implications for the philosophy of scientific explanation.

4.4.1 Contextuality and historical dynamics

A striking example of how standards of intelligibility can vary in the course of time, and of the role of contextual factors, is provided by the history of gravitational theory. As this case will be analyzed in full detail in chapter 5, I will here present only a sketch of the episode to introduce my thesis regarding the historical dynamics of intelligibility. In 1687, Newton published his now famous theory of gravitation, mathematically expressed by the inverse-square law, which seemed to imply that all material bodies act upon each other instantaneously, without any intervening medium. His contemporaries Huygens and Leibniz expressed grave doubts about the theory because they considered the idea of action at a distance unintelligible (in fact, Newton himself struggled with this apparent implication of his theory). Their objections can be traced

---

23. While my study focuses on historical contextuality, variation in the way explanatory understanding is achieved can be observed also across cultural contexts. Empirical study has revealed that different types of cultures favor different styles of explanations, not only with respect to human behavior but also regarding natural phenomena (see Keil 2006, 246–247, for a review of the literature on this topic).

back to metaphysics: the Cartesian corpuscularist worldview to which most seventeenth-century physicists adhered was based on the principle of contact action, leaving no room for action at a distance. But action at a distance has not always been regarded as incomprehensible, as a historical study by van Lunteren (1991) shows. On the contrary, opinions oscillated: after a time when it was deemed unintelligible, the period between 1700 and 1850 was dominated by proponents of action at a distance theories, among them Kant, Laplace, and Helmholtz. At the end of the eighteenth century, the tide had turned completely in favor of action at a distance. In this period, attempts to formulate theories of gravitation based on contact action (by, for example, Euler, Le Sage, and Herapath) were ignored by the scientific community. Only in the second half of the nineteenth century, with the successes of ether theories, contact action became acceptable once again.

At first sight, one might think that this is simply a case of a metaphysical worldview lagging behind scientific development and hampering the acceptance of a revolutionary theory. However, closer inspection of the controversy about the intelligibility of Newton's theory of gravitation reveals a more subtle and complex interaction between metaphysics and intelligibility. Descartes's mechanics, which was the most successful physical theory before Newton, was rendered intelligible by means of a specifically mechanistic conception of causality, in which contact action was essential. The widely accepted corpuscularist metaphysics associated with Cartesian mechanics was a "canonization" of the mechanistic tools that had contributed to the achievement of scientific understanding. This was the reason why Huygens rejected action at a distance as unintelligible. Huygens's adherence to corpuscularism was rooted in the fact that he had learned to understand the natural world scientifically by means of mechanistic principles and models. The notion of action at a distance flatly contradicted the principle of contact action and was therefore unacceptable as an explanatory resource. In due course, however, scientists acquired the skills to work with Newtonian theory and achieved many scientific successes with it. This led to the acceptance of action at a distance, which was used successfully as a tool for constructing explanations of phenomena in new domains such as electricity and chemistry (see section 5.3). As a result, around 1800 action at a distance had replaced contact action as the preferred tool for scientific understanding. But the tide turned once again in the nineteenth century. Since the notion of contact action proved helpful for qualitative reasoning in the theory of electromagnetism (think of Maxwell's famous mechanical model of the ether; see chapter 6 for further discussion), it became a central element of the nineteenth-century conceptual toolkit.

The history of theories of gravitation shows that there is contextual variation in the availability and acceptability of tools for understanding. It appears
that metaphysics is one element in that context: it may supply conceptual
tools, but it can also prohibit the use of alternative tools, as the examples of
contact action and action at a distance show. What more general conclusions
can be drawn about the historical variation of conceptual tools? What contextual factors may affect such variation? To answer these questions, it is helpful
to consult the work of James McAllister, who presents an extensive analysis of
the role of aesthetic factors in theory evaluation. McAllister (1996, 78) argues
that scientists' aesthetic preferences are formed and updated by what he calls
"aesthetic induction": "A community compiles its aesthetic canon at a certain
date by attaching to each property a weighting proportional to the degree of
empirical adequacy then attributed to the set of current and recent theories
that have exhibited that property." Interestingly, many of the properties that
McAllister labels "aesthetic" are theoretical qualities which, according to my
analysis of scientific understanding, may provide conceptual tools for achieving understanding (e.g., visualizability and symmetry). Thus, conceptual toolkits are (at least partly) overlapping with aesthetic canons and are plausibly
formed in a similar inductive manner.

In fact, my theory of understanding complements McAllister's model: their
combination provides a more realistic, more credible account of the historical
dynamics of aesthetic canons and conceptual toolkits. Note that McAllister
presupposes that scientists simply select one theory from a given set of available theories that have a given degree of empirical success. If many successful scientific theories in the past had aesthetic property *AP*, scientists will be
inclined to select a new theory that exhibits *AP* in favor of alternative theories
that do not have this property. This bias is allegedly rational because there is
inductive support for the claim that theories exhibiting *AP* are empirically
more successful than rival theories that do not have *AP*. However, there are
several problems with McAllister's assumptions concerning theory selection.
First and foremost, the fact that it is highly idealized and unrealistic: scientists
do not choose from a given set of theories, but they construct and develop
them. Moreover, empirical success is not a given property of a theory; instead,
as has been argued in section 2.2, it has to be produced by constructing models of phenomena. (Note that if empirical success was given, there would
be no need to select on the basis of aesthetic evaluations, except in cases of
empirically equivalent theories.) My theory of understanding is based on an
analysis of this process of model construction and the subsequent production of explanations and prediction. It does not merely assert that theories
with a particular quality (aesthetic property) are or have been successful, it

explains why this quality is conducive to empirical success; namely, because it enhances the intelligibility of theories for scientists who possess skills to use the associated conceptual tools. Accordingly, achieving empirical and explanatory success is due to the understanding-providing power of the tools in question. Consequently, scientists do not make inductive inferences directly about the aesthetic properties of theories that have been empirically successful in the past, but rather they assess the usefulness of a conceptual tool in the light of its previous successes in providing understanding. For example, if visualization has successfully functioned as a tool for rendering physical theories of the recent past intelligible, then visualizability will figure prominently in the contemporary physicist's conceptual toolkit for understanding. Incidentally, since scientific understanding is typically a community achievement, it should not surprise us that conceptual toolkits, like aesthetic canons, are first and foremost established at the meso-level (cf. section 4.1).

This account of the dynamics of understanding suggests that understanding a scientific theory is, in a sense, a matter of becoming familiar with it: theories can become intelligible when we get accustomed to them and develop the ability to use them in an "intuitive" way (which shows if, for example, CIT_1 applies).[24] In this way, my analysis rehabilitates a viewpoint that has often been discredited: the idea that understanding is related to familiarity. Friedman (1974, 9), for example, deems the view that "scientific explanations give us understanding of the world by relating (or reducing) unfamiliar phenomena to familiar ones"—the so-called "familiarity view" of scientific understanding—"rather obviously inadequate." Indeed, there is a well-known argument against it: science often explains phenomena that are directly known and quite familiar to us by means of theories and concepts of a strange and unfamiliar (sometimes even counterintuitive) character; see Toulmin (1963, 60–61) and Hempel (1965, 256–258; 1966, 83–84) for similar criticisms. Nonetheless, the idea behind the familiarity view should not, and need not, be relinquished completely. The thesis that intelligibility requires conceptual tools, and associated skills, implies that only if tools are familiar to their users (if these users have developed relevant skills), can they be used for their purpose, namely making predictions without entering into explicit calculations. However, this familiarity does not necessarily involve the idea that the user should be acquainted with the concepts in question from everyday experience. One can get accustomed to the mathematical concepts used

---

24. As mentioned in section 4.3, the idea that intuitive skills are related to familiarity was also endorsed by Herbert Simon and Daniel Kahneman: "Intuition is nothing more and nothing less than recognition" (Simon quoted by Kahneman 2011, 11, 237).

in a theory or to an initially strange physical interpretation of a theory, to such an extent that it becomes possible to reason using the associated terms in an intuitive manner. In this way, my theory of understanding incorporates the insight on which the familiarity view is based; but it does not lead to the consequence that we should understand phenomena in terms of things which are more familiar from everyday experience than the phenomena themselves. It gives a more sophisticated explanation of the role of familiarity in achieving understanding than the standard familiarity view and is not vulnerable to the objections that demonstrate the failure of that view.

4.4.2 Contextuality and the intuitions of philosophers

The contextual theory of understanding defended in this book is based upon empirical studies of science. The thesis that standards of intelligibility and explanatory understanding vary with the context is derived from, and supported by, historical evidence and analysis of explanatory practice. By contrast, traditional philosophical accounts of explanation typically bypass in-depth study of actual scientific practice, instead justifying their employed conception of understanding by invoking intuitions.[25] Barnes (1992, 8), for example, after having reproached Friedman and Kitcher for not supplying any argument for the understanding-providing virtues of unification, defends the causal conception by arguing that it rests on a "sound intuition." Similarly, Cushing (1994, 11) defends visualizability as a criterion for understanding by referring to "the intuition ... that understanding of physical processes involves a story that can, in principle, be told on an event-by-event basis." No one who looks back on sixty years of debate about scientific explanation will fail to notice the central role of intuitions about what a good (read: understanding-providing) explanation should consist in; theorists of explanation use such intuitions in their attempts to substantiate their own position and invalidate opposing views. These intuitions are usually employed as "basic facts": for example, the well-known problem of asymmetry (which supposedly refutes Hempel's covering law model and supports the causal model) involves the intuition that

---

25. Note that these are not the same intuitions as those discussed in section 4.3. The latter refer to a type of judgment in scientific (and more generally, human) reasoning, while the intuitions discussed here are allegedly incontrovertible beliefs employed by philosophers in arguments for or against a particular philosophical position. In both cases, knowledge seems to be produced in an a priori manner, hence the term "intuition"; however, I argue that in fact both types of intuitions are determined by the context (since our most basic intuitions have developed in an evolutionary process of adaptation to our environment, it is not surprising that these appear to be a priori).

the length of a flagpole can explain that of its shadow, and not the other way around. My contextual analysis of scientific understanding does not deny the value of these intuitions. But I do not accept them as rigid directives given once and for all. Intuitions depend partly on the historical and scientific context, and may therefore be subject to change or development.

By acknowledging the relativity of intuitions, my approach does not fall prey to the kind of criticism that has proved effective against Hempel's deductive-nomological model of scientific explanation. At first sight, it might be argued that all familiar counterexamples to this model (deduction of causes from effects, deduction of a law from the conjunction of itself and another irrelevant law, causally irrelevant deductions, and so on; for an overview, see Salmon 1990, 46–50) are also counterexamples to a theory of understanding based on CUP and CIT_1. Indeed, it would seem that one could just add the stipulation that a scientist arrived at the results of the deductions intuitively (i.e., without detailed calculations) without weakening the strength of the counterexamples. I will discuss some concrete examples to show how my theory of understanding evades this potential criticism.

In the well-known barometer case, the standard objection is that the mere deduction of the future occurrence of a storm from the reading of a barometer does not yield an explanation of the storm and does not make its occurrence understandable. Instead, a common cause is responsible and provides the explanation, namely the very low air pressure. First, note that the prediction of an upcoming storm from present barometer readings does not satisfy criterion CUP because it does not refer to any scientific theory. Actually, there is no theory about relations between barometer readings, as theoretical quantities, and weather conditions: according to the meteorological theory that actually connects barometer readings to weather conditions, barometers are just indicators of air pressure. On criterion CIT_1, this theory is intelligible if it can be foreseen qualitatively that, for example, the future occurrence of a storm can be the consequence of very low air pressure obtaining now. A meteorologist able to make a global deduction on the basis of meteorological theory, and using the data provided by the barometer, will possess scientific understanding.

But suppose, to get closer to the heart of the matter, that situations exist in which there are correlations between different events (analogously to those between barometer readings and weather conditions) but in which no theoretical explanation in terms of a common cause is available. In that case, one can deduce and predict the occurrence of an event from the occurrence of its correlate, but will this lead to scientific understanding? On my analysis, this is perfectly well possible. CUP merely requires that the correlations are embedded in a scientific theory; this theory does not have to be causal (which means that the correlations do not necessarily have to be explained in terms of either direct causal connection or a common cause). The theory may equally well contain the correlations as scientifically basic, and not as substitutes for something else (as in the barometer case). Such a theory is not per se unintelligible, and scientists who understand this theory (for example, according to CIT_1) can acquire scientific understanding of the phenomena in its domain. Perhaps these scientists would proceed in a rather abstract mathematical way, having developed an intuitive feeling for the equations describing the correlations. In fact, this is the case for quantum physicists who have developed intuitions about the outcomes of experiments with so-called entangled states, in which case causal-mechanical reasoning fails and the equations are the main guide.

So my response to the barometer case is twofold. First, the example itself provides no real challenge, because it does not deal with actual scientific theories and scientific understanding. Second, in situations in which correlations between events do figure in basic scientific theory, it is not clear why deductions using these correlations could not lead to scientific understanding. The EPR correlations (in which entangled states play an essential role) constitute a case in point. The outcome at one wing of the experiment can be understood on the basis of the outcome at the other side (plus quantum theory), even though there is no causal contact between these events (see also section 3.2). In this case, our causal intuitions fail as tools for understanding and the context requires that we develop alternative mathematical intuitions.

What about other putative counterexamples? Cases of irrelevant deductions (Kyburg's famous hexed salt example, or Salmon's case of men consuming birth-control pills) seem to fall in the same category as the barometer problem. There is no scientific theory correlating these (redundant) conditions to the effect in question. If such a theory did exist, it would not be evident that the correlations could not provide understanding. Putative counterexamples in which laws or theories are trivially derived from themselves do not hit the mark either, since my analysis pertains to the understanding of natural phenomena on the basis of theories, and not to the derivation of theories themselves.

The asymmetry problem, exemplified by the flagpole case, is more interesting. In line with what has been argued, I hold that it depends on the context whether the length of the flagpole makes it understandable how long the shadow is, or vice versa. In this respect, I agree with van Fraassen (1980, 130ff.). The common sense intuition of asymmetry is based upon a preference for everyday causal reasoning; and in many scientific contexts (e.g., classical optics) such causal reasoning is useful as well. But it would be unjustified to attribute a context-independent privileged epistemological role to it. As has been shown in this chapter and in chapter 3, causal explanations do not have a unique position in modern science, not even if the notorious case of quantum mechanics is disregarded (for arguments to this effect, see also Ruben 1993, 10; Berger 1998). If non-causal tools are admitted, there is no reason to hold on to the idea that there is a fixed direction in all understanding-providing arguments. Moreover, even if preference is given to causal reasoning, physical science does not automatically fit in with everyday causal thinking and does not always single out earlier events as the causes of what happens later. A famous example in which causal chains can be read in both time directions is furnished by electromagnetic theory in the version of Wheeler and Feynman (1945).[26] In this time-symmetric theory of electrodynamics the force on a charged particle is considered to be caused both by antecedent conditions and by circumstances in the future. Actually, a similar interpretation can already be given within the context of ordinary electrodynamics: the electromagnetic field at a particular instant can be viewed either as coming from the earlier motions of charged particles or as originating from later motions of these particles (so-called "retarded" and "advanced" solutions of the equations). That such ideas have been accepted as serious proposals shows that there are no a priori absolute obstacles to giving scientific causal explanations in a direction we normally do not consider in everyday life. Our everyday preferences and intuitions are not absolute but contextually determined.

4.4.3 Contextuality and pragmatics

The context dependence of scientific understanding is inherently related to the pragmatic nature of understanding and its correlate intelligibility. Accordingly, the question can be asked how my account of scientific understanding relates to existing pragmatic theories of scientific explanation. Various philosophers of science have defended a pragmatic approach to explanation and articulated it in different ways.[27] Like my theory of scientific understanding, their pragmatic theories of explanation can be regarded as attempts to account for the plurality of explanatory strategies in scientific practice. The possibility of a pragmatic interpretation of explanation was already acknowledged by Hempel, but rejected by him as philosophically insignificant (see

---

26. See Panofsky and Phillips (1969, 394–398) for an introduction.

27. Notable examples are van Fraassen (1980), Achinstein (1983), and Sintonen (1999). See Faye (2007, 2014) for reviews of the pragmatic approach to explanation and a defense of his own "pragmatic-rhetorical theory." The present section will focus on van Fraassen's theory of explanation.

section 2.1). On a pragmatic interpretation, Hempel (1965, 425–426) states, explanation is a term that "requires reference to the persons involved in the process of explaining" and it is therefore "a relative notion: something can be significantly said to constitute an explanation in this sense only for this or that individual." This conception of explanation, and its implication that the meaning and value of an explanation is relative to the context in which it is uttered, has been hailed—*pace* Hempel—as the quintessence of explanation by advocates of the pragmatic approach. Their accounts of explanation are built on the idea that explanations are given and received by particular people in particular contexts for particular purposes. Different contexts, people, and purposes may require different types of explanation. (For this reason I have not discussed pragmatic theories in chapter 3: these theories have a different goal and do not provide concrete tools for achieving explanatory understanding; instead, they attempt to unify the various models of explanation discussed in chapter 3). In this subsection, I will briefly discuss the pragmatic approach to explanation and examine how it relates to my theory of understanding.

The first full-fledged pragmatic theories of explanation were developed in the late 1970s and early 1980s. (Following Hempel, in the 1950s and 1960s most philosophers ignored the pragmatic aspects of explanation, with the notable exception of Michael Scriven). The best known and most influential pragmatic theory is that of van Fraassen, presented in chapter 5 of *The Scientific Image* (1980, 97–157). As mentioned in section 2.2, van Fraassen draws a sharp distinction between an epistemic and a pragmatic dimension of theory acceptance. On his constructive empiricist view of science, empirical adequacy is the sole epistemic aim of science. To be sure, individual scientists may have other aims as well, but according to van Fraassen (1980, 87–88) these are pragmatic because they are rooted in "specifically human concerns, a function of our interests and pleasures." Among these pragmatic aims is explanation, which is not an intrinsic aim of science but a human activity in which scientific knowledge may be employed. Van Fraassen presents an elaborate account of (the pragmatics of) explanation, which has interesting parallels with my theory of understanding, as we shall see below. First, however, let me emphasize that I disagree with his thesis that explanation, and *ipso facto* understanding, falls outside the epistemic domain of science. As I argued in section 2.2, van Fraassen's sharp demarcation between an epistemic and a pragmatic dimension of science is untenable: the epistemic and the pragmatic are inextricably intertwined in scientific practice, and explanatory understanding may legitimately be regarded as an epistemic aim of science, even though it is inherently pragmatic. More generally, van Fraassen's distinction rests on a false dichotomy between "the aims of science" and "human concerns." On a naturalistic approach, science is a human activity, and it makes no sense to speak of "the aims of science" in the absence of human concerns.

How does van Fraassen analyze the contextuality of explanatory practices? His starting point is the idea that explanations are answers to why-questions, which are generally of the form "Why P?" However, when taken in isolation, a why-question does not determine the kind of answer that is asked for. For example, the question "Why did Don Giovanni kill the Commendatore?" can be interpreted in different ways, depending on which part of the sentence is emphasized. In these interpretations different kinds of answers are expected. For example, if "the Commendatore" is emphasized, a suitable answer is: because it was the Commendatore who challenged him to fight a duel. If "kill" is emphasized, however, an answer might be: because Don Giovanni is a reckless person who cannot control himself. This reveals that an explanation-seeking question always (at least implicitly) refers to a contrast class $X(P_1, P_2, \ldots, P_n)$ of alternative possibilities: "Why P_i [rather than another member of X]?." Often, this contrast class is not made explicit because it is clear from the context what the relevant contrast class is. In the famous story of a priest visiting the notorious bank robber Willie Sutton in prison and asking him: "Why do you rob banks?", Willie's answer "because that's where the money is" clearly violates the expectations provided by the context.[28] The contrast class is a first important contextual element, which determines the set of candidate explanations.[29] Subsequently, when we want to answer the why-question—in other words, when we want to choose the best explanation of P_i—a further contextual influence enters the scene. First, a satisfactory answer A must be scientifically relevant: it must be acceptable (likely to be true), it must favor P_i over its alternatives, and it must not be made irrelevant by other answers. However, according to van Fraassen, not all scientifically relevant factors are explanatorily relevant to a particular explanation request: explanations single out "salient factors" among the scientifically relevant factors. No general criteria

---

28. The Willie Sutton example is borrowed from Garfinkel (1981, 21–22), another early proponent of the idea that explanation is contrastive.

29. Sometimes an explanation-seeking question does have an answer in one context and not in another. This allows for a satisfactory treatment of the notorious paresis case (see Salmon 1990, 49, 59–60 for a summary of this case). On van Fraassen's (1980, 105) analysis, the question "Why did the mayor contract paresis?" has an answer if the contrast class is the set of all inhabitants of the town in which the mayor lives, but does not have an answer if the contrast class is the set of all other syphilitics. Van Fraassen's account allows for legitimate rejection of explanation requests, which can indeed be observed in scientific practice (e.g., physicists admitting that individual, probabilistic quantum-mechanical events defy explanation).

for explanatory relevance exist; it is the context that determines what is explanatorily relevant: "the salient feature picked out as 'the cause' in that complex
process, is salient to a given person because of his orientation, his interests,
and various other peculiarities in the way he approaches or comes to know
the problem—contextual factors" (van Fraassen 1980, 125).[30] This applies, for
example, to the asymmetry cases, such as the flagpole and the shadow: since
the context determines the relevance relation, in particular contexts the length
of the flagpole can be explained by the length of the shadow (van Fraassen
1980, 130–134).

   Although van Fraassen's pragmatic theory of explanation is in some
respects fundamentally at odds with my contextual theory of scientific understanding, there seem to be prospects for using elements of the one theory
to further elaborate the other (and vice versa). Let me start with the fundamental disagreements. First and foremost, van Fraassen assumes that the
epistemic aspects of a situation in which an explanation-seeking question is
posed, are pre-given and unrelated to the pragmatics of the situation. In other
words, which potential answers to the question are scientifically relevant is
not affected by pragmatic, contextual factors. By contrast, I have argued that
intelligibility, which is a pragmatic notion, is a necessary requirement for
reaching the epistemic aim of explanation. Second, as regards the nature of
the contextual factors, van Fraassen locates them in "human concerns"; in
the fact that, for example, interests of people may vary across different contexts. While I would not disagree that such contextual differences exist and are
important, my theory implies that in addition there is contextual variation in
the tools that scientists—or, for that matter, anybody who wants to explain or
understand a phenomenon—have at their disposal, and possess the skills for,
in order to construct explanations.

   While these are important differences, there are notable similarities as
well. Most importantly, our approaches agree in that they are both attempts
to accommodate the specific models of explanation discussed in chapter 3
as possible ways to answer explanation-seeking questions in particular
contexts. They imply that it depends on contextual factors what kinds of
answers are explanatorily relevant. As van Fraassen (1980, 156) asserts,
explanation "is a three-term relation between theory, fact, and context." The
classic example of a context-dependent explanation is the car accident: "the

---

30. Van Fraassen's use of the term "cause" in this quotation should not be taken as an
endorsement of a specifically causal conception of explanation, as he defines causation in an
extremely general way: "the causal net = whatever structure of relations science describes"
(1980, 124).

lawyer, highway engineer, automobile mechanic, and psychologist may offer quite different accounts of why the Princess of Wales had a fatal accident" (Kitcher 2001, 74). In such cases, people with varying, context-dependent interests focus on different aspects of the situation and accordingly present different explanations. Contextuality of this kind is not incompatible with assuming the existence of a complete objective explanatory account of the situation, from which different people single out different elements as the crucial explanatory factor.[31] Another type of contextuality is exemplified by situations in which different types of explanation are preferred by people with different skills. Think of the example given in section 4.3, in which three different ways of understanding the deflection of light by matter (as predicted by general relativity) were presented. Preference for one or the other may be traced back to differences in skills or background knowledge. One might think that this case is also compatible with the assumption of a non-contextual, objective explanatory account, where the different ways of achieving understanding are merely different (complementary) ways of reading this objective explanatory text. However, as I have argued at length in section 3.3, this "complementarity thesis" cannot be sustained and a radically pragmatic and contextual approach to explanatory understanding should be adopted instead.

Van Fraassen's theory of explanation has been criticized by Kitcher and Salmon for allegedly implying that "anything goes" because it does not place any constraints on the relation of explanatory relevance.[32] Although van Fraassen (1980, 126) states that "no factor is explanatorily relevant unless it is scientifically relevant," he does not specify formal criteria for explanatory relevance. According to Kitcher and Salmon, van Fraassen faces a dilemma of choosing between (1) admitting that any relation can be explanatory in some context (e.g., an astrological account is explanatory in an astrological context), or (2) acknowledging the existence of additional, as yet unspecified, objective criteria for explanatory relevance (e.g., causal relevance). Since he explicitly denies (2), he is forced to accept (1), or so Kitcher and Salmon argue.[33] The way out of this dilemma is to follow the course I have outlined

---

31. Having such a complete objective account would provide us with what Michael Strevens calls "exhaustive understanding"; see section 3.2.

32. This criticism was first published in Kitcher and Salmon (1987); see Salmon (1990, 141–146) for a summary.

33. However, Kitcher (2001, 76n6) later withdrew his criticism, stating that "we overlooked an important possibility, that variable interests might promote different topics and different relevance relations."

in section 4.1, by adding the requirement that to provide scientific understanding, an explanation should conform to the two basic scientific values of empirical adequacy and internal consistency. Thus, relations that are (in some context) perceived as explanatorily relevant may still fail to produce models that are empirically (that is, descriptively and predictively) adequate (as appears to be the case for astrology and intelligent design). However, as has been explained in section 4.2 (and illustrated by figure 4.1), explanatory understanding and empirical adequacy are intrinsically related and cannot be achieved without each other, since the construction of empirically adequate models of the phenomena requires intelligible theories. While saving van Fraassen's pragmatic theory from relativism, this solution implies that understanding and explanation belong to the epistemic aims of science, contrary to van Fraassen's suggestion.

If one accepts this consequence, van Fraassen's theory of explanation and my theory of understanding complement and reinforce each other. Van Fraassen's analysis of the logic of why-questions and their answers (in terms of contrast classes and relevance relations) provides a formal account of pragmatics that can be added to my theory, which in turn supplies a pragmatic analysis of understanding that enriches van Fraassen's account of explanation—and indeed of empirical adequacy itself—by adding an analysis of how precisely scientific explanations and predictions are constructed. Of course, this undermines van Fraassen's strict separation of an epistemic and a pragmatic dimension of science, but I submit that this distinction can be abandoned without making his approach inconsistent.

4.5 Realism, reduction, and understanding

Explanation and understanding have traditionally been related to other issues in the philosophy of science, in particular the debates about scientific realism and reductionism. It has been argued by many authors that accepting the idea that science does provide understanding of phenomena commits one to a realist position with respect to the theories that are used in the understanding-providing explanations. Furthermore, explanation and reduction have often been linked: many philosophers of explanation have suggested that reduction is always conducive to—and perhaps even essential for—the achievement of scientific understanding. In the present section, I will discuss the implications of my theory of understanding for the issues of reductionism and scientific realism, and I will argue against the traditional positions that assume a strong link between understanding, realism, and reductionism.

4.5.1 Understanding and realism

In the previous sections, we have encountered cases in which understanding is achieved through models that cannot be taken as accurate representations of reality. For instance, meteorologists use the PV picture, which represents atmospheric conditions in terms of potential vorticity, to obtain qualitative understanding of the behavior of cyclones, even though this picture defies a realistic interpretation. Another example is the MIT bag model used in quantum chromodynamics, which facilitates understanding of the phenomenon of quark confinement but which cannot be taken realistically. Apparently, scientists have no difficulty with using models that resist a straightforwardly realistic interpretation in order to enhance their understanding of the phenomena. Explaining a phenomenon by constructing a model of it gives us scientific understanding even if such models are unrealistic, highly idealized representations of the target system. Since the account of model-based explanation sketched in section 2.2 does not draw an essential distinction between models and theories, the same appears to hold for the theories on which the explanation is based. Thus, it seems that the goal of scientific understanding may be achieved independently of whether one interprets scientific theories and models in a realistic fashion, namely as being—at least approximately— accurate representations of (unobservable) reality.

   This idea runs counter to a popular argument in favor of realism. Scientific realists often argue that the widely accepted idea that science provides explanatory understanding commits one to a realist position. The argument is based on the thesis that understanding can only result from explanations based on theories that are (at least approximately) true.[34] An attempt to explain a phenomenon by deducing it from a false theory would not yield genuine understanding. This thesis was endorsed also by Hempel, who stated an "empirical condition of adequacy" for covering law explanations: "The sentences constituting the explanans must be true" (Hempel 1965, 248). Obviously, how precisely this condition should be interpreted depends on what theory of truth one adopts. While Hempel surely was not committed to a correspondence theory of truth, scientific realists either adopt some version of the correspondence theory or at least hold that "good theories are reasonably successful in describing the nature of a mind-independent world" (Chakravartty 2007, 13). On this assumption, Hempel's condition implies that an acceptable explanation can only be based on theories and models that are (at least approximately)

---

34. In De Regt (2015) and De Regt and Gijsbers (2017) this "realist thesis" is examined in more detail.

correct representations of reality. While today Hempel's model of explanation has been discarded by most philosophers of science, the basic idea that the explanans (whatever its precise form and whatever its exact relation to the explanandum) must be true appears to be maintained by many philosophers.

Scientific realists have tried to provide further support for this idea by presenting it as a special case of the general rule of Inference to the Best Explanation (IBE), which asserts that one should infer from the available evidence to the truth of the hypothesis that best explains this evidence. IBE is an abductive method typical of scientific practice, which suggests that explanatory understanding is a guide to truth. Scientific realists argue that we should follow this rule across the board, also in cases where the best explanation is couched in terms of unobservable entities, structures, or processes. A classic statement is due to Richard Boyd (1984, 67): "If the fact that a theory provides the best available explanation for some important phenomenon is not a justification for believing that the theory is at least approximately true, then it is hard to see how intellectual inquiry could proceed." This intuition was also endorsed by Peter Lipton, even though he found some IBE-type arguments for scientific realism (such as the "miracle argument") ultimately wanting. Lipton (2004, 206) quotes Charles Darwin, who wrote in *The Origin of Species*: "It can hardly be supposed that a false theory would explain, in so satisfactory a manner as does the theory of natural selection, the several large classes of facts above specified."

The thrust of the realist argument is that only if the theories one invokes to explain the phenomena are (at least approximately) true descriptions of an underlying reality, can they provide understanding of those phenomena. Unwittingly, anti-realists may have provided the ammunition for this argument, when they endorsed the view that the aim of science is merely to describe the observable phenomena and not to explain or understand them in terms of an unobservable reality. Where Mach and the logical positivists argued that scientific theories are nothing but instruments to describe and predict observable phenomena, it is not surprising that their opponents turned this argument on its head and reasoned from an assumed explanatory goal of science to a realist interpretation of theories. And although today's most prominent anti-realist Bas van Fraassen acknowledges, in contrast to Mach and the positivists, that scientific knowledge can be used in explanations (and has even developed a theory of explanation; see the previous section), he does not regard the achievement of explanatory understanding as an epistemic aim of science, and certainly not as a sign that some truth about unobservable reality has been discovered. Accordingly, Alan Musgrave (1985, 221) correctly observes, when comparing scientific realism with Bas van

Fraassen's constructive empiricism: "The realist values theoretical science as an attempt to understand the world ... the constructive empiricist jettisons understanding."

But are the realists correct? Is a realistic interpretation of theories and models required for explanatory understanding? I submit that it is not: we can have genuine understanding of phenomena on the basis of theories and models that defy realistic interpretation. The theory of scientific understanding developed above allows for this possibility; it is not committed to the idea that the aim of understanding necessitates a realist conception of scientific theories and models. An important argument in favor of this position is that it accommodates much of what goes on in scientific practice that presents problems for the realist (examples were already given and more will follow). Moreover, it renders harmless the well-known "pessimistic induction" from the history of science (Laudan 1981), which forces us to take seriously the possibility that not only many past theories but plausibly also our current best theories are false. If understanding requires a realistic interpretation of scientific models and theories, the pessimistic induction implies that we do not have any explanatory understanding at all.

The key to seeing why understanding and realistic representation are independent lies in the contextuality of scientific understanding. Theories and models are employed by scientists in particular contexts for particular explanatory purposes. They do not need to be a literally true representation of the target system; what matters is that they suit their purpose in the relevant context. Once we acknowledge this, it becomes clear why we can still use "outdated" theories for explaining and understanding phenomena, and why we can employ different, incompatible theories or models for explaining different aspects of target systems. For example, although Newtonian mechanics has been superseded by Einstein's theory of relativity, and is therefore strictly speaking false, it can be and indeed still is used to explain phenomena, and in this way genuine understanding can be obtained. In order to understand tidal phenomena, Newton's theory of gravitation is much more useful than Einstein's theory of general relativity; in this context, for this purpose, Newtonian theory appears to be more intelligible and thereby more suitable for constructing an explanatory model of the tides.[35] Similarly, incompatible models of water may be used to explain and understand different aspects of the behavior of water. If we want to understand the properties of water as a solvent, we can best represent the target system as

---

35. I owe this example to Paul Teller (workshop presentation, Bochum, April 25, 2013).

a collection of molecules. However, understanding its behavior as a fluid is better achieved by representing water as a continuum, since this allows for application of the hydrodynamical Navier-Stokes equations.[36] For example, to understand the phenomenon of turbulence, one needs a model of the target system (water) that selects specific aspects, at a specific scale, with a specific degree of accuracy, in such a way that the model can be used and manipulated to make inferences about the system, to predict and control its behavior. It appears that the most detailed and realistic representation, one that best approximates the truth, is typically not the most useful for understanding the behavior of the system.

One might object that contextualizing understanding in this way is too liberal, because it would imply that one can achieve understanding of phenomena even on the basis of theories that are now definitively rejected. For example, why not use eighteenth-century phlogiston theory (which was discarded in favor of Lavoisier's oxygen theory) to understand particular chemical phenomena? My answer is that there is in principle no objection to doing so. To be sure, phlogiston (denoting a very subtle, inflammable substance) is now regarded as a non-referring term, but so is Newtonian gravitational force, and this is not the reason that it cannot be used to explain and understand phenomena. Before I defend this, let me first note that in the eighteenth-century context phlogiston theory was an intelligible theory by virtue of which many chemical phenomena could be explained and understood. It would surely be awkward to assume that eighteenth-century chemists like Stahl and Priestley, did not possess any scientific understanding at all, a view which is implied by the realist thesis, as well as by Hempel's empirical condition of adequacy.[37] Phlogiston theorists were able to explain many (though not all) aspects of combustion, and they classified chemical substances and reactions in ways that bear close resemblance to our current understanding.[38] There is no reason to deny them having some degree of understanding. But even if this is granted, it is clear that we do not use phlogiston theory to achieve scientific

---

36. Teller (2009, 243–244). Note that both representations are incorrect from the viewpoint of fundamental physics, if we take the ontology of quantum field theory as basic. Thanks to Paul Teller for pointing this out.

37. Hempel (1965, 248) mentions the case of phlogiston as an example of a potential explanation that fails the empirical condition of adequacy.

38. See Hankins (1985, 94–100) for a summary of phlogiston theory and the transition to oxygen theory. See Chang (2010) and Allchin (1997) for sophisticated accounts of the historical case of phlogiston, showing that the transition was more gradual than traditionally assumed, and for criticisms of philosophers' use of the case.

understanding today. Aren't realists right when they say that this is because we now know that the term does not refer? No, they are not. The reason we do not use phlogiston anymore is that today there appears to be no context in which a phlogiston explanation is empirically adequate and more intelligible than an oxygen explanation.

Explanations provide understanding by presenting a systematic line of reasoning that connects a phenomenon with other accepted knowledge items (see section 2.2). In the context of contemporary chemistry, based on the modern system of chemical elements, phlogiston fails to play an explanatory role because it does not appear to be helpful for constructing such explanations. The point is, however, that this is not a matter of principle but of fact: any understanding-providing function that phlogiston still might have, is performed equally well or better by more modern notions. (A similar argument can be set up for the case of the caloric versus the kinetic theory of heat.) Here the difference with the Newton-Einstein case comes to the fore: in particular contexts (in which we want to understand phenomena on a particular scale), Newton's theory is still equally adequate from an empirical perspective and more intelligible than Einstein's theory. Whether or not theories or models can be used for understanding phenomena does not depend on whether they are accurate representations of a reality underlying the phenomena.

While the examples given so far derive from the physical sciences (and more examples from physics will be given in the next chapters), illustrations can also be found in the life sciences and social sciences, which are concerned with complex systems and typically use highly unrealistic models, the central goal of which is to provide understanding in a way that accords with the theory of scientific understanding presented in this chapter. In economics, for example, basic models and assumptions are typically highly unrealistic or straightforwardly false, the *homo economicus* being an obvious case in point. This fact is acknowledged by economists, as well as philosophers of economics, and has given rise to the "realism of the assumptions debate" (for a review, see Knuuttila 2009). A classic appraisal of the situation was made by economist Milton Friedman, who stated in 1953: "Truly important and significant hypotheses will be found to have assumptions that are wildly inaccurate descriptive representations of reality and, in general, the more significant the theory, the more unrealistic the assumptions" (quoted in Knuuttila 2009, 208). Tarja Knuuttila analyzes the use of models in economics and concludes that the problem of their unrealistic, or even fictional, nature dissolves if one recognizes that their function is "productive" rather than representational. A model is a constructed "epistemic artefact," the aim of which is to "render the situation more intelligible and workable" and to "gain understanding and draw inferences from using or 'manipulating' it" (Knuuttila 2009, 222–223). Accordingly, unrealistic models provide understanding by answering what-if-things-had-been different questions, which remain unanswerable on the basis of a too detailed description of complex economic reality. The understanding that economic models afford is not the kind favored by scientific realists, but rather understanding of a more pragmatic sort: it allows for prediction, manipulation, and control.[39]

A comparable situation obtains in ecology, a discipline in which models—and computer simulations in particular—are employed to investigate complex environmental systems.[40] As may be gleaned from a debate in the *Bulletin of the Ecological Society of America*, opinions diverge about the value of models in ecology. In an editorial entitled "Why Don't We Believe the Models?" John Aber (1997) suggests that models are rightly distrusted by many ecologists because model presentations contain too much "hand-waving" and lack rigorous standards for testing. In response, environmental scientists Virginia Dale and Webster Van Winkle (1998) published a piece called "Models Provide Understanding, Not Belief." Their point is that the purpose of models is not, as Aber thinks, to represent a system completely accurately, so that we would have "perfect understanding" of a system and would be justified in "believing" the model. Rather, "models should be used to improve understanding or insight," and they do so by synthesizing our understanding of a system on the basis of available, incomplete information. Even when detailed empirical information is available, models are useful for interpreting or predicting how a real-world complex system will behave, especially in the context of decision-making. Dale and Van Winkle are scientists, not philosophers, and their terminology may accordingly deviate from philosophical usage, but it is telling that they explicitly contrast "understanding" with "belief." In contrast to scientific realists, who associate understanding with truth, they hold that belief in a model (as an accurate representation of a target system) should be separated from using the model to understand the system (which allows for interpretation, prediction, and control). Consequently, their view of the function of

---

39. The account of models as epistemic artefacts is also defended by (Knuuttila and Merz 2009), who support it by cases studies of computer models used in particle physics (event generators) and linguistics (constraint grammar parsers). For a different view on how economists achieve understanding through modeling, see Lehtinen and Kuorikoski (2007).

40. Computer simulations play a central role in present-day meteorology and climate science as well; see Petersen (2012, 35–37) and Parker (2014) for accounts of how they are used to achieve understanding.

models appears to agree quite well with Knuuttila's account of models as productive epistemic artefacts.[41]

The life sciences provide ample evidence that explanatory understanding can be achieved by means of models of which the realistic status is contestable. This applies, for instance, to the mechanisms that populate contemporary biology and neuroscience. Machamer, Darden, and Craver (2000, 21) suggest that mechanistic explanations may be "merely" how-possibly explanations, but still provide understanding of phenomena. Illustrations are supplied by Craver (2007), who discusses various proposed explanations of the action potential that qualify as how-possibly explanations at best. The 1952 Hodgkin and Huxley model, for example, represents neurons in terms of an electrical circuit containing ion channels, of which a realistic interpretation was highly contestable, as acknowledged by Hodgkin and Huxley themselves (Craver 2007, 49–61, see esp. 57–58). Similarly, later explanations of the action potential proposed by Armstrong and Hille contained how-possibly mechanisms that defied realistic interpretation (Craver 2007, 116–118). Although there is no agreement as to whether such how-possibly models qualify as fully adequate explanations, their central role in scientific practice cannot be denied. Even if one regards (which I do not) only how-actually explanations as truly explanatory and grants how-possibly explanations "only" a heuristic function,[42] it seems plausible that the latter provide at least some degree of understanding. How do they achieve this? In line with Machamer's emphasis on intelligibility as a key concept, I submit that they do so by enhancing the intelligibility of the basic theory (e.g., by allowing for qualitative predictions of the behavior of the target system), thereby facilitating the construction of better models (which may ultimately produce how-actually explanations).[43]

It can be concluded that unrealistic models are the rule rather than the exception in explanatory practices across the sciences. The reason is that in many cases such models help us to understand the target system better than a more realistic representation would do. Such understanding consists in being able to use and manipulate the model in order to make inferences about the

---

41. A similar analysis is provided by Lenhard (2006), who discusses how computer simulations in nanoscience provide understanding. Against the objection of their "epistemic opacity" he argues that they can still result in "the ability to control phenomena, to gain power to perform interventions, and thus to gain pragmatic understanding" (Lenhard 2006, 613).

42. This is argued by Resnik (1991) and Craver (2007, 112); see also Persson (2009) for discussion.

43. Lipton (2009, 49–52) presents interesting arguments for the thesis that potential (how-possibly) explanations can provide understanding. His view is compatible with my analysis.

system, to predict and control its behavior. Accordingly, an approximately true description of the system is no precondition for understanding; on the contrary, if one wants to understand a complex system it is often advisable to abandon the goal of a realistic description. Typically, representations that are closer to the truth are less intelligible and accordingly less useful for achieving scientific understanding.

We can see why by comparing scientific models and theories to maps, as suggested by Giere (2006, 72–78). Maps are representations, but they never aim at a fully realistic picture. Instead, the respects and degrees in which they should be accurate are determined by the context in which they are used. A typical subway map, for example, is a highly distorted representation of the actual subway system, but these distortions facilitate its use: a fully accurate map (of which the topology is exactly isomorphic to that of the real system) would be far more difficult to use. Subway maps have just the right kind of accuracy to move around in the subway system. They represent the system in a way that gives the kind of understanding that is just right in the relevant context. Of course, maps are useful only when they correctly represent the relevant aspects of reality: a good, useful subway map, for example, must represent the order of the stations and the connections between the lines correctly. But while this means that there is a role for truth, this is not unqualified, objective truth but truth relative to a particular context and a particular purpose (cf. Giere 2006, 81–82). The way in which scientific theories and models provide understanding is comparable to the way maps help us to move around in the world, and is context-dependent in a similar manner. Newton's theory of gravitation is more useful than Einstein's in the context of understanding tidal phenomena, and a continuum model of water is preferable to a molecular model if one wants to understand its behavior as a fluid. If one wants to understand a phenomenon such as turbulence, one needs a representation of the target system (water) that selects specific aspects, at a specific scale, with a specific degree of accuracy, on the basis of which an explanation can be constructed. The most detailed and realistic representation is typically not the most useful one for this purpose.

This conclusion does not entail that scientific realism itself needs to be abandoned. Since I have argued that understanding may be achieved independently of whether one interprets scientific theories and models realistically, one might think that I endorse an instrumentalist view according to which models and theories are merely "tools" that can produce understanding without truly or accurately representing (unobservable) reality. But although my analysis is compatible with anti-realism (and provides indirect ammunition against realism, as it shows that realists have more difficulty than anti-realists to make sense of how representations are used for achieving understanding in scientific practice), it is not a defense of anti-realism: its aim is to present a more sophisticated picture of the relation between realistic representation and explanatory understanding and to refute the idea that they are necessarily connected. On my account, even anti-realists (who do not believe that scientific theories aspire to be true descriptions of the unobservable world) can endorse understanding as an epistemic aim of science. Moreover, there are various forms of realism that may be compatible with my analysis of understanding. For example, Giere's view on models and theories, which I have endorsed and used, is the basis of what he calls "perspectival realism" (Giere 2006, 88–93). Accordingly, this variety of realism is quite congenial to my account of understanding.[44]

4.5.2 Understanding and reduction

It is often suggested, by philosophers of science and by scientists themselves (particularly by theoretical physicists), that inter-level reduction and explanatory understanding go hand in hand. Many hold not only that reductive explanation enhances our understanding of phenomena, but that reduction is a *sine qua non* for the advancement of scientific understanding. In his book *Depth*, Michael Strevens (2008, 136) claims that "science is said to be deep just when it provides understanding." He elaborates this idea in reductionist fashion, arguing that "in order to understand a phenomenon fully, you must grasp the workings of the relevant causal mechanism in fundamentally physical terms. An explanation that cites only high-level laws will, unless supplemented, fail to engender such understanding, because it fails to describe completely what it cites." (Strevens 2008, 130–131).[45] In a similar vein, Machamer, Darden, and

---

44. In this section I have analyzed how representation functions as a means to the end of scientific understanding, and I have argued against the thesis that understanding requires realistic representation. Of course, representation is widely regarded as in itself an aim of science. It is beyond the scope of this book, however, to give a full-fledged account of the representational aim of science, and I do not want to commit myself to a particular view about scientific representation in general nor to a specific position in the realism debate. Giere (2006) and Van Fraassen (2008) do provide such analyses, which are compatible with my account of the relation between representation and understanding. A similarly nuanced view, called "instrumental realism," is defended by Woodward (2003a, 112–116) and matches my analysis very well in this respect. See also section 2.2.

45. To be sure, Strevens (2008, 117–119) admits that one particular event can have many "standalone explanations," which may all be satisfactory and sufficient for understanding. However, he argues that some are better than others and that in particular "deepening" explanations, which give a lower-level account of why higher-level causal laws obtain, are superior from an explanatory point of view (Strevens 2008, 130–132).

138 UNDERSTANDING SCIENTIFIC UNDERSTANDING

Craver (2000, 21) defend "the contemporary mechanical world view" as a "conviction about how phenomena are to be understood," where "intelligibility consists in the mechanisms being portrayed in terms of a field's bottom out entities and activities."

At first sight, this is not surprising. Most models of explanation discussed in chapter 3 specify criteria for explanatory understanding that are compatible with, or even identical to, the idea that explanatory theories are reductive theories. There is, for example, a direct link between unification and reduction. Kitcher's model of explanation by unification not only shows how understanding is produced but also provides a sophisticated analysis of reductive explanation, avoiding the problems of Nagel's classic account: inter-level reduction consists in the extension of the range of phenomena explained by the same argument pattern (Kitcher 1989, 447–448). This idea is in line with the view of reductionist scientists, such as Steven Weinberg (1993), who suggest that the "final theory" of physics will be a Theory of Everything that unifies all phenomena by reducing them to fundamental particle physics. Salmon's causal-mechanical model of explanatory understanding is also fully compatible with a reductionist view in which knowledge of the fundamental (causal) structure of the world comprises the deepest understanding. In addition to etiological explanations (where antecedent causes explain effects), Salmon (1984, 270) allows for "constitutive explanations," which reductively explain phenomena on the basis of underlying causal mechanisms.[46]

On my account of understanding, however, reduction and understanding are not essentially related. Consider the case of gas theory. In section 4.2, I argued that the kinetic theory (or more generally, statistical mechanics) supplies understanding of the behavior of gases by providing conceptual

---

46. Although functional explanation, as an autonomous mode of explanation used in higher-level sciences, is typically associated with anti-reductionism, the currently popular mechanistic approach to functional explanation has a reductionist flavor, as the quotation from Machamer, Darden, and Craver given at the beginning of this section shows. In his later work, however, Craver (2007, 256–267) has argued that on this approach explanation should not be identified with reduction but rather with "inter-level integration." Erik Weber (2012b) argues that my theory of scientific understanding is at odds with mechanistic accounts, since these allegedly assume that part–whole relations are essential for understanding. Contra Weber, I deny that explanation is asymmetric in the sense that explanatory understanding can only be achieved in a bottom-up, reductive manner. However, while my account thereby implies that mechanistic analyses are not intrinsically intelligible, nor essential to understanding, it does not entail that complex-system mechanists are mistaken about the intelligibility of many mechanistic accounts. It is only the alleged intrinsic intelligibility of mechanisms that is a mistake. Merely asserting that intelligibility is produced by descriptions in terms of bottoming-out entities and activities would be apodictic and not very convincing. An argument for the intelligibility of such descriptions is needed. My theory of scientific understanding suits this purpose: it shows how mechanistic analyses produce understanding and enhance intelligibility.

tools with which one can obtain qualitative insight in the relations between temperature, pressure, and volume of a gas. Such qualitative understanding is the motivation and starting point for constructing detailed models, which allow for quantitative predictions and explanations. By describing gases as aggregates of molecules in motion, the kinetic theory offers a microscopic reduction of macroscopic phenomena. But it is not by virtue of the reduction that the theory provides understanding of the phenomena: the reductive nature of the kinetic theory is a contingent feature, not a necessary condition for intelligibility. Scientific understanding of gaseous phenomena may also be achieved without a reductive microscopic theory, for example, with the help of thermodynamics (see, e.g., Feynman et al. 1963–1965, 1:44–1ff.). Even if thermodynamic laws can be reduced to statistical-mechanical laws, the theory of statistical mechanics would not be preferable to thermodynamics for achieving understanding in all contexts. To be sure, statistical mechanics explains more phenomena than thermodynamics (think of Brownian motion), but this does not entail that it is a more intelligible theory or that descriptions of microscopic mechanisms are essential to scientific understanding. There are no essential or in-principle restrictions on the nature of theories used in explanations. Often it is counter-productive to search for microscopic explanations and more fruitful to analyze the situation at the macroscopic level. For example, suppose someone lights a cigarette in a crowded room and after a while everyone in the room smells the cigarette smoke. The fact that the cigarette smoke has spread through the room is better understood by citing the second law of thermodynamics than by giving an exact microscopic description of the paths of the individual smoke particles.[47] Alan Garfinkel (1981, 59) has summarized this idea nicely: "Explanation seeks its own level."[48]

---

47. Cf. Woodward (2003b, 231–233), who argues that macroscopic explanations are sometimes preferable to microscopic ones because they provide better answers to "what-if-things-had-been-different questions."

48. Garfinkel (1981, 53–58) defends this thesis by analyzing an example from population biology, which describes a predator-prey system by the Lotka-Volterra equations, which describe the dynamics of population densities. Consider a system with only foxes and rabbits. The death of rabbit R might be explained through a macro-explanation ("R died because the fox population was high") or a micro-explanation ("R died because he passed through the capture space of fox F_1 at time t"). Garfinkel argues that the macro-explanation is superior because it refers to the contrast class that we (and R) are interested in: [R dies, R survives]. The micro-explanation refers to a different contrast class: [R was killed by F_1 at t, R was killed by F_2 at t_2, R was killed by F_3 at t_3, ..., R was not killed]. Thus, the micro-explanation does not pick out a crucial difference for the death/survival contrast we are interested in, for if R had not been killed by F, it might well have been killed by another fox at some later time. Of course, the context determines which contrast class we are interested in. In this case, the typical context is one in which a macro-explanation is preferable to a micro-explanation.

I do not mean to deny the value that reductions may have in science. Scientific research often aims at discovering inter-level relations, and finding one is usually considered an important scientific success. One motivation for developing lower-level theories is their generality: they have a wider field of application than the higher-level theories and cover more phenomena. If the kinetic theory, for example, would not have generated successful novel predictions about fluctuations or transport phenomena, it would probably not have superseded classical thermodynamics. However, I object to the thesis that inter-level reduction is desirable because it leads by definition to more, or deeper, understanding. On my analysis, understanding requires intelligibility of the theory used to explain phenomena. Scientific theories typically pertain to a specific level of description of reality, and they may well be rendered intelligible while remaining on this level. Accordingly, the quest for understanding does not automatically lead to the investigation of deeper layers of reality. What is more, descending to deeper levels may even go counter to the wish to obtain better understanding. The case of the cigarette smoke is one example; another is the case of water cited in the previous section. The behavior of water as a fluid is best understood by representing water as a continuum (Teller 2009). The macroscopic continuum model of water can be reduced to a microscopic model that represents water as a collection of molecules, but this reduction does not enhance our understanding of hydrodynamics.

Further reflection on the example of kinetic theory leads to the same conclusion. While observable relations between pressure, volume, and temperature of gases can be understood on the basis of kinetic theory, most people would not gain additional understanding if they would proceed to a quantum-mechanical description. Going to the still deeper levels of quantum field theory, string theory, and so on, makes matters still more complicated, and would for most people—even for most physicists—result in an account unintelligible to them. The crucial point here is that understanding is pragmatic and contextual: in some contexts (for some people) reduction may enhance understanding, but consideration of scientific practice reveals that in many contexts (for many people) understanding is achieved without reduction and reductive approaches would hamper rather than increase understanding of the phenomena.

4.6 Contextualism: risky relativism?

In this chapter, I have presented a contextual theory of scientific understanding that accounts for the role of understanding in scientific practice and accommodates the historical diversity of conceptions of understanding. While allowing for contextual variation, the theory comprises a general, non-trivial characterization of scientific understanding. At the macro-level understanding phenomena (UP) is a universal epistemic aim of science, and such understanding is provided by explanations. The construction of explanations requires pragmatic understanding of the relevant theories (UT): these theories must be intelligible to the scientists who use them, where intelligibility is defined as the positive value that scientists attribute to the theoretical qualities that facilitate the construction of models of phenomena. Since intelligibility is not an intrinsic property of a theory but a pragmatic, context-dependent value (related both to the theoretical qualities and to the scientists' skills), there can be meso- and micro-level variation in scientists' assessments of intelligibility. This is because the availability and acceptability of suitable conceptual tools for rendering theories intelligible, and the associated skills, vary with the historical or disciplinary context. The next chapters will present more detailed examples of such variation.

My theory implies that when two scientists possess exactly the same theories and background knowledge, it may still be the case that one understands a phenomenon while the other does not—as the theories may be intelligible to the former and not to the latter scientist. Accordingly, scientific understanding is not objective in the traditional sense of being completely independent of human subjects. At this point some readers might object that this makes scientific understanding, and thereby science itself, a subjective and individual affair; in other words, that it implies a type of relativism that denies the real value of science and should accordingly be avoided. But this worry is unfounded. First of all, as emphasized in this chapter and in chapter 2, scientific understanding is a community achievement: scientific progress is possible only if there is shared understanding within a community, which requires communication between scientists and shared standards of intelligibility. In line with this demand, skills for rendering theories intelligible are acquired within a scientific community, and it is the community that decides whether or not understanding has been achieved. Indeed, as was argued in section 2.2, skills are based on "collective tacit knowledge," which can only be obtained in a social context, by participating in the shared practices of a social group (Collins 2010, 119–138).[49] Consequently, skills and intelligibility standards are typically shared at the meso-level of scientific communities. In Kuhnian terminology, they are elements of the disciplinary matrix. To be sure, Kuhn did not use the terms "understanding" or "intelligibility," but Rouse (2003) convincingly argues that the main feature of Kuhnian paradigms is

---

49. Moreover, as Radder (1996, 35–36) argues, the fact that science essentially depends on

in fact that they provide shared ways of understanding the world, rather than shared beliefs about the world. This view is confirmed by Harold Brown's analysis of the role of judgment in science, which was discussed in section 2.2. According to Brown, the accomplishments of science depend on the ability to exercise judgment, an ability that scientists develop as they learn and practice their craft. Scientists develop judgment in the specific fields that they have mastered, and this results in the existence of a set of cognitive skills in the scientific community. These skills are fallible, but their fallibility does not make them epistemically worthless (Brown 2000, 201–202).

Accordingly, intelligibility judgments are not idiosyncratic but firmly rooted in the shared practices of the scientific community. There is therefore no need to worry about relativism in the latter sense: scientific understanding does not vary capriciously from one individual scientist to the next.

Still, intelligibility is context relative at the meso-level: it may vary across communities and historical periods. In this sense, my account of scientific understanding is a relativist one. But is this a relativism that threatens our view of science as a reliable source of knowledge? I submit that it is not. As we saw in section 2.3, the fact that intelligibility depends on (context-relative) value judgments does not preclude the possibility that scientific understanding is objective. That would be impossible only on the traditional conception of objectivity, which excludes any values from the reasoning process. My analysis, on which intelligibility is a necessary condition for understanding phenomena, undermines such a strongly objectivist view of science. Following Douglas (2009b), I have replaced the traditional, value-free conception of objectivity with more realistic conditions for producing reliable knowledge, namely detached objectivity at the individual level, and concordant or interactive objectivity at the social level. To be sure, while these conditions together eliminate many individual biases, they do not guarantee that scientific understanding is completely value-free at the meso-level; the shared skills and intelligibility standards lead to a community-wide bias toward theories exhibiting particular qualities. But even this bias does not result in surrender to relativism: intelligibility is necessary but insufficient for scientific understanding. Criterion CUP includes accepted logical and empirical requirements to which explanations have to conform. These requirements can be listed as a set of theoretical qualities that generally play a role in the evaluation of scientific theories, which together provide a shared basis for assessing explanations (cf.

---

skills does not entail that it remains forever bound to a local context: scientific knowledge gained in experiments, for example, has to be reproducible, and is constantly reconstructed in order to make it more stable.

Kuhn 1977, 322). In particular, as argued in section 2.3, this list should include what I have called the two "basic scientific values": empirical adequacy and internal consistency. While any intelligible theory may be employed in the construction of an explanatory model, the resulting explanation is a scientific explanation only if it conforms to these basic scientific values to a sufficient extent. Intelligibility is not the only requirement for scientific theories, but an essential one if one wants to understand the phenomena.

5

Intelligibility and Metaphysics

UNDERSTANDING GRAVITATION

TODAY, EVERY HIGH-SCHOOL student learns that the falling of objects to the Earth and the orbiting of planets around the sun is caused by one and the same force: gravitation. The concept of gravitational force is part and parcel of our scientific worldview and is not difficult to understand for most of us. However, when Newton published his theory of universal gravitation in 1687, the idea of gravitational attraction between material bodies was regarded as highly problematic. Newton himself wrote, in an oft-quoted letter to Richard Bentley: "It is inconceivable that inanimate brute matter should, without the mediation of something else which is not material, operate upon and affect other matter without mutual contact" (Newton 2004, 102). The fact that not only his contemporaries but even Newton himself had difficulty with the idea of a gravitational force—that they regarded this idea in some sense as unintelligible—is often cited as an argument for the thesis that intelligibility is merely a matter of familiarity. It takes time to get used to a new, revolutionary idea or theory, but after a while one will automatically come to view it as intelligible (perhaps as a result of the "mere-exposure effect"; Kahneman 2011, 66–67), or so it is argued. But is this really all there is to it? On the account of scientific understanding presented in the previous chapters, intelligibility is more than just familiarity. To support this thesis, I will present a detailed analysis of the debate between Isaac Newton and his contemporaries, in particular, Christiaan Huygens, about the (un)intelligibility of the theory of gravitation, and of the subsequent development of physicists' views on contact action versus action at a distance in the eighteenth and nineteenth centuries.

In chapters 2 and 4, the intelligibility of a theory was defined as the value scientists attribute to the cluster of its qualities facilitating its use, and it was argued that scientists need intelligible theories to construct explanations that provide scientific understanding. In the present chapter, and in the next two chapters, I will apply my theory to cases from the history of physics, in order to see whether it can account for the way understanding is achieved in actual scientific practice. All case studies are concerned with episodes in which the scientists involved explicitly debated issues concerning understanding or intelligibility. It will turn out that physicists had diverging views of what intelligibility consists in and of when scientific understanding is achieved, which accords with my thesis that intelligibility and understanding are contextual notions. However, it is not to be expected that whenever scientists have explicitly referred to "intelligibility," they have done so in full agreement with my definition. It may well be that they meant something different, or that there is only a partial overlap between their interpretation of the term and mine. Therefore, when describing and analyzing historical episodes, I will carefully distinguish between various uses of the term and make sure there is no conflation of terms used by historical actors and my own terminology (see also section 5.2). I submit, however, that my philosophical account of understanding and the associated definition of intelligibility shed new light on the historical debates on intelligibility and demonstrate their significance for the advancement of scientific understanding.

In this respect, the history of Newtonian gravitation provides an important test case. While intelligibility clearly played a central role in seventeenth-century discussions on gravitation, it is sometimes difficult to pinpoint what exactly the participants in the debate meant when they used this term (or related terms such as "comprehensibility" and "conceivability"). Newton's famous letter to Bentley is an example: as we shall see, scholars disagree on what precisely Newton found "inconceivable," and why. What cannot be doubted, however, is that the main obstacle to the intelligibility of Newton's theory was the fact that the gravitational force "acts at a distance." It was this aspect of the theory that appeared unintelligible to many of Newton's contemporaries, and perhaps also to Newton himself. It seems that their worries were first and foremost concerned with metaphysics: they found it inconceivable that "a thing can act where it is not" because this would be in flagrant contradiction with the current metaphysical doctrine of Cartesian corpuscularism. Their rejection of the metaphysics of action at a distance did not seem to inhibit their capacity to work with Newtonian theory, however. Huygens, for example, obviously understood Newton's *Principia* and was able to use it and apply it to concrete examples. So is there a role for intelligibility in my sense of the term? And if so, what is its relation to the notion of intelligibility used by seventeenth-century scientists? Answering these questions is an important goal of the present chapter, which serves as a case study of the relations between metaphysical worldviews and scientific understanding.

The chapter is structured as follows. In section 5.1, I will introduce the historical case and review traditional analyses of it by positivist philosophers of science and an alternative interpretation offered by James Cushing. In section 5.2, I will examine the seventeenth-century debate in detail, focusing on Newton and Huygens. First, I give a descriptive account of their scientific work on gravitation, of their relevant metaphysical views, and of their discussions of the nature and import of intelligibility. Subsequently, I analyze the episode in terms of the theory of scientific understanding presented in chapters 2 and 4, by investigating how the historical actors' claims regarding intelligibility relate to my definition of it, and by assessing how their views of understanding and intelligibility affected their scientific work. Section 5.3 examines how scientists' attitudes toward (the intelligibility of) action at a distance developed in the eighteenth and nineteenth centuries. Section 5.4 presents conclusions of the case study, particularly with respect to the relation between metaphysics and scientific understanding.

5.1 The (un)intelligibility of Newton's theory of universal gravitation

Newton's theory of gravitation was one of the cornerstones of physics until it was superseded by Einstein's general theory of relativity in 1915. But in a sense it remains a cornerstone: despite the superiority of Einstein's theory, Newton's law of gravitation is still useful in almost all practical situations (as more generally is the case with Newtonian mechanics). The central idea of Newton's theory—the notion of a universal force of gravitation inherent in all matter—was daring and revolutionary. To many of Newton's contemporaries it seemed a relapse into the magical world-picture of the Renaissance, in which occult qualities such as active powers and affinities were basic, a world-picture that had been abandoned in favor of the Cartesian mechanical philosophy. In contrast to the Cartesian principle that only direct contact between material bodies, for example through collisions, can effect changes in their motion, Newton assumed that every material body exerts a force of attraction F_g on every other body in the universe, the magnitude of which is proportional to the masses of the two bodies involved (m_1, m_2) and inversely proportional to the square of the distance r between them:

$$F_g = G \frac{m_1 m_2}{r^2}.$$
(5.1)

After the publication of Newton's *Principia* in 1687, in which the theory of universal gravitation was developed, many natural philosophers, in particular, Huygens and Leibniz, objected to this theory because the idea of a force that acts at a distance appeared unintelligible to them.[1] They were unable to understand how bodies could act upon each other directly and instantaneously, without an intervening medium, as the theory seemed to suggest. In other words, they could not understand it in terms of their Cartesian world-picture: the notion of *actio in distans* conflicted with Cartesian corpuscularism, and Newton's theory of gravitation did not allow (at least not *prima facie*) for an interpretation in terms of contact action. In his *Discours de la cause de la pesanteur* (Treatise on the cause of gravity, 1690), Huygens criticized Newton's theory and said of the idea of gravitational attraction: "That I would not know how to admit, because I believe to see clearly that the cause of such an attraction is not explicable by any principle of mechanics, nor by rules of motion."[2] Huygens's theory of mechanics was a version of Cartesian corpuscularism: although he disproved the laws of motion that Descartes had presented in his *Principia Philosophiae* (1644), Huygens's own theory retained the idea that only contact forces can cause changes of motion.

In section 5.2, I will describe and analyze this historical episode in more detail, but first I will review both the standard philosophical account of it and a more recent, alternative interpretation. The traditional account derives from positivist philosophers who suggested that intelligibility is merely a matter of familiarity.[3] In his 1957 book *Philosophy of Science: The Link between Science and Philosophy*, Philipp Frank explicitly discusses the role of "intelligible principles" in the development of science. The idea that natural phenomena can and should be explained on the basis of intelligible, self-evident principles is central to the rationalist approach, which dates back to Plato and Aristotle. According to Descartes, physics is a tree that grows on the trunk of metaphysics, which provides the intelligible principles. An intelligible principle is an idea that is so clear and distinct (*clair et distinct*) that, as soon as one understands it, one also understands that it is true. Descartes considered his laws of motion to be examples of such intelligible principles. With the demise of rationalism in favor of empiricism, the demand for intelligibility had not been given up, however. Frank (1957, 32–33) observes a pattern in the history

---

1. N.B.: here the term "intelligibility" is not used in the specific sense of my definition, but in accordance with the historical actors' use of the term; see section 5.2 for detailed analysis.

2. Huygens (1888–1952, 21:471); translation in Dijksterhuis (2004, 245).

3. Compare Pauli's approach to *Anschaulichkeit*; see section 7.3.

of science: initially, a revolutionary new scientific theory that successfully accounts for observable data is accepted as descriptively adequate despite its unintelligibility; after some time, its practical success lends a reputation of intelligibility to it; finally, however, in the face of anomalous data, the theory is overturned by a new revolutionary theory, which is considered descriptively adequate but unintelligible; and so on. Newton's mechanics, containing the laws of inertia and gravitation, provides an excellent example, according to Frank:

> Newton's theory was accepted because of its technical excellence as a scientific "truth," but originally it was not recognized as a "philosophic truth." The greatest scientists of his time, men like Huygens and Leibniz, were reluctant to accept principles which were not "intelligible." ... Newton ... agreed that if his laws of gravitation and inertia could be derived from an intelligible principle, this would make for progress in understanding, but he preferred to restrict himself to what we have called the "purely scientific" aspect, and to abandon the search for intelligible principles. ... However, after the great technical successes of the Newtonian laws, since the beginning of the nineteenth century there has been a steady growth of the belief that the Newtonian laws are themselves intelligible. ... They were declared to be self-evident statements which would be valid in any future system of physics. ... Every new physical theory that contradicted Newtonian physics was now absurd. (Frank 1957, 34–36)

This belief was shattered in the twentieth century, with the advent of relativity theory and quantum mechanics. Frank's analysis suggests that clinging to intelligible principles hinders rather than advances the progress of science. For this reason, he regards the appeal to intelligibility as superfluous from a scientific point of view. Its only function is to relate science and common sense, and thereby to provide a kind of psychological comfort. Indeed, the main reason why many of us believe in intelligible principles is psychological: we long for them "to give us back the feeling that we can understand the general scientific principles other than and better than by their observable results" (Frank 1957, 41).

From a historiographical point of view, Frank's reconstruction of this episode appears an oversimplification. To identify intelligibility with self-evidence, for example, does scant justice to the views of eighteenth-century scientists and philosophers: while Kant defended Newton's laws as intelligible, he would surely deny that they are self-evident. However, Frank's account rightly suggests that there is a connection between intelligibility and familiarity. This is confirmed by the analysis of historian of science Eduard Dijksterhuis, author of *The Mechanization of the World Picture* (1950), an influential account of the history of science up to Newton. Dijksterhuis discussed the issue in his 1955 inaugural lecture *Ad Quanta Intelligenda Condita* (Designed for understanding quantities). Emphasizing the role of familiarity, he argues that Cartesian contact action is intelligible because it is familiar to us from daily experience: "In the seventeenth century explanations by means of the contact action of material corpuscles had appeared persuasive because the phenomena of pressure and impact, with which daily life makes us familiar, were regarded as sufficiently intelligible" (Dijksterhuis [1955] 1990, 124). Newton's theory of gravitation, by contrast, was considered unintelligible because it assumed forces acting at a distance. However, Dijksterhuis states that the notion of attraction, which Leibniz and Huygens had condemned as an unintelligible occult quality, soon became "so familiar and well-known to investigators of nature that they began to declare it a fundamental principle and to aim at turning it into the cornerstone of as many domains of science as possible." According to Dijksterhuis,

> judgments on the acceptability and manageability of a scientific concept appear to depend on the extent to which we have become familiar with it, which is determined in its turn by the environment in which we undergo our scientific education. Again and again a younger generation learns to handle effortlessly the concepts and conceptions that their great predecessors had introduced with much hesitation and in face of the opposition of their contemporaries, and then the new generation goes on to develop these further in an equally laborious process. It is this collective growth of human thought that makes progress in science possible. (Dijksterhuis [1955] 1990, 124)

In contrast to Frank, who takes the practical success of Newtonian science for granted and regards intelligibility as a psychological byproduct, Dijksterhuis emphasizes that this practical success has to be produced; and scientists who have become familiar with scientific concepts and theories will find them more manageable and will more easily achieve such success. Thus, despite their comparable accounts, Frank sees intelligibility as a mere hindrance to progress, while Dijksterhuis views it as positively contributing to it.

The account of Frank can be classified as positivist because it takes empirical accuracy as primary and relegates the appeal to intelligibility to the domain of psychology. It accords with Hempel's idea (discussed in chapter 2) that understanding and intelligibility are psychological notions that are irrelevant from an epistemological perspective. What is more, in Frank's positivist view they may hamper scientific progress—a view recently reiterated by J. D. Trout (2002). It will therefore come as no surprise that Ernst Mach, one of the founding fathers of positivist philosophy, advanced a similar analysis of the history of gravitational theory. In his *History and Root of the Principle of the Conservation of Energy*, Mach ([1872] 1911, 55–58) discusses the question of the intelligibility of Newtonian gravitation in the context of his philosophical approach to science and scientific explanation. He argues that scientific explanation is nothing but the economical systematization of facts, which is achieved by reducing many complicated facts to a few simple facts. Mach ([1872] 1911, 55): "These simplest facts ... are always unintelligible [*unverständlich*] in themselves, that is to say, they are not further resolvable." Mach cites the fact that a mass conveys acceleration to another mass as an example of such a basic "unintelligible" fact. But, he continues, most people are not satisfied with unintelligibility, so they tend to think that the fundamental facts must somehow be intelligible. Accordingly, they make up some argument that these facts follow from intuition [*Anschauung*]. In fact, however, understanding [*Verstehen*] is merely a matter of reducing "uncommon unintelligibilities to common unintelligibilities" (56). Subsequently, Mach argues that the historical context determines which facts are considered fundamental, illustrating his thesis with the case of gravitation:

> What facts one will allow to rank as fundamental facts, at which one rests, depends on custom and on history. For the lowest stage of knowledge there is no more sufficient explanation than pressure and impact. The Newtonian theory of gravitation, on its appearance, disturbed almost all investigators of nature because it was founded on an uncommon unintelligibility. People tried to reduce gravitation to pressure and impact. At the present day gravitation no longer disturbs anybody: it has become a common unintelligibility. (Mach [1872] 1911, 56)

Intelligibility, according to Mach, is merely an illusion, which results from becoming familiar with ideas and theories that were previously perceived as strange and unintelligible. The idea that eighteenth-century scientists came to regard Newton's concept of gravitational force as intelligible through a process of habituation is also defended by James Cushing, in his book *Quantum Mechanics: Historical Contingency and the Copenhagen Hegemony* (1994).[4] However, Cushing gives a very different interpretation of it, which turns the positivist account on its head. He suggests that Newtonians wrongly regarded action at a distance as intelligible; notwithstanding the illusion to the contrary it has in fact always remained unintelligible. According to Cushing, true understanding of gravitational phenomena was gained only with Einstein's general theory of relativity (which does not assume action at a distance). Thus, he holds that there exist universal conditions for understanding, among which causality, visualizability, and locality are most important. He claims that our experience and the history of science show that "understanding of physical processes involves a story that can, in principle, be told on an event-by-event basis. This exercise often makes use of picturable physical mechanisms and processes" (Cushing 1994, 11).

In support of this thesis, Cushing (1994, 13–14 and 18–19) discusses the historical debate on the interpretation of Newton's theory of gravitation. First, he argues that Newton's theory does not give understanding but merely "formal explanation." Understanding can be obtained only through an interpretation of the formalism:

[Newton's law of gravitation] gives us no understanding of what physical process causes the planet to follow an elliptical orbit. One attempt at a causal explanation would be to invoke the notion of (instantaneous) action at a distance. It seems implausible that anyone fully *understood* such action at a distance. (Cushing 1994, 13, original italics)

However, Cushing (1994, 18) claims that, since the Newtonian formalism was so successful in "explaining" the data, "action at a distance was essentially bracketed as a problem for two hundred years or so." This suggests that there had always been a (latent) desire for a more satisfactory, intelligible interpretation of gravitation, namely an interpretation in terms of contact action. Cushing (1994, 19): "The basic motivating factor in demanding contact action was that of *intelligibility*." He concludes that understanding was regained only with Einstein's general theory of relativity because this provides an intelligible (read: local and causal) explanation without recourse to forces acting at a distance. Thus, physicists could happily reject action at

---

4. Cushing's argument is part of a defense of Bohm's hidden-variable interpretation of quantum mechanics. He argues that Bohm's interpretation provides better understanding than the standard (Copenhagen) interpretation.

a distance as a "failed attempt at an intelligible explanatory discourse."[5] In sum, Cushing suggests, like Frank and Mach, that the empirical success of Newton's theory led scientists to accept action at a distance in the eighteenth century.[6] But he gives a different assessment of this development: in his view, these scientists swept a problem under the carpet, as action at a distance is inherently unintelligible. By contrast, Mach and Frank held that the search for an "intelligible" cause of gravity was rightly abandoned, since empirical success is all that counts.

Which is the correct interpretation? The history of gravitational theory clearly shows that appraisals of intelligibility may vary and are plausibly related to familiarity. But what precisely is the relation between intelligibility and familiarity, and how do judgments of intelligibility affect scientific development? In order to answer these questions, I will investigate the historical case in more detail.

5.2 The seventeenth-century debate on gravitation

In the seventeenth-century debate about gravitation, the notions of intelligibility and understanding played a central role. In this section, I will examine this debate, focusing on the contributions of Newton and Huygens. My aim is to discover whether, and if so, how precisely, this episode fits the theory of understanding presented in the previous chapters. Of course, it should not be assumed that seventeenth-century scientists used the terms "intelligibility" and "understanding" in my sense; on the contrary, one of my aims is to uncover how their use of these terms compares to my definitions. Therefore, it is important not to conflate different meanings of the terms. When describing the historical episode in the present section, I will stick as closely as possible to the original terminology of Newton, Huygens, and others (as some of the relevant literature is in Latin or French, I will always provide the original of the translated terms). When I use the terms

---

5. Cushing (1994, 18). He adds a footnote that says: "This statement (perhaps too sweepingly) greatly simplifies a complex historical story in that several outstanding physicists did challenge the doctrine of absolute action at distance (van Lunteren 1991), but no successful, generally accepted alternative to instantaneous action at a distance emerged." As I will show in section 5.3, this wrongly interprets Van Lunteren's work as supporting Cushing's thesis.

6. A comparable account is given by McAllister (1996, 56–58), who analyzes the episode in terms of shifting aesthetic criteria, which favor theories with specific "metaphysical allegiances" and are updated in the light of empirical success.

"understanding" and "intelligibility" in the sense defined in chapters 2 and 4, this will be stated explicitly.

The publication of Newton's *Principia* (full title: *Philosophiae Naturalis Principia Mathematica*, 1687) marked the end of the Scientific Revolution; it was the culmination of the *anni mirabiles* that had started with Copernicus's *De Revolutionibus Orbium Celestium* (1543). But Newton's theory of mechanics, based on his three laws of motion, was not only the climax of a long-term development—it constituted itself a revolution and the beginning of a new era in physical science. A key role was played by his theory of gravitation, which constituted a departure from the established scientific worldview. Seventeenth-century physical science was dominated by the mechanical philosophy championed by René Descartes, Pierre Gassendi, and Robert Boyle. It is difficult to give an exact definition of this mechanical philosophy, as it is an umbrella term for a number of related theories about nature (Gabbey 2002, 337–338). In 1661, Boyle suggested the term "mechanical philosophy" (or, alternatively, "corpuscular philosophy") for the view that material reality consists of small particles (corpuscles) and that natural phenomena can be explained in terms of the motion of these particles. Boyle emphasized the intelligibility of the mechanical, or corpuscular, philosophy: "as to Natural Philosophy in general I do not expect to see any Principles propos'd more comprehensive and intelligible than the Corpuscularian or Mechanical" (Boyle [1680] quoted in Jones 2012, 341). The ontology of corpuscularism is, according to Boyle, inherently intelligible: one understands the phenomena as soon as one has identified underlying mechanical entities and processes (Gabbey 2002, 338; Jones 2012, 343–344). In other words, Boyle associated intelligibility with a specific metaphysical doctrine.

Newton's theory of gravitation was perceived as conflicting with the mechanical philosophy because the notion of gravitational attraction (a force that acts at a distance) was incompatible with corpuscularist metaphysics. Indeed, it seemed to be a clear case of an active power, a type of occult quality central to the Renaissance world-picture. The mechanical philosophers had rejected active powers and viewed matter as fundamentally passive. According to Descartes, matter can be characterized exhaustively in geometrical terms (extension), and this is what makes it intelligible: "I described this matter, trying to represent it so that there is absolutely nothing, I think, which is clearer and more intelligible, with the exception of what just has been said about God and the soul" (Descartes [1637] 1985, 132). In line with this conception of matter, Cartesian philosophers assumed that only by means of direct impact—collisions, pushes, and pulls—can material bodies affect the motion of other bodies. This principle of contact action was part of the core of Descartes's theory of mechanics and a basic tool for rendering natural phenomena intelligible.[7] Moreover, Descartes assumed that the universe is a *plenum*: there is no vacuum; all space is filled with material particles, which combine into a system of interlocking vortices. Newton's law of gravitation seems to imply, by contrast, that changes in the motion of bodies can be caused without impact, as a result of forces emanating from distant bodies (and across a vacuum).

5.2.1 Isaac Newton: reluctant revolutionary

In his formative years, in the 1660s, Isaac Newton (1642–1727) studied the works of Descartes and was strongly attracted to the mechanical philosophy. He developed his own mechanical system of nature, based on the assumption of an all-pervading ether consisting of tiny particles, which he presented in his 1675 paper "An Hypothesis Explaining the Properties of Light." But while his early natural philosophy was clearly a variety of Cartesian corpuscularism, Newton was fascinated by phenomena that posed a challenge to the mechanical philosophy, such as electricity, magnetism, and gravitation (Westfall 1977, 140–141). In addition, he worked on alchemy, a field that seemed hard to reconcile with the mechanical philosophy. According to Gabbey (2002, 338–342), this makes it difficult to answer the question to what extent Newton adhered to the mechanical philosophy, and it is unclear "if Newton ever was a mechanical philosopher of 'the canonical' sort" (340).

Newton's first speculations on gravitation date from 1665 to 1666, when he hypothesized that terrestrial gravitation extends to the moon and calculated that the force that keeps the planets in their orbits obeys an inverse-square law (Westfall 1980, 143). But it was only in 1684–85, two years before the publication of the *Principia*, that he developed a full-fledged theory of universal gravitation (Cohen and Smith 2002, 6). Several important steps had to be taken to get from these first speculations and calculations to his definitive theory of gravitation. Newton's first estimation of an inverse-square law was based on the notion of a centrifugal force, in line with Cartesian mechanics.[8] He calculated that the magnitude of the centrifugal force of orbiting planets decreases proportionally to the square of their distance to the sun. This does not yet imply the existence of a centripetal force emanating from the sun. Also, he

---

7. In section 5.2.2, the Cartesian ideal of intelligibility will be discussed in more detail.

8. Descartes assumed a principle of inertia, according to which bodies keep in motion (the mechanical philosophy did not allow for an active principle that causes bodies to move—so motion must be a state of matter). Inertia entails that the moon and the planets have a centrifugal tendency.

did not yet consider the idea of a mutual attraction between the sun and the planets (or between material bodies in general). These innovations required the completely new conceptions of force and mass that Newton presented in the *Principia* (see Cohen 2002). In sum, in the period between 1665 and 1687, Newton's ideas about gravitation were gradually moving away from Cartesian mechanical philosophy. It should be noted that this development was facilitated by his interest in alchemy, which assumed active principles, and by his theological views. Newton's belief that God actively and continuously interferes in the world allows for the possibility that He causes gravitational attraction between bodies, in contrast to the Cartesian idea that God, after having created matter and set it in motion, does not actively intervene in the material world (see Dobbs 1991).

Newton presented his theory of universal gravitation in Book III of the *Principia* ("The system of the world"). It is important to distinguish between the law of gravitation (formula 5.1) and the cause of gravitation. In a famous passage from the General Scholium, which concludes the second edition (1713) of the *Principia*, Newton (1999, 943) claims that he has deduced the law of gravitation from the phenomena but that he does not "feign hypotheses" about the cause of gravitation. The law of gravitation is presented in the form of two theorems, which are derived from the laws of motion (in particular, the first and second law) and various celestial phenomena.[9] This is an example of Newton's method of "deduction from the phenomena," which he deemed central to the "experimental philosophy."[10] In Newton's view, "whatever is not deduced from the phenomena must be called a hypothesis; and hypotheses, whether metaphysical or physical, or based on occult qualities, or mechanical, have no place in experimental philosophy" (Newton 1999, 943). Thus, he claimed that he had established the truth of his theory of gravitation, insofar as he had proved that gravity is a centripetal force that exists in all bodies universally and obeys the inverse-square law (formula 5.1). The notion of centripetal force, defined as "the force by which bodies are drawn from all sides, are impelled or in any way tend toward some point as to a center" (Definition 5 in

---

9. In particular Theorems 7 and 8 (Newton 1999, 810–811). It is often, wrongly, assumed that Newton derived the law of gravitation on the basis of Kepler's laws. Strictly speaking, Kepler's laws are only approximately correct, while the correct laws were derived by Newton (see Cohen 1980, 221–229).

10. See, e.g., Worrall (2000) and Harper (2002, 2012). Most philosophers (Worrall, and before him Duhem, Popper, and Lakatos) argue that Newton's professed methodology is misguided and not in line with his actual reasoning, but Harper defends it. The universality of gravitation, as expressed in Theorem 7, is inferred on the basis of the third Rule for the Study of Natural Philosophy (Newton 1999, 795), which is essentially an inductive principle.

Newton 1999, 405), was new and foreign to traditional Cartesian mechanical philosophy, which assumed contact forces only.

As mentioned already, Newton refrained from speculating about the cause of gravitation in the *Principia*.[11] The question of whether there is some deeper cause or principle that explains the existence of the force of gravitation is not answered in the *Principia* because Newton did not want to "feign hypotheses" [*hypotheses non fingo*]. This does not mean, however, that Newton thought that it is impossible or undesirable to answer that question. As we shall see, he did consider various hypothetical causes of gravitation in other writings. In the General Scholium, however, he stated that "it is enough [*satis est*] that gravity really exists and acts according to the laws that we have set forth and is sufficient to explain all the motions of the heavenly bodies and of our sea" (Newton 1999, 943). This statement shows that Newton's views on explanation were anti-foundationalist. He held that it is possible to explain phenomena by means of a concept or theory that is itself as yet unexplained (in the sense that its cause is unknown). One does not need an ultimate explanation in terms of an intelligible metaphysics in order to be able to explain phenomena.[12] Positivist philosophers of science like Mach suggested, on the basis of this passage, that Newton was a positivist *avant la lettre*, who restricted himself to the goal of describing observable phenomena and objected to the search for a deeper understanding. This is a misinterpretation: Newton did not reject the goal of understanding and wanted to find the cause of gravitation (Cohen 1999, 277–279). According to Cohen (279), the phrase *satis est* was probably intended to stimulate other physicists to work with the theory even though such an explanation had not yet been found. Newton's view that his theory of gravitation provides understanding of the phenomena even though the cause of gravity is as yet unknown can also be gleaned from a letter of 1712 in which he stated:

> And to understand this without knowing the cause of gravity, is as good a progress in philosophy as it is to understand the frame of a clock & the dependence of the wheels upon one another without knowing the cause of the gravity of the weight which moves the machine is in the

---

11. An exception is the final paragraph of the General Scholium, discussed later.

12. Cf. Query 31 of the *Opticks*: "To tell us that every species of things is endowed with an occult specific quality by which it acts and produces manifest effects, is to tell us nothing: but to derive two or three principles of motion from phenomena, and afterwards to tell us how the properties and actions of all corporeal things follow from those manifest principles, would be a very great step in philosophy, though the causes of those principles were not yet discovered" (Newton 1931, 401–402; 2004, 137).

philosophy of clockwork, or the understanding of the bones & muscles by the contracting or dilating of the muscles without knowing how the muscles are contracted or dilated by the power of the mind is [in] the philosophy of animal motion.[13]

Newton contemplated various possible ways of explaining gravitation. The main problem was the fact that it is a force that acts at a distance: it is a mutual interaction between bodies that are separated in space. This is why Cartesians, who accepted only contact action, had difficulty with it. For them, the preferred solution would be to explain (away) the apparent action at a distance by assuming an intervening medium in which only contact forces are at work. However, in the General Scholium (1713) Newton showed that it is fundamentally impossible to account for gravitation by mechanical causes of this kind:

[Gravity] arises from some cause that penetrates as far as the centers of the sun and planets, without any diminution of its power to act, and that acts not in proportion to the quantity of the surfaces of the particles on which it acts (as mechanical causes are wont to do) but in proportion to the quantity of solid matter, and whose action is extended everywhere to immense distances, always decreasing as the square of these distances. (Newton 1999, 943)

While explanations in terms of contact action are thus ruled out, Newton speculated about different types of explanations of gravitation involving an intervening medium. Thus, in the final paragraph of the General Scholium, he suggested the possible existence of a "very subtle spirit."[14] Moreover, in the famous Queries that conclude his *Opticks*, Newton discussed the idea that an extremely rare, elastic ether serves as the cause of gravitational attraction. In Query 21, Newton (1931, 350–351) suggested that the density of this ether is higher at greater distances from celestial bodies, so that smaller bodies are driven to regions where the density is lower, that is, to the larger celestial bodies (e.g., the planets to the sun). However, it is not clear how this hypothesized explanation would eliminate action at a distance. For, as Ducheyne (2011, 157) and Henry (2011, 14) observe, it implies that this ether

---

13. Newton (1959–1977, 5:300); quoted in Ducheyne (2009, 232).

14. Newton (1999, 943–944). This paragraph refers to electrical attraction and does not explicitly mention gravitation. It shows, however, that Newton took ether explanations of action at a distance seriously. See Cohen (1999, 280–292) for discussion.

consists of repellent particles acting at a distance, which in turn implies that action at a distance is not explained away.

It is obvious why Cartesians objected to Newton's theory: it seemed irreconcilable with the metaphysics of the mechanical philosophy, the corpuscularist ontology that Boyle deemed inherently intelligible. If one accepts Newton's theory, one accepts action at a distance and one needs a metaphysics that is compatible with it. Cartesian metaphysics is incompatible with Newtonian gravitation, so Cartesians deemed it unintelligible.[15] Newton himself wanted to find an alternative, non-mechanical explanation that would make gravitation acceptable from a metaphysical point of view. Many scholars have claimed that Newton searched for a cause of gravity because he considered action at a distance unintelligible.[16] As evidence for this, they usually cite his correspondence with Richard Bentley, specifically the famous letter of 1693 in which he wrote:

> It is inconceivable that inanimate brute matter should, without the mediation of something else which is not material, operate upon and affect other matter without mutual contact, as it must be, if gravitation in the sense of Epicurus, be essential and inherent in it. And this is one reason why I desired you would not ascribe innate gravity to me. (Newton 2004, 102)[17]

Newton added that this idea is "so great an absurdity that I believe no man who has in philosophical matters any competent faculty of thinking can ever fall into it." It would be wrong, however, to conclude from this passage that Newton found *actio in distans* unintelligible per se. As noted, the gravitational force acts at a distance and acceptance of Newton's theory implies acceptance of action at a distance (certainly for Newton himself, who realized that gravitational attraction cannot be reduced to contact forces). What Newton intended to convey to Bentley was, rather, that he rejected the metaphysical idea that gravitation is an innate property of matter, a property that is "essential and

---

15. See section 5.2.2, where Huygens's response to Newton is discussed.

16. For example, Dijksterhuis ([1955] 1990, 123–124); Dear (2006, 27–28). In an earlier paper (De Regt and Dieks 2005, 160), I endorsed this account, but the work of Henry (2011) and Ducheyne (2011, 2009) has convinced me that it is incorrect.

17. Epicurus regarded weight as an essential quality of atoms. N.B.: Newton almost literally repeats Bentley's phrase: "It is inconceivable that inanimate brute matter should (without a divine impression) operate upon and affect other matter without mutual contact, as it must, if gravitation be essential and inherent in it" (Bentley quoted in Henry 2011, 13).

inherent" to it. In the quoted passage Newton referred to his previous letter to Bentley, in which he begged:

> You sometimes speak of gravity as essential and inherent to matter. Pray, do not ascribe that notion to me; for the cause of gravity is what I do not pretend to know, and therefore would take more time to consider of it. (Newton 2004, 100)

In his correspondence with Bentley, Newton distanced himself from a conception of gravitation as an essential property of matter. That material bodies possess an active power to attract other bodies was not metaphysically unacceptable to Newton. His work on alchemy and theology reveals that he was not opposed to active powers (see Gabbey 2002). What was important to Newton, however, was the idea that such active powers were not inherent to matter but enforced on it by God. Accordingly, God should be regarded as the ultimate metaphysical cause of gravitation. So, Newton did not regard action at a distance as unintelligible *tout court*, he regarded it as inconceivable only if not mediated by "something else, which is not material" (or, as Bentley wrote, "divine impression").[18]

Analysis: the role of intelligibility

In the seventeenth-century debate on the acceptability of Newton's theory of gravitation conceptions of intelligibility played a central part. The Cartesians objected to Newton's theory because they deemed it unintelligible (more on this in section 5.2.2, where Huygens is discussed). What they meant was that the theory was incompatible with Cartesian corpuscularism, an ontology that was regarded as inherently intelligible. Thus, intelligibility was associated with a particular metaphysics. Newton, however, was not committed to Cartesian metaphysics and was thereby better disposed to develop a theory of gravitation that implied action at a distance. The fact that his theory was fundamentally at odds with the Cartesian mechanical philosophy was not a fatal objection for him: he was more than willing to consider an alternative metaphysics to

---

18. Newton scholars disagree on the exact interpretation of Newton's views regarding action at a distance, and on how his metaphysical and theological views relate to his conception of gravitation. Ducheyne (2009, 2011) and Henry (2011) argue that Newton did not find action at a distance intrinsically unintelligible, while Kochiras (2011) and Janiak (2013) defend the opposite view. See also Stein (2002, 282ff.) for a discussion of Newton's metaphysics in relation to his theory of gravitation. For my purposes, the intricacies of Newton's metaphysics and theology may be ignored. What matters is that Newton, in contrast to the Cartesians, was willing to take action at a distance seriously (on the condition that it was associated with an acceptable metaphysics).

associate with his theory. Indeed, as Gabbey (2002, 339) observes, Newton rejected important aspects of the mechanical philosophy:

> For Newton the mathematical way went hand-in-hand with a denial of the mechanistic necessity, a denial of the purely corporeal world and an insistence on the existence of non-corporeal active powers at work in nature under God's stewardship, and a deep antipathy to the dogmatic assurance of the Cartesians and others who claimed that in a mechanical universe the causes of phenomena are already known, or are readily accessible to human inquiry.

Newton's remarks on the "conceivability" of the theory of gravitation (in the letters to Bentley) reveal that he, too, interpreted intelligibility in terms of how it fitted in with a specific metaphysics, although not necessarily Cartesian metaphysics. Action at a distance was not necessarily unintelligible to him, as it was for the Cartesians, but had to be "mediated" by something immaterial. What was metaphysically unacceptable for Newton was the idea of gravitation as an active power that is inherent and essential to matter.

For Newton, as well as for the Cartesians, intelligibility was connected with metaphysics. The type of intelligibility they demanded from a theory may be called *metaphysical intelligibility*, where a theory is metaphysically intelligible if it harmonizes with extant, or preferred, metaphysics.[19] Thus, the seventeenth-century debate about the intelligibility of gravitation was first and foremost a debate about metaphysics. And the basis of Newton's revolutionary achievements was a changed view of the relation between metaphysics and science ("natural philosophy"). In this respect, two factors were crucial for his development of the theory of universal gravitation. The first was Newton's willingness to abandon Cartesian metaphysics and his penchant for alternative metaphysical doctrines in which action at a distance is a viable option. The second crucial factor was his strategy of separating metaphysics, physics, and mathematics, which allowed him to develop a theory of gravitational forces without specifying the cause of gravitation. Part of this strategy is what I. B. Cohen has called the "Newtonian Style," the essence of which is "an ability to separate the study of the exact sciences in two parts: the developments of the mathematical consequences of imaginative constructs or systems and the subsequent application of

---

19. Note that metaphysical intelligibility differs from intelligibility as defined in section 2.3. However, as will be argued below, there can be overlap and interaction between the two.

the mathematically derived results to the explanation of phenomenological reality" (Cohen 1980, xii; cf. Cohen 1999, 60–64). This approach enabled Newton to analyze idealized systems of (centripetal) forces, specified in a purely mathematical way, compare the results to real-world systems only afterwards, and postpone the question of the causes of such forces. In this way, it became possible to do natural philosophy without first having to engage in metaphysics. In an unpublished preface to the *Principia*, Newton (1999, 53–54) stated this clearly:

> First, the phenomena should be observed, then their proximate causes—and afterward the causes of their causes—should be investigated, and finally it will be possible to come down from the causes of the causes (established by phenomena) to their effects, by arguing a priori. Natural philosophy should be founded not on metaphysical opinions, but on its own principles; and [MS breaks off].

The Newtonian Style implied a revolutionary change in the aims and methods of science (natural philosophy), and accordingly in the conception of scientific explanation. Before Newton, explanation was tied to metaphysics: to explain a phenomenon meant to specify its metaphysical cause. Thus, for Cartesians, a phenomenon was explained when the underlying mechanism that produces it was discovered. In other words, one had obtained understanding of the phenomenon if one had described it in terms of the corpuscularist ontology that the mechanical philosophy considered inherently intelligible. By contrast, Newton's approach made it possible to explain a phenomenon by providing a mathematical model of it, even when its metaphysical basis was not yet known (cf. Gingras 2001, 398–399). Accordingly, metaphysical intelligibility was no longer a precondition for achieving scientific understanding (which results from explanations). It is not surprising that positivist philosophers like Mach interpreted this development as a defeat of metaphysics and a victory for a purely positivistic view of science in which intelligibility plays no role at all. However, it is not that simple. For a start, Newton himself did not abandon the search for the ultimate metaphysical cause of gravitation. Newton's novel approach rendered metaphysics and natural philosophy distinct but not disconnected. The theory of scientific understanding that I have presented in the previous chapters allows us to see how scientific explanation and understanding, on the one hand, and metaphysical intelligibility, on the other hand, are related.

The notion of intelligibility plays a pivotal role in my theory of scientific understanding. As I emphasized at the beginning of section 5.2, seventeenth-century conceptions of intelligibility should not be conflated with intelligibility as I have defined it in chapter 2. We have seen that seventeenth-century physicists associated intelligibility with metaphysics (ontology). The question is how metaphysical intelligibility relates to scientific intelligibility, defined in chapter 2 as: the value that scientists attribute to the cluster of qualities of a theory (in one or more of its representations) that facilitate the use of the theory.

I submit that the case of gravitation shows that the two types of intelligibility can interact. On the one hand, metaphysics may provide conceptual tools that help to render a scientific theory intelligible in the above sense.[20] Cartesian corpuscularism not only provided an ontology that was considered inherently intelligible by the mechanical philosophers, it also supplied conceptual tools to facilitate reasoning about the phenomena in terms of accepted theories, such as Descartes's or Huygens's theories of mechanics. Contact action, in particular, functioned as such a tool. The idea that the motion of material bodies can only be affected by contact forces was inextricably connected with the Cartesian metaphysical conception of matter (as geometrically defined and passive), and was accordingly a basic tenet of the mechanical philosophy. In addition, however, the principle of contact action could be used to reason qualitatively about many observable phenomena, of which billiard ball collisions are typical examples. As noted by Dijksterhuis ([1955] 1990, 124), this benefit is reinforced by the fact that the principle accords with much of our daily experience. In sum, metaphysical doctrines can have pragmatic import. This thesis will be further substantiated in section 5.2.2, where Huygens's work is discussed in detail.

On the other hand, if the (scientific) intelligibility achieved by means of specific conceptual tools is successfully employed in the construction of explanations that produce scientific understanding, the metaphysical worldview that supplies these tools will be bolstered. This was one reason why Cartesian corpuscularism superseded the magical worldview of the Renaissance. If application of conceptual tools leads to sustained scientific success, these tools will plausibly be "canonized": they will come to be regarded as indispensable for achieving understanding. This interaction between metaphysical intelligibility and scientific intelligibility can be visualized as a region of overlap between two domains: the domain of metaphysical doctrines and concepts with which scientific theories should harmonize in order to be regarded as metaphysically intelligible, and the domain of conceptual tools that contribute to the scientific intelligibility of the theory (see figure 5.1).

---

20. See section 4.3, where the function of conceptual tools for understanding is discussed.

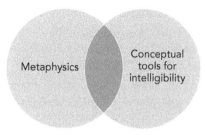

FIGURE 5.1 The domains of metaphysical and scientific intelligibility.

The region of overlap contains tools that contribute to scientific intelligibility and are associated with (extant or preferred) metaphysics. This picture should not be regarded as static but as dynamic: the domains and their overlap can change; thus, scientific successes can lead to canonization of conceptual tools, which may lend them metaphysical status. However, such a canonization will sometimes have to be overcome, in order to advance scientific understanding to a new level. This was what happened in the Newtonian revolution. (For further support of this thesis, see the discussion of Huygens in section 5.2.2).

How was scientific understanding achieved by Newton's theory of gravitation, when corpuscularist metaphysics and reasoning with contact action appeared useless? Which qualities enhanced the scientific intelligibility of the theory? This becomes clear by looking at a few concrete examples. An important success of Newton's theory was the explanation of the tides. If gravitation is a universal force, the waters in the seas must be affected by the gravitational forces of both the sun and the moon. Qualitative reasoning about the joint action of these two forces of attraction leads to the insight that, depending on the relative positions of the sun and the moon, these forces may be in or out of phase, so that the combined force will vary. This suggests an explanation of tidal phenomena, which Newton elaborated in Propositions 24, 36, and 37 of Book III of the *Principia*.[21] A similar line of reasoning can be followed in the case of the motion of the moon. The moon's motion was known to be irregular and Newton's theory of gravitation suggested a possibility of explaining this on the basis of the combined gravitational action of the earth and the sun on the moon. Newton did not succeed in developing a wholly satisfactory account of the motion of the moon because of the enormous complexity of the problem, but his work

---

21. Newton (1999, 835–839, 874–880); see Cohen (1999, 238–246) for an analysis of Newton's reasoning.

provided the basis on which eighteenth-century astronomers constructed a complete explanation.[22]

Another example of qualitative reasoning with forces acting at a distance can be found in Query 21 of the *Opticks*. Here Newton (1931, 350–351) suggests that gravitational attraction between celestial bodies can be explained by assuming a rare, elastic ether of repellent particles acting at a distance. If its density increases with the distance to celestial bodies, then smaller bodies (e.g., the planets) will be driven to regions where the density is lower, that is, to the larger celestial bodies (e.g., the sun). These examples show that it is possible to reason in a qualitative manner with forces acting at a distance, and that Newton's explanations of particular phenomena proceeded from a qualitative understanding of the theory. Criterion CIT_1, which was proposed as a test for the intelligibility of theories (section 4.2), is thus fulfilled—at least for Newton—and the theory is thereby rendered (scientifically) intelligible.

So what are the specific intelligibility-enhancing qualities of the theory? Steffen Ducheyne (2009, 253) argues that "Newton's argument for universal gravitation contains several intelligibility-enhancing virtues," citing causal explanation, unification, and (de)composition as examples.[23] Regarding causal explanation, Ducheyne states that Newton "rendered it intelligible that mechanical theories cannot account for the celestial motions (negative aspect), and that a non-mechanical cause needs to be introduced in natural philosophy (positive aspect)" (2009, 253). This claim concerns first of all metaphysics: the theory of universal gravitation cannot be rendered metaphysically intelligible via a causal explanation of the mechanical kind, so a non-mechanical (e.g., divine) cause needs to be found. But how does this change in metaphysics affect the scientific intelligibility of the theory, if at all? Since the mechanistic tool of contact action fails in this respect, alternative conceptual tools for understanding gravitational phenomena need to be found. The crucial question is whether an alternative, non-mechanical metaphysics can provide such conceptual tools.[24] While Newton accepted action at a distance, the divine metaphysics he associates with it does not seem relevant

---

22. Newton (1999, 832–834, 839–869); see Cohen (1999, 247–264) for a discussion of Newton's work and that of eighteenth-century scientists Clairaut and Euler.

23. Note that this supports the thesis, presented in section 3.2, that the various modes of explanation discussed in chapter 3 are different ways to achieve scientific understanding, making use of different conceptual tools.

24. Not every metaphysical doctrine provides useful conceptual tools that can be fruitfully employed to achieve scientific intelligibility and understanding. Intelligent Design, for example, trades on the *prima facie* unintelligibility of evolutionary accounts of how particular complex features of organisms have developed. However, the notion of Intelligent Design

for rendering the theory scientifically intelligible. Whether a divine cause is assumed, or gravity is regarded as an active power inherent to matter, does not make a difference when it comes to reasoning with forces acting at a distance. The examples given (e.g., the ether explanation involving repellent particles) show, however, that Newton engaged in qualitative causal reasoning using action-at-a-distance forces. In this way, his theory of gravitation could be rendered scientifically (albeit not yet metaphysically) intelligible. Newton had added a new tool to the conceptual toolkit (in which contact forces still had their own place and function). His new conception of force included the idea of centripetal forces acting at a distance, next to the forces of "percussion" and "pressure," acknowledged by the mechanical philosophy (see Cohen 2002, 62–63). In the case of action at a distance, the tool for scientific understanding was not supplied by metaphysics. But, as we shall see in section 5.3, in the eighteenth century its success led to its canonization and to renewed attempts to provide a metaphysical basis for it, most notably by Immanuel Kant.

Ducheyne (2009, 253) observes, moreover, that unification is an intelligibility-enhancing virtue of Newton's theory. It plays a role, for example, in the famous "moon test," which gives "insight in the fact that the moon, the motions of the primary and secondary planets, and the terrestrial motions are produced by the same force," and in his argument that mass-weight proportionality is present in terrestrial as well as celestial bodies.[25] Finally, (de)composition of forces is crucial for Newton's argument that the gravitational force of a physical body obeys an inverse-square law emanating from the center of mass. It also plays a central role in the qualitative treatment of the tides and of the motion of the moon. In sum, among the conceptual tools that Newton employed were the novel concept of centripetal force acting at a distance, unification, and (de)composition of forces. These tools do not appear to have their source in extant metaphysics; rather, as will be argued, their success as tools for intelligibility would later lead to their canonization.

Thus, it appears that Newton found ways to render his own theory scientifically intelligible. But was it also intelligible to others? Ducheyne (2009,

---

does not appear to supply alternative conceptual tools with which evolutionary theory (or any alternative theory, for that matter) can be rendered intelligible, so that empirically adequate models of the relevant phenomena can be constructed (see section 4.1). Another example, comparable to Newton's departure from Cartesian mechanistic philosophy but less successful, will be discussed in section 7.4: the non-mechanical force (*unmechanischer Zwang*), introduced by Wolfgang Pauli as an alternative to failed mechanical models of atomic structure. Pauli's suggestion remained sterile and was replaced by the fruitful notion of electron spin.

25. See Harper (2002, 182–183) and Cohen (1999, 64–70, 204–206) for discussion of Newton's moon test.

253–256) argues that my theory of scientific understanding cannot account for Huygens's opposition to Newton's theory (that is, for the fact that Huygens considered Newton's theory unintelligible). I submit, however, that here the distinction between metaphysical and scientific intelligibility plays a crucial role: Huygens's criticisms of Newton's theory were first and foremost motivated by its metaphysical unintelligibility. In order to see whether it was also scientifically unintelligible to him, let us have a closer look at Huygens's ideas on gravitation and his response to Newton's theory.

5.2.2 Christiaan Huygens: the conscience of corpuscularism

The mechanical philosophy found its culmination in the work of Christiaan Huygens (1629–1695), who started as a mathematician but focused his attention more and more on physics from the 1650s onward.[26] Combining excellent mathematical skills with an empiricist attitude, Huygens showed that all but one of Descartes's laws of motion were false and derived correct laws for elastic collisions. An important role in the argument was played by the principle of relativity of motion, which Huygens accepted unconditionally.[27] Despite the fact that Huygens was highly critical of Descartes's philosophy and physics (especially in his later years), his own physical theories remained true to the Cartesian spirit. The reason was that in his view mechanical explanation was the only route to scientific understanding. In 1693, in a commentary on a biography of Descartes, Huygens stated that in his youth he was deeply impressed with Descartes's work, but that he later discovered many flaws in it and eventually disagreed with almost everything in Cartesian physics and metaphysics. However, he immediately added that the merit of Cartesianism was that

> one understood [*entendoit*] what Mr. Descartes said, unlike the other philosophers who used words that caused nothing to be understood [*que ne faisoient rien comprendre*], such as qualities, substantial forms, intentional species, etc. He rejected this impertinent rubbish more completely than anyone had ever done. But what especially recommends his philosophy is that he has not only expressed disgust for the old [philosophy], but he

---

26. Historically, Huygens preceded Newton. I discuss his work after Newton's because this chapter focuses on Newton's theory of gravitation and its reception by Huygens.

27. See, e.g., Dijksterhuis (1950, 411–419) and Westfall (1977, 125–128).

has dared to substitute causes which one can understand [*comprendre*] of all there exists in nature.[28]

Thus, like Descartes and Boyle, Huygens emphasized the intelligibility of the mechanical philosophy. However, as will be argued, his views on intelligibility were inspired not only by commitment to a metaphysical worldview but also by methodological concerns.

That Huygens never renounced the goal of mechanical explanation is clear from his *Traité de la lumière* (Treatise on light, 1690). The goal of this book is, as stated in the introduction, to explain the properties of light and optical phenomena by "intelligible reasoning [*raisons intelligibles*]" (Huygens [1690] 1912, 1–2). According to Huygens, this can be achieved on the basis of "the principles accepted in the philosophy of today," by which he clearly refers to the mechanical philosophy. His discussion of the properties of light, in the next paragraph, starts with the claim: "It is inconceivable to doubt that light consist in the motion of some sort of matter" (3). Huygens's arguments are that light is produced by fire and that it has effects that resemble those of fire and burning, which undoubtedly involves particles in rapid motion. He concludes:

> This is assuredly the mark of motion, at least in the true Philosophy [*la vraye Philosophie*], in which one conceives [*conçoit*] the cause of all natural effects by reasons of mechanics [*raisons de mechanique*]. This, in my opinion, we must necessarily do, or else renounce all hopes of ever comprehending [*comprendre*] anything in Physics. (Huygens [1690] 1912, 3)

What are *raisons de mechanique*, in Huygens's approach? Historian of science Fokko-Jan Dijksterhuis, in his in-depth study of Huygens's optics, argues that the essence of Huygens's view of explanation by *raisons de mechanique* was to give an account of microscopic mechanisms (of imperceptible matter) that conforms to the (macroscopic) laws of the established science of motion (Dijksterhuis 2004, 192). In this respect, he followed the general approach of Cartesian mechanical philosophy, even though he rejected Descartes's theory of light: "Even Mr. Des Cartes, whose aim has been to treat all the subjects of Physics intelligibly [*intelligiblement*], and who assuredly has succeeded in this better than anyone before him, has said nothing that is not full of difficulties, or even inconceivable [*inconcevable*], in dealing with Light and its properties" (Huygens [1690] 1912, 7).

---

28. Huygens (1888–1952, 10:403); translation in Westman (1980, 95–96).

Huygens's own theory was based on the idea that light consists of waves that are produced by colliding ether particles, and a central element was his principle of wave propagation: each point on a wave front is the source of a new wave spreading in all directions. According to Dijksterhuis (2004, 196), Huygens's approach involved a conception of comprehensibility that combines two features: mechanistic conceptualization and mathematical representation. First, explanations of phenomena should be phrased in terms of corpuscles that obey the established laws of motion (read: Huygens's laws of collision). In the case of light, phenomena like reflection and refraction are explained in terms of the motion of (unobservable) ether particles. Second, the explanations should be given a mathematical form. In Huygens's theory, the propagation of light waves can be treated in a purely geometrical way. Dijksterhuis (2004, 196): "To Huygens, sound mechanistic concepts were those that could be represented mathematically." Dijksterhuis's analysis implies that, for Huygens, comprehensibility (intelligibility) was not only rooted in a particular metaphysics but had a methodological aspect as well: the requirement that the theory could be represented mathematically, which greatly enhanced its fertility.[29]

Huygens employed this approach also in his attempts to explain gravitation. In Paris, in August 1669, at a meeting of the newly founded *Académie des Sciences*, Huygens entered in a public discussion with Gilles de Roberval on the topic.[30] Roberval attempted to account for gravitational phenomena in terms of mutual attraction and criticized Huygens for dogmatically opposing such an approach. According to Roberval, Huygens "excludes from nature without proof attractive and expulsive qualities and he wants to introduce without foundation solely sizes, shapes and movement."[31] Huygens replied by emphasizing the importance of intelligibility:

I search for an intelligible cause of gravity, as it seems to me that it would be saying as much as nothing when attributing the cause why heavy bodies descend to the earth to some attractive quality of the earth or of these bodies themselves, but for the movement, the shape and the sizes of bodies I do not see how one can say introduce them without

29. According to Dijksterhuis (2004, 202), Huygens's principle of wave propagation functioned as an intermediary between the microscopic and macroscopic pictures: it allowed for a mathematical derivation of the laws of optics (the macroscopic laws of the behavior of light rays) from the microscopic, mechanistic account of the motion of ether-particles. Dijksterhuis claims that for Huygens such a reduction amounted to explanation.

30. Papers and discussion published in Huygens (1888–1952, 19:628–644).

31. Huygens (1888–1952, 19:640).

foundation since the senses make us know that these things are in nature.[32]

This statement shows that Huygens considered Roberval's approach unintelligible because it relied on an occult, active power, while he regarded the mechanical philosophy, which strives to explain phenomena in terms of shape, size, and motion, as the only route to intelligible explanations. Huygens presented an empiricist argument for the Cartesian mechanical philosophy: he countered Roberval's objection by arguing that the primacy of shape, size, and motion is supported by sensory experience. Thus, at first sight, Huygens's endorsement of the mechanical philosophy seems to be motivated by ontological and epistemological considerations. However, as Dijksterhuis (2004, 241–242) argues, it was not only for these reasons that Huygens had problems with Roberval's use of attractive forces. An equally important motivation to reject the idea of attractive forces was the fact that he considered it mathematically sterile. Huygens was strongly influenced by Galileo, who had introduced a purely kinematical conception of motion, which had the advantage that it could be described in mathematical, geometrical terms (cf. Westfall 1977, 77). Dijksterhuis (2004, 241) claims that, at the time of the dispute with Roberval, "Huygens found that whatever could not be expressed in terms of velocities escapes mathematical treatment." It appears that his endorsement of the intelligibility of mechanical explanations was perhaps more inspired by Galileo's mathematics than by Descartes's metaphysics: "He understood mechanistic philosophy as an ultimately mathematical idiom. Not the ontological idiom of the *Principia Philosophiae*, but the mathematical idiom of the laws of motion of the *Discorsi*" (Dijksterhuis 2004, 242).

Thus, Huygens's rejection of the idea of an attractive force of gravitation was based as much on methodological, pragmatic considerations as on metaphysical commitments. It was in line with his conception of comprehensibility (intelligibility) as a combination of mathematical representation and mechanistic conceptualization.

Huygens presented his own mechanical theory of gravitation in his paper for the 1669 Paris meeting.[33] This theory is in line with the Cartesian mechanical philosophy and follows Descartes's earlier attempt to explain gravitation as an effect of contact action (pressure and impact) of ether particles on heavy bodies. Huygens assumed that the atmosphere is filled with a "subtle matter,"

---

32. Huygens (1888–1952, 19:642); translation in Dijksterhuis (2004, 241).

33. See Koyré (1965, 118–122) for a summary and excerpts from Huygens's paper.

which consists of particles that move rapidly in all directions, and which permeates heavy bodies. However, as the particles cannot escape the atmosphere, they move around the center of the earth. Since their motion is accordingly partially circular, they have a centrifugal tendency, which makes them move away from the center of the earth, thereby pushing heavy bodies toward this center. (Huygens argued that the heavy bodies will not follow the ether particles, since these act on them very quickly and from all sides). Thus, gravity "is the effort made by the subtle matter that circles around the center of the earth in all directions, to move away from this center, and to push into its place bodies that do not follow its movement."[34]

Huygens illustrated his theory with an experiment with a rotating vessel, which he had constructed "especially for that purpose, which is worthy of being noticed as it makes accessible to the eye an image of gravity."[35] The vessel is filled with water and pieces of wax (which are heavier than water). If it is set into rotation on a table around its axis, the pieces of wax will move away from center. However, if the table is suddenly stopped when the water rotates with the same speed as the vessel, the pieces of wax will move toward the center. The second stage of this experiment simulates Huygens's ether model of the atmosphere, with the water as the "subtle matter" in rapid motion and the pieces of wax as the heavy bodies. It shows, by analogy, how a centrifugal tendency may produce gravitational phenomena. The experiment is an example of how visualizability and analogy contribute to the intelligibility of Huygens's mechanical theory of gravitation.

Huygens published his paper on gravitation almost twenty years later in *Discours de la cause de la pesanteur* (Treatise on the cause of gravity), as an appendix to the *Traité de la lumière* of 1690. This was motivated, obviously, by the publication of Newton's *Principia*, to which Huygens felt he should respond. In addition to his 1669 paper, the *Discours* contained a critique of Newton's theory of gravitation. Huygens had first learned about Newton's theory from Fatio de Duillier, who wrote him about the upcoming publication of the *Principia* in June 1687. Not surprisingly, he was skeptical of the notion of an attractive force of gravitation. According to Huygens, an intelligible explanation of gravitation can only be based on the Cartesian mechanical philosophy, in which the material world is exhaustively characterized by size, shape, and motion. Since size and shape cannot explain the tendency of bodies to fall, it must be caused by motion. His own theory of gravitation provides such

---

34. Huygens (1888–1952, 21:456); my translation.

35. Huygens (1888–1952, 21:453); translation in Koyré (1965, 119).

an explanation, assuming only contact action and ether particles in motion. Therefore, Huygens found the idea of mutual attraction unnecessary as well as unacceptable: "That is something I would not be able to admit because I believe that I see clearly that the cause of such an attraction is not explainable by any of the principles of mechanics, or of the rules of motion."[36]

Huygens admitted that Newton's theory of gravitation was innovative and successful because it unified celestial and terrestrial phenomena. He stated politely: "I have nothing against the *Vis Centripeta*, as Mr. Newton calls it,"[37] but emphasized that this force must be explained mechanically, that is, it must be reduced to pressure and impact. Newton's inverse-square law, Huygens wrote, is "a new and very remarkable property of gravity, of which it is well worth to seek the cause [*raison*]," and he added: "I cannot doubt the truth either of these hypotheses concerning gravity or of the system of M. Newton, in so far as it is based upon it."[38] What Huygens meant was that Newton had provided correct mathematical descriptions of gravitational phenomena. However, he was able to endorse Newton's system only because in the *Principia* Newton professed agnosticism with respect the cause of gravity. Huygens made it clear what his own view was:

> It would be a different matter if one supposes that gravity is a qual-
> ity inherent to corporeal matter. But that is what I do not believe Mr.
> Newton agrees with, because such a hypothesis would lead us far from
> Mathematical or Mechanical Principles.[39]

Huygens suggested that his own theory of gravitation could be added to Newton's system as the underlying mechanism, providing the cause [*raison*] of the centripetal force of gravitation. This was an act of despair, however, because Huygens knew that in Book II of the *Principia* Newton had proved that Cartesian vortices are irreconcilable with Kepler's second law, thus pre-venting explanations of the gravitational attraction of the planets by the sun in terms of Cartesian mechanisms. In 1688, after having read the *Principia*,

---

36. Huygens (1888–1952, 21:471); translation in Koyré (1965, 118). Also in 1690, he wrote to Leibniz that Newton's "Principle of Attraction . . . to me seems absurd" (quoted in van Lunteren 1991, 45).

37. Huygens (1888–1952, 21:472); translation in Koyré (1965, 121). See Koyré (1965, 121–123) and Dijksterhuis (2004, 243–247) for more excerpts and further discussion.

38. Huygens (1888–1952, 21:472); translation in Koyré (1965, 122).

39. Huygens (1888–1952, 21:474); translation in Dijksterhuis (2004, 245).

Huygens wrote in his notebook: "Vortices destroyed by Newton. Vortices of spherical motion in their place," and "To rectify the idea of vortices. Vortices necessary."[40]

Analysis: the role of intelligibility

The story of Huygens's work on gravitation and his resistance to Newton's theory sheds light on how conceptions of intelligibility develop and how they relate to metaphysics. After the discussion of Newton's work, I observed that the seventeenth-century controversy about the intelligibility of theories of gravitation was essentially a debate about metaphysics. Cartesians considered action at a distance unintelligible because it contradicts the corpuscularist ontology, which was regarded as inherently intelligible. Although Huygens was not a dogmatic Cartesian and criticized many of Descartes's ideas, throughout his life he remained committed to the mechanical philosophy. As has been amply illustrated, he believed that one can understand natural phenomena only if one accepts "the true philosophy" (read: the mechanical philosophy), and that "intelligible reasoning" is to be identified with "mechanical reasoning." Huygens was more a physicist than a philosopher and never engaged in explicit discussions of metaphysics. Nonetheless, it seems fair to say that he was committed to corpuscularist metaphysics: he did not envisage any other conception of nature (cf. his statement that he could not accept gravity as a quality inherent to corporeal matter). His main problem with Newton's theory of gravitation was the notion of mutual attraction, which he was unable to accept as long as it could not be reduced to impact and pressure.

Huygens's commitment to the corpuscularist ontology was partially rooted in the fact that he could easily subject it to mathematical analysis. It enabled him to construct models of phenomena that could be represented mathematically (that is, geometrically). Huygens employed this approach with great success in his mechanics and his theory of light. In other words, Cartesian metaphysics provided him with suitable tools for achieving scientific understanding: theories based on Cartesian metaphysics were, for Huygens, (scientifically) intelligible: they had qualities that, for him, facilitated use of the theory.

However, Huygens's successful use of the mechanical philosophy as a source of conceptual tools for achieving scientific understanding eventually hampered his work. Because of their fertility in the past, he clung so strongly

---

40. *Chartae Astronomicae*, unpublished notes; quoted in Huygens (1888–1952, 21:437, 439); translation in Koyré (1965, 117).

to these tools that he regarded them as the only suitable ones, even when their fertility appeared to be exhausted. This had happened when Huygens, in his later years, was confronted with Newton's theory of gravitation. Newton's novel approach, using forces of attraction, turned out to be more successful in dealing with gravitation than the mechanical approach of Huygens and Descartes. Huygens could not deny this, so he reluctantly praised Newton's discovery of the inverse-square law. But he still associated the notion of attraction with Roberval, whose work he had rightly rejected because it contained only vague, speculative ideas which could not be treated mathematically (see Koyré 1965, 59–60). Newton's new conception of centripetal force, however, differed fundamentally from Roberval's notion of attraction: it was cast in mathematical form, part of a consistent system, and accordingly far more fruitful. While Huygens was clearly aware of this, it appeared impossible for him to accept it because the notions of attraction and action at a distance were metaphysically unintelligible to him.

Steffen Ducheyne has criticized the account of Huygens's response to Newton that was presented in De Regt and Dieks (2005, 160–161) because our claim that Huygens did not regard Newton's theory of gravitation intelligible seems to imply that he was unable to work with it. Ducheyne (2009, 255–256) agrees that "Huygens found a key element of Newton's theory of universal gravitation unintelligible: the very notion of attraction," but he adds: "Despite all this, Huygens had a profound *operative understanding* of Newton's theory, i.e. he had a genuine grasp of what Newton's theory encompassed and how conclusions were to be derived from it." I agree with Ducheyne in this respect; surely Huygens was able to use Newton's theory and recognized its consequences. The analysis presented in our 2005 paper is inaccurate because it was based on a too simple, rigid view of the relation between metaphysics and (scientific) intelligibility. There is no one-to-one correspondence between metaphysical intelligibility and scientific intelligibility. They are different notions which can partly overlap and interact. On the one hand, metaphysics can be a source of conceptual tools for scientific intelligibility. But metaphysical intelligibility does not guarantee scientific intelligibility, and conversely, metaphysical unintelligibility does not preclude scientific intelligibility. On the other hand, scientific intelligibility can affect metaphysical commitments. Although it does not guarantee metaphysical intelligibility, it may bolster a particular metaphysics and lead to canonization of the tools provided by it. Huygens's response to Newton illustrates the latter mechanism: because corpuscularist metaphysics had helped him to achieve scientific understanding, he rejected action at a distance categorically and could not accept Newton's theory of gravitation, despite the fact that it was scientifically intelligible to him. This does not imply, however, that metaphysics is always only a hindrance to scientific progress (as positivists like Mach maintain). On the contrary, conceptual tools supplied by metaphysics often play a crucial role in scientific development. But sometimes these tools will have to be exchanged for new ones to further scientific understanding on a higher level, as exemplified by the Newtonian revolution.

5.3 *Actio in distans* and intelligibility after Newton

After the Newtonian revolution, the relation between science and metaphysics, and the standards of scientific explanation, had changed. In the seventeenth century, metaphysical intelligibility was considered a precondition for explanatory understanding: a phenomenon was explained—and thereby understood—if and only if it was embedded in accepted metaphysics. Newton and his followers, by contrast, held that constructing a mathematical model of a phenomenon can provide explanatory understanding even when its metaphysical cause is unknown. For Newton himself metaphysical intelligibility remained the ultimate goal: throughout his life he was committed to the search for an underlying cause of gravity. Eighteenth-century Newtonians, however, abandoned this search; they considered Newton's theory of gravitation as not being in need of further explanation.

In section 5.1, two opposing interpretations of this development have been discussed. Philipp Frank and Ernst Mach regard it as a victory of science over metaphysics and conclude that the quest for intelligibility is misguided: we simply have to get used to new theories and concepts and judge them by their empirical success only. James Cushing (1994, 18), by contrast, claims that the problem of action at a distance "was essentially bracketed": gravitation was never truly understood during the eighteenth and nineteenth century. According to Cushing, it was only with the advent of Einstein's general theory of relativity that intelligibility was regained and understanding of gravitation achieved. I submit that both interpretations are off the mark because they disregard the distinction between metaphysical and scientific intelligibility, and thereby misconstrue the nature and significance of intelligibility. Mach and Frank ignore the epistemic relevance of intelligibility. They suggest that talk of intelligibility is mere metaphysical window-dressing, which serves to provide psychological comfort but does not have any positive role in scientific progress. But, as my analysis of Newton's and Huygens's work has shown, intelligibility does serve an epistemic, scientific purpose. Cushing, by

contrast, acknowledges that intelligibility is a legitimate requirement for scientific theories, but he neglects its contextuality and historical variation. His
view of intelligibility criteria is too static, and he fails to see that Newtonian
mechanics, including the theory of gravitation, rightly acquired the status of a
scientifically intelligible theory that provided understanding.

   In this section I will briefly review the development of scientists' views
on intelligibility, action at a distance, and gravitation after Newton. I rely in
part on the account given by historian of science Frans van Lunteren in his
dissertation "Framing Hypotheses: Conceptions of Gravity in the 18th and
19th Centuries" (1991). Van Lunteren's history reveals that, contrary to what
Cushing claims, action at a distance has not always been regarded as incomprehensible.[41] On the contrary, in the course of the eighteenth century more
and more scientists accepted an action-at-a-distance theory of gravitation as
fully satisfactory and saw no need to look for a "deeper" explanation. Around
1800, many scientists even preferred action at a distance over contact action,
arguing that not the former but the latter was unintelligible.

   An important event in this development was the publication of the second,
substantially revised edition of the *Principia* (1713), which included a preface
by mathematician Roger Cotes, who had assisted Newton with the revisions.
In his preface, Cotes presented an eloquent defense of Newton's theory of
gravitation, arguing that "gravity belongs to all bodies universally" and is a
"primary quality" that cannot and need not be reduced to (Cartesian) mechanical causes (Newton 1999, 391–392). The view that gravity is an occult quality,
and should therefore be banished from natural philosophy, was refuted by
Cotes with the following argument: first, its existence had been demonstrated
empirically; and second, the fact that its cause had not yet been found did not
imply that gravity itself should be regarded as occult; for this was the case for
all "simplest causes" and if these were banished, the causes that depend upon
these should also be banished, and so on, "until philosophy is emptied and
purged of all causes" (392). Cotes clearly rejected the Cartesian dogma that
only mechanical causes are inherently intelligible, and thereby paved the way
for the idea that action at a distance may be scientifically intelligible, in spite
of its alleged metaphysical unintelligibility. A similar view had been advanced
earlier by the empiricist philosopher John Locke.[42]

---

41. Cushing (1994, 222n50) claims that van Lunteren's study "demonstrates that a quest for
intelligibility was uppermost for several major physicists who attempted ether-type explanations for action at a distance." This may be the case, but, as I will argue, van Lunteren's
study does not support Cushing's thesis that action at a distance has never been regarded as
intelligible in the period between Newton and Einstein.

42. See Locke (1699) quoted in Koyré (1965, 155); cf. Buchdahl (1970, 86–88).

In the first half of the eighteenth century, Newtonianism—exemplified by Cotes—became the dominant philosophy of nature, first in Britain and subsequently on the European continent. An important spokesman of Newton was Samuel Clarke, who in his correspondence with Leibniz (1715–16) defended universal gravitation while acknowledging its incompatibility with the mechanical philosophy: "the means by which two bodies attract each other may be invisible and intangible, and of a different nature from mechanism, and yet, acting regularly and constantly, may well be called natural" (Leibniz and Clarke [1717] 2000, 35). In France, the resistance to Newtonianism lasted somewhat longer, as the Cartesian conception of intelligibility continued to hold sway. Bernard le Bovier de Fontenelle, for example, wrote in 1719: "It is certain that whenever one wishes to understand one's words, there is only impulse, and when one does not care to understand, there are attractions and whatever you like, but then nature will be so incomprehensible to us, that it might be wiser to leave it for what it is" (quoted in van Lunteren 1991, 60). However, as van Lunteren (1991, 63) observes, the Newtonians had conquered the Paris academy by the mid-eighteenth century. At this time, the search for an underlying cause of gravity had been abandoned; instead, gravity was now regarded as an "irreducible principle" (68).

The second half of the eighteenth century was dominated by proponents of action-at-a-distance theories, among whom Roger Boscovich, Pierre-Simon Laplace, and Immanuel Kant. To be sure, this period witnessed several attempts to formulate theories of gravitation based on contact action, most notably by Leonhard Euler and George-Louis Le Sage (see van Lunteren 1991, 95–121). However, these theories were largely ignored by the scientific community. Leading eighteenth-century Newtonians not only gave up the quest for a mechanical explanation of gravity but also explicitly attacked the Cartesian view that only explanations in terms of contact action are intelligible (Heilbron 1979, 56–57). They argued, following Locke, that the essence of matter is beyond human comprehension. Accordingly, it is equally impossible to understand why motion is transferred by contact action as why it can be caused by action at a distance. In sum, both are at bottom incomprehensible. Thus, in 1749, Etienne Bonnot de Condillac wrote: "The Cartesians reproach the Newtonians for having no idea of attraction. They are right, but there is no basis for their judgment that impulse is any more intelligible" (quoted in Heilbron 1979, 57). In the same vein, John Playfair stated in 1773: "The action of one body on another by contact is as inexplicable as *actio in distans*" (57).

A well-known, influential action-at-a-distance theory was Boscovich's theory of point-particles (1745). Boscovich's motivation for constructing his theory was that he regarded the Cartesian theory of collision unintelligible and, moreover, in conflict with Leibniz's principle of continuity (Heilbron 1979, 66; van Lunteren 1991, 128). He sought to resolve these problems by conceiving of material particles as points and unifying the various interactions between particles (such as attraction, repulsion, and collision) in terms of a single, spherically symmetric force function $f(r)$. When the distance r is small, the force f is repulsive, such that if r approaches zero, f goes to infinity, which accounts for the impenetrability of matter. At intermediate distances r, f oscillates between attraction and repulsion, and at great distances it approximates the inverse-square law of gravitational attraction. In this way, Boscovich's theory aspired to unify chemical and physical interactions (e.g., cohesion, electrical, and magnetic interactions). Thus, in contrast to Cartesian mechanics, Boscovich's theory "provided continuity, and although ultimately perhaps no more intelligibility than one invoking impulse, it had (he says) the very great merit of explaining everything with the same 'felicity': bodies exchange motions in collision as they do in any other process, through forces that begin to operate before, and ultimately prohibit, contact" (Heilbron 1979, 66–67). Thus, Boscovich eliminated contact action, replacing it by action at a distance.

As the case of Boscovich makes clear, the changed philosophical stance toward action at a distance was not merely a *post hoc* rationalization of Newton's theory of gravitation but was also related to the perceived fertility of action-at-a-distance theories in other domains of physical science, especially in the science of electricity and magnetism. Allesandro Volta, for example, observed in 1778: "The dominion of the principle of mutual forces in chemistry and physics is today extensive and, in particular, it is becoming continually more evident in the phenomena of electricity" (quoted in Heilbron 1979, 71). Accordingly, expectations were only confirmed when, in 1785, Charles-Augustin Coulomb measured the attractive and repulsive forces of electricity and found these to obey an inverse-square law analogous to Newton's law of gravitation. Other physical and chemical phenomena, such as cohesion and capillarity, were also explained in terms of attractive forces acting at a distance, and although some still regarded such forces as "impossible to conceive" (Jan Hendrik van Swinden quoted in Heilbron 1979, 71), they did not consider their (metaphysical) unintelligibility an obstacle to using these forces in scientific explanations.

John Heilbron, in his *Electricity in the 17th and 18th Centuries* (1979, 71–72), concludes that most eighteenth-century physicists were instrumentalists, who abandoned the view that science aims at understanding and theories should be intelligible. On the final page of his book, Heilbron (1979, 500) states that "the chief moral of this long *History* may be that, when confronted with a choice between a qualitative model deemed intelligible and an exact description lacking clear physical foundations, the leading physicists of the Enlightenment preferred exactness." At first sight, this conclusion might seem to contradict my analysis and favor the account of Mach and Frank. However, what these physicists abandoned was the requirement of metaphysical intelligibility, especially in its Cartesian variant. The fact that they had learned to work with action-at-a-distance theories, which they employed with great success in the explanation of phenomena in new scientific domains, shows that the notion of action at a distance had become a useful conceptual tool. Scientists had become familiar with it: not only had they grown accustomed to it, but they had also developed the skills to use it effectively to construct models of phenomena. In other words, action-at-a-distance theories had become scientifically intelligible.

The result was that, at the end of the eighteenth century, the tide had turned in favor of *actio in distans*, and that attempts were made to establish its metaphysical superiority over contact action. Van Lunteren (1991, 126) observes: "The former truism 'nothing can act where it is not' was changed for the canon that 'a thing can only act where it is not.'" John Leslie used this argument to defend action-at-a-distance theories:

> Some writers, indeed, are unwilling to admit the possibility of *action at a distance*, and like the poor Indian who placed the world on the back of a tortoise, they have to recourse to some intervening medium. But is it more difficult to conceive an effect produced at the distance of 1000 miles, or at the 1000th part of an inch? . . . To maintain, *that no body can act where it is not*, is in fact, to assert, that the same body can be in two places at the same time; which is a contradiction in terms, and therefore completely absurd. (Leslie 1824, 17–18)[43]

The most notable attempt to provide a metaphysical foundation for action at a distance was made by Immanuel Kant, whose aim was to incorporate Newtonian physics in a rationalist metaphysical framework. Kant opposed the instrumentalist conception of science which, some eighteenth-century physicists adopted in response to the perceived metaphysical unintelligibility

---

43. A similar argument was advanced by Kant; see Watkins (2001, 150–152).

of action-at-a-distance theories. Instead of rejecting the demand for intelligibility, Kant sought to erect a new metaphysical framework in which Newtonian physics would be intelligible. But his approach differed fundamentally from that of earlier theories in metaphysics. He argued that the Newtonian concepts of space, time, motion, and force are neither metaphysical causes behind the phenomena, nor mere inductive generalizations from the phenomena, but a priori conditions for our sensory experience. On this basis, Kant explicated the concept of matter in such a way that attractive and repulsive forces, acting at a distance, belong essentially to it.[44] Moreover, he suggested that the law that gravitational attraction is inversely proportional to the square of the distance between bodies is a necessary truth, which can be known a priori. In the *Prolegomena to Any Future Metaphysics*, Kant formulates his central thesis as follows: "The understanding does not draw its (a priori) laws from nature, but prescribes them to it" (Kant [1783] 1997, 73–74). As an example of such a law, he discusses the "physical law of reciprocal attraction" (read: Newton's law of gravitation), arguing that it is "cognizable a priori" and that "no other law of attraction besides the relation of the inverse square of the distances can be conceived as suitable for a system of the world" (75).[45]

In the first half of the nineteenth century, action at a distance had become a canonized tool for scientific understanding. Important proponents of action-at-a-distance theories in physics were Wilhelm Weber and Hermann von Helmholtz. In the 1840s, Weber developed a unified theory of electricity and magnetism on the basis of central forces acting at a distance. Weber's theory was highly successful and produced many empirically accurate results, but was later abandoned in favor of Maxwell's theory.[46] Helmholtz, who was strongly influenced by Kant's philosophy, regarded action at a distance as a

---

44. See Buchdahl (1970, 94–95).

45. See Friedman (2001, 10–12) for a brief account of Kant's attitude toward Newtonian physics. Buchdahl (1970) and Friedman (1992) provide extensive treatments of Kant's approach to Newtonian gravitation. Friedman (1992) contains a fifty-page chapter on section 38 of Kant's *Prolegomena* (from which the passages on gravitation, quoted in the main text, derive). Kant's remarks on the a priori nature of the law of gravitation are abstruse, and Friedman tries to make sense of them in the light of Kant's other writings. For my purposes, it suffices to note that Kant regarded action at a distance as an irreducible principle, and that his attempt at providing a metaphysical foundation for it confirms my thesis that tools for scientific understanding may be canonized in metaphysics (see section 5.2).

46. See Harman (1982, 103–105) and Jungnickel and McCormmach (1986, 1:142–146) for discussions of Weber's theory. Harman (1998, 170–171) discusses Maxwell's criticism of it.

necessary condition for intelligibility. In the introduction to *Über die Erhaltung der Kraft* (1847), his famous treatise on the conservation of energy, he stated:

> In any case it is clear that science, the goal of which is the comprehension of nature [*die Natur zu begreifen*], must begin with the presupposition of its comprehensibility [*Begreiflichkeit*] and proceed in accordance of this assumption until, perhaps, it is forced by irrefutable facts to recognize limits beyond which it may not go. (Helmholtz [1847] 1971, 4) . . .
>
> Thus we see that the problem of the physical sciences is to trace natural phenomena back to inalterable forces of attraction and repulsion, the intensity of the forces depending upon distance. The solution of this problem would mean the complete comprehensibility [*Begreiflichkeit*] of nature. (Helmholtz [1847] 1971, 6)

The tide turned again in the second half of the nineteenth century, when electromagnetic ether and field theories rose to prominence. The first ether theories, most notably the successful ether theory of light proposed by Augustin Fresnel in 1819, were still formulated in terms of particles that interacted via repulsive forces acting at a distance (see van Lunteren 1991, 140). In the course of the nineteenth century, the ether came to be regarded as the fundamental entity of physics, which promised to be the basis for the unification of all physical forces (an idea that had become popular under the influence of German *Naturphilosophie*). When Joseph Fourier's mathematical methods allowed for a continuum description of the ether, physicists were converted to contact action once again and rediscovered the unintelligibility of action at a distance. But this does not imply that Cushing is correct in stating that the problem of *actio in distans* was merely "bracketed." As my account has shown, eighteenth-century and early-nineteenth-century scientists had good reasons to prefer action at a distance over contact action. Intelligibility is a contextual value, and in this historical period (roughly 1750–1850) action-at-distance theories were intelligible to most scientists. Accordingly, the conversion of the physics community to ether theories was a relatively slow process, and not the rapid change one would expect had action at a distance been categorically unintelligible. Indeed, the first ether theories met with much opposition, as Maxwell explains in one of the final sections of his *Treatise on Electricity and Magnetism* (1873):

> There appears to be . . . some prejudice, or *a priori* objection, against the hypothesis of a medium in which the phenomena of radiation of light and heat and the electrical actions at a distance take place. It is

true that at one time those who speculated as to the causes of physical phenomena were in the habit of accounting for each kind of action at a distance by means of a special aethereal fluid. They ... were invented merely to "save the appearances," so that more rational enquirers were willing rather to accept not only Newton's definite law of attraction at a distance, but even the dogma of Cotes, that action at a distance is one of the primary properties of matter, and that no explanation can be more intelligible than that. (Maxwell [1873] 1954, 2:492)

The success of ether and field theories stimulated some late-nineteenth-century physicists, most notably Hendrik Antoon Lorentz, to propose electromagnetic theories of gravitation, but without much success.[47] Newton's theory of gravitation was superseded only in 1915, when Einstein advanced his general theory of relativity. In the next chapter, we will have a closer look at nineteenth-century ideals of intelligibility.

5.4 Metaphysics as a resource for scientific understanding

When we look back at the history sketched in this chapter, we see a remarkable pattern: over a period of more than two centuries, scientists' attitudes toward the intelligibility of action at a distance oscillated. Seventeenth-century Cartesian philosophers (among them Huygens) found the idea that material bodies act at a distance completely incomprehensible; they demanded an explanation of gravitation in terms of contact action. Newton himself had somewhat less difficulty with the idea; yet he searched for an intelligible cause of gravitation, not via contact action but in terms of a divine metaphysics. Many eighteenth-century Newtonians, by contrast, rejected the demand for intelligibility, arguing that both contact action and action at a distance are at bottom unintelligible. The pendulum swung to the other extreme when late-eighteenth-century and early-nineteenth-century scientists defended the intelligibility of action at a distance; they suggested that contact action is unintelligible and should be explained in terms of repulsive forces acting at a distance. Finally, in the second half of the nineteenth century, the trend was reversed and the unintelligibility of action at a distance re-emerged.

---

47. See Harman (1982, 116–119) for a review of Lorentz's "electromagnetic world view," of which his electromagnetic theory of gravitation was part, and Jungnickel and McCormmach (1986, 2:237–238) and van Lunteren (1991, 289–294) for more detailed discussions of Lorentz's theory.

Philosophers and historians of science have given diverging interpretations of this historical development and have assigned different roles to the historical actors' views on intelligibility. Positivists have suggested that demands for intelligibility reflect a conservative attitude, typically rooted in dogmatic adherence to a particular metaphysics. Novel scientific theories that conflict with accepted metaphysics invite resistance. Seventeenth-century physicists, for example, rejected Newton's theory because it did not square with the reigning Cartesian metaphysics, even though it successfully accounted for many phenomena. Eighteenth-century Newtonians, however, abandoned these metaphysical scruples and embraced the theory. Positivists conclude that metaphysics is merely a hindrance to scientific development, and that demands for intelligibility are misguided: theories will "automatically" become intelligible, if they are empirically successful and once scientists have grown accustomed to them.

It seems plausible that intelligibility is related to familiarity. However, my analysis of the history of theories of gravitation shows that the positivist picture is too simple. A closer look at the episode shows that intelligibility, metaphysics, and scientific understanding are intertwined, and can fruitfully interact. Metaphysics is not necessarily an obstacle to scientific progress, but can play a positive, productive role as well. The main flaw in the positivist account is that it regards the production of the empirical success of science as unproblematic. It neglects the fact that scientists need to use theories to construct empirically accurate models of phenomena, and productive use requires relevant skills. In a word, the theories need to be intelligible to them. Accordingly, intelligibility is not a psychological byproduct of empirical success but a condition for achieving it.

To be sure, intelligibility in this sense does not coincide with intelligibility in the sense of harmonizing with a preferred metaphysical worldview, but there is often overlap and interaction between the two. On the one hand, the former (scientific intelligibility) can be boosted by the latter (metaphysical intelligibility). Metaphysical worldviews are part of the context in which science is practiced; and they can provide conceptual tools for achieving scientific understanding. Metaphysics is a resource for scientific understanding.[48] For example, Huygens effectively employed Cartesian metaphysics to achieve

---

48. N.B.: I do not want to suggest that the only function of metaphysics is to provide conceptual tools for scientific understanding, or that all of metaphysics is merely a canonization of such tools. Metaphysics has many more dimensions and many more functions. My analysis shows only that science and metaphysics can and do interact, and highlights the impact of metaphysics on the advancement of scientific understanding.

scientific understanding of mechanical and optical phenomena. On the other hand, fruitful conceptual tools may be "canonized" in metaphysics. Huygens's adherence to Cartesian metaphysics was rooted in, and reinforced by, the fact that he had learned to understand the natural world scientifically by means of corpuscularist principles and models. However, as the case of Huygens shows, there can be a downside to this: if metaphysical commitments are canonized they may hinder scientific understanding. Huygens rejected action at a distance as unintelligible for metaphysical reasons. While the conceptual tools supplied by metaphysics often play a crucial positive role in scientific development, they sometimes need to be replaced by new ones to advance scientific understanding to another level, as happened in the Newtonian revolution.

Scientific revolutions typically involve changes of metaphysical worldviews and associated standards of intelligibility. However, according to some scholars, most notably I. B. Cohen, the Newtonian revolution stands out as a special case. Cohen argues that it changed the nature of explanation itself, laying the foundation for the modern conception of scientific explanation and understanding. Before Newton, explanation was tied to metaphysics: to explain a phenomenon meant to specify its metaphysical cause. After Newton, phenomena could be explained mathematically, even when their metaphysical basis was (as yet) unknown. In my terminology: metaphysical intelligibility was no longer regarded as a requirement for a scientific understanding of phenomena. This was indeed a crucial turning point in the history of science, in which metaphysics lost its dominant position in natural philosophy and room was made for scientific understanding without metaphysical intelligibility. However, as I have attempted to show in this chapter, this does not imply that the part of metaphysics is played out: even in modern science it can be a resource of tools for understanding.

6

Models and Mechanisms

PHYSICAL UNDERSTANDING IN
THE NINETEENTH CENTURY

IN HIS 1884 *Baltimore Lectures on Molecular Dynamics and the Wave Theory of Light*, William Thomson (Lord Kelvin) famously declared: "It seems to me that the test of 'Do we or do we not understand a particular subject in physics?' is, 'Can we make a mechanical model of it?'" (Kargon and Achinstein 1987, 111). Thomson's dictum expresses a view that was held by many nineteenth-century physicists: the idea that scientific understanding can only be achieved by devising mechanical models. As we saw in the previous chapter, scientists' views on how gravitation can be understood changed dramatically with the historical context. Around 1687, when Newton published his *Principia*, contact action was the ideal of intelligibility, but in the eighteenth and early nineteenth century action at a distance became an acceptable and even preferred tool for understanding. The mid-nineteenth century, however, witnessed a revival of theories based on contact action. In 1845, Michael Faraday introduced the concept of an electric field, as an alternative to extant action-at-a-distance theories of electricity. Such a field was regarded as either a force field or a (continuous or discrete) mediating ether (Harman 1982, 72–73). Faraday's approach was adopted by Thomson and James Clerk Maxwell, who successfully employed it to develop theories of electricity, magnetism, and light. The resurgence of contact-action physics, and its empirical successes, led to the establishment of the so-called mechanical program of explanation, which strove to account for all physical phenomena in mechanical terms. The proponents of this program regarded mechanical modeling as an indispensable tool for scientific understanding, as Thomson's statement shows.

In this chapter, I analyze the role of mechanical modeling in nineteenth-century physics, showing how precisely mechanical models were used to enhance scientific understanding. Section 6.1 examines the nineteenth-century ideal of mechanical explanation and understanding, by investigating the work and ideas of three key representatives of the mechanical approach in physics: William Thomson, James Clerk Maxwell, and Ludwig Boltzmann. These physicists advanced explicit views on the function and status of mechanical models, and on their importance for providing understanding. Section 6.2 contains a detailed case study of the role of these ideas in scientific practice. The case concerns the construction of molecular models in order to explain the so-called specific heat anomaly on the basis of the kinetic theory of gases. Using the theoretical framework presented in chapters 2 and 4, I show how the intelligibility of the kinetic theory was enhanced by the use of mechanical models and conceptual tools. Section 6.3 examines the account of the status and value of mechanical models that was proposed by Boltzmann in the late nineteenth century: the so-called picture theory (*Bildtheorie*). This theory was developed in response to the problems and criticisms that the program of mechanical explanation confronted at the end of the nineteenth century. Boltzmann associated his *Bildtheorie* with a pragmatic conception of understanding that has affinities with the theory of scientific understanding defended in the present book. Finally, section 6.4 briefly discusses the situation around 1900 and Ernst Mach's criticism of the mechanical program.

6.1 Mechanical modeling in nineteenth-century physics

Mechanical explanation occupied center stage in nineteenth-century physics. In fact, it was only in this century that physics was regarded as a separate discipline, which "came to be defined in terms of the unifying role of the concept of energy and the program of mechanical explanation," as historian of science P. M. Harman observes in his survey *Energy, Force and Matter* (1982, 1). Mechanical explanation was often also called "dynamical explanation." In his 1879 *Encyclopedia Britannica* article, "Physical Sciences," Maxwell (1986, 269) writes that physics is based on "the fundamental science of dynamics, or the doctrine of the motion of bodies as affected by force" (where dynamics can be further divided into kinematics, statics, kinetics, and energetics). The ideal of mechanical explanation—the program to explain all physical phenomena in dynamical terms—guided much of physical research and led to many successes and to the unification of many phenomena and branches of physics.

A key role in this development was played by the mechanical theory of heat, proposed by James Prescott Joule in the 1840s. This theory, which stated that heat and mechanical work are equivalent and convertible, replaced the caloric theory of heat, according to which heat is a substance. It provided the basis for the unification of different types of energy and for the formulation of the laws of thermodynamics by Rudolf Clausius and William Thomson in the 1850s. The first law of thermodynamics is a general expression of the principle of energy conservation, the idea that the total amount of energy in a closed system is conserved and that accordingly energy cannot be created or destroyed but only be transformed from one form to another. The success of the mechanical theory of heat led mid-nineteenth-century physicists to adopt the doctrine that all energy is mechanical energy. The unifying concept of energy and the associated program of mechanical explanation provided a new framework for the whole of physical science. In the 1850s, Thomson and W. J. M. Rankine elaborated this program into a unified "energy physics," or "energetics" as Rankine called it (Harman 1982, 58–59).

The program of mechanical explanation had its roots in the science of heat, and it led directly to the development of the kinetic theory of gases by Clausius, Maxwell, and Boltzmann in the 1860s and 1870s. Of its extension to other domains of physics, the application to electricity and magnetism was most important. The first half of the nineteenth century had witnessed the rise of ether theories to explain electrical and magnetic phenomena. In the mid-nineteenth century, the idea of an ether as the medium for electrical and magnetic forces was well-established, and physicists such as Thomson and Maxwell attempted to give mechanical interpretations of the ether, of which Maxwell's famous 1862 model is best known (this model is discussed in more detail in section 6.1.2).

The program of mechanical explanation is often associated with a specific ontology: the metaphysical worldview that assumes that everything consists of particles of matter in motion. While this ontological view may have been attractive to many nineteenth-century scientists, the ideal of mechanical explanation does not necessarily imply the adoption of a corresponding mechanistic metaphysics. As the case studies in this chapter show, the main goal of mechanical explanation and mechanical modeling was to provide understanding of phenomena in a way that is not dependent on a realistic interpretation of the theories or models. Harman (1982, 9) argues that physicists used mechanical explanation in three different ways. First, by developing dynamical theories of systems of particles in motion, which explain phenomena in terms of the configuration of particles and the forces between them. Second, by constructing (real or hypothetical) mechanical models of phenomena that render them intelligible (without pretending to represent reality). Third, by appealing to abstract mathematical formalisms (such as the Lagrangian formulation of mechanics) to account for the phenomena without speculating about their underlying physical structure. In this chapter, I will focus on the first and second modes of mechanical explanation, which were employed with great success by William Thomson, James Clerk Maxwell, and Ludwig Boltzmann. The dynamical theories of molecular motion that Maxwell and Boltzmann developed to explain gas phenomena will be analyzed in detail in section 6.2. First, however, I will investigate the general views of Thomson, Maxwell, and Boltzmann on mechanical explanation and mechanical models.

6.1.1 William Thomson: master modeler

William Thomson, Lord Kelvin, (1824–1907) epitomizes the nineteenth-century physicist: his life spanned the greater part of the century; he was a key figure in the British scientific establishment; and he was involved in a great variety of scientific debates and made many important contributions to developments in physics and engineering.[1] Although his genius and lasting fame is perhaps eclipsed by that of Maxwell, Thomson's influence on physics can hardly be overestimated. His work, which was guided by the ideal of mechanical explanation, is highly characteristic of the nineteenth-century way of doing physics, and he lived long enough to witness the decline and downfall of the mechanical program. Until the end of his life Thomson clung to the idea that mechanical models are essential in physical science—that mechanical modeling is the only route to understanding physical phenomena. But some problems in physics—the "nineteenth-century clouds over the dynamical theory of heat and light," as Thomson dubbed them in his famous 1900 address—turned out to be unsolvable by means of the traditional mechanical approach; they sparked the development of quantum theory and relativity theory (see section 6.3). According to his biographers Smith and Wise (1989, 491), Thomson's approach was "a methodology that grounded mathematical physics in steam-engines, vortex turbines, and telegraph lines; a methodology for industrialization and Empire." It fitted the nineteenth-century context and was highly conducive to scientific progress for at least five decades. Twentieth-century physics, however, required a novel approach.

---

1. Thomson's life and achievements are documented in *Energy and Empire*, a biography by Crosbie Smith and M. Norton Wise (1989).

Before investigating Thomson's ideas about mechanical explanation and mechanical modeling in more detail, I will briefly review his most important scientific achievements. As noted, Thomson's scientific work was guided by the idea of a unified physics based on the concept of energy. The main domains of physics that would be unified in this way were, on the one hand, the phenomena of heat and thermodynamics, and on the other hand, those of electricity, light, and magnetism. Thomson played a key role in the development of the science of thermodynamics: in the late 1840s he studied the work of Carnot and Joule, observing a conflict between Carnot's theory of the motive power of heat—which was based on the caloric theory—and Joule's experiments, which seemed to show that mechanical work can be converted into heat and vice versa. His investigations into irreversible thermal phenomena, which appear to involve a loss of mechanical energy, led him to accept Joule's mechanical theory of heat and to use it to develop a modified version of Carnot's theory into a general thermodynamics (a similar result was achieved by Clausius around the same time). Thomson's important 1851 paper "On the Dynamical Theory of Heat" states the two laws of thermodynamics. The first law expresses the idea of energy conservation, or, in Thomson's words, the principle of the indestructibility of energy. The second law is the principle of energy dissipation, which asserts that irreversible processes involve a transformation (dissipation) of mechanical work into a form of energy that is unrecoverable.[2]

Thomson's contributions to the development of the physics of electricity and magnetism were equally influential (Harman 1982, 79–84). While it was Maxwell who constructed the unifying theory of electromagnetism, this theory was inspired by and based on Thomson's work.[3] In his early papers, from the 1840s, Thomson had developed analogies between electricity and heat flow (as described by Fourier's theory) and between magnetism and hydrodynamics.[4] The purpose of these analogies was merely to arrive at a descriptive mathematical theory of electrical and magnetic phenomena; Thomson refrained from making assertions about an unobservable physical reality underlying these phenomena. At this time, Thomson wanted to construct "positive" theories that described macroscopic phenomena (Smith and Wise 1989, 279); he rejected theories based on physical hypotheses

2. See Harman (1982, 45–58) for a more detailed account.

3. See the preface to the first edition of Maxwell's *Treatise on Electricity and Magnetism* ([1873] 1954, viii–ix).

4. See Smith and Wise (1989, 203–212 and 263–275).

regarding electrical and magnetic fluids. In the 1850s, however, after having accepted Joule's mechanical theory of heat, Thomson changed his approach to the analysis of electromagnetic phenomena. He adopted the unifying ideal of mechanical explanation and set out to explain electromagnetism in terms of the mechanical motion of an all-pervading ether. Strictly following the mechanical program—assuming nothing but matter and motion—he developed a hydrodynamical account of the ether, as a "Universal Plenum" that should serve as the basis for the explanation of all physical phenomena.[5] In Thomson's words: "The explanation of all phenomena of electro-magnetic attraction or repulsion, and of electro-magnetic induction, is to be looked for simply in the inertia and pressure of the matter of which the motions constitute heat."[6]

The mechanical program guided Thomson's work for the rest of his life. Its ultimate goal was the development of a unified dynamical theory of ether and matter. The 1867 *Treatise on Natural Philosophy*, written in collaboration with Peter Guthrie Tait, was intended as a textbook that would provide the basis for such a theory.[7] Ultimately, however, Thomson's mechanical approach did not succeed. This became most apparent in his desperate attempts to rescue the idea of a mechanical theory of the ether. In the final decade of the century, Thomson discussed Maxwell's theory with younger physicists such as G. F. FitzGerald, Joseph Larmor, and Oliver Heaviside. Thomson clung to a mechanical theory of the ether while the new generation of "Maxwellians" endorsed Hertz's dictum that "Maxwell's theory is Maxwell's system of equations" (Hertz 1893, 21) and adopted a strictly mathematical approach that Thomson labeled "nihilistic."[8] FitzGerald, by contrast, accused Thomson of "lending his overwhelming authority to a view of the ether which is not justified by our present knowledge" and thereby "delaying the progress of science."[9]

In his 1884 *Baltimore Lectures*, Thomson defended the program of mechanical explanation by pointing at the understanding-providing power of mechanical models. The famous quote with which I started this chapter clearly illustrates his view. Because of his insistence on mechanical modeling,

---

5. See Smith and Wise (1989, 396–444); Harman (1982, 79–85). Thomson quoted by Smith and Wise (1989, 409).

6. Thomson (1856) quoted by Smith and Wise (1989, 408).

7. Harman (1982, 69–71); Smith and Wise (1989, 348–395).

8. Smith and Wise (1989, 488–494). Cf. Harman (1982, 98–103).

9. FitzGerald quoted in Smith and Wise (1989, 461).

Thomson had difficulties with Maxwell's theory of electromagnetism—
he regarded it as unintelligible because it lacked a completely satisfactory
mechanical model:

> I never satisfy myself until I can make a mechanical model of a thing.
> If I can make a mechanical model I can understand it. As long as I can-
> not make a mechanical model all the way through I cannot understand;
> and that is why I cannot get the electromagnetic theory. (Kargon and
> Achinstein 1987, 206).[10]

Thomson thus identified scientifically understanding a phenomenon with
making a mechanical model of it. But what exactly counts as a mechanical model, according to Thomson? Bailer-Jones (2009, 27) observes that
nineteenth-century physicists saw models as concrete, tangible constructions
in three dimensions (as is nicely illustrated by Boltzmann's entry "Model"
in the 1902 edition of the *Encyclopedia Britannica*, discussed in section 6.3).
Accordingly, their conception of model was much narrower than the present one, which includes mathematical models, computer models, and so on.
The mechanical models of Thomson, who was not only a physicist but also
an engineer,[11] clearly belonged to the category of concrete physical models
(while not always actually constructed, they were constructible in principle).
For example, in 1883 Thomson tried to construct a model for Cauchy's theory
of refractive dispersion, which consisted of "a series of wooden bars attached
crosswise to a wire suspended from the ceiling. A periodic twist at one end
would produce wavelike oscillations in the ends of the bars, regarded as a series of identical molecules" (Smith and Wise 1989, 442).

Why, and how, do such mechanical models yield understanding? Bailer-
Jones (2009, 29) claims that "Thomson does not tell us why he thinks
that mechanical models promote understanding. He simply takes this for
granted." A closer look at Thomson's writings reveals more about his reasons,

---

10. Thomson continued: "I firmly believe in an electro-magnetic theory of light, and that
when we understand electricity and magnetism and light, we shall see them all together as
part of a whole. But I want to understand light as well as I can without introducing things
that we understand even less of" (Kargon and Achinstein 1987, 206). To be sure, attempts
had been made—by Thomson himself and earlier by Maxwell (see section 6.1.2)—to construct mechanical models of the electromagnetic ether, but these confronted problems (see
Harman 1982, 99–101).

11. Thomson was involved in the Atlantic Telegraph project, and he held many patents for
inventions related, for example, to telegraphy and navigation at sea (Smith and Wise 1989,
649–798).

however. In their monumental biographical study of Thomson, *Energy and Empire*, Smith and Wise (1989, 463–471) present an original and convincing analysis of his views in terms of what they call the "methodology of look and see." They argue that Thomson's preference for mechanical models is part of a methodology that emphasizes that theoretical physicists can obtain knowledge and understanding only if they "look" and "touch" in order to "see" and "feel" (Smith and Wise 1989, 464). For Thomson, to know and understand something means to see and feel it. If we cannot see and feel something directly (such as a molecule, which is too small), we must find alternative ways to get acquainted with it, to see and feel it. Making a mechanical model is one way to achieve this. The aim of a mechanical model (e.g., of a molecule) is to allow one to acquire a feeling for how it behaves: "A mechanical model of a possible molecule enabled one to manipulate it in all its variety of circumstances; to touch it, turn it, look at it, and thereby to know it intuitively as a potentially real thing" (Smith and Wise 1989, 465). Thus, the "feeling" that Thomson deems so important corresponds to the "feeling" for the qualitative consequences of a theory that was suggested as a sufficient condition for intelligibility in section 4.2.

But mechanical modeling is not the only way to achieve this aim. Smith and Wise observe that Thomson's *Baltimore Lectures* contain, parallel to the well-known methodological maxims concerning the necessity of mechanical models, equally important (but lesser known) suggestions for an "arithmetical laboratory." In the arithmetical laboratory students have to make calculations in order to become familiar with physical magnitudes, to acquire a feeling for them. Thomson: "I have no satisfaction in formulas unless I feel their arithmetical magnitude at all events when formulas are intended for definite dynamical or physical problems" (Kargon and Achinstein 1987, 67). According to Smith and Wise (1989, 464), both mechanical models and the arithmetical laboratory "provide a direct 'feeling' for how things vary under varying conditions." In other words, they supply tools for understanding.

In the *Baltimore Lectures* Thomson characterized these tools as "brain savers": of a model of polarized light using a bowl of jelly, he said: "It saves brain very much" (Kargon and Achinstein 1987, 74). He repeatedly emphasized the limitations of our brains, and accordingly of abstract thought. In line with his practical, engineering orientation, he valued direct visual and tactile experience more highly than abstract reasoning, and recommended mechanical modeling as a better and more secure way of achieving understanding. For example, Thomson presented a mechanical model of a system of coupled ether-molecules (figure 6.1). After having described the motion of this system, he added: "From looking at the thing, and learning to understand it by making

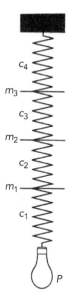

FIGURE 6.1 Thomson's model of coupled molecules: a series of springs c_i connecting masses m_i can be pulled from below by the bell-pull P. Smith and Wise (1989, 468) observe: "The experimenter can both see and feel the various periods at which accumulation and loss of energy in the different masses occurs." Reprinted from C. Smith and M. N. Wise, *Energy and Empire: A Biographical Study of Lord Kelvin* (Cambridge: Cambridge University Press, 1989), 468.

the experiment, if you do not understand it by brains alone, you will see that everything I am saying is obvious" (Kargon and Achinstein 1987, 37).

Seeing and feeling are quicker and safer routes to understanding than abstract thinking. A mechanical model provides a visualization of the phenomenon, and one that can be manipulated. Thus, one can see it and develop a feeling for its behavior in changing circumstances. As Smith and Wise (1989, 230–236) argue, geometrical visualization had always played a central role in Thomson's methodology. As early as 1847, he developed a "purely geometrical method of images" in order to obtain an intuitive grasp of mathematical theory (Smith and Wise 1989, 230). For Thomson, scientific understanding was essentially related to the ability to manipulate and to visualize, and mechanical models were well-suited to this purpose. Whether or not these models should be interpreted realistically was of little concern to Thomson (see, e.g., Kargon and Achinstein 1987, 110–111).

In the early twentieth century, Thomson's views on the indispensability of models were famously criticized by Pierre Duhem in his 1906 book *La Théorie Physique: Son Objet, Sa Structure* (The aim and structure of physical theory). Distinguishing between the "narrow but strong" French mind and the "ample but weak" English mind, Duhem (1954, 63–75) regarded the penchant for mechanical models as an example of the latter. After having quoted Thomson's famous statements from the *Baltimore Lectures*, he observed: "Understanding a physical phenomenon is, therefore, for the physicist of the English school, the same thing as designing a model imitating the phenomenon; whence the nature of material things is to be understood by imagining a mechanism whose performance will represent and simulate the properties of the bodies" (Duhem 1954, 72). While he admitted that mechanical modeling sometimes produced valuable results, he claimed that "neither in Lord Kelvin's nor in Maxwell's work has the use of mechanical models shown that fruitfulness nowadays attributed so readily to it" (Duhem 1954, 98). According to Duhem, reasoning with abstract theories (the preferred way of the French mind) was a far more secure way to achieve progress in physics.

Duhem's criticism reflected the situation around 1900, in which mechanical modeling had run out of steam. At that time, it had become clear that twentieth-century physicists would need different tools for understanding. Clearly, however, Duhem was too harsh on the mechanical program: models and mechanisms may still be conducive to understanding. But they are not, as Thomson believed, necessary conditions for it; whether or not they are considered useful and acceptable depends on both the scientific and the broader philosophical and sociocultural context.[12]

6.1.2 James Clerk Maxwell: advocate of analogies

Mechanical models also played a key role in the work of James Clerk Maxwell (1831–1879), who was perhaps the greatest physicist of the nineteenth century. Maxwell was an extremely versatile scientist: in his relatively short life he made fundamental contributions to numerous branches of physical science. His two most important achievements, however, were his theory of electromagnetism and his contributions to the development of the kinetic theory of gases. In both cases, Maxwell fruitfully employed mechanical models, and while his attitude toward the epistemological status of such models gradually changed, like Thomson he always valued them highly for their intelligibility and understanding-providing power. I will review the role of mechanical

---

12. See Smith and Wise (1989) for an elaborate account of how Thomson's physics and philosophy of science were embedded in the political and economic climate of Victorian society. Dear (2006, 115–140) presents a more general discussion of nineteenth-century British physics that highlights its relations with contemporary socioeconomic developments.

models in Maxwell's scientific work and examine his philosophical views on the status and function of such models in some more detail.

Maxwell's theory of electromagnetism was developed in a series of papers from 1856 onward, culminating in *A Treatise on Electricity and Magnetism* (1873). In his first paper, "On Faraday's Lines of Force" (1856), he suggested that there is an analogy between "lines of force," introduced by Michael Faraday to account for effects such as electromagnetic induction, and streamlines in an incompressible fluid (following a suggestion made by Thomson in an 1847 paper; see Harman 1998, 98). This mechanical—more specifically: hydrodynamical—analogy was further developed in his second paper, "On physical lines of force" (1862), which contains Maxwell's famous mechanical model of the ether (figure 6.2).

This model represents the medium for electrical and magnetic fields (the electromagnetic ether) as a system of vortices in an incompressible fluid. The axes of rotation of the vortices represent the lines of the magnetic field, and their angular momenta the intensity of the field. In order to allow the vortices to rotate in the same direction, Maxwell introduced counter-rotating "idle

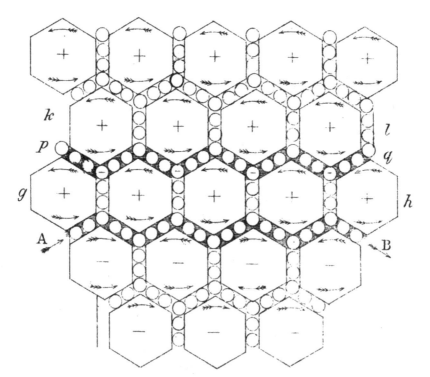

FIGURE 6.2 Maxwell's model of the electromagnetic ether (Maxwell 1965, 1:489).

wheels" in between vortices. These idle wheels "play the part of electricity" (Maxwell 1965, 1:486): in conductors they can move freely, giving rise to an electric current, while in insulators they remain attached to the vortices. As Dear (2006, 132) observes, considerations of intelligibility and understanding were central to Maxwell's model, in particular, to his introduction of idle wheels: the model is presented as the only way in which the motion of the vortices can be intelligibly represented (Maxwell 1965, 1:468). On the basis of this mechanical model, Maxwell was able to deduce a number of known laws of electricity (such as Coulomb's law of the attraction and repulsion between electrically charged bodies). Moreover, it led him to important new discoveries, namely the existence of the so-called displacement current and the electromagnetic theory of light.[13] The latter discovery was announced at the end of Maxwell's 1862 paper: it turned out, quite surprisingly, that the properties of the medium (the electromagnetic ether) were identical to those of the medium for light propagation (the luminiferous ether), and that the predicted velocity of electromagnetic waves was identical to the observed velocity of light. Maxwell (1965, 1:500, original italics): "We can scarcely avoid the inference that *light consists in the transverse undulations of the same medium which is the cause of electric and magnetic phenomena.*"

Notwithstanding Maxwell's enthusiasm about the achieved theoretical unification of electricity, magnetism, and light, he emphasized that his mechanical ether model should be regarded as an analogy and not be interpreted realistically. The notion of "analogy" was crucial in Maxwell's early work. He began his 1856 paper with an explicit statement of his method of physical analogy, which allowed him to attach physical meaning to his statements and derivations without being committed to a hypothesis in advance:

> In order to obtain physical ideas without adopting a physical theory we must make ourselves familiar with the existence of physical analogies. By a physical analogy I mean that partial similarity between the laws of one science and those of another which makes each of them illustrate the other. (Maxwell 1965, 1:155)

Such physical analogies may be discovered if one finds that completely different phenomena can be described by laws that have the same form. But one can also actively search for analogies, by treating a phenomenon under study as a system that is analogous to another phenomenon of which the

---

13. Chalmers (2001, 429) disputes that Maxwell discovered the displacement current via his ether model; but this is not the generally accepted view (see Chalmers 2001, 437n10).

laws are well-known. If such analogical treatment appears to be consistent with the empirical facts, a physical analogy has been established. The main motivation for finding physical analogies is the understanding they provide.[14] Analogies—in particular, mechanical models—may provide visualizations or illustrations of phenomena, thereby making them more intelligible. When one has established a physical analogy between phenomena from two different branches of science, one has gained insight in both branches, and possibilities to make new discoveries in either of them may emerge. So analogies also have heuristic value. In sum, according to Maxwell, their main purpose was "to assist the imagination, to render the phenomena intelligible" (Harman 1998, 98).[15]

In the preface to the first edition of *A Treatise on Electricity and Magnetism* (1873), Maxwell stated that his aim was to illuminate the relations between a mathematical theory of electromagnetism and "the fundamental science of Dynamics, in order that we may in some degree be prepared to determine the kind of dynamical phenomena among which we are to look for illustrations or explanations of the electromagnetic phenomena" (Maxwell [1873] 1954, 1: vi). After having discussed a mechanical analogy of the electromagnetic phenomenon of self-induction in the second volume of the *Treatise*, Maxwell explained why mechanical analogies are so helpful in achieving understanding:

> It is difficult . . . for the mind which has once recognised the analogy between the phenomena of self-induction and those of the motion of material bodies, to abandon altogether the help of this analogy, or to admit that it is entirely superficial and misleading. The fundamental dynamical idea of matter, as capable by its motion of becoming the recipient of momentum and of energy, is so interwoven with our forms of thought that whenever we catch a glimpse of it in any part of nature,

---

14. It should be added that, in Maxwell's view, the discovery that some phenomenon is analogous to another phenomenon constitutes knowledge about that phenomenon, even though the analogy should not be interpreted as real: "the recognition of the formal analogy between the two systems of ideas leads to a knowledge of both, more profound than could be obtained by studying each system separately" (Maxwell 1986, 94). Therefore, Maxwell considers the search for analogies as an important aim of science. See Olson (1975, 330), who relates this view of Maxwell's to the "Common Sense" doctrine that only relations between phenomena can be known.

15. Harman (1998, 98–99) claims that in Maxwell's 1856 paper the analogy was still "illustrative, not explanatory," but in his 1862 paper he proposed a "physical analogy in the sense of a causal, explanatory model."

we feel that a path is before us leading, sooner or later, to the complete understanding of the subject. (Maxwell [1873] 1954, 2:196–197)

The intelligibility of concepts and theories was a serious concern for Maxwell. As Harman (1998, 147) states, Maxwell considered geometry as "the keystone of intelligibility," following the tradition of Scottish mathematics and philosophy. In this he agreed with his fellow Scotsman Thomson, who also emphasized that geometrical visualization fosters understanding. Harman (1998, 27–36) observes that Maxwell, influenced by William Hamilton and William Whewell, adopted a Kantian view of space and time, regarding them as necessary conditions of thinking and therefore of intelligibility, rather than as structures in reality. For example, Maxwell described geometric figures as "forms of thought and not of matter" (quoted in Harman 1998, 30). This Kantian strain is clearly present in the quoted passage. Maxwell's analogies, such as his mechanical model of the ether, aimed at providing understanding of phenomena, for which their geometrical nature was essential (Harman 1998, 87–88, 90). Their goal was intelligibility rather than truth: even if they failed to be correct representations of reality, mechanical models served to render phenomena intelligible. Thus, when evaluating the status of his ether model, Maxwell stated: "I do not bring it forward as a mode of connexion existing in nature." He added, however, that the model is "mechanically conceivable" and "it serves to bring out the actual mechanical connexions between the known electro-magnetic phenomena" (Maxwell 1965, 1:486).

Maxwell's second great achievement lies in his work on the kinetic theory of gases. The kinetic theory assumes that gases are composed of small particles (atoms or molecules), and that heat is nothing else than the motion of such particles. On the basis of these ideas and some simple statistical assumptions, Rudolf Clausius (1857) had derived the ideal-gas law.[16] However, in the 1850s both the hypothesis that gases consist of atoms or molecules and the identification of heat with mechanical motion were not yet universally accepted. Maxwell was not convinced of the truth of the kinetic hypothesis and the reality of molecules either; but he studied Clausius's theory because he was interested in applications of statistics. In his first article on the topic, "Illustrations of the Dynamical Theory of Gases" (1860), Maxwell presented a further development of Clausius's theory.[17] In its main part, he treated the

---

16. R. Clausius, "Über die Art der Bewegung, welche wir Wärme nennen" (1857), English translation in Brush (1965, 111–134).

17. J. C. Maxwell, "Illustrations of the Dynamical Theory of Gases" (1860), reprinted in Maxwell (1986, 285–318).

particles as elastic spheres and showed that many properties of real gases can be deduced from this hypothesis. He described his method as follows:

> If the properties of such a system of bodies are found to correspond to those of gases, an important physical analogy will be established, which may lead to more accurate knowledge of the properties of matter. If experiments on gases are inconsistent with the hypothesis of these propositions, then our theory, though consistent with itself, is proved to be incapable of explaining the phenomena of gases. In either consequence it is necessary to follow out the consequences of the hypothesis. (Maxwell 1986, 287)

Accordingly, Maxwell's aim was to discover a *physical analogy*, and not to prove that gases really consist of elastic, spherical particles. Indeed, in the passage immediately following this quotation, he stated that the gas particles could equally well be conceived as centers of force, as this would yield identical results. The question of whether the particles really are spheres or centers of force was of minor importance to him.

Maxwell's approach was quite successful: using refined statistical methods, he derived a law of the distribution of molecular velocities, and equations governing transport phenomena (diffusion, viscosity, heat conduction). There was one serious problem, however: the theoretical prediction for the value of the ratio of specific heats could not be reconciled with the experimentally obtained value. This discrepancy between theory and experiment came to be known as the specific heat anomaly (in section 6.2, this anomaly will be discussed in more detail). Maxwell himself, in a summary written for the British Association, concluded that "this result of the dynamical theory, being at variance with experiment, overturns the whole hypothesis, however satisfactory the other results may be" (Maxwell 1986, 321). Notwithstanding this seemingly radical conclusion, he continued his research on the kinetic theory of gases. This suggests that, although he had not yet succeeded in establishing the kinetic theory as an "important physical analogy," Maxwell still regarded it as a fruitful "potential" analogy. Indeed, he was able to continue his research precisely because he employed the analogical method, the aim of which was "to obtain physical ideas without adopting a physical theory" (Maxwell 1965, 1:155). In other words, Maxwell remained convinced that the kinetic analogy was a useful tool for understanding gaseous phenomena.

This indeed turned out to be the case. Maxwell's later work on the kinetic theory yielded many successful predictions, and partly due to this work the reality of molecules and atoms was, by the end of the 1860s, generally accepted; only their specific nature remained a subject of discussion. Maxwell himself gradually moved toward a more realistic view of the kinetic theory, and abandoned the method of physical analogy in favor of what he called "Newtonian deduction from the phenomena," described as follows in an 1876 article: "The true method of physical reasoning is to begin with the phenomena and to deduce forces from them by a direct application of the equations of motion" (Maxwell 1965, 2:309). Obviously, deduction from the phenomena is possible only if at least one theoretical premise is accepted because one cannot deduce theories from empirical evidence only. Maxwell took this premise to be the presupposition that all physical systems are "material systems," that is, systems which are subject to the fundamental laws of Newtonian mechanics and of energy conservation (see, e.g., Maxwell 1986, 219). Consequently, these laws can be used as premises in deductions. Although, strictly speaking, these premises are hypotheses, Maxwell regarded them as minimal, even necessary, presuppositions. In some places, he attempted to give a justification of them, adopting a position which is again reminiscent of Kant (see Chalmers 1973, 110). Kantian elements can also be discerned in Maxwell's 1875 description of the ultimate goal of the scientific method as the establishment of "dynamical explanations":

> When a physical phenomenon can be completely described as a change in the configuration and motion of a material system, the dynamical explanation of that phenomenon is said to be complete. We cannot conceive any further explanation to be either necessary, desirable, or possible, for as soon as we know what is meant by the words configuration, motion, mass, and force, we see that the ideas which they represent are so elementary that they cannot be explained by means of anything else. (Maxwell 1986, 217)

Throughout his career Maxwell used mechanical models and dynamical explanations to achieve understanding of phenomena. As the quotation shows, he regarded mechanical explanation as the only route to scientific understanding because it accounts for the phenomena purely in terms of concepts that are intrinsically intelligible.[18] While Maxwell's attitude toward the representational value of his mechanical models varied (from seeing them as mere "illustrations" to interpreting them in a realistic fashion), he

---

18. Maxwell (1965, 2:781) regarded the concept of matter "as perfectly intelligible as a straight line or a sphere."

valued them first and foremost for their intelligibility and the understanding they provided.

6.1.3 Ludwig Boltzmann: promoter of pictures

The mechanistic tradition in physics was continued by Ludwig Boltzmann (1844–1906), who is famous for his contributions to the kinetic theory and statistical mechanics. His first important article, published in 1868, built upon Maxwell's work and presented an important generalization of Maxwell's distribution law, containing the well-known Boltzmann factor.[19] Philosophically, the young Boltzmann was less scrupulous than Maxwell: he accepted the kinetic theory and the reality of atoms unconditionally. To be sure, the article consisted purely of abstract analytical mechanics, which might suggest that it aimed at the establishment of a Maxwellian analogy. However, according to Boltzmann, the analysis of systems of moving point masses serves to elucidate "the tenets of the mechanical theory of heat, which do refer to such motions and which hitherto have remained so unconnected and so defective in their analytical foundation" (Boltzmann 1968, 1:49; my translation). In the 1870s, Boltzmann continued his work on the kinetic theory, producing such crucial results as the theorem of equipartition and the H-theorem. Notwithstanding its successes, the kinetic theory was faced with serious problems, most notably the specific heat anomaly. Boltzmann was among those who tried to find a solution of this anomaly (see section 6.2 for a detailed account), and he was well aware that the mechanical systems he analyzed were idealizations that could not pretend to be accurate representations of real physical systems such as gases. Nevertheless, Boltzmann believed the development of a mathematical theory of particles in empty space to be "of the greatest importance for the investigation of the true nature of the gas molecules" (Boltzmann 1968, 1:258; my translation).

Throughout his life, Boltzmann remained committed to the program of mechanical explanation. He believed that the laws of mechanics constitute an indispensable basis of natural science, and that to explain a phenomenon is to provide a mechanical model of it. A clear illustration can be found in his *Vorlesungen über Gastheorie* (Lectures on gas theory, 1896–1898), which begin with an introductory section entitled "Mechanical Analogy for the Behavior of a Gas." Boltzmann sets out by introducing Clausius's distinction between the

---

19. L. Boltzmann, "Studien über das Gleichgewicht der lebendigen Kraft zwischen bewegten materiellen Punkten" (1868), reprinted in Boltzmann (1968, 1:49–96).

general theory of heat (phenomenological thermodynamics) and the special theory of heat (the kinetic theory of gases based on the atomistic hypothesis that heat is molecular motion). The latter theory, says Boltzmann (1964, 26), should be considered as a mechanical analogy, a term that indicates "how far removed we are from that viewpoint which would see in visible matter the true properties of the smallest particles of the body." The remaining part of the section is devoted to a purely qualitative analysis that leads to the conclusion that a gas can be pictured as a collection of freely moving molecules in a container (this passage has been discussed in more detail in section 4.2).

However, mechanical models and analogies can be applied in many more areas of physics, according to Boltzmann. Examples abound in his *Vorlesungen über Maxwells Theorie der Elektricität und des Lichtes* (Lectures on Maxwell's theory of electricity and light, 1891–1893), which according to Klein (1972, 73) "can surely be paired with Kelvin's *Baltimore Lectures* as representing the High Baroque phase of the mechanical world view." In the first volume, Boltzmann discusses a mechanical analogy of the second law of thermodynamics to illustrate the physical significance of the Lagrangian equations of motion. Having explicated the analogy, Boltzmann (1982, Part I, 13–14) concludes the lecture with a section entitled *Die Theorien sind blosse Bilder der Naturprocesse* (Theories are mere pictures of natural processes). He states that the sketched analogy also helps to clarify the nature of the theories to be discussed in his *Vorlesungen*, and indeed of many physical theories. They do not pretend to give literally true accounts of states of affairs and processes in nature, but only to describe mechanisms that have a strong analogy with the natural phenomena in question. Boltzmann reminds us of Maxwell's "dynamical illustrations" and emphasizes the advantages and heuristic value of their clear and well-defined character. Figure 6.3 depicts two examples of mechanical models of electromagnetic phenomena.

In the second volume (1893) of the *Vorlesungen*, Boltzmann (1982, Part II, 22) introduces a distinction between two different interpretations of mechanical pictures. First, a physical theory in itself can be regarded as a picture, as an *Analogon*. Second, specific mechanical analogies can be employed in order to obtain visualizations (*Versinnlichung*) of the consequences of a theory.[20] This is one of the first statements of Bolzmann's *Bildtheorie*, which I will discuss in more detail in section 6.3. As representations of reality, *Bilder* are necessarily limited: there is never a complete one-to-one correspondence between theory and reality. But in addition to their representative role, *Bilder* can provide understanding: they serve to make phenomena intelligible to us. And it is in

---

20. See also Miller (1986, 91) for a discussion of this passage.

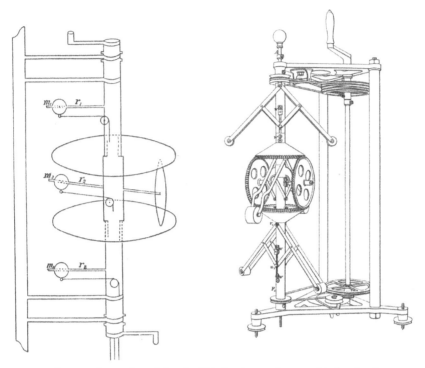

FIGURE 6.3 Mechanical models of self-induction and mutual induction between coupled electric circuits in Boltzmann's *Vorlesungen über Maxwells Theorie der Elektricität und des Lichtes*. Reprinted with permission from Boltzmann (1982, Part 1, 26 and Taf. II). Copyright (1982) by the Akademische Druck- und Verlagsanstalt.

this respect that *mechanical* pictures and models are highly valuable: according to Boltzmann, mechanical pictures are superior when it comes to explaining the phenomena.

Boltzmann saw giving explanations of natural phenomena as a central aim of science, in contrast to merely describing and predicting observable phenomena; see, for example, Boltzmann (1974, 16), where he argues against Kirchhoff's positivist view of science. In his 1902 inaugural address, "On the Principles of Mechanics," Boltzmann (1974, 149) expressed his view as follows: "It is the ubiquitous task of science to explain the more complex in terms of the simpler; or, if preferred, to represent [*anschaulich darstellen*] the complex by means of clear pictures [*Bilder*] borrowed from the sphere of the simpler phenomena." This statement shows that in Boltzmann's philosophy of science *Bilder* were essential to the explanatory aim of natural science.

Having asserted that the aim of science is explanation, Boltzmann observed (in the passage following the statement) that this induced physicists to develop mechanical explanations of various physical phenomena. Why mechanical? Because mechanical pictures are the most intelligible ones. The simplest conceivable phenomena consist of particles in motion, and therefore the scientist would try to explain all phenomena by means of the science of motion: mechanics. At various places, Boltzmann suggested that he held mechanical explanations to be the most intelligible and therefore the most satisfying ones. For example, in his 1900 inaugural address "On the Principles of Mechanics" he stated:

> If . . . all apparently qualitative changes were representable by the picture of motions or changes of arrangements of smallest parts, this would lead to an especially simple explanation of nature. In that case nature would appear to us at its most comprehensible [*begreiflichsten*], but we cannot compel her to this, we must leave open a possibility that this will not do and that we need in addition other pictures of other changes; understandably, it is precisely the more recent developments of physics that have made it prudent to allow for this possibility. (Boltzmann 1974, 143)

This statement seems to carry the idea that there exist a priori criteria for assessing when scientific theories provide understanding, criteria which imply that theories giving mechanical pictures provide maximal understanding because of their simplicity.[21] Such arguments might suggest that Boltzmann's preference for mechanical explanations, like Maxwell's, can be associated with a Kantian view, according to which our intellectual faculties determine the form of our scientific theories. However, this impression would be mistaken: Boltzmann was certainly not a Kantian (see D'Agostino 1990). Indeed, in a passage immediately preceding the quotation, Boltzmann stated that he did not think highly of attempts to give a priori proofs of the mechanical program of explanation. His opposition to Kantianism is especially apparent in his rejection of Hertz's view of *Bilder* as corresponding to "laws of thought" (see De Regt 1999a, 116–117).

What reasons could Boltzmann have had to prefer mechanical pictures as being most intelligible, if there were no a priori arguments for it? In order to answer this question we must turn to Boltzmann's views about laws of thought (*Denkgesetze*), which he proposed as an alternative to the ideas of Hertz and Kant. As D'Agostino (1990, 388–390) has observed, Boltzmann

---

21. See Boltzmann (1974, 149) for similar arguments in favor of mechanical explanation.

adhered to an evolutionary, Darwinist conception of laws of thought. On this view, there are indeed laws of thought, which are in some cases innate and in this sense a priori. However, these laws have achieved this status through their evolutionary success. They have become innate and apparently immutable because of their lasting utility in the struggle for survival. But this does not imply that such laws are absolutely infallible or a priori in the traditional sense: there is always the possibility that new, unexpected situations turn up in which they fail.[22] Boltzmann held that explanation through mechanical pictures corresponds with our laws of thought in this evolutionary sense and is therefore preferable but not infallible.[23]

We can now see why Boltzmann favored mechanical explanation. Although he did not believe in the traditional notion of immutable laws of thought (allegedly necessitating mechanical explanation), he acknowledged the existence of laws of thought formed in the evolutionary sense. These laws have made explanation through mechanical pictures a preferable mode of explanation, albeit not an infallible one. Accordingly, the intelligibility of mechanical pictures is only a contingent fact. It is the practical success of mechanical modeling—possibly linked with our familiarity with mechanical systems from daily experience—that has made it into a criterion for intelligibility in science.

In the quoted passage from his inaugural address, Boltzmann (1974, 143) stated that we cannot compel nature to be explicable by means of mechanical pictures. He added that "more recent developments in physics" illustrate this situation. Here he hinted at the fact that at the end of the nineteenth century the project of mechanical explanation was meeting with difficulties, which induced physicists to search for alternatives. One of these was the electromagnetic worldview, based on the assumption that mechanical phenomena should be explained in electromagnetic terms rather than the other way around (it suggested, for instance, explaining inertial mass from the motion of charges). On this view the fundamental electromagnetic entity—the ether—served as the most fundamental mechanism that had to explain all physical phenomena. Boltzmann (1974, 150) observed: "It was no longer a question of explaining everything mechanically, but of finding a mechanism to explain all mechanisms."

---

22. See Boltzmann (1974, 105, 195) for arguments to this effect.

23. An extensive discussion of the nature and status of *Denkgesetze* can be found in Boltzmann's notes for his Lectures on Natural Philosophy (1903–1906), posthumously published as *Principien der Naturfilosofi* (Fasol-Boltzmann 1990). See De Regt (1999a, 120–121) for a summary and evaluation.

Notwithstanding this qualification of the status of mechanical explanations, Boltzmann hoped and believed that mechanical pictures would finally be victorious when it came to assessing their fruitfulness. Thus, he concluded his 1900 inaugural address with the following words: "Summing up in conclusion, our result is that one side of all processes of inanimate and animate nature is representable through purely mechanical pictures, or, as the phrase goes, made intelligible [*begreiflich*] with a measure of exactness not hitherto achieved in any other way, while at the same time none of the higher endeavors and ideals are in the least impaired" (Boltzmann 1974, 146).[24] Although at the turn of the century the mechanical program faced serious problems and had become implausible as a metaphysical worldview, Boltzmann still believed in the pragmatic value of mechanical pictures and models, in their use as tools for understanding. In section 6.3, I will investigate Boltzmann's view of this pragmatic role of mechanical models in more detail. But first I will zoom in on a specific episode in the history of the kinetic theory of gases, in order to examine how intelligibility standards and tools for understanding function in scientific practice.

6.2 Molecular models for understanding gas phenomena

In the previous section, I have reviewed the nineteenth-century mechanical tradition by means of a general discussion of the work and ideas of some of its chief proponents. It appeared that a main motivation for using mechanical models was the idea that such models provide understanding of the phenomena. Mechanical models and mechanical explanations were preferable for their intelligibility, or so many nineteenth-century physicists believed. But how precisely did mechanical modeling advance understanding in practice, if at all? In the present section, I will answer this question by investigating a particular episode in the development of the kinetic theory of gases, analyzing it with the theory of scientific understanding presented in chapters 2 and 4. The central issue in this episode is the so-called specific heat anomaly (mentioned already in the previous section), which was a serious empirical problem that

---

24. I have slightly revised Paul Foulkes's (1974) translation by adding the phrase "through purely mechanical pictures." The German original reads: "Wenn wir nun zum Schlusse das Resultat unserer Betrachtungen resumieren, so können wir als solches bezeichnen, daß sich eine Seite aller Vorgänge der unbelebten und belebten Natur durch rein mechanische Bilder in einer Exaktheit darstellen, wie man sich ausdrückt, begreiflich machen läßt, wie es sonst in keiner anderen Weise bisher gelungen ist, während anderseits doch alle höheren Bestrebungen und Ideale keine Einbuße erleiden" (Boltzmann 1979, 190).

the kinetic theory confronted. I will examine how Maxwell and Boltzmann, the key figures in this episode, enhanced their understanding of the behavior of gases on the basis of the kinetic theory and associated mechanical models, and how they attempted to solve the anomaly.

Again, as in chapter 5, a preliminary remark on terminology is in order before we begin our analysis. In my theory of scientific understanding the terms "intelligibility" and "understanding" are employed in quite specific ways, and the notions of "model" and "theory" function in specific ways. Of course, the ways in which scientists such as Maxwell and Boltzmann used these terms may be different from—or at least not precisely identical to—my use of them. In the previous section, I have simply followed scientists' own use of the terms. But in the present section I will analyze a historical episode from the perspective of my theory of understanding, so I will strictly keep to my own terminology. This is especially important in the following cases:

- Intelligibility: This term has been used loosely in the previous section because scientists used the term in various ways: sometimes they spoke about rendering phenomena intelligible through models, at other times they referred to the intelligibility of the models themselves (e.g., when arguing that only mechanical models are intelligible, a claim that Maxwell justified with a Kantian argument). In the analysis that follows, the epithet "intelligible" will be used only for theories or models, not for phenomena.
- Model and theory: As noted earlier, nineteenth-century physicists typically reserved the term "model" for concrete, tangible objects such as scale models (Bailer-Jones 2009, 27–29). Abstract models, such as Maxwell's mechanical model of the ether, were usually called "analogies." The notion of "model" is used in a different way in my theory of understanding, although it will turn out that the models and analogies of nineteenth-century physicists often functioned in accordance with my theory. In the analysis that follows, the notions of model and theory will be used as defined in section 2.2. A model represents a target system (the phenomenon-to-be-explained) in such a way that a theory can be applied to it. In Morgan and Morrison's (1999) terms, the model "mediates" between theory and the phenomenon. If this is successful, one has constructed an explanation and achieved understanding of the phenomenon.

As was noted in section 2.2, the distinction between theory and model cannot always be drawn sharply. The kinetic theory of gases provides a clear example. This theory represents real gases (its target systems) as aggregates of particles that behave according to the laws of Newtonian mechanics. Thus, the

theory already provides a general model of gases. In order to explain particular gas phenomena on the basis of the kinetic theory, more specific models
(e.g., of particle structure) have to be constructed.[25] In this case there is good
reason for drawing the distinction between theory and model as follows: the
representation of gases as aggregates of molecules in motion is part of the theory, while the representation of molecules as, for example, elastic spheres is a
specific model. This is because all kinetic theories share the former model of
a gas while the latter model of a molecule is not an essential part of the theory
(kinetic theory can operate on different molecular models).

The first mature versions of the kinetic theory were published by Rudolf
Clausius in 1857 and by James Clerk Maxwell in 1860. In both cases, the core
of the theory consisted in an application of the laws of classical mechanics to
aggregates of particles (molecules), where the description of the system did
not consist in tracing the motion of each particle individually but in a statistical
treatment (Clausius used a simple averaging procedure, Maxwell's statistical
treatment was more advanced). The elementary model used by both Clausius
and Maxwell was that of the molecule as a hard elastic sphere.[26] Having modeled molecules in this way, kinetic theory supplies equations for the behavior
of the system. Clausius thus succeeded in explaining well-known experimental gas laws such as the Boyle-Charles law and Gay-Lussac's law, and Maxwell
provided explanations for the transport phenomena of viscosity, heat conduction, and diffusion. Both Clausius and Maxwell also tried to account for experimental knowledge about the so-called specific heat ratio γ, that is, the ratio
between the specific heat at constant pressure and the specific heat at constant
volume. It was known from experiment that different gases have different
specific heat ratios, and such differences can be explained by modeling these
gases as poly-atomic molecules with different energies of translation and/or
rotation. Crucial in these explanations is the so-called equipartition theorem,
which asserts that there is a constant and equal distribution of kinetic energy
over the various possible "modes of motion" (translation, rotation, and/or
vibration) of the molecule.

---

25. Alternatively, one might claim that the kinetic theory consists only of the laws of
Newtonian mechanics (and some additional statistical laws and assumptions), and accordingly does not contain a model of gases. However, this makes it difficult to view the kinetic
theory as a distinct theory, that is, about gases. Thus, it appears that the particle model of
gases forms an essential part of the kinetic theory.

26. Clausius (in Brush 1965, 113) assumed that atoms are absolutely rigid, elastic spheres (or
point particles) and that molecules that are composed of several atoms are capable of rotation and vibration. Maxwell (1986, 286–287) treated atoms as centers of force, or smooth
hard elastic spheres, and poly-atomic molecules as constituted of such atoms.

The first equipartition theorem was formulated by Clausius, who postulated that the total amount of energy of translatory motion of the particles was uniformly distributed over the three directions of translation. It is important to note that Clausius's postulate differed from later versions of the theorem of equipartition. Whereas in later years equipartition was assumed (and eventually proved) to apply to all modes of motion, in Clausius's theory it was applied only to translatory motion. Nonetheless, Clausius did recognize the possibility of internal motion (rotation and/or vibration) of the particles, and he assumed that the amount of energy of internal motion was proportional to the amount of translatory energy.[27] With these hypotheses about the partition of kinetic energy, Clausius was able to deduce some consequences concerning the specific heats of gases. In particular, he predicted that specific heats are independent of the temperature of the gas, in accordance with experimental data. Furthermore, he derived a formula for the relation between the ratio of specific heat at constant pressure (C_p) to specific heat at constant volume (C_v) and the ratio of translatory energy to total kinetic energy (K/H):[28]

$$\gamma = \frac{C_p}{C_v} = 1 + \frac{2}{3} \cdot \frac{E_{trans}}{E_{kin}}, \qquad (6.1)$$

in which H is the total kinetic energy (*vis viva*) of the molecules and K the kinetic energy of translatory motion. From the experimentally known fact that for most gases $\gamma = 1.421$ Clausius calculated that $K/H = 0.6315$, and he concluded that in this case there is internal motion of the gas particles. To explain the presence of such internal motion, he suggested that the particles in question are molecules consisting of at least two atoms, permitting rotation and vibration. Thus, Clausius had no difficulty in handling the known facts about specific heats. Nevertheless, he set the stage for what would soon turn out to be the severest problem the kinetic theory had to cope with.

It was Maxwell who, in 1860, hit upon the problem in his first article on the kinetic theory, which was briefly discussed in section 6.1. In this article, Maxwell presented his analysis of gases in terms of a system of elastic, spherical particles as a physical analogy. When turning to specific heats, Maxwell followed Clausius's suggestion and used a poly-atomic, non-spherical molecular

---

27. Clausius (in Brush 1965, 114): "In one and the same gas the translatory motion of the whole molecules will always have a constant relation to the . . . motions of the constituents."

28. This formula is equivalent with formula (12) in Clausius's article; see Brush (1965, 133). N.B.: I have adapted the original formulae to modern usage, but I have tried to keep the changes to a minimum.

model, thus allowing internal motion to take up part of the kinetic energy. Moreover, Maxwell derived a more specific version of the equipartition theorem: in a state of thermal equilibrium the energy of translation equals the energy of rotation of the molecules.[29] This result, however, could not be reconciled with the experimentally obtained value $\gamma = 1.408$ for many common gases, such as oxygen and nitrogen (Maxwell 1860, 318). While the theorem implied that the ratio β of total kinetic energy to translatory energy had to be $\beta = K/H = 2$, from the value $\gamma = 1.408$ it followed that this ratio was 1.634, in agreement with Clausius's results. It was this discrepancy between theory and experiment that later came to be known as the specific heat anomaly.

In his second article "On the Dynamical Theory of Gases" (1867), Maxwell appeared to have accepted the kinetic theory unconditionally.[30] This strengthened commitment is especially clear from his treatment of specific heats, in which he draws a veil over the anomaly (see De Regt 1996, 48–49). But the anomalous data would not disappear so easily. In 1871, Boltzmann, who had been working on the kinetic theory since 1866, brought the anomaly back on stage by generalizing the equipartition theorem.[31] Assuming, like Clausius and Maxwell, that molecules are poly-atomic and thereby capable of translatory as well as internal motion, he proved that the kinetic energy is uniformly distributed over all modes of motion. From this Boltzmann derived the theoretical value $\gamma = 1.33$ for the ratio of specific heats, which implied that the anomalous experimental value $\gamma = 1.41$ was still unexplained.

In 1875, Maxwell reviewed the state of the art in molecular science in his lecture "On the Dynamical Evidence of the Molecular Constitution of Bodies."[32] He argued that the kinetic theory was immensely successful in many respects, but he also showed a renewed awareness of the anomaly. At this point he employed a new tool, the notion of "degree of freedom," to model molecules.[33]

---

29. Maxwell (1986, 316–317): "the average *vis viva* [kinetic energy, HdR] of translation along each of the three axes is the same in all the systems, and equal to the average *vis viva* of rotation about each of the three principal axes of rotation of each particle." His reasoning was, however, fallacious; see Brush (1976, 344–345). In his 1860 article Maxwell did not consider vibrational motion.

30. J. C. Maxwell, "On the Dynamical Theory of Gases" (1867), reprinted in Maxwell (1986, 415–472).

31. L. Boltzmann, "Über das Wärmegleichgewicht zwischen mehratomigen Gasmolekülen" (1871), reprinted in Boltzmann (1968, 1:237–258).

32. J. C. Maxwell, "On the Dynamical Evidence of the Molecular Constitution of Bodies" (1875), reprinted in Maxwell (1986, 216–237); see esp. 229–231.

33. Maxwell had introduced the concept of "degrees of freedom" in 1870 (Maxwell 1965, 2:171).

Maxwell assumed that "the position and configuration of the molecule can be completely expressed by a certain number of variables" and added:

> Let us call this number n. Of these variables, three are required to determine the position of the centre of mass of the molecule, and the remaining $n - 3$ to determine its configuration relative to its centre of mass. To each of the variables corresponds a different kind of motion. (Maxwell 1986, 230)

Subsequently, Maxwell presented a new formula for the specific heat ratio:

$$\gamma = \frac{C_p}{C_v} = 1 + \frac{2}{3} \cdot \frac{E_{trans}}{E_{kin}}, \tag{6.2}$$

where n is number of degrees of freedom, and e is a quantity depending on the binding forces in the molecule; e accounts for the relative amount of heat that is stored as potential energy in the molecule. Comparison with experimental values of specific heats led Maxwell to conclude that $n + e$ "for air and several other gases cannot be more than 4.9," since the experiments have determined that $\gamma = 1.408$. Furthermore, these gases cannot consist of monatomic molecules: such molecules have no internal structure and therefore only three degrees of freedom ($n = 3$), which yields $\gamma = 1.66$, a value not yet observed for any gas. Moreover, spectroscopic research had shown that most gases emit spectral lines, the best explanation of which seemed to lie in internal vibration of the molecules. This implies at least six additional degrees of freedom, so that $n \geq 6$ and thereby $\gamma \leq 1.33$. The observed ratio of $\gamma = 1.408$ was thus unexplainable. Maxwell (1986, 232) concluded that this anomaly is "the greatest difficulty yet encountered by the molecular theory."

Only one year after Maxwell's desperate statement, Ludwig Boltzmann proposed a simple and straightforward solution of the specific heat anomaly. Two factors played a crucial part in Boltzmann's train of thought: the concept of degrees of freedom and an experiment by August Kundt and Emil Warburg. Boltzmann's 1876 paper "Über die Natur der Gasmoleküle," in which the solution is described, begins with a treatment of molecules in terms of degrees of freedom (for which Maxwell and H. W. Watson receive credit[34]),

---

34. Boltzmann (1968, 2:103) cites the English term "degrees of freedom" and uses *Beweglichkeitsarten* as German translation. He refers to H. W. Watson's *A Treatise on the Kinetic Theory of Gases* (1876).

leading to a derivation of formula (6.2) for the ratio of specific heats. Next, Boltzmann cites the recent (1875) experimental result of Kundt and Warburg, who had measured the specific heat ratio of mercury vapor and found it to be $\gamma = 1.66$, a value which the kinetic theory predicts for monatomic gases but which had never been observed experimentally. This result was striking because it implied that the mercury molecules behave as material points with only three degrees of freedom, while the observed emission of spectral lines by mercury vapor suggested that the molecules possess an internal structure, implying the presence of additional vibrational degrees of freedom. The observation was thus an unexpected and important, but also paradoxical, success for the kinetic theory. Kundt and Warburg's experiment paved the way for Boltzmann's proposal. In his 1876 article, he interpreted their result as follows:

> From this it does not yet follow, of course, that a molecule of mercury vapor really is a mathematical point, which we know to be already refuted by the spectrum of mercury vapor, but merely that in collisions the mercury molecules behave almost like material points or, if one prefers, like elastic spheres. (Boltzmann 1968, 2:105; my translation)

Subsequently, Boltzmann advanced the hypothesis that the molecules of the gases possessing the anomalous ratio $\gamma = 1.4$ consist of two atoms—material points or smooth elastic spheres—which are rigidly connected (figure 6.4). Such "rigid dumbbells" possess only five degrees of freedom: three of translation and two of rotation, hence $n = 5$. Moreover, since the molecules are absolutely rigid, they cannot store potential energy, hence $e = 0$. Consequently, $\gamma = 1.4$, almost precisely in accordance with the measured value.

This simple model thus provides explanatory understanding of the anomalous specific heat ratios. However, Boltzmann (1968, 2:107) admitted that the "dumbbell model" cannot be a completely realistic description of diatomic molecules, because real gas molecules also have vibrational degrees of freedom, as the emission of spectral lines supposedly showed. Boltzmann stressed that, just as mercury molecules cannot in reality be material points, the molecules of diatomic gases cannot in reality be rigid dumbbells. But it may be concluded, analogously to the case of mercury, that in collision processes diatomic molecules behave as if they are such rigid dumbbells. But how can it be explained that the vibrational degrees of freedom do not affect the specific heats? Boltzmann suggested that the molecular vibrations occur only during a very short time after a collision and are immediately transferred to the surrounding ether, a process comparable to the production of sound by

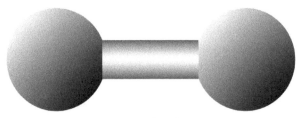

FIGURE 6.4 Boltzmann's dumbbell model of diatomic gases.

colliding billiard balls. In a footnote, he admitted that this hypothesis implies a loss of kinetic energy to the ether and thus requires the additional hypothesis that the molecules absorb energy, for example, from radiation of the walls and other bodies. Boltzmann summarized his conclusion as follows:

> The entire aggregate, which forms a single gas molecule, and which may consist of both ponderable atoms and ether atoms perhaps connected with them, probably *behaves* in its progressive motion and in its collision with other molecules *almost like* a solid body. (Boltzmann 1968, 2:109; my translation and italics)

Maxwell responded to Boltzmann's hypothesis in a review of H. W. Watson's *Treatise on the Kinetic Theory of Gases*. He admitted that this hypothesis yields results that are "in striking agreement with the phenomena of the three groups of gases." Nevertheless, while calling Boltzmann's idea politely a "somewhat promising hypothesis," Maxwell also raised an objection to it. He argued that the rigid elastic bodies that Boltzmann assumed cannot exist:

> It will not do to take a body formed of continuous matter endowed with elastic properties, and to increase the coefficients of elasticity without limit till the body becomes practically rigid. For such a body, though apparently rigid, is in reality capable of internal vibrations, and these of an infinite variety of types, so that the body has an infinite number of degrees of freedom. (Maxwell 1877, 245)

There are two aspects to this criticism of Boltzmann's model. First, Maxwell objects that the dumbbell model is at variance with the laws of mechanics, for rigidity of extended bodies is incompatible with elasticity (see Brush 1976, 354–355). This objection reveals that in his later years Maxwell shifted to a realist view of the kinetic theory and associated mechanical models, as described in section 6.1. On Maxwell's later view, physical reasoning must start from the assumption that all physical systems are governed by the laws of mechanics; he criticized Boltzmann's model for being inconsistent with these laws. The fact that Maxwell himself had used rigid elastic bodies as molecular models in his earlier work on gas theory shows that he changed his attitude toward models. The inconsistency is no obstacle for models that "merely" function as analogies, but it is problematic for a realistic interpretation of models (N.B.: Maxwell did not use the term "model" or "analogy" in his review; he referred to Boltzmann's proposal as a "hypothesis").

Second, Maxwell objected that Boltzmann's hypothesis was at variance with experiment, since rigid molecules are incapable of internal vibration, whereas experiments show that real molecules emit spectral lines, which allegedly implies that they can vibrate.[35] As mentioned, Boltzmann hoped to counter the second objection by invoking a special hypothesis about the interaction with the ether. Maxwell considered this hypothesis but rejected it because the theorem of complete equipartition (which, ironically, had been proven by Boltzmann himself) entailed that any such interaction would lead to an increase of specific heats; an interaction of the kind that Boltzmann suggested was forbidden by the theorem. Maxwell's conclusion was that the specific heat anomaly remained unsolved.

Boltzmann's dumbbell model clearly illustrates that model-building is a non-deductive process. The model is not entailed by the kinetic theory, and it cannot be derived from experimental data either: approximations and idealizations are necessary in order to achieve a fit between model and data.[36] At least one approximation and two idealizations are essential in the case of the dumbbell model:

- Approximation: the value $\gamma = 1.4$ (from which $n + e = 5$ follows) is an inexact description of the experimental data. Maxwell (1860 and 1875) used the experimental value of $\gamma = 1.408$, which entailed $n + e = 4.9$. Clausius (1857) calculated with $\gamma = 1.421$, which would have led to $n + e = 4.75$. Boltzmann used the approximate value $\gamma = 1.4$, "which deviates not too far from the experimentally found values for air and other simple gases" (1968, 2:106; my translation).
- Idealization 1: The dumbbell model represents molecules as absolutely rigid, which implies that heat cannot be stored as potential energy. This entails that $e = 0$.

---

35. Maxwell did not discuss the experimental result of Kundt and Warburg.

36. See Norton (2012, 209) for precise characterizations of the notions of "approximation" and "idealization."

- Idealization 2: The dumbbell model assumes that internal vibrational degrees of freedom do not contribute to specific heats.

Decisions to approximate and idealize in this way belong to the pragmatic dimension of explanation. Boltzmann was the first who was willing to make these pragmatic decisions and to construct the model. Why was Boltzmann's solution not proposed earlier? Clausius and the early Maxwell possessed all relevant theoretical knowledge and experimental data, so why did they not consider the possibility that the molecules of the anomalous gases were rigid dumbbells? I submit that this was because the concept of "degree of freedom," which was introduced only in 1870, functioned as a crucial pragmatic tool for constructing this model. Representing molecules in terms of degrees of freedom allowed scientists to construct different kind of molecular models and to "see" new explanations and predictions on the basis of the kinetic theory. To be sure, the kinetic theory itself remained the same, and it might be objected that the notion of "degrees of freedom" merely offered a new way of representing extant knowledge and did not add new knowledge. But it is precisely this view that I want to challenge. The new tool facilitated the construction of new models, mediating between the theory and the phenomena, and was accordingly crucial to the production of new explanatory and descriptive knowledge. It enhanced the intelligibility of the kinetic theory, and paved the way, via equation (6.2), for the construction of the dumbbell model.

It is important to note that even with the notion of "degrees of freedom" in hand the dumbbell model ($n = 5$ solution) does not follow logically from theory and data: a scientist with suitable skills was needed to "see" the solution by making the necessary approximations and idealizations. This scientist was Ludwig Boltzmann: his skillful use of the tool led him to construct a model for the anomalous gases that provides scientific understanding of the specific heat ratio.[37] The anomalous specific heat ratios could now be understood because an appropriate explanation had become available on the basis of the kinetic theory, which had become more intelligible with the help of the tool of "degrees of freedom." Of course, intelligibility alone is not sufficient: in addition, CUP demands that the explanation should conform to the basic epistemic values of empirical adequacy and internal consistency. It is precisely these two additional requirements that lie at the basis of Maxwell's objections to the dumbbell model and explain his disagreement with Boltzmann.

---

37. Today, every physics student acquires these skills in the course of his or her education, as the dumbbell model has become an exemplary problem solution that is presented in undergraduate textbooks.

First, Maxwell objected to the idealization regarding rigidity, which made the model inconsistent from the perspective of mechanics. Different philosophical commitments lie at the basis of Maxwell's and Boltzmann's opposing attitudes toward this idealization, as described in more detail in De Regt (1996). Second, Maxwell rejected Boltzmann's explanation because it appeared to contradict empirical evidence concerning spectral emission. Here the Maxwell–Boltzmann controversy supports the thesis, defended in section 2.3, that empirical adequacy and consistency do not function as absolute criteria but as values, whose application is not as straightforward and unambiguous as is often assumed. In this case (which is far from unusual) value judgments have to be made, first, about which part of the available evidence is considered most important, and second, about the weight of the model's inconsistency with mechanical principles. Boltzmann and Maxwell made different judgments, and accordingly valued the empirical adequacy and inconsistency of the model differently. This explains why it was Boltzmann and not Maxwell himself who proposed the dumbbell model, even though Maxwell had introduced the concept of degrees of freedom and surely had the skills to construct the model.[38]

Today the dumbbell model is still used by physicists, despite its limitations as an accurate representation.[39] From our current perspective we understand why one of the idealizations that allowed Boltzmann to propose the dumbbell model was justified, despite Maxwell's objections. The crucial assumption that internal vibrational degrees of freedom do not contribute to specific heats hinted at the failure of the equipartition theorem, one of Thomson's clouds that contributed to the breakdown of classical physics and foreshadowed the advent of quantum theory. Because it is quantized, vibrational energy only contributes to the internal energy above certain very high temperatures. For the case of hydrogen (H_2), this temperature is 5400°K; below 5400°K the vibrational degrees of freedom are "frozen" (see Feynman et al. 1963–1965, 1:40–9).[40] This does not imply, however, that idealizations are merely intermediary stages that will be overcome when we have achieved "true knowledge" about the phenomenon. On the contrary, idealizations are part and parcel of scientific practice. Thus, Boltzmann's second idealization

---

38. Cf. Kelp and Douven (2012), who cite this case as an example of what they call "rational disagreement."

39. For an example, see Netz et al. (2006).

40. The same holds for rotational vibration, but here the temperature of "freezing" is much lower: 60°K, so that these degrees of freedom contribute to specific heats at room temperature. For other diatomic gases the freezing temperatures are different.

(the assumption of rigidity) still applies in a quantum-mechanical treatment of diatomic molecules.

6.3 Boltzmann's *Bildtheorie*: a pragmatic view of understanding

In spite of Maxwell's criticisms, Boltzmann did not abandon his dumbbell model. Almost twenty-five years later, in "On the Development of the Methods of Theoretical Physics in Recent Times" (1899), he claimed that "the distinctively molecular theory of the ratio of the two specific heats of gases has ... resumed an important role today" (Boltzmann 1974, 98). He did not mention the problem of molecular vibrations and spectral lines, which was still unsolved. But in response to these and other problems of the kinetic theory, Boltzmann abandoned his earlier hard-headed realism and adopted the view that scientific theories are "mental pictures" that do not coincide with reality but may still help us to reveal some of nature's secrets. To be sure, he believed that the fundamental hypothesis of the kinetic theory of gases must be true: "[The Theory of Gases] agrees in so many respects with the facts, that we can hardly doubt that in gases certain entities, the number and size of which can be roughly determined, fly about pell-mell." But he added immediately:

> Can it be seriously expected that [these entities] behave exactly as aggregates of Newtonian centres of force, or as rigid bodies of our Mechanics? And how awkward is the human mind in divining the nature of things, when forsaken by the analogy of what we see and touch directly? (Boltzmann 1974, 202)

Although Boltzmann weakened his position, he did not become an anti-realist: he still adhered to a form of realism by asserting the reality of atoms and molecules as such. His mature epistemological view, the so-called "picture-theory" or *Bildtheorie*, complemented this realism: it provided a philosophical justification for the use of theories that resist a completely realistic interpretation. Boltzmann's *Bildtheorie* has been discussed extensively in the literature (Hiebert 1981; Miller 1986; Wilson 1989, 1993; D'Agostino 1990; Blackmore 1995). It is usually taken to be an answer to the epistemological question of whether (and if so, how) scientific theories are representations of reality.[41] In his book *Scientific Representation* (2008), Bas van Fraassen

---

41. Heinrich Hertz defended a similar conception of scientific theories; see De Regt (1999a, 116–117) for an assessment of the relation between Boltzmann's and Hertz's views.

presents Boltzmann's *Bildtheorie* as an inspiration for a structuralist view of representation in science (defending an empiricist alternative to structural realism). However, as was described in section 6.1, Boltzmann also saw a central role for pictures (*Bilder*) in relation to the explanatory task of science. Mechanical pictures and models, in particular, may facilitate understanding of phenomena, even if they cannot always be interpreted realistically. In this section, I will examine the *Bildtheorie* in more detail, drawing attention to the pragmatic conception of scientific understanding that Boltzmann associated with it.

The earliest formulation of the *Bildtheorie* can be found in the 1890 address "On the Significance of Theories," where Boltzmann (1974, 33) stated that the "task of theory consists in constructing a picture of the external world that exists purely internally and must be our guiding star in all thought and experiment." His 1899 essay "On the Development of the Methods of Theoretical Physics in Recent Times" contains a more elaborate exposition of the *Bildtheorie*, which Boltzmann (1974, 90–91) traces back to Maxwell and Hertz: "Hertz makes physicists properly aware of something philosophers had no doubt long since stated, namely that no theory can be objective, actually coinciding with nature, but rather that each theory is only a mental picture of phenomena, related to them as sign is to designatum."[42] He adds that this implies that "it cannot be our task to find an absolutely correct theory but rather a picture that is as simple as possible and represents the phenomena as accurately as possible." As D'Agostino (1990, 383) observes, with the *Bildtheorie* "Boltzmann succeeds in obtaining a remarkable balance between the opposite pretensions of crude phenomenology and crude (ontological) atomism."[43]

However, the controversy between Boltzmann and phenomenalists like Ernst Mach and Gustav Kirchhoff did not only concern the epistemological interpretation of theories (realism vs. instrumentalism) but also the issue of whether the aim of science is explanatory or descriptive. While Mach and Kirchhoff considered the aim of science to be mere (economical) description of observable phenomena, Boltzmann held that science must strive for explanations of the phenomena. In the case of atomism, this means that the

---

42. For similar formulations of the *Bildtheorie*, see Boltzmann (1974, 83, 104, 141, 225). Van Fraassen (2008, 1–2) claims that Boltzmann's conception of *Bilder* as "mental representations" involves an outdated philosophy of mind. Even without the idea of mental representation, however, the *Bildtheorie* remains a viable account of the relation between models and the real-world systems they aim to represent.

43. In De Regt (1996), I have analyzed Boltzmann's philosophy by distinguishing between an epistemological and a methodological component, which combine to a form of "constructive realism."

question is not only whether the atoms postulated by the kinetic theory really exist or are merely instruments for describing and predicting observable gas phenomena. An equally important question is whether an atomistic approach gives more understanding of the behavior of gases than a phenomenological one (such as thermodynamics). If the answer to the latter question is affirmative, as Boltzmann claimed, then what accounts for this difference? Boltzmann's *Bildtheorie* blocks the simple and straightforward answer of the naïve realist, to wit that the kinetic theory provides understanding because it describes the "deeper truth" about the constitution of gases. But how can a scientific theory provide understanding in a different way? My own view has been given in section 4.5.1, and we shall now see that Boltzmann answered the question along similar lines.

In section 6.1, I observed that Boltzmann regarded explanation as a central aim of science, suggesting that explanation of complex phenomena is possible by developing theories that employ "clear pictures borrowed from the sphere of the simpler phenomena" (Boltzmann 1974, 149). According to Boltzmann, mechanical models are the prime examples of such clear pictures; their intelligibility can be traced back to our laws of thought, which have been formed by evolution. But Boltzmann's evolutionary view of laws of thought implies that the intelligibility of mechanical pictures is merely contingent and that mechanical explanation may fail when one enters new, as yet unknown domains of physical reality. This is exactly what turned out to be the case at the end of the nineteenth century, when fundamental problems in electromagnetic theory, on the one hand, and thermodynamics and statistical mechanics, on the other, resisted explanation in mechanical terms. These "clouds over the dynamical theory of heat and light," as William Thomson called them, ultimately gave rise to relativity and quantum theory, respectively. The first cloud was related to the failure to detect the motion of the ether by the Michelson-Morley experiment, an anomaly that was resolved by Einstein's theory of special relativity of 1905. The second cloud concerned questions about the validity of Boltzmann's equipartition theorem, of which the specific heat anomaly had been a harbinger. Among the difficulties surrounding the equipartition theorem was the failure to derive an empirically adequate distribution law for blackbody radiation, a problem that led Max Planck to postulate the existence of energy quanta in 1900.

Toward the turn of the century, Boltzmann was well aware of the limitations of the program of mechanical explanation and of the fact that a scientific metaphysics based only on mechanics appeared untenable. His *Bildtheorie* dealt with this by rejecting a naïvely realistic interpretation of mechanical models while regarding them as useful tools for achieving explanatory understanding of observable phenomena (and thus more than merely instruments for economical description of the phenomena, as Mach would have it). In Boltzmann's own words: "we invent [*fingieren*] the atoms for the explanation [*Erklärung*] of the phenomena" (Fasol-Boltzmann 1990, 275; my translation). In the lemma "Model" for the 1902 edition of the *Encyclopaedia Britannica*, Boltzmann elucidated the explanatory function of mechanical models in relation to their *Bild*-character in more detail:

> But while it was formerly believed that it was allowable to assume with a great show of probability the actual existence of such mechanisms in nature, yet nowadays philosophers postulate no more than a partial resemblance between the phenomena visible in such mechanisms and those which appear in nature. Here again it is perfectly clear that these models of wood, metal and cardboard are really a continuation and integration of our processes of thought; for ... physical theory is merely a mental construction of mechanical models, the working of which we make plain to ourselves by analogy of mechanisms we hold in our hands, and which have so much in common with natural phenomena as to help our comprehension of the latter. (Boltzmann 1974, 218)

Thus, while Boltzmann qualified the representational value of mechanical pictures and models, he remained convinced of their value as tools for understanding. But what kind of understanding do mechanical models provide, if they cannot be conceived as accurate representations of reality? When trying to answer this question, Boltzmann found himself drawn to pragmatism:

> The task of our thinking is so to use and combine [mental pictures] that by their means we always most readily hit upon the correct actions and guide others likewise. In this, metaphysics follows the most down-to-earth and practical point of view, so that extremes meet. (Boltzmann 1974, 104)

Reflecting upon the scope of mechanical explanation, Boltzmann (1974, 149–150) considered the possibility that electromagnetism is more fundamental than mechanics, so that the electromagnetic ether would be the "mechanism" that explains mechanical phenomena. His conclusion was quoted already in section 6.1: "It was no longer a question of explaining everything mechanically, but of finding a mechanism to explain all mechanisms." Boltzmann continued:

What, then, is meant by having perfectly correct understanding of a mechanism? Everybody knows that the practical criterion for this consists in being able to handle it correctly. However, I go further and assert that this is the only tenable definition of understanding a mechanism. (Boltzmann 1974, 150)[44]

Accordingly, Boltzmann had a thoroughly pragmatic view of understanding. Boltzmann identifies "understanding" with "knowing the right thing to do in all circumstances." This pragmatic stance is related to his commitment to Darwinism, particularly his evolutionary view of laws of thought, which implies that criteria for understanding are grounded in, and justified by, their practical success. While the Darwinist traits in Boltzmann's philosophy are generally acknowledged, his penchant for pragmatism has gone largely unnoticed. Only John Blackmore (1995, 78–82) has paid serious attention to the elements of pragmatism in Boltzmann's philosophy of science. Erwin Hiebert (1981, 181) had earlier called Boltzmann a "pragmatic realist" but did not relate this to philosophical pragmatism. In the remaining part of this section, I will investigate Boltzmann's inclination to pragmatism, elaborating on Blackmore's analysis, and argue that it lies at the root of his views on scientific understanding.

Philosophical pragmatism, founded by Charles Sanders Peirce and William James, is first of all a theory of meaning and truth. It was Peirce who introduced the term "pragmatism." In his version of it the central idea is that the meaning of a concept is given by its practical uses and effects. In Peirce's own words: "Consider what effects, which might conceivably have practical bearings, we conceive the object of our perception to have. Then our conception of these effects is the whole of our conception of the object" (Peirce 1878, 293). William James further developed pragmatism and turned it into a theory of truth, which asserts that a doctrine (theory, statement) is true if it has desirable consequences: "an idea is 'true' so long as to believe it is profitable to our lives" (James 1907, 75). I will argue that there are similarities between such pragmatic ideas and the views of Boltzmann. A very clear example is the following remark, which seems an explicit endorsement of Peircian pragmatism: "How we are to form our concepts cannot be defined and is indeed quite indifferent, so long as they always lead to the correct mode of action" (Boltzmann 1974, 150).[45]

---

44. The German original contains the terms *Verstehen* and *Verständnis*, respectively, which are here both translated as "understanding" (Boltzmann 1979, 196).

45. Whether there has been a direct influence of Peirce or James on Boltzmann, for example, whether they met during Boltzmann's travels in the United States, is doubtful. Boltzmann

Boltzmann's first step in the direction of pragmatism was taken in the 1890s, when he had to defend atomic theory against the attacks of phenomenalists and energeticists. In these debates, Boltzmann argued that atomism was preferable for its practical virtues: theories that employ mechanical pictures are heuristically more fruitful. His strategy was to avoid having to claim that atoms do exist, and to lay emphasis on their indispensability in scientific practice. Several authors have noticed Boltzmann's pragmatically oriented argumentation and have related it in one way or another to the attenuated realism of Boltzmann's *Bildtheorie* (Hiebert 1981, 180–181; D'Agostino 1990, 383–384,). On the other hand, the thesis that atoms are merely "a useful picture" might have been just an "extremely cunning" argumentative strategy against the anti-atomists, as Gerhard Fasol claims (Fasol-Boltzmann 1990, 66), having no implications for Boltzmann's own position regarding the existence of atoms (which according to Fasol was still uncompromisingly realist). We will see, however, that the argumentation is more plausibly regarded as a first step toward the more radical philosophical pragmatism held by Boltzmann after 1900.

Already in 1897, in his essay "On the Question of the Objective Existence of Processes in Inanimate Nature," Boltzmann had hinted at applying a pragmatic conception of truth to scientific theories:

Actions that are followed by things we desire and ideas under whose guidance we act in this manner we denote as correct [*richtig*]. We must aim at having ideas that are correct and economical as well, that is we are to be able always to reach the correct mode of action with the least expenditure of time and effort. The demand on any theory is that it be correct and economical. (Boltzmann 1974, 58)

Nevertheless, it was only after the turn of the century that Boltzmann came out in defense of pragmatism more strongly, as first noticed by Blackmore (1995, 78–82).[46] Blackmore relates this to Boltzmann's view of *Bilder* as idealizations: theoretical physics cannot do without idealizations and therefore it needs a non-correspondence theory of truth. Thus, in 1904, Boltzmann (1974, 261) stated: "We call these mental pictures true only because they are useful in predicting future phenomena as completely and effortlessly as possible." Of

---

never referred to them in his writings or lectures. According to Blackmore (1995, 80), there is a possible but as yet unproven influence.

46. Blackmore (1995, 81) adds, however, that Boltzmann's attachment to pragmatism "was not complete since he could not go all the way maintaining with James . . . that what didn't work was 'meaningless.'"

course, this claim might also be interpreted in plainly instrumentalist, anti-realist terms. However, further evidence that Boltzmann tended to pragmatism abounds in his *Lectures on Natural Philosophy 1903–1906*. Again and again Boltzmann employed the term *zweckmäßig* (efficient) and stated that formation and appraisal of concepts, laws of thought, and scientific theories should be based on considerations of efficiency only. The reason for this is that science, like any other human activity, is a Darwinian struggle to cope with our environment: a scientific theory "should always enable us to intervene appropriately [*richtig*] in nature, so that we can attain appropriate effects" (Fasol-Boltzmann 1990, 168, cf. 85, 161, 163). As noted, according to Boltzmann, innate ideas are not infallible a priori truths but selected for their efficiency in the course of human evolution. This view led him to endorse a pragmatic conception of truth: "Both the innate and the acquired should be tested by experience again and again; only if it proves its mettle always, if it leads to correct action always, . . . is it correct" (Fasol-Boltzmann 1990, 164). Boltzmann regards practical success as the sole criterion for being correct (*richtig*). It is telling that he always uses the term *richtig*, which means "correct" or "true" in a more pragmatic sense, and never the term *wahr*, which means "true" but is more easily associated with a correspondence theory of truth.

It is crucial to assess Boltzmann's inclination to a pragmatic theory of truth in the broader context of his Darwinist worldview. Boltzmann's admiration for Darwin was unlimited and induced him to regard all human cognitive faculties—and therefore science—as products of evolution. Thus, he arrived at a form of naturalistic, evolutionary epistemology, in which the *Bildtheorie* is connected with a pragmatic approach to cognition: "To think means to form oneself pictures with which one can act correctly" (Fasol-Boltzmann 1990, 71). One of the implications of this all-pervading Darwinism seems to be his position with respect to scientific understanding and explanation, which is reflected in his definition of understanding, quoted above. In the 1902 inaugural lecture in which Boltzmann proposes this definition, pragmatism appears to be a basic thread. Moreover, it contains repeated allusions to a Darwinist worldview. The lecture begins with a description of the development of mechanics with strong emphasis on its practical significance, hinting at the survival value of mechanical tools. Boltzmann then moves on to discuss abstract analytical mechanics and arrives at his characterization of the explanatory aim of science. This leads him to his pragmatic definition of the notion of understanding. He defends it by invoking a pragmatic theory of meaning, which is in turn illustrated with a pragmatic argument against solipsism.[47]

---

47. Boltzmann (1974, 150) claims that he had proven solipsism false when he discovered that "it led to my failing to take the right practical action and caused me great damage."

In conclusion, in Boltzmann's philosophy of science, there is an intimate relationship between Darwinism, pragmatism, and the status and function of *Bilder*. On the one hand, Boltzmann's *Bilder* have a representative function. As representations they are "merely" idealizations and therefore a pragmatic conception of truth is applicable, as emphasized by Blackmore (1995, 80–81). Moreover, *Bilder* have an explanatory function. The way in which they fulfill this task, namely by being tools for understanding (and thus ultimately for survival), also has a pragmatic foundation. Obviously, these aspects are two sides of the same coin.

6.4 The uses and limitations of mechanical models

Mechanical models were important tools for understanding phenomena in nineteenth-century physics. In this chapter, I have examined the scientific work and philosophical ideas of leading nineteenth-century physicists Thomson, Maxwell, and Boltzmann, who regarded mechanical explanation as the best if not the only way to achieve understanding. The way in which mechanical models functioned has been illustrated by a detailed study of their use in explaining gas phenomena on the basis of the kinetic theory. My account of Boltzmann's construction of the dumbbell model for diatomic molecules to explain the specific heat anomaly highlights the role of conceptual tools in achieving understanding of the phenomena. In particular, the concept of "degrees of freedom" served as a conceptual tool that facilitated the construction of new models, mediating between the kinetic theory and the observed phenomena regarding specific heats. This tool enhanced the intelligibility of the kinetic theory and allowed for the construction of the dumbbell model.

Toward the end of the nineteenth century, the program of mechanical explanation ran into serious difficulties. It became clear that some physical phenomena resisted explanation in mechanical terms, and younger physicists turned away from the mechanical models advocated by Thomson. It was no longer believed, for example, that mechanical models of the ether were useful for understanding electromagnetic phenomena. Instead, the new generation of theoretical physicists followed Hertz's suggestion that "Maxwell's theory is Maxwell's system of equations" (Hertz 1893, 21). Thomson's famous dictum, quoted at the beginning of this chapter, had become a thing of the past: the idea that mechanical models are a *sine qua non* for intelligibility and understanding was abandoned. This development went hand in hand with a rising tide of philosophical criticism of the mechanical approach, of which Mach and Duhem were the most prominent representatives. Duhem's attack on the "ample but weak English mind," which could not understand without mechanical models, has been discussed in section 6.1. An earlier critic of the mechanical program was Mach, who denounced it—and atomism in particular—as being without a proper foundation. In his influential 1883 book *Die Mechanik in ihrer Entwicklung*, he stated: "The view that makes mechanics the basis of the remaining branches of physics, and explains all phenomena by mechanical ideas, is in our judgment a prejudice" (Mach [1883] 1960, 596). He argued that from a historical point of view it is understandable that the program of mechanical explanation had dominated the scientific scene for such a long time, but that there was no reason to regard it as a priori superior to alternative modes of explanation. In particular, Mach claimed that the tendency to regard mechanical models and explanations as inherently intelligible is misguided, and merely a result of the historical fact that people have been more accustomed to mechanical phenomena (cf. the discussion of Mach's views in section 5.1):

> It is the result of a misconception, to believe, as people do at the present time, that mechanical facts are more intelligible [*verständlicher*] than others, and that they can provide the foundation for other physical effects. This belief arises from the fact that the history of mechanics is older and richer than that of physics, so that we have been on terms of intimacy with mechanical facts for a longer time. Who can say that, at some future time, electrical and thermal phenomena will not appear to us like that, when we have come to know and to be familiar with their simplest rules? (Mach [1872] 1911, 56)

According to Mach ([1872] 1911, 55–57), the only aim of science is to provide economical descriptions of empirical facts, and explaining phenomena means nothing more than analyzing them and relating them to simple facts in such a way that the most economical systematization results. It is a mistake to think that these simple facts are more intelligible, and that explanation consists in a reduction of the unintelligible to the intelligible. On the contrary: "These simplest facts, to which we reduce the more complicated ones, are always unintelligible in themselves, that is to say, they are not further resolvable." (55). In sum, Mach believed that the idea that science provides understanding by reducing phenomena to inherently intelligible basic facts is an illusion.

   Apart from his claim that one cannot ascribe an intrinsic intelligibility to mechanical explanations such as provided by the kinetic theory of gases, Mach ([1872] 1911, 57) criticized atomism and the molecular theory for being purely speculative and not adding anything useful to science: "molecules are merely a valueless image [*werthloses Bild*]." This radical claim was disputed by Boltzmann, and rightly so, for both the episode described in section 6.3 and the subsequent development of physics in the twentieth century have proved that atomism remains a highly productive thesis, notwithstanding the limitations of the mechanical view of nature. To be sure, Mach's analysis of the intelligibility of mechanical models is partly correct: intelligibility is a historically contingent property and accordingly not absolute but contextual. Mach was also right to claim that mechanics should not be regarded as an a priori foundation of science, as quantum mechanics has made abundantly clear. But he threw out the baby with the bathwater when denying intelligibility a positive role and rejecting the use of mechanical models of molecules. The history of the kinetic theory of gases, and Boltzmann's work on the specific heat anomaly, in particular, shows that the (contextual) intelligibility of the kinetic theory and associated mechanical models has had epistemic value and has contributed to the advancement of scientific understanding.

Accordingly, a molecular model is indeed an image, as Mach writes, but not a "valueless image." Boltzmann's *Bildtheorie*, developed in response to Mach's philosophical critique and to the scientific problems of the mechanical program, specifies the limits as well as the value of molecular models. The fact that mechanical models of molecules do not mirror real processes in nature does not preclude them from having an explanatory function. However, while mechanical models were the ideal tools for understanding in the nineteenth-century context, their appeal and applicability lessened in the twentieth century, when classical physics was replaced by relativistic and quantum physics. Contrary to what Lord Kelvin once believed, it became clear that mechanical modeling has limitations and hence cannot be essential for scientific understanding. In the next chapter we will examine how physicists searched for new tools to cope with the unexpected challenges of twentieth-century atomic physics.

7

Visualizability and Intelligibility

INSIGHT INTO THE QUANTUM WORLD

ORDINARY LANGUAGE OFTEN uses visual metaphors in connection with understanding. When we finally understand what someone is trying to point out to us, we exclaim: "I see!" When someone really understands a subject-matter, we say that she has "insight." There appears to be a link between visualization and understanding, and between visualizability and intelligibility. As we saw in chapter 4, this applies equally well in science: visualization is regarded as a useful guide to achieving scientific understanding, even in the most esoteric and abstract areas of science. Theoretical physicist Richard Feynman, for example, was so successful in scientific research and teaching because he employed visualization in a highly effective way. When dealing with the very abstract mathematical theories of quantum electrodynamics and quantum chromodynamics, physicists happily rely on visualizations, such as Feynman diagrams and the MIT bag model, to achieve understanding of particular phenomena. In sum, visualization appears to be an important tool for understanding.

In chapter 4, it was observed that for many scientists visualizability enhances the intelligibility of a theory, and some examples have been given to show how exactly visualization can yield understanding. In the present chapter, I will investigate the relation between visualizability and intelligibility in more detail, by means of an in-depth study of the case that was already presented in chapter 1: the transition from classical physics to quantum physics in the first decades of the twentieth century. In this development, which concerned the construction of a theory of the structure of atoms, the issue of visualizability played a central role. The possibility and desirability of visualization in atomic theory was debated chiefly by physicists who wrote in German. The German word for visualizability is *Anschaulichkeit*, a term that can also mean "intelligibility" in a more general sense. This linguistic connection between visualizability and intelligibility was fruitfully employed by Erwin Schrödinger, one of the protagonists in this turbulent episode in the history of physics. He argued that the only way to obtain understanding of nature is to construct theories that are visualizable in space and time because:

> we cannot really alter our manner of thinking in space and time, and what we cannot comprehend within it we cannot understand at all. There *are* such things—but I do not believe that atomic structure is one of them. (Schrödinger 1928, 27)[1]

Science is based on the presupposition that nature is understandable, Schrödinger ([1954] 1996, 278–279) argues, and such understanding can only be achieved in space and time. In other words, spatiotemporal visualizability is a necessary condition for scientific understanding. Schrödinger's conclusion was that any acceptable scientific theory must be visualizable. He employed this argument in defense of his quantum theory of wave mechanics, the *Anschaulichkeit* of which supposedly made it superior to the rival quantum theory: Heisenberg's abstract, non-visualizable theory of matrix mechanics. As my analysis of this episode will show, Schrödinger's emphasis on *Anschaulichkeit* was not merely a rhetorical strategy: the visualizability of his theory turned out to be an epistemically significant feature of it, contributing to the understanding of atomic phenomena. Nevertheless, Heisenberg's approach carried the day and subsequently Heisenberg proposed a reinterpretation of the notion of *Anschaulichkeit*. This reinterpretation, which implies that visualizability is not a necessary condition for intelligibility, inspired the criterion for intelligibility CIT_1 (see section 4.2). It implies that visualization is but one out of many tools for understanding, albeit one that has proved very effective in science.

The chapter is structured as follows. Section 7.1 examines the role of visualizability in classical physics. Three subsequent sections present a description of the gradual loss of visualizability in the development of quantum theory, and an investigation of how quantum physicists Bohr, Pauli, Heisenberg, and Schrödinger assessed the relation between visualizability and intelligibility. This is done by analyzing the historical development of Bohr's ideas and the so-called old quantum theory (7.2), the contest between Schrödinger's wave

---

1. The German original contains the term *verstehen* twice, which is translated as "comprehend" and "understand," respectively.

mechanics and Heisenberg's matrix mechanics (7.3), and the discovery of electron spin (7.4). Finally, section 7.5 analyzes the role of visualization in postwar quantum physics, focusing on Feynman diagrams as tools for understanding.

7.1 Visualizability and intelligibility in classical physics

Expositions of the strange and counterintuitive features of quantum theory often draw a contrast with the theories of classical physics, which are allegedly intuitively clear and in accordance with our experiences from daily life. It is typically taken for granted that, in contrast to quantum physics, classical physics is causal, deterministic, continuous, local, and visualizable. But is this really true? If we restrict ourselves to the issue of *Anschaulichkeit*, of visualizability and intelligibility, what was the situation before the advent of quantum theory? Are all theories of classical physics *anschaulich*: Are they visualizable and thereby intelligible?

In his book *Zum Weltbild der Physik*, Carl Friedrich von Weizsäcker (1970, 81) observes that physicists tend to identify *anschaulich* with "classical" because "classical physics describes all physical phenomena as states of quantities in three-dimensional, Euclidean space and as changes of these states in one-dimensional, objective time." This idea is in line with Immanuel Kant's project of establishing a philosophical foundation for Newtonian mechanics, the paradigm theory of classical physics. A basic tenet of Kant's epistemology is that our sensory impressions are structured by the *Anschauungsformen* ("forms of intuition") of space and time. Consequently, our knowledge of the phenomena is necessarily of a spatiotemporal kind and *Anschaulichkeit* in the sense of space-time visualizability is a prerequisite for natural science.[2] Newtonian mechanics was exemplary in this respect and at the end of the eighteenth century and in the early nineteenth century, when Newtonian physics reigned supreme, nobody questioned the idea that intelligibility and visualizability were inherently connected. Von Weizsäcker's analysis is supported by Dennis Dieks (2001), who emphasizes that classical theories of physics can always be formulated as space-time theories in which physical quantities are represented as functions on a manifold of space-time points. According to Dieks (2001, 223), "the space-time points, forming the arena in which the

---

2. For Kant this was a necessary but not a sufficient condition for knowledge and understanding: sensory impressions have to be grasped by means of concepts in order to yield intelligible knowledge. Compare his famous dictum: "Thoughts without content are empty, intuitions without concepts are blind."

game of theory is played, guarantee *Anschaulichkeit* and the associated kind of intelligibility." However, it seems that, at least in practice, not all classical theories are immediately visualizable. Consider, for example, thermodynamics. Of course, this theory describes physical systems in three-dimensional space and their evolution in time. But it appears quite difficult to visualize thermodynamic properties of these systems (such as pressure, temperature, and entropy), their evolution and the relations between them. Other cases in point are Maxwell's theory of electromagnetism and the theory of statistical mechanics. To be sure, there does not seem to be an argument against the in-principle possibility of visualization in these cases (as would be the case with theories that cannot be formulated as space-time theories). Nonetheless, visualization seems practically impossible in some cases. The reason is that nineteenth-century physics had already become more abstract and had drifted away from the paradigm visualizable theory of classical mechanics. It follows that the space-time character of a theory is a necessary condition for its visualizability, but does not appear to be a sufficient condition: cases like thermodynamics indicate that space-time theories are sometimes hardly visualizable. The *Anschaulichkeit* of classical physics is therefore less trivial than is often suggested.

Does the apparent non-visualizability of some classical theories inhibit their intelligibility? Did nineteenth-century scientists have problems with lack of visualizability, and did they doubt the intelligibility of those theories, just as Schrödinger questioned the intelligibility of quantum theory? As we saw in the previous chapter, leading physicists such as William Thomson and James Clerk Maxwell regarded mechanical explanation as the best way to achieve understanding and intelligibility. An important reason for this was the geometrical nature and visualizability of mechanical models (for Maxwell this was connected with his Kantian view of space and time; see section 6.1.2). Toward the end of the nineteenth century, however, the program of mechanical explanation ran into serious difficulties, and rival approaches burst onto the scene: phenomenalism, energetics, and the electromagnetic worldview. In the context of the debates between these different viewpoints, Ludwig Boltzmann developed his *Bildtheorie*, discussed in section 6.3. While Boltzmann's conception of a scientific theory as a "picture" (*Bild*) is first of all intended as a warning against taking theories as a true representations of states of affairs and processes in nature, it also emphasizes the role of pictures in the more specific sense of visualizations. In his *Vorlesungen über Maxwells Theorie der Elektricität und des Lichtes*, which contains many mechanical models of electromagnetic phenomena, Boltzmann argued that a mechanical analogy may help us to obtain a visualization (*Versinnlichung*) of the consequences of a scientific theory. And an important function of visualization is that it may enhance our understanding. Indeed, Boltzmann (1974, 143) argued that explanation by means of mechanical pictures is preferable because it leads to the most intelligible accounts of nature: "In that case nature would appear to us at its most comprehensible [*begreiflichsten*]." Although it is a contingent fact that mechanical pictures appear most intelligible to us, and nature might ultimately resist this desired mode of understanding, we cannot easily change our intellectual capacities and therefore we must continue to look for mechanical pictures. That is why Boltzmann continued the program of mechanical explanation even after 1900 and remained committed to mechanical pictures as an ideal of intelligibility.

In sum, reflection on the nature of classical physics leads to the conclusion that the space-time framework, in which classical theories are formulated, is a necessary condition for visualizability, but not a sufficient condition. Many theories of nineteenth-century classical physics had already such a degree of abstraction that visualization was not immediately possible. This was one of the reasons that nineteenth-century physicists did not take the intelligibility of classical theories for granted, as is clear from the fact that they tried hard to construct pictorial, mechanical models of, for example, electromagnetic and thermodynamic phenomena. As we saw in chapter 6, these attempts were only partially successful, and the hope that all physical phenomena could be explained mechanically was abandoned by many around the turn of the century. However, the move away from visualizability and the associated intelligibility had already set in earlier, and therefore the transition from classical physics to quantum physics was—at least in this respect—less revolutionary than is often believed.

7.2 Quantum theory and the waning of *Anschaulichkeit*

The theories of classical physics presuppose a space-time framework, thereby meeting at least a necessary requirement for visualizability. We have seen that this does not yet guarantee visualizability: it is not a sufficient condition. But it was only in the twentieth century that a theory appeared on the scene that seemed to be unvisualizable in principle: quantum theory. Again, it should be emphasized that this was a gradual process: the idea that quantum theory is unvisualizable did not arrive at once. Only in 1925, with the advent of matrix mechanics, did the unvisualizability of quantum theory become complete. But intimations of unvisualizability were present in quantum theory from the very

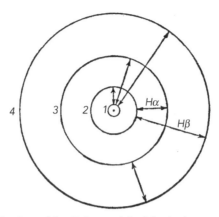

FIGURE 7.1 Visualization of the Bohr model of the hydrogen atom in simplified form, with circles instead of ellipses (Kramers and Holst 1923, 119).

beginning. In this section, I will describe the first stage of the process toward unvisualizability, focusing on the work of Niels Bohr, the central figure in the development of quantum theory until 1925. Bohr's famous atomic model of 1913, associated with the "old quantum theory," is semi-mechanical: it is an adaptation of Rutherford's classical-mechanical model, which depicts atoms as miniature solar systems of a nucleus with electrons revolving around it. In order to account for the observed discrete spectra of radiation, Bohr assumed that electrons remain in discrete "stationary states" and emit radiation only when they make a discontinuous, instantaneous "jump" from one state to another. Accordingly, the model was only partly visualizable: the stationary states could be visualized in terms of electron orbits, but the transitions between states (the infamous "quantum jumps") were unvisualizable (see figure 7.1).

Bohr deemed space-time description highly important, believing that theories for explaining quantum phenomena should be formulated in a spatio-temporal framework (Camilleri 2009, 48, 52–53). However, around 1922 he began to take seriously the possibility that quantum theory failed in an essential way to provide visualizable pictures. His considerations, combined with a conviction that "every description of natural processes must be based on ideas which have been introduced and defined by the classical theory,"[3] led him to an analysis of the way in which atomic theory departed from "the causal description in space and time that is characteristic of the classical mechanical

---

3. Bohr (1976, 3:458); from his 1923 article "On the Application of the Quantum Theory to Atomic Structure."

description of nature."[4] His search finally resulted in his conception of complementarity, which specifies the extent to which quantum phenomena can be understood in terms of classical concepts.

Although visualizability was not an explicit subject of discussion in Bohr's work before 1922, it was implicitly contained in the conceptual problems that had occupied him from 1911 onward, namely those concerning the relation of the quantum theory to classical theories. As we saw in section 7.1, classical space-time description appears to be a necessary condition for visualizability. Therefore, the question of whether the classical concepts "position" and "momentum" (of particles) can be retained in quantum theory needs to be answered in order to find an answer to the question of whether atomic processes are visualizable.

The relation between Bohr's quantum theory and classical theory is expressed in the correspondence principle, which asserts that in the region of large quantum numbers the predictions of quantum theory and classical theory should be the same. According to Radder (1991, 203–208), one can distinguish three stages in Bohr's interpretation of the correspondence principle. In the first stage, from 1913 to 1916, the relation between classical physics and quantum theory was seen as numerical correspondence: the correspondence only concerns the numerical results of calculations of the values of quantities. Bohr spoke of "agreement of calculations," and in this way stressed the conceptual discontinuity between the two theories. From 1916 on, however, Bohr's attitude toward the correspondence principle changed, issuing in an idea of conceptual correspondence: he now believed that there exists a far-reaching analogy between classical theory and quantum theory. Quantum theory is a "rational generalization" of classical theory: the transition probabilities are non-classical but the relation between radiation and motion is analogous to that in classical electrodynamics. This view nurtured expectations of being able to develop semi-classical accounts of the "mechanism" of radiation. Unfortunately, these expectations were not fulfilled, as all semi-classical approaches failed. Consequently, the idea of conceptual correspondence was rejected, and a conception of numerical and formal correspondence was adopted (1923–1925). In this third stage, every hope of a visualizable, mechanistic understanding of the transitions between stationary states was abandoned.

What are the implications of this development for the question of visualizability? In 1913, Bohr's restricted view of a merely numerical correspondence

---

4. Bohr (1976, 3:571); from an unpublished manuscript "Problems of the Atomic Theory," written in 1923 or 1924.

reflected his awareness of the conceptual discontinuity between his model and classical theory, which had its source in the unvisualizable part of his model: the transitions ("quantum jumps"). On the other hand, the stationary states are still described in a classical, visualizable manner and Bohr's model is thereby partly visualizable. From 1916 onward, the successes of the application of the correspondence principle led Bohr to believe that the conceptual discontinuity between quantum and classical theory might not be as great as previously thought. This development, in which the role of classical concepts in the foundation of the theory increased, suggests that for Bohr there were in principle no objections to a possible visualization of his atomic model. Nevertheless, Bohr was too well aware of the failure of classical physics to search for a complete return to classical representations, and it is unlikely that he would have supported a naively realistic interpretation of such a semiclassical representation (an orbital model in which electrons jump instantaneously from one orbit to another). The idea of conceptual correspondence was rejected again in the early 1920s. The reasons for this change were that Bohr's orbital model faced insoluble problems: it failed to account for the spectrum of helium and for the anomalous Zeeman effect (which concerns the splitting of spectral lines in magnetic fields and which played a key role in the search for a new quantum mechanics and the discovery of electron spin; see sections 7.3 and 7.4). In this period, Bohr began to examine the role of pictures in physical theory. In 1922 he wrote, in a letter to philosopher Harald Høffding: "One must in general and especially in new fields of work constantly be aware of the apparent or possible inadequacy of pictures," and "my personal viewpoint is that these difficulties are of a kind that hardly leaves room for the hope of accomplishing a spatial and temporal description of them that corresponds to our usual sense impressions."[5]

A central factor in Bohr's worries about the possibility of pictures was the wave-particle dilemma concerning light. Bohr did not accept Einstein's concept of light quanta as a description of reality. However, light quanta appeared to be necessary to account for phenomena that involved interaction between radiation and matter. Consequently, it appeared "hardly possible to propose any picture which accounts, at the same time, for the interference phenomena and the photoelectric effect, without introducing profound changes in the viewpoints on the basis of which we have hitherto attempted to describe the natural phenomena."[6] Nevertheless, Bohr's reluctance to accept light quanta

---

5. Bohr to Høffding, September 22, 1922, quoted in Favrholdt (1992, 24–25).

6. Bohr (1976, 3:235); from the 1920 lecture "On the Interaction between Light and Matter."

was so strong that even Compton's experiments of 1923, which were generally regarded as a confirmation of the light-quantum hypothesis, did not change his opinion.

Instead, he proposed, together with H. A. Kramers and J. C. Slater, an alternative theory of radiation—the BKS theory—in which strict energy conservation is renounced in order to describe interaction processes without the light quantum.[7] The central idea of the BKS theory is that atoms in stationary states are accompanied by a classical "virtual radiation field," which is identical to the field of a set of harmonic oscillators of all possible frequencies of the atom (a set of so-called virtual oscillators). The field, which is called "virtual" because it is not observable and does not carry momentum or energy, transmits probabilities for transitions in other atoms. Accordingly, any atom experiences a virtual field which is the sum of the virtual fields of all atoms that are present, including its own. Hence, through the field there is a communication between distant atoms, which is non-causal because it merely changes the probability that a transition will occur (contrary to an emitted light quantum, which, when absorbed, always induces a transition).

Since the main purpose of the BKS theory was to show that a quantum theory of radiation without light quanta remained possible, it can be regarded as an attempt to preserve the possibility of an unambiguous space-time picture, and thus visualization, of atomic events. It is therefore not surprising that Schrödinger appreciated the theory (see De Regt 1997, 472–473). Whereas the wave-particle duality of radiation fundamentally excludes unambiguous visualization, the BKS theory restores it by resolving the dichotomy in favor of the wave-picture. The price that had to be paid for this was, besides a renunciation of causality, an explicit anti-realist view of the postulated virtual entities. Moreover, Bohr stressed that the BKS theory has a formal character, analogously to his earlier emphasis on the formal nature of his 1913 atomic theory. He thus wanted to emphasize that the theory lacks explanatory force in the sense that it does not specify a physical mechanism of the actual probability transmissions, a defect which perhaps could be repaired in the future.[8]

---

7. N. Bohr, H. A. Kramers, and J. C. Slater, "The Quantum Theory of Radiation" (1924); reprinted in Bohr (1976, 5:99–118). My account of the BKS theory draws mainly upon Dresden (1987, 159–178).

8. Bohr (1976, 5:101) wrote: "At the present state of science it does not seem possible to avoid the formal character of the quantum theory which is shown by the fact that the interpretation of atomic phenomena does not involve a description of the mechanism of the discontinuous processes, which in the quantum theory of spectra are designated as transitions between stationary states of the atom." See also Dresden (1987, 171), who defines Bohr's conception of a "formal theory" as "a theory which contains rules, relations, and connections

It appeared, however, that Bohr was willing to pay this price for retaining the possibility of unambiguous visualizable description. As such, the BKS theory exemplifies a fundamental difficulty for understanding phenomena in the quantum domain: causal-mechanical description appears to be irreconcilable with visualization. This is essentially different from the situation in classical physics, where, as we saw in chapter 6, it was precisely the visualizability of mechanical models that contributed to their intelligibility. In quantum physics, however, the two ideals of intelligibility diverged. At least in the early 1920s, Bohr preferred visualizability as ideal of intelligibility.

The BKS theory was experimentally disproved in April 1925 by Bothe and Geiger. Bohr's response confirms the interpretation already given. He accepted that the experiment proved that there was a "coupling through radiation of the changes of state of widely-separated atoms." This causal coupling refuted the virtual-radiation-field hypothesis, but it did not yet prove the reality of light quanta. Instead, Bohr concluded that the result did "so thoroughly rule out the retention of the ordinary space-time description of phenomena, that in spite of the existence of coupling, conclusions concerning a possible corpuscular nature of radiation lack a sufficient basis."[9] In other words, the existence of coupling "precludes the possibility of a simple description of the physical occurrences by means of visualizable pictures [*anschaulicher Bilder*]."[10]

The refutation of the BKS theory marks the transition to a new phase in the development of quantum theory, a phase in which Bohr began to examine the limitations of space-time description and which finally led to his conception of complementarity. He was convinced that the refutation of the BKS theory pointed to "an essential failure of the pictures of space and time on which the description of natural phenomena has hitherto been based."[11] Above all, the fact that even the spatiotemporal picture of radiation (the wave theory of light) had its limitations worried Bohr. From 1925 on he had to accept the wave-particle duality of light. Initially he emphasized its formal character, particularly of the particle picture.[12] He admitted that there was a duality in the mathematical description, but refrained from giving a physical interpretation to it. In December 1925, he discussed the issue with Einstein,

---

between physical quantities, but the theory does *not* and sometimes *cannot* provide a physical mechanism or a physical justification for such relations."

9. Bohr to Geiger, April 21, 1925, in Bohr (1976, 5:345); translation in Murdoch (1987, 29).

10. Bohr to Born, May 1, 1925, in Bohr (1976, 5:311); translation in Murdoch (1987, 29).

11. Bohr (1934, 34–35); from the 1925 lecture "Atomic Theory and Mechanics."

12. Bohr (1934, 29).

and afterwards stated: "In my opinion the possibility of obtaining a space-time picture based on our usual concepts becomes ever more hopeless."[13] It appears that Bohr was still worried by the inadequacy of pictures "based on our usual concepts," that is, visualizable pictures. Indeed, despite their apparent limitations, he became ever more convinced that these "usual"—read: classical—concepts were indispensable for rendering atomic physics intelligible.

7.3 The new quantum mechanics: a struggle for intelligibility

In the early 1920s, Bohr's young students Wolfgang Pauli and Werner Heisenberg began to work on the development of Bohr's semi-mechanical atomic model. They invested all their energy in attempts to solve its problems, particularly the anomalous Zeeman effect, but to little avail. Heisenberg made ingenious adaptations to the model, but these violated basic principles of quantum theory and were therefore ultimately unsatisfactory (De Regt 1999b, 412–413). Pauli's attempts were equally unsuccessful and even led him to a temporary retreat from atomic physics. When he took up the subject again in the autumn of 1924, Pauli started a radically new program for quantum theory in which all mechanical concepts, such as momenta and orbits, were relinquished completely. This implied that quantum numbers do not correspond with classical properties anymore, and that one may invoke as many quantum numbers as appears to be necessary. Thus, Pauli simply assigned a new quantum number to the electron, which accounted for the Zeeman splitting. He further elaborated his program by formulating the famous "exclusion principle."[14] This principle, according to which no quantum state (characterized by the four quantum numbers) can ever be occupied by more than one electron, provided an explanation of the shell structure of the atom and thus of the periodic system.

Pauli's attack on mechanical models went hand in hand with a renunciation of visualizability: the rejection of the applicability of concepts of classical mechanics in the atomic domain entailed the impossibility of visualization in the classical sense. Though Pauli did not explicitly regard this

---

13. Bohr to Slater, January 28, 1926, in Bohr (1976, 5:497).

14. See Pauli's 1925 article "Über den Zusammenhang des Abschlusses der Elektronengruppen im Atom mit der Komplexstruktur der Spektren"; reprinted in Pauli (1964, 2:214–232).

as an advantage, he certainly did not consider it a serious problem. Pauli's letter to Bohr of December 12, 1924, reveals his attitude toward the aspect of unvisualizability (in fact, in this letter the notion of *Anschaulichkeit* is referred to for the first time in the Pauli correspondence). In it Pauli expressed the conviction "that not only the dynamic concept of force but also the kinematic concept of motion of the classical theory shall have to undergo fundamental changes." In an appended note, he remarked with characteristic sarcasm:

> I consider this certain—despite our good friend Kramers and his colorful picture books—"and the children, they love to listen." Even though the demand of these children for *Anschaulichkeit* is partly a legitimate and a healthy one, still this demand should never count in physics as an argument for the retention of fixed conceptual systems. Once the new conceptual systems are settled, then also these will be *anschaulich.*[15]

Thus, Pauli rejected *Anschaulichkeit* if it was conceived as the visualizability of mechanical models. The concepts of classical mechanics had to be replaced by new ones, which would after some time become *anschaulich* as well, in the sense of "intelligible." With respect to the way in which these new concepts had to be discovered, Pauli advocated an operationalist methodology.[16] After crediting the energies and angular momenta of stationary states for being far more real than orbits, he stated:

> The (still unattained) goal must be to deduce these and all other physically real, observable characteristics of the stationary states from the (fixed) quantum numbers and quantum-theoretical laws. However, we should not want to clap the atoms into the chains of our preconceptions (to which in my opinion belongs the assumption of the existence

---

15. Pauli (1979, 188); translations in Serwer (1977, 242, 234). Pauli referred to H. A. Kramers's popular book *The Atom and the Bohr Theory of its Structure* (Kramers and Holst 1923), which contains drawings of atoms and orbiting electrons (such as figure 7.1). N.B.: in translations of quotations I have replaced the original German terms *anschaulich, Anschaulichkeit*, etc., because they are often inadequately translated (e.g., as "intuitive").

16. This claim has been denied by Camilleri (2009, 23). However, there is direct evidence that Pauli adopted operationalism at a very early date, and his letter to Bohr (December 24, 1924) clearly shows that he applied it to electron orbits (cf. De Regt 1999b, 407). Moreover, Camilleri does not tell us in detail what Pauli's alternative reason was for rejecting orbits, except for the general remark that they are difficult to reconcile with observed phenomena. In private communication (July 9, 2010), Camilleri suggested that the problem of explaining optical dispersion might have played a role here.

of electron orbits in the sense of the usual kinematics) but we must on the contrary adjust our ideas to experience.[17]

Pauli's ideas significantly influenced Heisenberg's work in the spring and summer of 1925, which laid the foundation for matrix mechanics, the first "quantum mechanics" (as Max Born had coined the long-sought foundation for quantum theory).[18] The theory of matrix mechanics, which was further developed by Heisenberg in collaboration with Born and Jordan, refrained from any visualization of atomic structure, restricting itself to describing relations between observable quantities such as frequencies and intensities of spectral lines. It was recognized as successful and promising by quantum physicists from the Copenhagen circle, among whom Bohr and Pauli. Outside this relatively small group, however, the theory was largely ignored. One reason was that the theory is formulated in the mathematical language of matrices, which was difficult and unfamiliar to most physicists at that time. Moreover, its abstract, unvisualizable nature inhibited acceptance by the mainstream physics community. But the relatively small impact of matrix mechanics was not simply due to the conservative taste of contemporary physicists, a more important reason was that its scientific successes were severely limited. The theory was confronted with mathematical difficulties which made the solution of general cases impossible; only very simple cases could be solved by matrix treatment (see Beller 1999, 28–29). In November 1925, Pauli made a strenuous effort to account for the hydrogen spectrum with the matrix method, but only succeeded in calculating the Balmer terms and was unable to predict the fine structure and the intensities of the spectral lines. In other words, initially the actual results did not supersede those of the old quantum theory. Rejecting visualizability had paved the way for a conceptual revolution, but the price to be paid was a loss of intelligibility that—at least temporarily—reduced the actual problem-solving capacity of quantum theory.

Half a year later, early in 1926, a rival quantum-mechanical theory appeared on the scene: Schrödinger's wave mechanics.[19] Representing

---

17. Pauli to Bohr (December 24, 1924), reprinted in Pauli (1979, 189); translation in Serwer (1977, 243).

18. W. Heisenberg, "Über quantentheoretische Umdeutung kinematischer und mechanischer Beziehungen" (1925); English translation in Van der Waerden (1967, 261–276).

19. In the first half of 1926, Schrödinger published his theory in four papers "Quantisierung als Eigenwertproblem" (part I–IV); reprinted in Schrödinger (1984, 3:82–136 and 166–250); English translations in Schrödinger (1928).

atomic structure in terms of wave functions, this theory appeared quite different from matrix mechanics. Most notably, it seemed to promise visualization of atomic processes as wave phenomena. In wave mechanics there was no need for "quantum jumps" and for a renunciation of space-time description. In other words, Schrödinger's theory was an attempt to restore the place of *Anschaulichkeit* in physical science. In fact, for Schrödinger himself, this promise was the chief motivation for constructing wave mechanics. As was noted before, Schrödinger was strongly committed to the thesis that *Anschaulichkeit* is a necessary condition for intelligibility of theories.[20] He believed that scientific theories should be designed to understand nature and that only a theory which is *anschaulich* can provide understanding. Although *anschaulich* may be translated as "intelligible," it is clear that Schrödinger identified intelligibility with visualizability in space and time, since he held that "we cannot really alter our manner of thinking in space and time, and what we cannot comprehend within it we cannot understand at all" (Schrödinger 1928, 27).

Unfortunately, however, visualization of atomic structure in terms of a wave picture was not without problems. Most importantly, n-particle systems are represented by wave functions in $3n$-dimensional configuration space, not 3-dimensional real space, which implies that visualization is not as easy as it might seem to be. Moreover, describing free electrons by wave packets was troubled by dispersion. For these reasons, and because he did not want to give the impression that his was a reactionary attempt to return to classical physics, Schrödinger derived his famous equation (the Schrödinger equation, which describes the evolution atomic systems in terms of a wave function Ψ) in a purely mathematical way, without referring to the wave picture. Only in the final section of his first paper did he discuss a possible interpretation:

It is, of course, strongly suggested that we should try to connect the function Ψ with some *vibrational process* in the atom, which would more nearly approach reality than the electronic orbits, the real existence of which is very much questioned today. I originally intended to found the new quantum conditions in this more *anschaulich* manner, but finally gave them the above neutral mathematical form, because it brings more clearly to light what is really essential. (Schrödinger 1928, 9)

20. Schrödinger's commitment to *Anschaulichkeit* was inspired by his admiration for Boltzmann and his adoption of the *Bild*-conception of physical theory (see De Regt 1997).

What is "essential," according to Schrödinger, is that his analysis shows that the ad hoc quantum conditions can be explained by the conditions for the function Ψ. Thus, the energy levels of the hydrogen spectrum follow naturally as simple solutions of the Schrödinger equation. Schrödinger envisaged *anschaulich* understanding of the Bohr frequency condition by conceiving of the emission of light during transitions as a kind of "beat" caused by a change in the vibrations, and added:

> It is hardly necessary to emphasize how much more congenial it would be to imagine that at a quantum transition the energy changes over from one form of vibration to another, than to think of a jumping electron. The changing of the vibration form can take place continuously in space and time. (Schrödinger 1928, 10–11)

Subsequently, Schrödinger compared his wave interpretation with the views of the matrix theorists. He argued that his interpretation allows for the apparently necessary renunciation of the concepts of "position" and "path" of the electron, while it avoids the conclusion that a space-time description of atomic structure must be given up altogether, a conclusion that Schrödinger (1928, 26–27) regarded, from the philosophical standpoint, "as equivalent to a complete surrender." He stated that matrix mechanics is "in its *tendency*" very close to his own theory, but stressed that the strength of wave mechanics lies in its "guiding, physical point of view," promising "intuitive [*anschaulich*] understanding" (Schrödinger 1928, 30). See figure 7.2 for a visualization of atomic structure on the basis of wave mechanics.

A few weeks after his first two papers on wave mechanics, Schrödinger published a paper in which he argued that matrix mechanics and his own theory are mathematically, equivalent.[21] Having proved this, he went on to compare the physical content of the two theories, and observed that from a positivistic viewpoint mathematical equivalence may have the same meaning as physical equivalence, so that "there might perhaps appear to be a certain superiority in the matrix representation because, through its *Unanschaulichkeit*, it does not tempt us to form space-time pictures of atomic processes, which must perhaps remain uncontrollable" (Schrödinger 1928, 58). Against this conclusion, however, Schrödinger presented two arguments. First, because the mathematical equivalence is completely symmetrical, the

---

21. Schrödinger, "Über das Verhältnis der Heisenberg-Born-Jordanschen Quantenmechanik zu der meinen" (1926), reprinted in Schrödinger (1984, 3:143–165); English translation in Schrödinger (1928, 45–61).

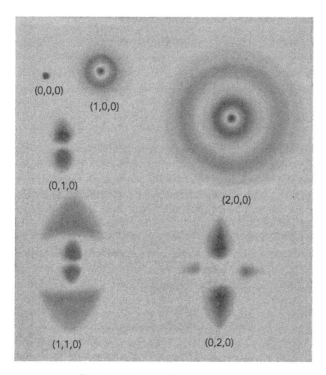

FIG. 24.—MODES OF HYDROGEN ATOM

The diagrams show the *intensity* of vibration at each place, and so indicate the probability of finding the particle-electron there. Each is supposed to be rotated about a vertical axis through its centre. Thus (0, 2, 0) would consist of a ring round the equator and two large lumps round the poles.

FIGURE 7.2 Visualization of stationary states in the wave representation (Darwin 1931, 115). Note that Darwin's caption acknowledges the statistical interpretation of the wave function.

formalism of wave mechanics does not contain a superfluous, "metaphysical" part that transcends the physical (empirical) content of matrix mechanics. In Schrödinger's own words (1928, 58): the wave functions "do not form, as it were, an *arbitrary* and *special* 'fleshy clothing' for the bare matrix skeleton, provided to pander to the need of *Anschaulichkeit*, [which] would establish the superiority of the matrices, from the epistemological point of view." Moreover, mathematically equivalent theories may differ in their possible extensions, and they can therefore differ in their fruitfulness. According to Schrödinger (1928, 59), atomic theory is confronted with problems that seem "extraordinarily difficult to tackle . . . as long as we feel obliged on epistemological grounds to repress *Anschauung* in atomic dynamics, and to operate only with such abstract ideas as transition probabilities, energy levels, etc." Thus, he contends that visualizable theories are preferable because they are heuristically more powerful. In sum, Schrödinger's appraisal of the *Anschaulichkeit* of wave mechanics is in full agreement with the definition of intelligibility presented in section 2.3.

Schrödinger's evaluation was confirmed: in the next couple of years wave mechanics turned out to be far more successful than matrix mechanics (see Beller 1999, 36–38). Because of its familiar mathematics and prospects for visualization, wave mechanics was happily received by many physicists outside the Copenhagen community. This was not merely a matter of taste, however. The visualizability and mathematical structure of the theory made it far more tractable: it suited the skills of physicists much better than matrix mechanics. It was easily applicable to concrete situations and allowed physicists to solve problems that matrix theory was unable to handle. For example, it yielded the spectrum of hydrogen quite straightforwardly, in contrast to Pauli's highly problematic treatment of the hydrogen atom with matrix methods. As a result, wave mechanics completely overshadowed matrix mechanics in the late 1920s.

The competition between the two quantum-mechanical theories led to emotionally charged debates in which the issue of *Anschaulichkeit* became the focus of attention. Schrödinger (1928, 46n) said of Heisenberg's matrix mechanics: "I naturally knew about his theory, but was discouraged, if not repelled, by what appeared to me as very difficult methods of transcendental algebra, and by the want of *Anschaulichkeit*." Schrödinger emphasized the connection between visualizability and intelligibility, arguing that, in contrast to matrix mechanics, wave mechanics is intelligible due to its *anschaulich*, visualizable nature. Since the larger physics community was receptive to this argument in favor of wave mechanics, the proponents of matrix mechanics strongly felt the need to defend their theory against it. Indeed, Heisenberg was well aware of Schrödinger's advantage in this respect, and he was far from pleased. In a letter to Pauli (June 8, 1926), he wrote:

> The more I think of the physical part of Schrödinger's theory, the more abominable I find it. What Schrödinger writes about *Anschaulichkeit* makes scarcely any sense, in other words I think it is crap.[22]

---

22. Heisenberg's letter is reprinted in Pauli (1979, 328). In October 1926, Schrödinger visited Copenhagen, at the invitation of Bohr. The heated and often emotional discussions on interpretational questions have been described by Heisenberg (1967). Bohr had a more favorable attitude toward Schrödinger's ideas than Heisenberg. However, he rejected Schrödinger's interpretation because it failed to explain the corpuscular aspects of matter. Bohr considered wave–particle duality the most fundamental feature of quantum theory. Schrödinger's ideas

Pauli had a more sophisticated response to Schrödinger's plea for *Anschaulichkeit*. Already in 1924—in the context of his criticism of mechanical models of the atom—he had argued that intelligibility did not necessarily have to be equated with visualizability. A radically new conceptual system was needed to solve the problems that quantum theory faced, and Pauli reasoned that this would involve replacing the traditional conception of intelligibility with a new one. As has been explained in section 7.1, the conceptual system of classical physics entails that its theories can be formulated in a space-time framework and are thereby at least in principle visualizable. Giving up the classical conceptual system in favor of an alternative that does not allow for space-time description would entail that intelligibility, if it is identified with visualizability, is given up as well. Pauli (1979, 188) argued, however, that intelligibility does not necessarily have to go when visualizability is abandoned: "Once the new conceptual systems are settled, they will also be *anschaulich*" (where *anschaulich* should be translated as "intelligible"). Thus, Pauli held that the traditional ideal of intelligibility could, and should, give way to new, revolutionary ideal. He argued that quantum mechanics will become intelligible as well when we have learned to use the theory. Note that Pauli's view on intelligibility corresponds with my thesis that intelligibility standards may vary contextually, and with the associated idea that this is partly a matter of becoming familiar with the new conceptual tools (see section 4.4.1). Although Pauli rejected Schrödinger's thesis that understanding requires visualization, he did not abandon intelligibility per se. Pauli's evaluation is consistent with my thesis that in the quantum-mechanical revolution traditional tools for understanding, such as visualization, had to be replaced with new tools.

Pauli's views on intelligibility were adopted by Heisenberg (see Camilleri 2009, 46–47), who made an attempt to flesh out the suggestion that a new conception of *Anschaulichkeit* was needed. The result can be found in Heisenberg's famous paper "Über den anschaulichen Inhalt der quantentheoretischen Kinematik und Mechanik" (1927), which contains the derivation

---

were demolished by Bohr and Heisenberg, and he returned rather discouraged. Reporting his defeat he wrote to Wien, on 21 October 21: "Certainly the standpoint of *anschaulich* pictures, adopted by De Broglie and me, is not yet far enough developed to account for even the most important facts" (quoted in Pauli 1979, 339; my translation). However, two days later he wrote to Bohr: "even if a hundred attempts miscarry, one would not give up the hope of achieving the goal of a representation of the true properties of space-time events through—I do not say classical pictures—but through representations that are free of logical contradictions. It is extremely probable that this is possible" (quoted in MacKinnon 1982, 249). Schrödinger never relinquished his ideal of visualization. Until the end of his life he was to remain a critic of the generally accepted Copenhagen interpretation (see Schrödinger 1952).

of the uncertainty relations. As is clear from its title, the paper intends to show that quantum theory (read: matrix mechanics) was not completely *unanschaulich*. As such, it was a direct response to Schrödinger's allegations.[23] But how could Heisenberg maintain that matrix mechanics was *anschaulich*? This remarkable conclusion depended on two feats: a redefinition of *Anschaulichkeit* and the derivation of the uncertainty relations. In the first sentence of his paper Heisenberg already presents his redefinition:

> We believe to understand [*anschaulich zu verstehen*] a physical theory when we can think through qualitatively its experimental consequences in all simple cases and when we have checked that the application of the theory never contains inner contradictions.[24]

He proceeds to discuss to what extent the usual kinematic and mechanical concepts (such as position, path, velocity, and energy) can be retained in quantum mechanics. He argues that under a suitable operationalist definition these concepts remain valid. However, discussion of a thought experiment in which the position of an electron is determined (the γ-ray microscope) leads Heisenberg to the conclusion that for any pair of canonically conjugate quantities p and q the relation $\Delta p \Delta q \approx h$ holds, where Δp is the precision with which the value of p can be determined (this result can be derived also from the quantum-mechanical commutation rules). Heisenberg's "uncertainty relation," when applied to momentum and position, precisely specifies the limitations of space-time description in the atomic domain. One might think that Heisenberg had definitively established the *Unanschaulichkeit* of quantum mechanics. Not so. He argued that the uncertainty relation allows one to analyze simple (thought) experiments, such as the γ-ray microscope and the Stern-Gerlach experiment, and to arrive at qualitative predictions. And this amounts precisely to *Anschaulichkeit*, given his redefinition of the notion. Therefore, he concluded that "as we can think through qualitatively the experimental consequences of the theory in all simple cases, we will no longer have to regard quantum mechanics as unintelligible [*unanschaulich*]

---

23. See Beller (1999, 67–78) for an analysis of the Heisenberg-Schrödinger "dialogue" in this paper.

24. Heisenberg (1927, 172; my translation). Original: "Eine physikalische theorie glauben wir dann anschaulich zu verstehen, wenn wir uns in allen einfachen Fällen die experimentellen Konsequenzen dieser Theorie qualitative denken könen, und wenn wir gleichzeitig erkannt haben, dass die Anwendung der Theorie niemals niemals innere Widerspruche enthält."

and abstract."[25] Thus, Heisenberg's analysis departs from the radical anti-mechanical program that Pauli had started. Classical notions such as position and momentum are not abandoned, but their applicability is restricted. While complete space-time description (and accordingly visualization) is impossible in principle, the restricted use of classical notions still allows for the intelligibility (*Anschaulichkeit*) of quantum theory.

Some authors have called Heisenberg's redefinition of *Anschaulichkeit* a rhetorical trick (Cushing 1994, 99; Beller 1999, 70). If regarded as nothing but a redefinition of visualizability, it might indeed seem dubious. But that is clearly not what Heisenberg intended. His aim was to offer a new perspective on understanding and intelligibility. It is an attempt to show how physical theories can be intelligible even when they are not visualizable in a straightforward sense. As Camilleri (2009, 49–52) makes clear, Heisenberg's idea should be viewed in the context of a tradition of empiricist critiques of Kantian epistemology that originated in the nineteenth century. It was, in particular, Hermann von Helmholtz (1876) who proposed an alternative conception of *Anschauung* ("intuition") that would apply to non-Euclidean geometries as well (in contrast to Kant's *Anschaulichkeit*, which was inherently related to the Euclidean geometry underlying Newtonian mechanics). Accordingly, Heisenberg's interpretation of intelligibility is not simply a redefinition tailored to the purpose of making matrix mechanics intelligible by definition—it is a substantial, general claim about what it means to understand a theory. Later physicists, among them Richard Feynman et al. (1963–1965, 2:2–1), have endorsed this characterization of intelligibility, but none of them has further elaborated on it. In my view, it is a highly valuable insight—it has inspired me to develop the theory of scientific understanding presented in this book.

7.4 Electron spin: the power of visualization

The aim of science is to explain phenomena, to generate understanding of phenomena. A central thesis of this book is that explanation and understanding require intelligible theories. The story of the development of quantum mechanics, and the heated discussions about its intelligibility or

---

25. Heisenberg (1927, 196, my translation). In a footnote appended to this statement, Heisenberg directly replies to Schrödinger's complaint about the *Unanschaulichkeit* of matrix mechanics. He acknowledges that Schrödinger's theory contributes to the mathematical understanding of the quantum-mechanical laws, and thereby to the intelligibility [*Anschaulichkeit*] of quantum mechanics in Heisenberg's own sense. But he rejects the visualizable interpretation that Schrödinger associates with wave mechanics, disqualifying it as an attempt at "popular intelligibility" [*populären Anschaulichkeit*].

Anschaulichkeit, provide ample support for my claim. The search for explanations of phenomena in the atomic domain first led to the rejection of classical atomic theories (such as Rutherford's), and when Bohr's old quantum theory failed to explain atomic behavior, quantum physicists looked for a new "quantum mechanics" that would be truly revolutionary and fully independent of classical theory. As a theory that radically departs from classical mechanics, Heisenberg's matrix mechanics seemed a very promising candidate. However, to possess a conceptually innovative theory is one thing, to construct explanations of phenomena with it is another. As I have argued throughout this book, the achievement of understanding via scientific explanations requires that theories be intelligible. Initially, as we saw in the previous section, matrix mechanics did not do very well in this respect and this had repercussions for its explanatory power: at the empirical level there was a long way to go before it would prove its superiority to the old quantum theory.

Intelligibility requires adaptation of the skills of scientists to the features of the relevant theories, and this implies that it takes time for a new theory to acquire the intelligibility that is needed for the construction of explanatory models. Scientists cannot simply abandon the skills they used previously and replace them with new skills. Visual skills had been very useful in pre-quantum physics and the average physicists remained inclined to employ this tool for understanding. This can be illustrated nicely with the story of the discovery of electron spin, an important episode in the transition from the old quantum theory to the new quantum mechanics.

Even after Heisenberg's discovery of matrix mechanics in the summer of 1925, the anomalous Zeeman effect, which played such an important role in the crisis of the old quantum theory, was difficult to understand. Pauli had suggested that it is caused by a peculiar property of the electron, namely a classically indescribable "two-valuedness" (*Zweideutigkeit*). The explanation of this *Zweideutigkeit* would in turn be an "unmechanical force" (*unmechanischer Zwang*). In the autumn of 1925, Samuel Goudsmit and George Uhlenbeck advanced the hypothesis of electron spin as an alternative explanation. The idea of a spinning electron was completely in the spirit of the old quantum theory, since it fitted into the visualizable orbital model. According to the spin hypothesis, the electron is a rotating particle, which has an angular momentum m_s ($= \pm\frac{1}{2}$) and a magnetic dipole moment $2\mu_B m_s$ (in which $\mu_B = eh/4\pi m_e$ is the Bohr magneton and the g-factor 2 follows if one assumes that the electron is a sphere with surface charge). The spin thus served as a mechanical explanation of the *Zweideutigkeit* of the electron, replacing Pauli's *unmechanischer Zwang*.

Ralph Kronig had been the first to propose the idea of spin in January 1925, when he was visiting Pauli and discussing the *Zweideutigkeit* of the electron. Pauli called it "a quite witty thought," but rejected it (Kronig 1960, 21). Obviously, the hypothesis was in flat contradiction with Pauli's anti-mechanical program. Moreover, it led to calculations of the doublet splitting in hydrogen that were wrong by a factor two, and it was therefore also empirically inadequate. Kronig was so discouraged by the negative response of Pauli, and later also of Heisenberg and Kramers, that he never published his idea. In October 1925 Goudsmit and Uhlenbeck, independently of Kronig's earlier proposal, conceived the idea of spin again. Looking back at the episode in 1995, Uhlenbeck recalled how they got at it after reading Pauli's paper on the exclusion principle:

> [In this paper] *four* quantum numbers were ascribed to the electron. This was done rather formally; no concrete picture was connected with it. To us, this was a mystery. We were so conversant with the proposition that every quantum number corresponds to a degree of freedom, and on the other hand with the idea of a point electron, which obviously had three degrees of freedom only, that we could not place the fourth quantum number. We could understand it only if the electron was assumed to be a small sphere that could rotate. (quoted in van der Waerden 1960, 213)

Uhlenbeck's account shows that their discovery was initiated by an attempt at visualization. Incidentally, Goudsmit and Uhlenbeck did not notice the problem of the incorrect factor two in the doublet splitting (they did not calculate it), but they realized that there was another problem: the rotational velocity at the surface of the electron would far exceed the speed of light. However, their supervisor Paul Ehrenfest considered the hypothesis valuable and submitted their manuscript to the journal *Naturwissenschaften*, in which it was published immediately (Uhlenbeck and Goudsmit 1925).

In the reception of Goudsmit and Uhlenbeck's proposal by Bohr, Heisenberg, and Pauli, *Anschaulichkeit* also played an interesting role. It was Bohr who was the first to accept the spin hypothesis and this is plausibly connected with his attitude toward visualizability. As described in section 7.2, after the refutation of the BKS theory, Bohr was convinced that there were limits to the possibility of visualization of atomic processes. Nonetheless, he was not willing to give up the idea of visualization completely. Instead, he had come to believe that classical concepts were indispensable for understanding phenomena in the atomic domain. Thus, although he considered Heisenberg's matrix mechanics a great step forward, he did not think that it was a satisfactory theory from the point of view of intelligibility. Of course, Bohr knew that a complete return to classically mechanical pictures was impossible, but he still wanted an intuitive, physical interpretation of the formalism, in which classical (e.g., mechanical) concepts had to play a role. This attitude might explain why Bohr was easily converted to the mechanical, visualizable spin hypothesis.

Pais (1986) presents the amusing story of Bohr's conversion, as Bohr himself told it to him. Initially, Bohr thought that the spin hypothesis was incapable of explaining doublet splitting, because this splitting can occur only in a magnetic field, whereas inside the atom there appears to be only the electric field of the nucleus. In December 1925, he traveled to Leiden to attend the Lorentz jubilee festivities. On the way, he met Pauli in Hamburg, who asked him what he thought about spin, and Bohr expressed his doubts. In Leiden, he met Einstein and Ehrenfest, who immediately asked Bohr what he thought about spin. Bohr again expressed his doubts. Then Einstein pointed out that, according to relativity theory, in the rest frame of the electron the nucleus is a moving charge and thus produces a magnetic field. This field is parallel to the angular momentum of the orbit, and the effect is a spin-orbit coupling, giving rise to doublet splitting. Pais tells us:

> Bohr was at once convinced. When told of the factor two he expressed confidence that this problem would find a natural resolution. . . . After Leiden Bohr travelled to Göttingen. There he was met at the station by Heisenberg and Jordan who asked what he thought about spin. Bohr replied that it was a great advance and explained about the spin-orbit coupling. . . . On his way home the train stopped at Berlin where Bohr was met at the station by Pauli, who had made the trip from Hamburg for the sole purpose of asking Bohr what he now thought about spin. Bohr said it was a great advance, to which Pauli replied: "eine neue Kopenhagener Irrlehre" (a new Copenhagen heresy). After his return home Bohr wrote to Ehrenfest that he had become a prophet of the electron magnet gospel. (Pais 1986, 278–279)

Goudsmit and Uhlenbeck's second paper on the spinning electron, dated December 1925, had an appended note by Bohr in which he wrote that spin "opens up a very hopeful prospect of our being able to account more extensively for the properties of elements by means of mechanical models, at least in the qualitative way characteristic of applications of the correspondence principle" (Uhlenbeck and Goudsmit 1926, 265). This statement confirms that Bohr still believed that mechanical models were valuable, although he knew that obviously such models could not be interpreted in a naively realistic manner. From that time on Bohr tried to convince Pauli and Heisenberg as well: "I have since [my trip to Leiden] had quite a difficult time trying to persuade Pauli and Heisenberg, who were so deep in the spell of the magical duality that they were most unwilling to greet any outway of the sort."[26]

Heisenberg was indifferent to the aspect of visualizability. For him the incorrect factor two in the doublet structure was the greatest obstacle. On November 21, he wrote to Goudsmit as well as to Pauli on spin and expressed his concern for this problem. However, he was not beforehand negative toward the idea.[27] Pauli apparently responded with a fierce disapproval, as can be read from Heisenberg's letter to Pauli of November 24. There Heisenberg stated that he still had strong reservations about spin. Nevertheless, he was working on a matrix-mechanical treatment of the model, which he hoped would solve the problems. Heisenberg's attitude toward spin changed under the influence of Bohr, and despite the unsolved empirical problems he gradually accepted the idea.[28]

Pauli, on the contrary, was persistent in his rejection of the visualizable spin-model. In December 1925, in a letter to Bohr, he stated objections of a technical nature. He admitted that a definitive appraisal of the model could only be made from the perspective of the new quantum mechanics, but until this was accomplished he maintained his opinion: "I don't like the thing!"[29] In February 1926, the difficulty of the factor two was resolved by L. Thomas, who had localized the problem in an incorrect treatment of the relative motion of the electron. Bohr happily communicated this result to Pauli, but Pauli responded negatively: he expressed the conviction that Thomas's calculations were not relevant to the problem. In March, Pauli presented an analysis of the disagreement about the spin hypothesis. Here the deeper motivation for his persistent rejection comes again to the fore. He explained that his disparaging remark about a "new heresy" (*neue Irrlehre*) was motivated by his conviction that the more fundamental, general problems regarding spin (i.e., consistency

---

26. Bohr to Kronig, March 26, 1926, in Bohr (1976, 5:235). The "magical duality" probably refers to Pauli's *Zweideutigkeit*.

27. See Heisenberg to Pauli, November 21, 1925, in Pauli (1979, 261–262); and Heisenberg to Goudsmit, November 21, 1925, quoted in Van der Waerden (1960, 214).

28. See Heisenberg's letters to Pauli of December 24, 1925, January 7, 1926, January 14, 1926, and January 27, 1926, in Pauli (1979, 271, 280, 281, 282).

29. Pauli to Bohr, December 30, 1925, in Pauli (1979, 275).

with matrix mechanics) had to be solved before spin could be accepted as an explanation of the hydrogen spectrum and the Zeeman effect.[30] One week later, however, Bohr had convinced Pauli that his objections to Thomas's calculations were unfounded. Pauli had made a mistake for which he now excused himself and concluded: "Now there is nothing else I can do but surrender completely!"[31] That even after this capitulation Pauli had reservations is clear from a letter to Gregor Wentzel, written in May 1926. In it he reported that the problems with respect to spin had been solved, and that one now had to believe that there is much truth in it, but he added: "I believe it only with a heavy heart, because the difficulties which it causes for the theory of the structure of the electron are very substantial."[32] The editors of the Pauli correspondence note that he probably referred to the fact that the rotational velocity of the electron, when conceived as a spinning particle, exceeds the speed of light. Pauli's reluctant surrender and his objection indicate that he was still convinced that a mechanical, visualizable interpretation of spin was misguided, even though he could not deny that the spin hypothesis successfully accounted for the empirical data. His dissatisfaction would, however, soon be removed, when in 1927 he managed to fit the concept into the formalism of quantum mechanics, thereby abandoning its classically visualizable interpretation. The resulting theory of spin is still used and contains what are now known as the "Pauli spin matrices." In 1955, Pauli looked back on this episode and remarked:

> After a brief period of spiritual and human confusion, caused by a provisional restriction to *Anschaulichkeit*, a general agreement was reached following the substitution of abstract mathematical symbols, as for instance psi, for concrete pictures. Especially the concrete picture of rotation has been replaced by mathematical characteristics of the representations of the group of rotations in three-dimensional space. (Pauli 1964, 1239)

While formally this is true, the fact remains that the concrete picture of rotation is still a useful guide for physical understanding of electron spin. To mention but one example, the experimental determination of magnetic moments of free electrons and muons in a so-called Penning trap, consisting of electric

30. Pauli to Bohr, March 5, 1926, in Pauli (1979, 302).

31. Pauli to Bohr, March 12, 1926, in Pauli (1979, 310).

32. Pauli to Wentzel, May 8, 1926, in Pauli (1979, 322).

and magnetic fields, is described as follows in Perkins (1982, 323): "The effect of the field is to confine the electron or muon in a potential well in which they make very small oscillations. Due to the magnetic field, the particle performs circular cyclotron orbits in the horizontal plane, and the particle spin also precesses about the field direction." One may agree with Pauli that no concrete picture should be attached to concepts such as precession, but it seems doubtful that many physicists could do completely without the visual imagery (which invites us to connect the concept of precession with the behavior of spinning electrons in particular circumstances).[33] The story of the discovery of electron spin shows that the demand for *Anschaulichkeit* did not only lead to confusion, as Pauli suggested, but also had a positive effect. It illustrates that visualization was a valuable aid in understanding the new quantum mechanics, and thereby in making new discoveries and in understanding the phenomena. Moreover, despite their limitations visual representations have remained useful tools for understanding quantum systems, as later developments and current practice in theoretical physics show.

7.5 Visualization in postwar quantum physics

So far, this chapter has focused on the early history of quantum theory. In this section, I will examine the later development of quantum physics and investigate the role of visualization in it. Since the late 1920s, physicists tried to apply quantum mechanics to phenomena that involve interactions between particles and electromagnetic fields. It was only after twenty years that a fully satisfactory quantum field theory emerged: quantum electrodynamics, a theory that combines quantum mechanics and special relativity and is mathematically far more intricate and abstract than standard quantum mechanics. In 1947–1948, Julian Schwinger and Sin-Itoro Tomonaga presented the first mathematically rigorous formulations of quantum electrodynamics: field-theoretical formalisms that were not amenable to visualization. Only one year later, Richard Feynman (1949) proposed his famous diagrammatic approach, which provides a visualization of interaction processes, albeit one that cannot be taken as one-to-one representation of actual occurrences in nature (see figure 7.3). As Feynman's presentation of his approach was not based on mathematical proof, it was initially regarded with suspicion (Miller 1986, 170). However, after Freeman Dyson had proved that Feynman's method was

---

33. Cf. Feynman et al. (1963–1965, 3:7–10), who puts inverted comma's around the term "precession" but whose description of the phenomenon invites a similar visualization.

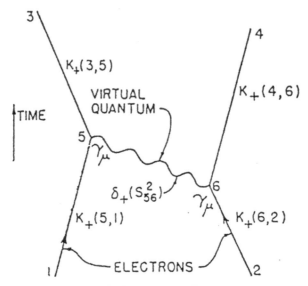

FIGURE 7.3 The first published Feynman diagram (Feynman 1949, 772). Reprinted with permission from Feynman (1949, 772). Copyright (1949) by the American Physical Society.

mathematically equivalent with that of Schwinger, most physicists were converted to Feynman's "intuitive method." One notices a striking similarity with the 1926 competition between matrix and wave mechanics, including the equivalence proof. The visual Feynman diagrams functioned as conceptual tools that made quantum field theory more intelligible for most theoretical physicists.

Rather than realistic representations of physical processes, Feynman diagrams are tools for solving problems and making calculations. In his in-depth study of the development and dispersion of Feynman diagrams, David Kaiser (2005) presents a strong case for the thesis that Feynman diagrams are tools (more generally, Kaiser argues that tools play a crucial role in theoretical physics). For the purposes of my study, three features of his analysis of Feynman diagrams as tools are important. First, Kaiser emphasizes that fruitful use of the diagrams requires specific skills. Acquisition of these skills is quite difficult if not impossible if one has to rely only upon textbooks or published papers. Rather, it is a matter of practicing under expert guidance. Although some physicists (notably in the Soviet Union) succeeded in learning how to calculate with Feynman diagrams from published sources only, they did not manage to use them as tools for dealing with completely new problem situations: "some form of understanding could be packaged and transmitted via texts, but not the more improvisational uses developed by those groups of physicists who shared informal contacts" (Kaiser 2005, 13, cf. 167–169). Accordingly, Kaiser argues, the successful "dispersion" of the diagrammatic method was facilitated by the specific infrastructure of the theoretical physics community after World War II, in which there was intensive traveling and exchange of experts and postdoctoral students between institutes and research groups around the globe. It was by means of personal contact and pedagogy that the specific skills for using Feynman diagrams were circulated and transmitted to younger physicists all over the world.

Second, Feynman diagrams were used in different ways, and applied to a wide variety of domains and contexts for which they were not originally developed. Precisely because they were not intended as realistic representations but functioned as tools, physicists could use them in flexible ways so as to fully exploit their heuristic power. The diagrams were molded in all kinds of ways, in order to solve problems in new domains, or even to develop completely new theoretical approaches. For example, around 1960 Geoffrey Chew refashioned Feynman diagrams and developed new rules for using them, which led to the S-matrix program, an alternative to quantum field theory (Kaiser 2005, 280–355). The history of Feynman diagrams shows that their function was not confined to one context and was independent of a specific theory. Originally, they were meant to make quantum field theory more intelligible, but they acquired independent status and were later used for understanding and developing other theoretical approaches.[34]

Third, the appeal of visualization was a key factor in the enormous success of Feynman's method. Richard Mattuck wrote in his textbook *A Guide to Feynman Diagrams in the Many-Body Problem*:

> It is in principle possible to do many-body perturbation theory without diagrams, just as it is possible to go through the jungles of the Amazon without a map. However, the probability of survival is much greater if we use them. (Mattuck 1976, 120)

When it comes to finding one's way in unknown territory, maps have obvious pragmatic advantages compared to linguistic descriptions—that is to

---

34. Kaiser (2005, 377–387) not only emphasizes the primacy of tools but even claims that in modern physics there are no theories of the sort conceived of in traditional philosophy of science. Although he criticizes Kuhn's account of science for its theory-dominance, his analysis appears compatible with a Kuhnian view, especially as it is interpreted by Rouse (2003), with emphasis on understanding and practice (see section 4.6).

say, if the user possesses basic map-reading skills—and these advantages can be traced back to the visual character of maps. For example, a visual representation such as a map provides an overview of the situation at a glance and can be read from different directions (perspectives), so that one can continue using it when circumstances change. Similarly, it was the visual nature of Feynman diagrams that made them suitable as tools for making quantum field theory intelligible. To be sure, the diagrams were not immediately and straightforwardly usable; on the contrary, as Kaiser (2005, 43–51) describes, shortly after their introduction by Feynman in 1948 there was much confusion about how they should be interpreted and used, and physicists had difficulty becoming acquainted with them. But not much later the diagrams were accepted and widely circulated in the physics community, and their success was not least due to their visual nature and their connection with older techniques of visualization, such as Minkowski diagrams: "Feynman diagrams were consistently drawn and taught as being of a piece with the reigning pictorial standards for studying particle trajectories through space and time" (Kaiser 2005, 365). This episode confirms the thesis, defended in section 4.4.1, that only if conceptual tools are to some extent familiar to their users can they be truly useful for their purpose: rendering theories intelligible.

Incidentally, Kaiser (2005, 366–370) argues that visualizability and tractability cannot be the whole story about the success of Feynman diagrams, for they succeeded where other diagrammatic tools failed (such as the so-called "dual diagrams," which were equally easy to use). One possible reason for this may have been their similarity to "real" pictures of "real" particle trajectories (such as bubble-chamber photographs). Kaiser (2005, 21–22) concludes: "Feynman diagrams thus functioned as many other influential scientific diagrams have done—ranging from stratigraphic columns, to chemical formulas and atomic orbitals, to pictures of immunological antibodies—subject to the same slippage between realistic depiction, convenient calculational device, and heuristic guide to further research."

For Feynman himself visualizability was essential. In an interview with Silvan Schweber (quoted in Schweber 1994, 465–466), Feynman stated that "visualization in some form or other is a vital part of my thinking." His description of how precisely his thinking worked fits in with my analysis of scientific understanding, and leads him to conclude: "I see the character of the answer before me—that's what the picturing is." On the relation between the visualizing and the calculating stage Feynman had this to say: "Ordinarily I try to get the pictures clearer but in the end, the mathematics can take over and can be more efficient in communicating the idea than the picture." As an example, he described how he solved the liquid helium problem by visualizing the situation:

> I didn't know how to write a damn thing and there was nothing I could do but keep on picturing ... and I couldn't get anything down mathematically. ... So the whole thing was worked out first, in fact was published first as a descriptive thing ... which doesn't carry much weight, but to me was the real answer. I really understood it and I was trying to explain it. (quoted in Schweber 1994, 466).

Note the distinction between understanding and explanation in the last sentence: the former is provided by visualization, the latter by mathematical derivation. Here Feynman's statement illustrates my analysis of intelligibility as a condition of explanation. First one needs intelligibility (i.e., understanding of the theory), which may be provided by visualization, and subsequently one can construct explanations, which may consist of mathematical derivations. Thus, visualization contributes to the intelligibility required for developing explanations. The success of Feynman's diagrammatic method indicates that most physicists prefer visualization as a tool for making theories intelligible. Incidentally, even Schwinger maintained that he employed visual imagery. Interviewed by Schweber (1994, 365), he said:

> I suppose you can't avoid having mental pictures. If somebody talks about an electron I don't think I see Schrödinger's equation. Everybody pictures something; it's a point moving. There has to be some sort of picture.

But, Schwinger continues, after the initial "physical impetus—which to some extent is visual, but certainly not in the elaborate way of Feynman," mathematical analysis takes over (Schweber 1994, 366). Like Schrödinger and Pauli a quarter century before, the difference between Feynman and Schwinger nicely illustrates the variation in conceptual tools that may be employed for obtaining understanding. Visualization is a very effective way to achieve intelligibility but it is not the only one.

7.6 Visualization as a tool
for scientific understanding

Erwin Schrödinger was strongly committed to the view that visualization is a necessary condition for scientific understanding. This was not an idiosyncrasy on his part but a principle in the venerable tradition of Kantian philosophy. Indeed, many nineteenth- and early-twentieth-century physicists supported the idea that understanding requires visualization and space-time description. However, as had happened before in history, an a priori philosophical thesis was refuted by scientific developments: the theory of quantum mechanics that resulted from combining the work of Schrödinger and Heisenberg does not allow for visualization, in the sense of unambiguous spatiotemporal description, of quantum phenomena. Any attempt to give a pictorial representation of processes and phenomena in the quantum domain will inevitably be incomplete, distorted or inconsistent. This gradually became clear during the 1920s and was definitively established in 1927, when Heisenberg derived the uncertainty relations.[35]

Schrödinger's hope for a visualizable interpretation of quantum mechanics was not fulfilled. But this does not entail that quantum mechanics cannot provide understanding of phenomena. While my analysis of this episode shows that there is no a priori relation between understanding and visualization, it also reveals that visualization remains an important tool for achieving scientific understanding. The overwhelming popularity of wave mechanics in the mainstream physics community was not so much an expression of conservatism, but rather due to the fact that the theory was much more tractable than matrix mechanics because of its visualizability and familiar mathematical structure. In a word, its epistemic success was based upon its intelligibility, and its intelligibility was due to its visualizability. The pragmatic virtue of visualizability facilitated the construction of models and explanations of specific phenomena, as is also illustrated by the discovery of electron spin and the development of Feynman diagrams. Accordingly, even in quantum physics, visualizability is a theoretical quality that may contribute to intelligibility.

---

35. To be sure, there have been proposals for so-called hidden-variable theories underlying quantum mechanics, most notably David Bohm's, which do allow for a spatiotemporal description of events. Proponents of such hidden-variable theories emphasize their visualizability and intelligibility as an advantage (Bohm and Hiley 1993; Holland 1993; Cushing 1994). These theories have other counterintuitive features, however, most notably pervasive non-locality.

This case study in the history of quantum physics shows, furthermore, that intelligibility varies not only diachronically but also synchronically, with the social and disciplinary context: a scientific theory considered unintelligible by one group of scientists may be regarded as intelligible by another, depending on the skills and tools that the scientists have at their disposal. The 1920s witnessed a divide between the mainstream physics community, to which Schrödinger belonged, and the Copenhagen school, of which Bohr, Pauli, and Heisenberg were members. While abstract matrix mechanics was intelligible to the latter group, physicists of the former group simply lacked the skills to make fruitful use of the theory. Schrödinger's wave mechanics, by contrast, was intelligible to the larger community of physicists because of its visualizability and its familiar mathematics. A similar diagnosis applies to the case of quantum field theory: the difference between Schwinger and Tomonaga's abstract approach versus Feynman's diagrammatic approach illustrates the variation in conceptual tools employed for obtaining understanding.

Although preferences for abstract or visualizable theories do vary among scientists, there appear to be more who prefer visualizability to abstractness, probably at any time in history. Apparently, the skills for using visualization as a tool for understanding have been widespread in the scientific community throughout history. Of course, this should not really surprise us as these skills seem to be deeply rooted in human nature. As Machamer, Darden, and Craver (2000, 22) suggest, it is plausible that "what we take to be intelligible is a product of ontogenetic and phylogenetic development of human beings in a world such as ours." Our sensory experience provides an important basis for intelligibility, which is then extended to realms beyond sense perception. Since seeing is for humans plausibly the most important way of grasping the world around us, it is not surprising that when we want to extend our grasp of the world beyond what we observe directly, we prefer to rely on our well-developed visual skills and employ visualization as a tool for understanding. Already in 1876, a similar suggestion was made by Helmholtz, when he argued against the Kantian thesis that space-time visualization based on Euclidean geometry is an a priori condition for perception and understanding:

It was rather a succession of everyday experiences, especially the perception of the geometrical similarity of great and small bodies, only possible in flat space, that led to the rejection, as impossible, of every geometrical representation at variance with this fact. . . . It is true that we have no word but *intuition* to mark this; but it is knowledge empirically gained by the aggregation and reinforcement of similar recurrent impressions in memory, and not a transcendental form given before experience. That other such empirical intuitions of fixed typical relations, when not clearly comprehended, have frequently enough been taken by metaphysicians for *a priori* principles, is a point on which I need not insist. (Helmholtz 1876, 320)

According to Helmholtz, Kant's "forms of intuition" (*Anschauungsformen*) should not be conceived of as necessary, a priori conditions for understanding. He suggests, however, that from an empiricist standpoint it is understandable that they have been regarded as such, since all our everyday sensory experience is structured in a spatiotemporal framework that conforms to them. Contemporary cognitive science provides us with insights that support this conclusion. As Gigerenzer (2007, 58–64) argues, the human mind can be regarded as an "adaptive toolbox," consisting of a great number of heuristic tools based on our evolved capacities. These evolved capacities (of which language, emotion, and object tracking are but a few examples) have been acquired via natural selection or cultural transmission. According to Gigerenzer (2007, 59), they "are always functions of both our genes and our learning environment," as they "evolved in tandem with the environment in which our ancestors lived and are shaped by the environment in which a child grows up."

In the light of these considerations, it appears only natural that most scientists prefer visualizable theories to abstract ones. Since, like all human beings, they possess the skills to visualize by nature, they will be inclined to use visualization as a tool for scientific understanding. For example, as we saw in section 3.2, visualizability is a key feature of mechanistic explanations that contributes to their popularity in the life sciences. As Bechtel and Abrahamsen (2005, 427–430) observe, diagrams of complex mechanisms are preferred to linguistic representations because the former directly convey the spatial organization of mechanisms and are thereby more tractable.[36] This does not imply, of course, that visualization can always be applied easily and immediately. In the case of quantum theory using visualization as a tool has to be learned, and in many scientific disciplines visual skills need to be developed and refined in

---

36. See Bechtel and Abrahamsen (2005, 430–431) for a brief discussion of neuroscientific explanations of the advantages of diagrammatic reasoning. Visual representation is also crucial for achieving understanding through computer simulations, as Humphreys (2004, 114) observes: "Because one of the goals of current science is human understanding, how the simulation output is represented is of great epistemological import when visual outputs provide considerably greater levels of understanding than do other kinds."

order to apply them fruitfully (Mathewson 1999; Titus and Horsman 2009). But visualizability is a theoretical quality that for most scientists will contribute to the intelligibility of theories. Although visualization is not indispensable for achieving scientific understanding, it remains a valuable tool in many contexts.

8

Conclusion

THE MANY FACES OF UNDERSTANDING

UNDERSTANDING THE PHENOMENA is a generally acknowledged aim of science, but the ways in which scientists attain this goal may vary widely. The philosophical theory of scientific understanding presented in this book acknowledges the diversity of conceptions of understanding in the history and practice of science, yet offers a general characterization of the nature of scientific understanding and criteria for achieving it. The core concept in the theory is "intelligibility," defined as the value that scientists attribute to the cluster of qualities of a theory that facilitate its use. Its central thesis is that attaining scientific understanding of phenomena requires intelligible theories. It should be emphasized, though, that these theories need not be fully articulated or formalized; a looser set of (implicit) theoretical principles may suffice. Hence, my theory is compatible with the idea that one can acquire scientific understanding without having a fully developed theory in hand; for example, through experimentation. It does assume, however, that all scientific activity—also experimentation—is guided by some theoretical principles. Thus, theories are needed, and these theories should be intelligible.

Which theories are intelligible, and which are not, is a contextual matter: scientists in different periods of history or in different communities often endorse quite different intelligibility standards. These intelligibility standards function as "tools" for achieving understanding in particular contexts. In this way the theory accounts for the historical variation of criteria for understanding employed by scientists in actual practice. Moreover, it supplies a framework for unifying the various philosophical theories of scientific explanation.

While extant theories of explanation differ greatly, they share the assumption that scientific explanations should give us understanding. My theory of understanding unifies these theories by showing how the various types of explanation offer different routes to the common goal of understanding, and why preferences for one or the other route may vary with the context. In this concluding chapter, I reflect on the results of my investigation by addressing three questions. First, what is the scope of my theory of scientific understanding? Second, does the theory imply a relativist philosophy of science? Third, can it serve as a basis for normative appraisal of scientific achievements?

8.1 Understanding across the sciences

A first issue that should be addressed is what the scope is of my theory of scientific understanding. Although the case studies and examples discussed in the book derive almost exclusively from the physical sciences, the theory aspires to have a wider validity, at least for the natural sciences more generally. It is to be expected that the ways in which understanding is achieved in, for example, biology, geoscience, or neuroscience, differ strongly from each other and from the way it is achieved in physics. The same will probably apply to the standards of intelligibility employed in these different disciplines. However, this is not a problem for my theory. On the contrary: since it acknowledges that scientific understanding is essentially contextual, such variation across disciplines can easily be accommodated. In the book, and especially in the case studies, the focus has been on understanding in different historical contexts, but the theory applies to variation across social and disciplinary contexts as well. Although I do not pretend to have offered sufficient evidence to support the claim that the theory is applicable outside the domain of the physical sciences, I have presented some examples that suggest the plausibility of this claim. Thus, cases from biology, meteorology, ecology, and neuroscience have been discussed briefly in chapters 3 and 4.

The focus on physical sciences led to special attention being paid to criteria for intelligibility that are suited to mathematized theories, which are the rule rather than the exception in this domain (in section 4.2). Thus, criterion CIT_1 is specifically designed for theories that are formulated in mathematical terms, since it refers to calculations and employs the qualitative-quantitative distinction. However, as mentioned in section 4.2, CIT_1 is but one of many possible criteria for testing whether a theory is intelligible to scientists in a particular context. For theories that are not cast in mathematical form other criteria for intelligibility need to be formulated. Accordingly, disciplinary variation in understanding will also be reflected in criteria for intelligibility. Incidentally, mathematized theories occur in the social and behavioral sciences as well, for example, in economics and in particular branches of psychology and cognitive science. I have presented some examples suggesting that also in these fields concrete qualitative models are employed to enhance the intelligibility of mathematized theories (see sections 4.1 and 4.5.1). So my theory of understanding, including criterion CIT_1, may apply beyond the natural sciences.[1]

It is generally agreed, however, that many disciplines in the social sciences differ fundamentally from the natural sciences in having different methods and aims. This holds even stronger for disciplines such as history and anthropology. Therefore, I make no claims as to whether or not my theory of scientific understanding is applicable to the human sciences generally.[2] Still, there is one issue related to the distinction between the natural sciences and the human sciences that merits special attention. This is the well-known *Verstehen-Erklären* dichotomy, introduced by the nineteenth-century philosophers Johann Gustav Droysen and Wilhelm Dilthey in order to clarify the difference between the natural sciences (*Naturwissenschaften*) and the humanities (*Geisteswissenschaften*). According to Droysen and Dilthey, the former aim at explanation (*Erklären*), whereas the latter have understanding (*Verstehen*) as their goal. Explanation is, in their view, a purely objective enterprise, which consists in uncovering the causes and general laws that underlie observed natural phenomena. Understanding, by contrast, is subjective and consists in interpreting the intentions of (historical) actors and the meaning of artefacts such as texts or works of art.[3]

Is this conception of understanding in any way related to my analysis of scientific understanding? It is not, if conceived as a specific aim and associated method that is distinctive of the human sciences and opposed to explanation.

---

1. Several contributions in De Regt, Leonelli, and Eigner (2009) discuss the applicability of my theory of understanding to disciplines outside the natural sciences; see esp. the chapters by Marcel Boumans (on understanding in economics), Kai Eigner (on understanding in psychology), Mieke Boon (on understanding in the engineering sciences), and Edwin Koster (on understanding in historical inquiry). Some of these authors argue for a revision of the criteria CUP and CIT_1 in the light of the specific disciplinary context.

2. The term "human sciences" refers to all disciplines that study (features and results of) human behavior or action. This includes social and behavioral sciences, as well as the humanities. The main reason for thinking that their methods and aims are fundamentally different is that their subject matter typically involves purposes, meanings, and intentions.

3. An insightful and accessible discussion of the two traditions, and a classic defense of the *Verstehen-Erklären* distinction, can be found in von Wright (1971).

In my account, understanding is associated with explanation: understanding of phenomena is produced by explanations, and understanding of theories (intelligibility) is a prerequisite for the construction of explanations. My theory applies to the natural sciences; whether or not it also applies to the human sciences is a question that remains to be answered. Accordingly, my notion of "scientific understanding" should not be confused with the concept of understanding employed by Droysen and Dilthey. However, there are some interesting connections between the two that deserve to be mentioned. First of all, I have made a case for the rehabilitation of understanding in the philosophy of science by arguing against the traditional view, championed by Hempel, that understanding is "merely" pragmatic, psychological, and subjective. These connotations of understanding were sufficient reason for Hempel to deny understanding any philosophical import, and thereby for rejecting the claim that historians should employ a distinct method of *Verstehen* (see section 3.1). My theory of scientific understanding, by contrast, assigns a crucial role to the pragmatic and the psychological, namely via the notion of intelligibility. Accordingly, I renounce the strongly objectivist approach of Hempel: understanding is important also in the natural sciences. This does not reduce scientific understanding to a completely subjective affair, as I have argued in section 2.3, but it does challenge the traditional ideal of value-free objectivity that Hempel endorsed. Both the systematic analysis in chapter 2 and the historical case studies in chapters 5–7 show that achieving scientific understanding through explanation necessarily involves values and judgment, not only in the human sciences—as emphasized by the advocates of *Verstehen*—but in the natural sciences as well.[4]

Second, the way in which scientific understanding advances, and its dependence on the context, is to some extent similar to the process of *Verstehen* in the humanities, in particular, to the so-called hermeneutic circle. The concept of the hermeneutic circle was originally conceived by Friedrich Schleiermacher to describe how texts are interpreted. On Schleiermacher's account, the interpretation—or understanding—of a text as a whole is always

---

4. See Koster (2009) for an analysis of the ways in which understanding is achieved in the study of history and a comparison with the conception of scientific understanding presented in De Regt and Dieks (2005). Koster notes that there are important similarities, in particular, "the tension between objectivity and subjectivity" (2009, 320). Subsequently, he argues that historical understanding is crucially dependent on "judgments," which he characterizes as: "nonobjective deliberations that are necessary to applying general features to particular situations and to determine which factors are more important than other ones" (2009, 330), and he suggests that judgment might be equally important for attaining understanding in the natural sciences. In the present book, I have followed this suggestion; see esp. section 2.2.

dependent on the understanding of its parts, while the understanding of any part depends on the understanding of the whole. This is not necessarily a vicious circle, but it suggests that texts cannot be fully understood on a first reading. It implies that if one reads a text for the first time one can only understand the parts on the basis of one's "pre-understanding" (gained by having read previous texts, having had certain experiences, etc.). Only after one has read the whole text can one reinterpret the parts and thereby the whole, which will result in a more comprehensive understanding. This is a process that may be repeated endlessly, leading to ever-increasing (or asymptotically converging) understanding. Context plays a crucial role in this process: one's understanding of some part of the text is affected by the context, which is given by one's understanding of the text as a whole and/or one's pre-understanding. This context is not fixed but changes in the process of gaining understanding.

While the hermeneutic circle applies to understanding and interpreting texts, there is an analogous process at work in the advancement of scientific understanding of phenomena. As I have shown in this book, scientific understanding is essentially contextual: the skills that are needed to construct explanations on the basis of particular theories are acquired in the context of scientists' education, and the scientific and philosophical context partly determines which tools are deemed suitable for rendering theories intelligible. Moreover, scientific background knowledge and familiarity with accepted scientific theories affect intelligibility judgments as well. Accordingly, scientists' understanding of phenomena depends on the broader context, but this context is not static. With the advancement of understanding it changes: new background knowledge appears, which might shed new light on previously accepted knowledge; skills are further developed; tools have proven effective, and so on. As in hermeneutics, there is a mutual interaction between context and object of understanding, and the process of furthering scientific understanding involves an analogous hermeneutic circle.

8.2 The relativity of understanding

My emphasis on the contextual nature of scientific understanding might worry some readers: they might think that it results in a relativist view that undermines the objectivity of science. Ever since Hempel, many philosophers of explanation have been at pains to avoid relativism. Indeed, as we saw in section 2.1, Hempel eschewed pragmatic conceptions of explanation and talk of understanding precisely for this reason. In a similar vein, Strevens (2008, 22), rejects relativist theories of explanation, which he defines as theories according to which "the nature of the explanatory relation changes according to preferences, cultural traditions, knowledge, conversational context, or some other observer-dependent factor." He cites van Fraassen's pragmatic theory of explanation as an example of a theory that may be regarded as partly relativist, and he therefore disapproves of it. As I have argued in section 4.4.3, van Fraassen's theory of explanation and my theory of scientific understanding go well together, most importantly because they share the idea that explanatory understanding is essentially contextual. Strevens (2008, 38) claims, by contrast, that even though explanatory practices have changed in the course of history, "there is an underlying set of principles that has always determined what does and does not count as a good explanation for us." So, does my contextual theory of scientific understanding imply relativism, and if so, is this a cause for concern?

Although I have addressed the relativism objection already in section 4.6, it may be worthwhile to explain once again, and in more detail, why there is no reason to worry about the relativistic implications of my theory. Although the theory obviously contains a relativist element by affirming the context-relativity of understanding, this does not entail the kind of relativism that many philosophers find unacceptable. First, it should be stressed that adopting a relativist theory of explanation and understanding does not necessarily imply relativism with respect to science as a whole. This clearly applies to van Fraassen, who combines his pragmatic theory of explanation with his well-known constructive empiricism, which is certainly not a relativist view of science. Second, merely asserting that understanding is context-dependent does not necessarily entail wholesale relativism regarding scientific understanding: as long as there are overarching criteria for assessing when understanding has been achieved, it is perfectly possible that specific tools for achieving understanding and specific standards for the intelligibility of theories vary across different contexts. My contextual theory of scientific understanding is based upon such an overarching criterion, namely CUP: A phenomenon P is understood scientifically if and only if there is an explanation of P that is based on an intelligible theory T and conforms to the basic epistemic values of empirical adequacy and internal consistency (section 4.1). Perhaps this does not yet persuade my critics, however, because they might object that CUP contains the notion of intelligibility, which—they might argue—makes it inherently relativist: the intelligibility of a theory is relative to the skills of the scientist, and a theory that is intelligible to one scientist may be unintelligible to another.

It is true that intelligibility is a contextual value, and it does indeed introduce a relativist element into my conception of understanding. However, as argued in section 4.6, this is not a relativism that puts the idea of science as a reliable source of knowledge in jeopardy. To begin with, it does not make scientific understanding a matter of individual idiosyncrasies at the micro-level. Variation in tools and intelligibility standards is typically found at the level of the scientific community. For example, in chapter 7, we saw that in the 1920s opposing views on the intelligibility of quantum theory were held by different groups: on the one hand, the mainstream physics community of which Schrödinger was a representative, on the other hand, the Copenhagen group around Bohr, including Pauli and Heisenberg. Although my account has focused primarily on the contributions of key figures in the debate, the controversy was one between different groups and the development of quantum mechanics was a community achievement. Postwar quantum physics featured a similarly crucial role for the community: the dispersion of Feynman diagrams as tools for understanding was made possible only through the interaction between physics communities around the world. These examples are typical, and they show that the contextual nature of intelligibility does not imply complete subjectivity. Intelligibility is based on skills, which are acquired through education and are relative to scientific communities rather than to individuals.

But even if this is granted, one might ask whether relativism at the community level is not equally problematic. By asserting that skills and standards of intelligibility are characteristic of scientific communities, my contextual theory of scientific understanding may suggest a Kuhnian view of science, and some will still associate this with an unacceptable kind of relativism. There are indeed parallels between my account of understanding and Kuhn's view, especially regarding the historical variation of standards and the role of the community. I concur with Rouse (2003), who observes that Kuhnian paradigms are best regarded as shared ways to understand the world, and that accepting a paradigm involves acquiring a set of skills (see also section 4.6). However, it might be objected that this leads us to the kind of relativism associated with Kuhn's theory of science: since members of different paradigms adhere to different standards of intelligibility, they may disagree fundamentally on whether or not phenomena can be understood on the basis of a particular theory (e.g., matrix mechanics versus wave mechanics). My reply is along the same lines as Kuhn's response to the relativism objection. Kuhn (1977) denied that his theory necessarily implied relativism, and supported this claim with an account of the role of values in theory choice. He identified a number of general characteristics that any good scientific theory should exhibit, among them accuracy and consistency. These characteristics function as values, shared by all scientists, which supply paradigm-transcending standards for evaluating theories. Accordingly, adherence to these values makes fruitful communication between members of different paradigms possible, thereby doing away with the relativist idea that paradigms are incomparable. In a similar manner, CUP features, next to intelligibility, the basic scientific values of empirical adequacy and internal consistency that protect us from unbridled relativism (see section 2.3 for an elaborate discussion of these basic scientific values, which do not function as rigid constraints but are nonetheless important requirements that guarantee the possibility of consensus and communication across paradigms).

An alternative approach to ward off the relativistic implications of Kuhn's view is defended by Michael Friedman in his *Dynamics of Reason* (2001). It is interesting to compare his analysis to my account of scientific understanding. Friedman presents a theory of the development of science in which relativized a priori principles play a central role, and which accounts for the occurrence of Kuhnian revolutions while retaining some continuity across revolutions. Friedman distinguishes three levels: (1) empirical laws; (2) constitutive a priori principles; (3) philosophical meta-paradigms. Drawing on Reichenbach's interpretation of Kantian a priori principles, Friedman argues that empirical laws only make sense in the light of certain constitutive a priori principles. For example, Newton's law of universal gravitation is meaningless without the notion of an inertial frame, which in turn requires Newton's laws of motion (since inertial frames are defined as frames in which these laws of motion hold). Consequently, Newton's laws of motion function as constitutive a priori principles in the Newtonian paradigm. While these principles are a priori in the sense that they precede empirical laws, they are not a priori in the sense of being immutable: they can be revised or replaced in the course of a scientific revolution. Such changes are often inspired by what Friedman (2001, 44, 105ff.) calls "meta-paradigms": frameworks that provide the basis for reflection and discussion on particular philosophical issues related to the scientific questions that gave rise to the revolutionary paradigm shift. Einstein, for example, developed his revolutionary theories of relativity in the context of long-standing philosophical debates on the problem of absolute versus relative motion and on the foundations of geometry. Although he abandoned the Newtonian paradigm by replacing its constitutive a priori principles with new ones (namely, the light principle and the equivalence principle), Einstein's involvement in philosophical debates that were widely regarded as fundamental and important by supporters of the Newtonian paradigm ensured that his theories were regarded as serious alternatives (Friedman 2001, 107–115). Hence, philosophical meta-paradigms allow for communication across scientific paradigms, and they thereby supply continuity and protect us from wholesale relativism.

The Einsteinian revolution is Friedman's prime example, but the two revolutionary developments discussed in chapters 5 and 7—the Newtonian revolution and the quantum revolution—can be interpreted along the same lines. As we saw in chapter 5, the seventeenth-century debate about the intelligibility of Newton's theory of gravitation was primarily concerned with metaphysical questions, in particular, with the question of whether action at a distance is metaphysically possible, and if so, what its metaphysical cause is. In Friedman's terminology, this was the philosophical meta-paradigm that constituted the common ground for rational communication and discussion among Cartesians and Newtonians.[5] When it comes to the quantum revolution Friedman (2001, 120–121) is less convinced of the applicability of his theory: he claims that "quantum mechanics simply has not been integrated with an ongoing meta-scientific tradition at all." However, my analysis of the genesis of quantum mechanics shows that a crucial role was played by philosophical debates regarding the status and function of visualizable pictures in science, within a meta-paradigm that had its roots in the nineteenth century. As described in sections 6.3 and 7.1, in the 1890s physicists like Boltzmann and Hertz developed sophisticated accounts of the idea that scientific theories are pictures (*Bilder*). In the 1920s, the central issue was the question of *Anschaulichkeit*: Is intelligibility in the sense of visualizability a necessary condition for scientific theories? While Schrödinger answered this question in the affirmative, Pauli argued that quantum theory can be intelligible without being visualizable and should be fully independent of classical concepts. Subsequently, Heisenberg redefined *Anschaulichkeit*, reintroduced classical concepts in quantum mechanics, and derived the uncertainty relations (see section 7.3).

Did the quantum revolution involve changes of constitutive a priori principles inspired by debates at the meta-paradigmatic level? Friedman (2001, 122) considers the correspondence principle the most plausible candidate for being a constitutive principle of quantum theory. Indeed, this principle expresses how quantum theory relates to the classical theories required for describing empirical phenomena (see section 7.2). My analysis of the quantum case suggests that also Heisenberg's uncertainty relations are among the constitutive a priori principles of quantum mechanics, since they define the possibilities and limitations of the use of classical concepts within the framework of quantum theory. Describing a quantum system in terms of positions and momenta of the particles that comprise it, for example, is possible only

---

5. See Friedman (2001, 44) for a brief discussion that matches my analysis.

to the extent specified by these relations. Although they embody the radical distinction between quantum mechanics and classical mechanics, they also establish a connection between their conceptual frameworks that enables scientists from the respective paradigms to communicate and understand each other. As we have seen, the formulation of the uncertainty relations was directly inspired by the debates between Schrödinger, Pauli, and Heisenberg on the *Anschaulichkeit* requirement. Accordingly, there appears to be a close relation between Friedman's relativized constitutive a priori and the standards of intelligibility in my theory of scientific understanding. However, whereas Friedman emphasizes the epistemological dimension, my account focuses on the pragmatic role of intelligibility. Traditional empiricists such as Philipp Frank have rejected intelligibility as an outdated requirement, a relic of the bygone days of rationalist philosophy.[6] Contrary to this view, and complementary to Friedman's analysis, I maintain that a generalized, relativized notion of intelligibility is crucial to scientific practice.

8.3 Norms for understanding

Finally, one important question remains to be discussed: Does the contextual theory of scientific understanding developed in this book have any normative force, or does it only allow us to describe and explain the way in which understanding actually has been achieved in the history and practice of science. Philosophy of science should be normative, according to many: it should tell us, for example, which methods are reliable and should be used by scientists, which scientific claims or results are justified, or how we can distinguish a good scientific explanation from a spurious one. The traditional view has it that it is this normative aspect that distinguishes philosophy of science from empirical studies of science such as history or sociology of science. While historians of science will typically confine themselves to a descriptive analysis of, for example, the transition from the Cartesian to the Newtonian theories of mechanics in the seventeenth century, philosophers of science should provide tools for normative appraisal: Did this development constitute progress? Was Newton's mechanics better justified than Descartes's theory, and if so, why? Were Newton's explanations of natural phenomena superior to the explanations given by Cartesians, and if so why? When it comes to understanding, the traditional view is that a philosophical theory of scientific understanding should offer tools to distinguish genuine understanding from spurious

---

6. See Frank (1957); his views have been discussed in section 5.1.

understanding (or misunderstanding), and should perhaps also provide guidelines for achieving genuine understanding.

As stated in chapter 1, the aim of this book-length study of scientific understanding has been to investigate and explicate the nature of the understanding that science can provide, and to develop a theory that describes the criteria for understanding employed in scientific practice and explains their function and historical variation. Accordingly, the study has first and foremost a descriptive and explanatory aim. It fits the integrated HPS approach outlined in section 1.2, and this in itself suffices to call it a philosophical study, as I have argued there. It transcends "mere" description of historical cases—if that were possible at all—and presents a general philosophical framework for the interpretation and explanation of historical episodes. In accordance with what Radder (1997, 649) identifies as the theoretical dimension of philosophy, my study reveals structural features that make sense of "non-local patterns" in the development of science. So, first of all, it should be emphasized that philosophy of science does not necessarily have to be normative in an explicit way, by offering rules or criteria for normative appraisal. But even though the normative dimension has not been the main focus of the study, it may be worthwhile to consider the question of whether my contextual theory of scientific understanding, in addition to its descriptive and explanatory aims, can serve as a basis for normative assessment of scientists' actions? The answer is: yes, it can, at least to a certain extent. In this final section of the book I will show how.

To answer this question, it is important to distinguish between two types of normativity, namely prescriptive and evaluative normativity. Prescriptive norms for understanding would supply rules that scientists should follow if they want to achieve scientific understanding of phenomena. Evaluative normative appraisal, by contrast, consists in assessing whether or not a particular scientific result (e.g., a model constructed to explain a particular phenomenon) does in fact provide genuine understanding. Evaluative norms do not immediately entail specific rules that can be applied to concrete practices.

Criterion CUP can be seen as implying a normative rule prescribing that scientists should construct explanations on the basis of intelligible theories in order to understand phenomena. Moreover, CUP refers to empirical adequacy and consistency as basic values that explanations should respect. However, a difficulty remains if one attempts to use CUP as a prescriptive norm. Since intelligibility is a contextual value, and accordingly no context-independent appraisal of the intelligibility of theories can be made, CUP does not offer scientists immediate concrete guidelines on which kinds of theories to use if they want to attain understanding of a phenomena. At most, it says that scientists should use intelligible theories, where the context determines when a theory is intelligible. So it might seem, at first sight, that contextualizing intelligibility reduces its normative import. What is more, it might be objected that my account runs the risk of trivializing the idea of intelligibility, as it implies that any theory can become intelligible if only one succeeds in learning to use it in a fruitful way. But does this make the notion of intelligibility vacuous? Not at all. It is true that the demand that theories be intelligible does not pose any universal, a priori restrictions on theories or theory choice, but it does entail that *in* a particular context certain theories are preferable over others. Thus, for most physicists in the 1920s wave mechanics was more intelligible than matrix mechanics, and that is why they preferred to work with Schrödinger's theory. But the fact that intelligibility is a contextual value also implies that no theory is intrinsically unintelligible.[7] Accordingly, with a change of context, matrix mechanics could become intelligible; and in a way it did: the theory of quantum mechanics—which combined matrix mechanics and wave mechanics—became intelligible for the general physics community in due course.

In sum, my theory does not provide concrete normative prescriptions in the sense that it recommends the use of specific types of theories (say, visualizable ones) because these would be inherently intelligible. However, my study does show that intelligibility is a crucial factor in science, where the context determines what the standards of intelligibility are. Thus, it can explain why theories with particular features are more successful in particular contexts. In this sense, it allows for normative evaluation of concrete scientific practices, and for the intelligibility of the theories employed in these practices. As has been argued in section 4.2, there are objective ways of testing whether or not theories are intelligible to scientists. Criterion CIT_1 was presented as one such test, which would be particularly suitable for the physical sciences. Accordingly, in a specific context there is the possibility of assessing whether a theory is intelligible to a scientist or a group of scientists, in other words, whether there is an appropriate combination of scientists' skills and theoretical properties. Thus, the normative content of my theory is of the evaluative kind, rather than of the prescriptive kind. On the basis of criteria such as CIT_1 one can assess whether or not a theory is intelligible to scientists. One might even turn prescriptive and adopt the policy that if theory T is more intelligible than theory T^* in context C, scientists in C should work with T. However, such a policy should never be turned into a rule. My theory of scientific

---

7. Of course, it may turn out that some theories are de facto unintelligible; for example, because they are too complex to be comprehended by the human mind.

understanding does not forbid scientists to work with unintelligible theories. The case of Schrödinger versus Pauli does not imply that scientists are not allowed to work on prima facie unintelligible theories, or should be discouraged to do so. On the contrary: sometimes progress can only be made by confronting the unintelligible. In such situations, new tools for understanding have to be developed.

Finally, some readers steeped in the traditional conception of philosophy of science might observe that my theory of understanding focuses mainly on the process of constructing scientific explanations, rather than on the evaluation of such explanations, and they might object that I have accordingly neglected the crucial normative dimension of science that is allegedly restricted to the latter process. However, as I have emphasized repeatedly in chapter 2, not only the construction but also the evaluation of explanations requires skills and judgment, hence intelligibility is a requirement that not only plays a role in the context of discovery but also in the context of justification. Still, proponents of the context distinction in its traditional form might demur that my analysis of such evaluations does not pertain to the "true" context of justification because it is concerned with describing and explaining the (historical) practice of science, and not with assessing how understanding of the phenomena can be achieved on the basis of criteria that transcend this practice (see Hoyningen-Huene 1987). As the case studies in the present book amply demonstrate, a search for such universal criteria for understanding is bound to fail. Accordingly, if normative philosophy of science is understood in the traditional sense, it will neither enhance our understanding of what real science is about, nor help practicing scientists in the quest for scientific understanding of the world. Philosophy of science should take the history and practice of science seriously, and should accordingly acknowledge the contextual nature of scientific understanding. As the physicist and philosopher Carl Friedrich von Weiszäcker observed:

> One should remember that with the historical development of science the structure of human thinking also changes. Scientific progress does not only consist in our discovering and understanding of new facts, but also in that, again and again, we learn new possible meanings of the word "understanding" itself.[8]

---

8. Carl Friedrich von Weiszäcker, discussing quantum mechanics and Kantian philosophy with Grete Hermann and Werner Heisenberg (1930–1932), recorded by Heisenberg in (1969, 173); my translation.

Bibliography

Aber, John D. 1997. "Why don't we believe the models?" *Bulletin of the Ecological Society of America* 78:232–233.

Achinstein, Peter. 1983. *The Nature of Explanation.* New York: Oxford University Press.

Allchin, Douglas. 1997. "Rekindling phlogiston: From classroom case study to interdisciplinary relationships." *Science and Education* 6:473–509.

Ambaum, Maarten H. P. 1997. "Large-scale dynamics of the tropopause." PhD dissertation, Technical University Eindhoven.

Avigad, Jeremy. 2008. "Understanding proofs". In *The Philosophy of Mathematical Practice*, edited by P. Mancosu, 317–353. Oxford: Oxford University Press.

Bailer-Jones, Daniela M. 2003. "When scientific models represent." *International Studies in the Philosophy of Science* 17:59–74.

Bailer-Jones, Daniela M. 2009. *Scientific Models in Philosophy of Science.* Pittsburgh: University of Pittsburgh Press.

Barnes, Eric. 1992. "Explanatory unification and scientific understanding." In *Philosophy of Science Association*, edited by D. Hull, M. Forbes, and K. Okruhlik, 3–12. East Lansing, MI: PSA.

Baumberger, Christoph, Claus Beisbart, and Georg Brun. 2017. "What is understanding? An overview of recent debates in epistemology and philosophy of science." In *Explaining Understanding: New Perspectives from Epistemology and Philosophy of Science*, edited by S. Grimm, C. Baumberger, and S. Ammon, 1–34. New York: Routledge.

Baumgartner, Michael. 2009. "Interdefining causation and intervention." *Dialectica* 63:175–194.

Bechtel, William. 2008. "Mechanisms in cognitive psychology: What are the operations?" *Philosophy of Science* 75:983–994.

Bechtel, William, and Adele Abrahamsen. 2005. "Explanation: A mechanist alternative." *Studies in History and Philosophy of Biological and Biomedical Sciences* 36:421–442.

Beller, Mara. 1999. *Quantum Dialogue: The Making of a Revolution.* Chicago: University of Chicago Press.

Berger, Ruth. 1998. "Understanding science: Why causes are not enough." *Philosophy of Science* 65:306–332.

Blackmore, John. 1995. *Ludwig Boltzmann: His Later Life and Philosophy, 1900–1906.* Book Two: *The Philosopher.* Dordrecht: Kluwer Academic Publishers.

Bohm, David, and Basil J. Hiley. 1993. *The Undivided Universe: An Ontological Interpretation of Quantum Theory.* London: Routledge.

Bohr, Niels. 1934. *Atomic Theory and the Description of Nature.* Cambridge: Cambridge University Press.

Bohr, Niels. 1976. *Collected Works.* Amsterdam: North-Holland.

Boltzmann, Ludwig. 1964. *Lectures on Gas Theory.* Translated by Stephen G. Brush. Berkeley: University of California Press.

Boltzmann, Ludwig. 1968. *Wissenschaftliche Abhandlungen.* Edited by F. Hasenöhrl. New York: Chelsea.

Boltzmann, Ludwig. 1974. *Theoretical Physics and Philosophical Problems.* Edited by B. McGuinness, translated by P. Foulkes. Dordrecht: Reidel.

Boltzmann, Ludwig. 1979. *Populäre Schriften.* Edited by E. Broda. Braunschweig: Vieweg.

Boltzmann, Ludwig. 1982. *Vorlesungen über Maxwells Theorie der Elektricität und des Lichtes. Ludwig Boltzmann Gesamtausgabe.* Vol. 2, edited by R. U. Sexl. Graz: Akademische Druck-und Verlagsanstalt.

Boyd, Richard. 1984. "The current status of scientific realism." In *Scientific Realism,* edited by J. Leplin, 41–82. Berkeley: University of California Press.

Bridgman, Percy W. 1950. *Reflections of a Physicist.* New York: Philosophical Library.

Brown, Harold I. 1988. *Rationality.* London: Routledge.

Brown, Harold I. 2000. "Judgment, role in science." In *A Companion to the Philosophy of Science,* edited by W. H. Newton-Smith, 194–202. Oxford: Blackwell.

Brush, Stephen G. 1965. *Kinetic Theory.* Vol. 1, *The Nature of Gases and Heat.* Oxford: Pergamon.

Brush, Stephen G. 1976. *The Kind of Motion We Call Heat: A History of the Kinetic Theory of Gases in the 19th Century.* Amsterdam: North-Holland.

Buchdahl, Gerd. 1970. "Gravity and intelligibility: Newton to Kant." In *The Methodological Heritage of Newton,* edited by R. E. Butts and J. W. Davis, 74–102. Oxford: Blackwell.

Camilleri, Kristian. 2009. *Heisenberg and the Interpretation of Quantum Mechanics.* Cambridge: Cambridge University Press.

Cartwright, Nancy. 1983. *How the Laws of Physics Lie.* Oxford: Clarendon Press.

Cartwright, Nancy, Towfic Shomar, and Mauricio Suárez. 1995. "The tool box of science." In *Theories and Models in Scientific Processes,* edited by W. Herfel, W. Krajewski, I. Niiniluoto, and R. Wojcicki, 137–149. Amsterdam: Rodopi.

Cat, Jordi. 1998. "The physicists' debates on unification in physics at the end of the 20th century." *Historical Studies in the Physical and Biological Sciences* 28:253–299.

Chakravartty, Anjan. 2007. *A Metaphysics for Scientific Realism.* Cambridge: Cambridge University Press.

Chalmers, Alan F. 1973. "Maxwell's methodology and his application of it to electromagnetism." *Studies in History and Philosophy of Science* 4:107–164.

Chalmers, Alan F. 2001. "Maxwell, mechanism, and the nature of electricity." *Physics in Perspective* 3:425–438.

Chang, Hasok. 2010. "The hidden history of phlogiston." *Hyle* 16:47–79.

Chang, Hasok. 2012. "Beyond case studies: History as philosophy." In *Integrating History and Philosophy of Science*, edited by S. Mauskopf and T. Schmaltz, 109–124. Dordrecht: Springer.

Clements, Wendy A., and Josef Perner. 1994. "Implicit understanding of belief." *Cognitive Development* 9:377–395.

Clements, Wendy A., Charlotte L. Rustin, and Sarah McCallum. 2000. "Promoting the transition from implicit to explicit understanding: A training study of false belief." *Developmental Science* 3:81–92.

Cohen, I. Bernard. 1980. *The Newtonian Revolution: With Illustrations of the Transformation of Scientific Ideas.* Cambridge: Cambridge University Press.

Cohen, I. Bernard. 1999. "A guide to Newton's Principia." In *Isaac Newton—The Principia—A New Translation and Guide*, edited by I. B. Cohen, 1–370. Berkeley: University of California Press.

Cohen, I. Bernard. 2002. "Newton's concepts of force and mass, with notes on the laws of motion." In *The Cambridge Companion to Newton*, edited by I. B. Cohen and G. E. Smith, 57–84. Cambridge: Cambridge University Press.

Cohen, I. Bernard, and George E. Smith, eds. 2002. *The Cambridge Companion to Newton.* Cambridge: Cambridge University Press.

Collins, Harry. 2010. *Tacit and Explicit Knowledge.* Chicago: University of Chicago Press.

Colyvan, Mark. 2008. "The ontological commitments of inconsistent theories." *Philosophical Studies* 141:115–123.

Cordero, Alberto. 1992. "Intelligibility and quantum theory." In *Idealization IV: Intelligibility in Science*, edited by C. Dilworth, 175–215. Amsterdam: Rodopi.

Craver, Carl F. 2001. "Role functions, mechanisms, and hierarchy." *Philosophy of Science* 68:53–74.

Craver, Carl F. 2007. *Explaining the Brain: Mechanisms and the Mosaic Unity of Neuroscience.* Oxford: Clarendon Press.

Cummins, Robert. 1975. "Functional analysis." *Journal of Philosophy* 72:741–756.

Cushing, James T. 1994. *Quantum Mechanics: Historical Contingency and the Copenhagen Hegemony.* Chicago: University of Chicago Press.

D'Agostino, Salvo. 1990. "Boltzmann and Hertz on the *Bild*-conception of physical theory." *History of Science* 28:380–398.

Dale, Virginia H., and Webster Van Winkle. 1998. "Models provide understanding, not belief." *Bulletin of the Ecological Society of America* 79:169–170.

Darden, Lindley. 2008. "Mechanisms: Beyond biology to psychology and chemistry." *Philosophy of Science* 75:958–969.

Darwin, Charles G. 1931. *The New Conceptions of Matter*. London: G. Bell and Sons.

Dear, Peter. 2006. *The Intelligibility of Nature: How Science Makes Sense of the World*. Chicago: University of Chicago Press.

Dembski, William A. 2004. *The Design Revolution: Answering the Toughest Questions about Intelligent Design*. Downers Grove, IL: InterVarsity Press.

De Regt, Henk W. 1996. "Philosophy and the kinetic theory of gases." *British Journal for the Philosophy of Science* 47:31–62.

De Regt, Henk W. 1997. "Erwin Schrödinger, *Anschaulichkeit*, and quantum theory." *Studies in History and Philosophy of Modern Physics* 28:461–482.

De Regt, Henk W. 1999a. "Ludwig Boltzmann's *Bildtheorie* and scientific understanding." *Synthese* 119:113–134.

De Regt, Henk W. 1999b. "Pauli versus Heisenberg: A case study of the heuristic role of philosophy." *Foundations of Science* 4:405–426.

De Regt, Henk W. 2001. "Spacetime visualisation and the intelligibility of physical theories." *Studies in History and Philosophy of Modern Physics* 32:243–266.

De Regt, Henk W. 2004a. "Discussion note: Making sense of understanding." *Philosophy of Science* 71:98–109.

De Regt, Henk W. 2004b. Review of James Woodward, *Making Things Happen*. *Notre Dame Philosophy Reviews*, http://ndpr.nd.edu/news/23818/?id=1455.

De Regt, Henk W. 2013. "Understanding and explanation: Living apart together?" *Studies in History and Philosophy of Science A* 44:505–509.

De Regt, Henk W. 2015. "Scientific understanding: Truth or dare?" *Synthese* 192:3781–3797.

De Regt, Henk W., and Dennis Dieks. 2005. "A contextual approach to scientific understanding." *Synthese* 144:137–170.

De Regt, Henk W., and Victor Gijsbers. 2017. "How false theories can yield genuine understanding." In *Explaining Understanding: New Perspectives from Epistemology and Philosophy of Science*, edited by S. R. Grimm, C. Baumberger, and S. Ammon, 50–75. London: Routledge.

De Regt, Henk W., Sabina Leonelli, and Kai Eigner. 2009. *Scientific Understanding: Philosophical Perspectives*. Pittsburgh: University of Pittsburgh Press.

Descartes, René. (1637) 1985. "Discourse on the Method." Translated by John Cottingham, Robert Stoothoff, and Dugald Murdoch. In *The Philosophical Writings of Descartes*, 109–151. Cambridge: Cambridge University Press.

Dieks, Dennis. 2001. "Space and time in particle and field physics." *Studies in History and Philosophy of Modern Physics* 32B:217–241.

Dieks, Dennis. 2009. "Understanding in physics: Bottom-up versus top-down." In *Scientific Understanding: Philosophical Perspectives*, edited by H. W. de Regt, S. Leonelli, and K. Eigner, 230–248. Pittsburgh: University of Pittsburgh Press.

Dijksterhuis, Eduard J. 1950. *De Mechanisering van het Wereldbeeld*. Amsterdam: Meulenhoff.

Dijksterhuis, Eduard J. (1955) 1990. "Ad quanta intelligenda condita (Designed for grasping quantities)." Translated by H. Floris Cohen. *Tractrix* 2:111–125.

Dijksterhuis, Fokko Jan. 2004. *Lenses and Waves: Christiaan Huygens and the Mathematical Science of Optics in the Seventeenth Century*. Dordrecht: Kluwer.

Dobbs, Betty Jo. 1991. *The Janus Faces of Genius: The Role of Alchemy in Newton's Thought*. Cambridge: Cambridge University Press.

Douglas, Heather E. 2004. "The irreducible complexity of objectivity." *Synthese* 138:453–473.

Douglas, Heather E. 2009a. "Reintroducing prediction to explanation." *Philosophy of Science* 76:444–463.

Douglas, Heather E. 2009b. *Science, Policy, and the Value-Free Ideal*. Pittsburgh: University of Pittsburgh Press.

Dowe, Phil. 1992. "Wesley Salmon's process theory of causality and the conserved quantity theory." *Philosophy of Science* 59:195–216.

Dowe, Phil. 2000. *Physical Causation*. Cambridge: Cambridge University Press.

Dresden, Max. 1987. *H. A. Kramers: Between Tradition and Revolution*. New York: Springer Verlag.

Ducheyne, Steffen. 2009. "Understanding (in) Newton's argument for universal gravitation." *Journal for General Philosophy of Science* 40:227–258.

Ducheyne, Steffen. 2011. "Newton on action at a distance and the cause of gravity." *Studies in History and Philosophy of Science A* 42:154–159.

Duhem, Pierre. 1954. *The Aim and Structure of Physical Theory*. Translated by Philip P. Wiener. Princeton, NJ: Princeton University Press.

Eddington, Arthur. 1920. *Space, Time and Gravitation*. Cambridge: Cambridge University Press.

Eigner, Kai. 2009. "Understanding in psychology: Is understanding a surplus?" In *Scientific Understanding: Philosophical Perspectives*, edited by H. W. de Regt, S. Leonelli, and K. Eigner, 271–297. Pittsburgh: University of Pittsburgh Press.

Eigner, Kai. 2010. "Understanding psychologists' understanding: the application of intelligible models to phenomena." PhD dissertation, VU University Amsterdam.

Elgin, Catherine Z. 1996. *Considered Judgment*. Princeton, NJ: Princeton University Press.

Elgin, Catherine Z. 2010. Review of De Regt, Leonelli, and Eigner, eds., *Scientific Understanding: Philosophical Perspectives*. *Notre Dame Philosophy Reviews*, http://ndpr.nd.edu/news/24266-scientific-understanding-philosophical-perspectives/.

Fasol-Boltzmann, Ilse, ed. 1990. *Boltzmann's Principien der Naturfilosofi: Lectures on Natural Philosophy, 1903–1906*. Berlin: Springer.

Favrholdt, David. 1992. *Niels Bohr's Philosophical Background.* Copenhagen: Munksgaard.

Faye, Jan. 2007. "The pragmatic-rhetorical theory of explanation." In *Rethinking Explanation*, edited by J. Persson and P. Ylikoski, 43–68. Dordrecht: Springer.

Faye, Jan. 2014. *The Nature of Scientific Thinking: On Interpretation, Explanation, and Understanding*. London: Palgrave MacMillan.

Feynman, Richard P. 1949. "Space-time approach to quantum electrodynamics." *Physical Review* 76:769–789.

Feynman, Richard P. (1965) 1992. *The Character of Physical Law.* London: Penguin Books.

Feynman, Richard P., Robert B. Leighton, and Matthew Sands. 1963–1965. *The Feynman Lectures on Physics*. Reading, MA: Addison-Wesley.

Frank, Philipp. 1957. *Philosophy of Science: The Link between Science and Philosophy*. Englewood Cliffs, NJ: Prentice-Hall.

Friedman, Michael. 1974. "Explanation and scientific understanding." *Journal of Philosophy* 71:5–19.

Friedman, Michael. 1992. *Kant and the Exact Sciences*. Cambridge, MA: Harvard University Press.

Friedman, Michael. 2001. *Dynamics of Reason*. Stanford, CA: CSLI Publications.

Frisch, Matthias. 2005. *Inconsistency, Asymmetry and Nonlocality: A Philosophical Investigation of Classical Electrodynamics*. New York: Oxford University Press.

Frisch, Matthias. 2014. "Models and scientific representations or: Who is afraid of inconsistency?" *Synthese* 191:3027–3040.

Gabbey, Alan. 2002. "Newton, active powers and the mechanical philosophy." In *The Cambridge Companion to Newton*, edited by I. B. Cohen and G. E. Smith, 329–357. Cambridge: Cambridge University Press.

Garfinkel, Alan. 1981. *Forms of Explanation*. New Haven, CT: Yale University Press.

Giere, Ronald N. 1999. *Science without Laws*. Chicago: University of Chicago Press.

Giere, Ronald N. 2004. "How models are used to represent reality." *Philosophy of Science* 71:742–752.

Giere, Ronald N. 2006. *Scientific Perspectivism*. Chicago: University of Chicago Press.

Gigerenzer, Gerd. 2007. *Gut Feelings: The Intelligence of the Unconscious.* London: Penguin Books.

Gijsbers, Victor. 2007. "Why unification is neither necessary nor sufficient for explanation." *Philosophy of Science* 74:481–500.

Gingras, Yves. 2001. "What did mathematics do to physics?" *History of Science* 39:383–416.

Glennan, Stuart. 2002. "Rethinking mechanistic explanation." *Philosophy of Science* 69:S342–S353.

Gopnik, Alison. 2000. "Explanation as orgasm and the drive for causal knowledge: The function, evolution, and phenomenology of the theory formation system." In *Explanation and Cognition*, edited by F. C. Keil and R. A. Wilson, 299–324. Cambridge, MA: MIT Press.

Grimm, Stephen R. 2009. "Reliability and the sense of understanding." In *Scientific Understanding: Philosophical Perspectives*, edited by H. W. de Regt, S. Leonelli, and K. Eigner, 83–99. Pittsburgh: University of Pittsburgh Press.

Hacking, Ian. 1983. *Representing and Intervening*. Cambridge: Cambridge University Press.

Halonen, Ilpo, and Jaakko Hintikka. 1999. "Unification—it's magnificent but is it explanation?" *Synthese* 120:27–47.

Hankins, Thomas L. 1985. *Science and the Enlightenment*. Cambridge: Cambridge University Press.

Harman, Peter M. 1982. *Energy, Force and Matter: The Conceptual Development of Nineteenth Century Physics*. Cambridge: Cambridge University Press.

Harman, Peter M. 1998. *The Natural Philosophy of James Clerk Maxwell*. Cambridge: Cambridge University Press.

Harper, William. 2002. "Newton's argument for universal gravitation." In *The Cambridge Companion to Newton*, edited by I. B. Cohen and G. E. Smith, 174–201. Cambridge: Cambridge University Press.

Harper, William. 2012. *Isaac Newton's Scientific Method: Turning Data into Evidence about Gravity and Cosmology*. Oxford: Oxford University Press.

Hartmann, Stephan. 1999. "Models and stories in hadron physics." In *Models as Mediators*, edited by M. S. Morgan and M. Morrison, 326–346. Cambridge: Cambridge University Press.

Heilbron, John L. 1979. *Electricity in the 17th and 18th Centuries: A Study of Early Modern Physics*. Berkeley: University of California Press.

Heisenberg, Werner. 1927. "Über den anschaulichen Inhalt der quantentheoretischen Kinematik und Mechanik." *Zeitschrift für Physik* 43:172–198.

Heisenberg, Werner. 1967. "Quantum theory and its interpretation." In *Niels Bohr as Seen by his Friends and Colleagues*, edited by S. Rozental, 94–108. Amsterdam: North Holland.

Heisenberg, Werner. 1969. *Der Teil und das Ganze: Gespräche im Umkreis der Atomphysik*. Munich: R. Piper & Co. Verlag.

Helmholtz, Hermann von. (1847) 1971. "On the conservation of force: A physical memoir." In *Selected Writings of Hermann von Helmholtz*, edited by R. Kahl, 3–55. Middletown, CT: Wesleyan University Press.

Helmholtz, Hermann von. 1876. "The origin and meaning of geometrical axioms." *Mind* 1:301–321.

Hempel, Carl G. 1965. *Aspects of Scientific Explanation and Other Essays in the Philosophy of Science*. New York: Free Press.

Hempel, Carl G. 1966. *Philosophy of Natural Science*. Prentice-Hall Foundations of Philosophy Series. Englewood Cliffs, NJ: Prentice-Hall.

Hempel, Carl G. (1983) 2001. "Valuation and objectivity in science." In *The Philosophy of Carl G. Hempel*, edited by J. H. Fetzer, 372–396. New York: Oxford University Press.

Henry, John. 2011. "Gravity and *De Gravitatione*: The development of Newton's ideas on action at a distance." *Studies in History and Philosophy of Science A* 42:11–27.

Hertz, Heinrich. 1893. *Electric Waves*. London: MacMillan.

Hiebert, Erwin N. 1981. "Boltzmann's conception of theory construction: The promotion of pluralism, provisionalism, and pragmatic realism." In *Probabilistic Thinking, Thermodynamics and the Interaction of the History and Philosophy of Science*, edited by J. Hintikka, D. Gruender, and E. Agazzi, 175–198. Dordrecht: Reidel.

Hofer-Szabó, Gabor, Miklos Rédei, and Laszlo E. Szabó. 1999. "On Reichenbach's common cause principle and Reichenbach's notion of common cause." *British Journal for the Philosophy of Science* 50:377–399.

Holland, Peter R. 1993. *The Quantum Theory of Motion*. Cambridge: Cambridge University Press.

Hoyningen-Huene, Paul. 1987. "Context of discovery and context of justification." *Studies in History and Philosophy of Science* 18:501–515.

Humphreys, Paul. 1993. "Greater unification equals greater understanding?" *Analysis* 53: 183–188.

Humphreys, Paul. 2000. "Analytic versus synthetic understanding." In *Science, Explanation and Rationality: The Philosophy of Carl G. Hempel*, edited by J. H. Fetzer, 267–286. New York: Oxford University Press.

Humphreys, Paul. 2004. *Extending Ourselves: Computational Science, Empiricism, and Scientific Method*. New York: Oxford University Press.

Huygens, Christiaan. (1690) 1912. *Treatise on Light*. Translated by S. P. Thompson. Chicago: University of Chicago Press.

Huygens, Christiaan. 1888–1952. *Oeuvres Complètes*. 22 vols. The Hague: Martinus Nijhoff.

IPCC. 2012. *Climate Change 2007—The Physical Science Basis, Working Group I Contribution to the Fourth Assessment Report of the IPCC*. Cambridge: Cambridge University Press.

James, William. 1907. *Pragmatism, a New Name for Some Old Ways of Thinking: Popular Lectures on Philosophy*. New York: Longmans Green.

Janiak, Andrew. 2013. "Three concepts of causation in Newton." *Studies in History and Philosophy of Science A* 44:396–407.

Jones, Jan-Erik. 2012. "Explaining how: The intelligibility of mechanical explanations in Boyle." *Philosophy Study* 2:337–346.

Jones, Todd. 1997. "Unification, reduction, and non-ideal explanations." *Synthese* 112:75–96.

Jung-Beeman, Mark, Edward M. Bowden, Jason Haberman, Jennifer L. Frymiare, Stella Arambel-Liu, Richard Greenblatt, Paul J. Reber, and John Kounios. 2004. "Neural activity when people solve verbal problems with insight." *PLoS Biology* 2: 500–510.

Jungnickel, Christa, and Russell McCormmach. 1986. *Intellectual Mastery of Nature.* 2 vols. Chicago: University of Chicago Press.

Kahneman, Daniel. 2011. *Thinking, Fast and Slow.* London: Allen Lane.

Kahneman, Daniel, and Gary Klein. 2009. "Conditions for intuitive expertise: A failure to disagree." *American Psychologist* 64: 515–526.

Kaiser, David. 2005. *Drawing Theories Apart: The Dispersion of Feynman Diagrams in Postwar Physics.* Chicago: University of Chicago Press.

Kant, Immanuel. (1783) 1997. *Prolegomena to Any Future Metaphysics.* Translated by Gary Hatfield. Cambridge: Cambridge University Press.

Kargon, Robert, and Peter Achinstein, eds. 1987. *Kelvin's Baltimore Lectures and Modern Theoretical Physics.* Cambridge, MA: MIT Press.

Keil, Frank. 2006. "Explanation and understanding." *Annual Review of Psychology* 57:227–254.

Kelp, Christoph, and Igor Douven. 2012. "Sustaining a rational disagreement." In *EPSA Philosophy of Science: Amsterdam 2009,* edited by H. W. de Regt, S. Hartmann, and S. Okasha, 101–110. Dordrecht: Springer.

Khalifa, Kareem. 2012. "Inaugurating understanding or repackaging explanation?" *Philosophy of Science* 79: 15–37.

Kitcher, Philip. 1981. "Explanatory unification." *Philosophy of Science* 48:507–531.

Kitcher, Philip. 1985. "Two approaches to explanation." *Journal of Philosophy* 82:632–639.

Kitcher, Philip. 1989. "Explanatory unification and the causal structure of the world." In *Scientific Explanation,* edited by P. Kitcher and W. C. Salmon, 410–505. Minneapolis: University of Minnesota Press.

Kitcher, Philip. 2001. *Science, Truth, and Democracy.* New York: Oxford University Press.

Kitcher, Philip. 2007. *Living with Darwin: Evolution, Design and the Future of Faith.* New York: Oxford University Press.

Kitcher, Philip, and Wesley C. Salmon. 1987. "Van Fraassen on explanation." *Journal of Philosophy* 84:315–330.

Klein, Martin J. 1972. "Mechanical explanation at the end of the nineteenth century." *Centaurus* 17:58–82.

Knuuttila, Tarja. 2005. "Models, representation and mediation." *Philosophy of Science* 72:1260–1271.

Knuuttila, Tarja. 2009. "Representation, idealization, and fiction in economics: From the assumptions issue to the epistemology of modeling." In *Fictions in Science*, edited by M. Suárez, 205–231. New York: Routledge.

Knuuttila, Tarja, and Martina Merz. 2009. "Understanding by modeling: An objectual approach." In *Scientific Understanding: Philosophical Perspectives*, edited by H. W. de Regt, S. Leonelli, and K. Eigner, 146–168. Pittsburgh: University of Pittsburgh Press.

Kochiras, Hylarie. 2011. "Gravity's cause and substance counting: Contextualizing the problems." *Studies in History and Philosophy of Science A* 42:167–184.

Koster, Edwin. 2009. "Understanding in historical science: Intelligibility and judgment." In *Scientific Understanding: Philosophical Perspectives*, edited by H. W. de Regt, S. Leonelli, and K. Eigner, 314–333. Pittsburgh: University of Pittsburgh Press.

Koyré, Alexandre. 1965. *Newtonian Studies* London: Chapman & Hall.

Kramers, Hendrik A., and Helge Holst. 1923. *The Atom and the Bohr Theory of Its Structure*. London: Gyldendal.

Kronig, Ralph. 1960. "The Turning Point." In *Theoretical Physics in the Twentieth Century: A Memorial Volume to Wolfgang Pauli*, edited by M. Fierz and V. F. Weisskopf, 5–39. New York: Wiley.

Kuhn, Thomas S. 1970. *The Structure of Scientific Revolutions*. 2nd ed. Chicago: University of Chicago Press.

Kuhn, Thomas S. 1977. "Objectivity, value judgment, and theory choice." In *The Essential Tension*, 320–339. Chicago: University of Chicago Press.

Lacey, Hugh. 1999. *Is Science Value Free? Values and Scientific Understanding*. London: Routledge.

Laudan, Larry. 1981. "A confutation of convergent realism." *Philosophy of Science* 48:19–49.

Laudan, Larry. 1984. *Science and Values*. Berkeley: University of California Press.

Laudan, Larry 1990. "Normative naturalism." *Philosophy of Science* 57:44–59.

Lear, Jonathan. 1988. *The Desire to Understand*. Cambridge: Cambridge University Press.

Lehtinen, Aki, and Jaakko Kuorikoski. 2007. "Computing the perfect model: Why do economists shun simulation?" *Philosophy of Science* 74:304–329.

Leibniz, Gottfried W., and Samuel Clarke. (1717) 2000. *Correspondence*. Indianapolis, IN: Hackett.

Lenhard, Johannes. 2006. "Surprised by a nanowire: Simulation, control, and understanding." *Philosophy of Science* 73:605–616.

Leonelli, Sabina. 2009. "Understanding in biology: The impure nature of biological knowledge." In *Scientific Understanding: Philosophical Perspectives*, edited by

H. W. de Regt, S. Leonelli, and K. Eigner, 189–209. Pittsburgh: University of Pittsburgh Press.

Leslie, John. 1824. "Observations on electrical theories." *Edinburgh Philosophical Journal* 11:1–39.

Lipton, Peter. 2004. *Inference to the Best Explanation.* 2nd ed. London: Routledge.

Lipton, Peter. 2009. "Understanding without explanation." In *Scientific Understanding: Philosophical Perspectives*, edited by H. W. de Regt, S. Leonelli, and K. Eigner, 43–63. Pittsburgh: University of Pittsburgh Press.

Longino, Helen E. 1990. *Science as Social Knowledge: Values and Objectivity in Scientific Inquiry.* Princeton, NJ: Princeton University Press.

Mach, Ernst. (1872) 1911. *History and Root of the Principle of the Conservation of Energy.* Translated by Philip Jourdain. Chicago: Open Court.

Mach, Ernst. (1883) 1960. *The Science of Mechanics: A Critical and Historical Exposition of Its Principles* Translated by Thomas J. McCormack. LaSalle, IL: Open Court.

Machamer, Peter K., Lindley Darden, and Carl F. Craver. 2000. "Thinking about mechanisms." *Philosophy of Science* 67: 1–25.

MacKinnon, Edward M. 1982. *Scientific Explanation and Atomic Physics.* Chicago: Chicago University Press.

Mäki, Uskali. 2001. "Explanatory unification: Double and doubtful." *Philosophy of the Social Sciences* 31:488–506.

Marchionni, Caterina. 2008. "Explanatory pluralism and complementarity: From autonomy to integration." *Philosophy of the Social Sciences* 38:314–333.

Mathewson, James H. 1999. "Visual-spatial thinking: An aspect of science overlooked by educators." *Science and Education* 83:33–54.

Mattuck, Richard. 1976. *A Guide to Feynman Diagrams in the Many-Body Problem.* 2nd ed. New York: Dover.

Mauskopf, Seymour, and Tad Schmaltz, eds. 2012. *Integrating History and Philosophy of Science.* Dordrecht: Springer.

Maxwell, James Clerk. (1873) 1954. *A Treatise on Electricity and Magnetism.* 2 vols. New York: Dover.

Maxwell, James Clerk. 1877. "The kinetic theory of gases." *Nature* 16:242–246.

Maxwell, James Clerk. 1965. *Scientific Papers.* 2 vols. Edited by W. D. Niven. New York: Dover.

Maxwell, James Clerk. 1986. *Maxwell on Molecules and Gases.* Edited by E. Garber, S. G. Brush, and C. W. F. Everitt. Cambridge, MA: MIT Press.

McAllister, James W. 1996. *Beauty and Revolution in Science.* Ithaca, NY: Cornell University Press.

McMullin, Ernan. 1983. "Values in science." In *PSA 1982*, edited by P. D. Asquith and T. Nickles, 3–28. East Lansing, MI: Philosophy of Science Association.

Meheus, Joke, ed. 2002. *Inconsistency in Science.* Dordrecht: Kluwer.

Miller, Arthur I. 1986. *Imagery in Scientific Thought.* Cambridge, MA: MIT Press.

Morgan, Mary S., and Margaret Morrison, eds. 1999. *Models as Mediators: Perspectives on Natural and Social Science*. Cambridge: Cambridge University Press.

Morrison, Margaret. 1999. "Models as autonomous agents." In *Models as Mediators*, edited by M. S. Morgan and M. Morrison, 38–65. Cambridge: Cambridge University Press.

Morrison, Margaret. 2000. *Unifying Scientific Theories: Physical Concepts and Mathematical Structures*. Cambridge: Cambridge University Press.

Morrison, Margaret. 2007. "Where have all the theories gone?" *Philosophy of Science* 74:195–228.

Morrison, Margaret. 2009. "Understanding in physics and biology: From the abstract to the concrete." In *Scientific Understanding: Philosophical Perspectives*, edited by H. W. de Regt, S. Leonelli, and K. Eigner, 123–145. Pittsburgh: University of Pittsburgh Press.

Morrison, Margaret. 2015. *Reconstructing Reality: Models, Mathematics, and Simulations*. New York: Oxford University Press.

Murdoch, Dugald. 1987. *Niels Bohr's Philosophy of Physics*. Cambridge: Cambridge University Press.

Musgrave, Alan. 1985. "Realism versus constructive empiricism." In *Images of Science*, edited by P. M. Churchland and C. A. Hooker, 197–221. Chicago: University of Chicago Press.

Netz, Paulo A., Sergey V. Buldyrev, Marcia C. Barbosa, and H. Eugene Stanley. 2006. "Thermodynamic and dynamic anomalies for dumbbell molecules interacting with a repulsive ramplike potential." *Physical Review E* 73:061504.

Newton, Isaac. 1931. *Opticks*. Reprint of the 4th ed. London: G. Bell & Sons.

Newton, Isaac. 1959–1977. *Correspondence*. Edited by W. Turnbull. Cambridge: Cambridge University Press.

Newton, Isaac. 1999. *The Principia: Mathematical Principles of Natural Philosophy*. Translation of the 3rd ed. by I. B. Cohen and Anne Whitman. Berkeley: University of California Press.

Newton, Isaac. 2004. *Philosophical Writings*. Cambridge: Cambridge University Press.

Norton, John D. 2012. "Approximation and idealization: Why the difference matters." *Philosophy of Science* 79:207–232.

Olson, Richard. 1975. *Scottish Philosophy and British Physics, 1750–1880*. Princeton, NJ: Princeton University Press.

Pais, Abraham. 1986. *Inward Bound: Of Matter and Forces in the Physical World*. New York: Oxford University Press.

Panofsky, Wolfgang K. H., and Melba Philips. 1969. *Classical Electricity and Magnetism*. Reading, MA: Addison-Wesley.

Parker, Wendy S. 2014. "Simulation and understanding in the study of weather and climate." *Perspectives on Science* 22:336–356.

Partridge, Derek. 1991. *A New Guide to Artificial Intelligence*. Norwood, NJ: Ablex.

Pauli, Wolfgang. 1964. *Collected Scientific Papers.* Edited by R. Kronig and V. F. Weisskopf. New York: Interscience Publishers.

Pauli, Wolfgang. 1979. *Wissenschaftlicher Briefwechsel.* Vol. 1, *1919–1929.* New York: Springer-Verlag.

Peirce, Charles S. 1878. "How to make our ideas clear." *Popular Science Monthly* 12:286–302.

Perkins, Donald H. 1982. *Introduction to High Energy Physics.* 2nd ed. Reading, MA: Addison-Wesley.

Persson, Johannes. 2009. "Three conceptions of explaining how possibly—and one reductive account." In *EPSA Philosophy of Science: Amsterdam 2009,* edited by H. W. de Regt, S. Hartmann, and S. Okasha, 275–286. Dordrecht: Springer.

Petersen, Arthur C. 2012. *Simulating Nature.* 2nd ed. Boca Raton, FL: CRC Press.

Pitt, Joseph C. 2001. "The dilemma of case studies: Toward a Heraclitian philosophy of science." *Perspectives on Science* 9:373–382.

Popper, Karl R. 1972. *Objective Knowledge.* Oxford: Clarendon Press.

Psillos, Stathis. 2002. *Causation and Explanation.* Chesham, UK: Acumen.

Putnam, Hilary. 1978. *Meaning and the Moral Sciences.* London: Routledge & Kegan Paul.

Quine, Willard V. O. 1992. *The Pursuit of Truth.* Cambridge, MA: Harvard University Press.

Radder, Hans. 1991. "Heuristics and the generalized correspondence principle." *British Journal for the Philosophy of Science* 42:195–226.

Radder, Hans. 1996. *In and about the World.* New York: SUNY Press.

Radder, Hans. 1997. "Philosophy and history of science: Beyond the Kuhnian paradigm." *Studies in History and Philosophy of Science A* 28:633–655.

Radder, Hans, ed. 2003a. *The Philosophy of Scientific Experimentation.* Pittsburgh: University of Pittsburgh Press.

Radder, Hans. 2003b. "Technology and theory in experimental science." In *The Philosophy of Scientific Experimentation,* edited by H. Radder, 152–173. Pittsburgh: University of Pittsburgh Press.

Railton, Peter. 1978. "A deductive-nomological model of probabilistic explanation." *Philosophy of Science* 45:206–226.

Railton, Peter. 1981. "Probability, explanation and information." *Synthese* 48:233–256.

Ramsey, Jeffry L. 2008. "Mechanisms and their explanatory challenges in organic chemistry." *Philosophy of Science* 75:970–982.

Reber, Arthur S. 1993. *Implicit Learning and Tacit Knowledge: An Essay on the Cognitive Unconscious.* New York: Oxford University Press.

Resnik, David. 1991. "How-possibly explanations in biology." *Acta Biotheoretica* 49:141–149.

Rouse, Joseph. 2003. "Kuhn's philosophy of scientific practice." In *Thomas Kuhn,* edited by T. Nickles, 101–121. Cambridge: Cambridge University Press.

286   *Bibliography*

Ruben, David-Hillel. 1993. *Explanation*. Oxford: Oxford University Press.

Salmon, Wesley C. 1984. *Scientific Explanation and the Causal Structure of the World*. Princeton, NJ: Princeton University Press.

Salmon, Wesley C. 1985. "Conflicting conceptions of scientific explanation." *Journal of Philosophy* 82:651–654.

Salmon, Wesley C. 1990. *Four Decades of Scientific Explanation*. Minneapolis: University of Minnesota Press.

Salmon, Wesley C. 1998. *Causality and Explanation*. New York: Oxford University Press.

Schickore, Jutta. 2011. "More thoughts on HPS: Another 20 years later." *Perspectives on Science* 19:453–481.

Schrödinger, Erwin. 1928. *Collected Papers on Wave Mechanics*. London: Blackie & Son.

Schrödinger, Erwin. 1952. "Are there quantum jumps?" *British Journal for the Philosophy of Science* 3:109–123.

Schrödinger, Erwin. (1954) 1996. *Nature and the Greeks*. Cambridge: Cambridge University Press.

Schrödinger, Erwin. 1984. *Gesammelte Abhandlungen*. Vienna: Verlag der Österreichischen Akademie der Wissenschaften.

Schurz, Gerhard. 1999. "Explanation as unification." *Synthese* 120:95–114.

Schurz, Gerhard, and Karel Lambert. 1994. "Outline of a theory of scientific understanding." *Synthese* 101:65–120.

Schweber, Silvan S. 1994. *QED and the Men Who Made It: Dyson, Feynman, Schwinger, and Tomonaga*. Princeton, NJ: Princeton University Press.

Scriven, Michael. 1959. "Truisms as the ground of historical explanations." In *Theories of History: Readings from Classical and Contemporary Sources*, edited by P. Gardiner, 443–475. New York: Free Press.

Scriven, Michael. 1962. "Explanations, predictions, and laws." In *Scientific Explanation, Space, and Time*, edited by H. Feigl and G. Maxwell, 170–230. Minneapolis: University of Minnesota Press.

Serwer, Daniel. 1977. "*Unmechanischer Zwang*: Pauli, Heisenberg, and the rejection of the mechanical atom, 1923–1925." *Historical Studies in the Physical Sciences* 8:189–256.

Shanks, David R. 2005. "Implicit learning." In *Handbook of Cognition*, edited by K. Lamberts and R. Goldstone, 202–220. London: Sage.

Sintonen, Matti. 1999. "Why questions, and why just why-questions?" *Synthese* 120:125–135.

Skipper, Rob A. 1999. "Selection and the extent of explanatory unification." *Philosophy of Science* 66:S196–S209.

Smith, Crosbie, and M. Norton Wise. 1989. *Energy and Empire: A Biographical Study of Lord Kelvin*. Cambridge: Cambridge University Press.

Stein, Howard. 2002. "Newton's metaphysics." In *The Cambridge Companion to Newton*, edited by I. B. Cohen and G. E. Smith, 256–307. Cambridge: Cambridge University Press.

Strevens, Michael. 2004. "The causal and unification approaches to explanation unified—causally." *Noûs* 38:154–179.

Strevens, Michael. 2008. *Depth: An Account of Scientific Explanation*. Cambridge, MA: Harvard University Press.

Suárez, Mauricio. 1999. "The role of models in the application of scientific theories: Epistemological implications." In *Models as Mediators*, edited by M. S. Morgan and M. Morrison, 168–196. Cambridge: Cambridge University Press.

Suárez, Mauricio. 2004. "An inferential conception of scientific representation." *Philosophy of Science* 71:767–779.

Suárez, Mauricio, and Nancy Cartwright. 2008. "Theories: Tools versus models." *Studies in History and Philosophy of Modern Physics* 39:62–81.

Teller, Paul. 2009. "Fictions, fictionalization, and truth in science." In *Fictions in Science*, edited by M. Suárez, 235–247. New York: Routledge.

Titus, Sarah, and Eric Horsman. 2009. "Characterizing and improving spatial visualization skills." *Journal of Geoscience Education* 57:242–254.

Toulmin, Stephen. 1963. *Foresight and Understanding: An Enquiry into the Aims of Science*. New York: Harper and Row.

Trout, J. D. 2002. "Scientific explanation and the sense of understanding." *Philosophy of Science* 69:212–233.

Trout, J. D. 2005. "Paying the price for a theory of explanation: De Regt's discussion of Trout." *Philosophy of Science* 72:198–208.

Trout, J. D. 2007. "The psychology of scientific explanation." *Philosophy Compass* 2:564–591.

Uhlenbeck, George E., and Samuel Goudsmit. 1925. "Ersetzung der Hypothese vom unmechanischen Zwang durch eine Forderung bezüglich des inneren Verhaltens jedes einzelnen Elektrons." *Naturwissenschaften* 13:953–954.

Uhlenbeck, George E., and Samuel Goudsmit. 1926. "Spinning electrons and the structure of spectra." *Nature* 117:264–265.

van der Waerden, Bartel L., ed. 1960. "Exclusion principle and spin." In *Theoretical Physics in the Twentieth Century: A Memorial Volume to Wolfgang Pauli*, edited by M. Fierz and V. F. Weisskopf, 199–244. New York: Wiley.

van der Waerden, Bartel L., ed. 1967. *Sources of Quantum Mechanics*. New York: Dover.

van Fraassen, Bas C. 1980. *The Scientific Image*. Oxford: Clarendon Press.

van Fraassen, Bas C. 1991. *Quantum Mechanics: An Empiricist View*. Oxford: Clarendon Press.

van Fraassen, Bas C. 2008. *Scientific Representation: Paradoxes of Perspective*. Oxford: Oxford University Press.

van Lunteren, Frans H. 1991. "Framing hypotheses: conceptions of gravity in the 18th and 19th centuries." PhD dissertation, Utrecht University.

Vickers, Peter. 2013. *Understanding Inconsistent Science*. New York: Oxford University Press.

von Weizsäcker, Carl F. 1970. *Zum Weltbild der Physik*. Stuttgart: Hirzel.

von Wright, Georg H. 1971. *Explanation and Understanding*. Ithaca, NY: Cornell University Press.

Waskan, Jonathan, Ian Harmon, Zachary Horne, Joseph Spino, and John Clevenger. 2014. "Explanatory anti-psychologism overturned by lay and scientific case classifications." *Synthese* 191:1013–1035.

Watkins, Eric, ed. 2001. *Kant and the Sciences*. New York: Oxford University Press.

Watson, Henry W. 1876. *A Treatise on the Kinetic Theory of Gases*. Oxford: Clarendon Press.

Wayne, Andrew. 1996. "Theoretical unity: The case of the Standard Model." *Perspectives on Science* 4:391–407.

Weber, Erik. 1996. "Explanation, understanding and scientific theories." *Erkenntnis* 44:1–23.

Weber, Erik. 1999. "Unification: What is it, how do we reach it, and why do we want it?" *Synthese* 118:447–499.

Weber, Erik. 2012a. "Two problems for the contextual theory of scientific understanding." *The Reasoner* 6:60–62.

Weber, Erik. 2012b. "Two gaps in the contextual theory of scientific understanding." *The Reasoner* 6:130–131.

Weinberg, Steven. 1993. *Dreams of a Final Theory*. New York: Pantheon Books.

Westfall, Richard S. 1977. *The Construction of Modern Science: Mechanisms and Mechanics*. Cambridge: Cambridge University Press.

Westfall, Richard S. 1980. *Never at Rest: A Biography of Isaac Newton*. Cambridge: Cambridge University Press.

Westman, Robert S. 1980. "Huygens and the problem of Cartesianism." In *Studies on Christiaan Huygens*, edited by H. J. M. Bos, M. J. S. Rudwick, H. A. M. Snelders, and R. P. W. Visser, 83–103. Lisse: Swest & Zeitlinger.

Wheeler, John A., and Richard P. Feynman. 1945. "Interaction with the absorber as the mechanism of radiation." *Reviews of Modern Physics* 17:157–181.

Wilson, Andrew D. 1989. "Hertz, Boltzmann and Wittgenstein reconsidered." *Studies in History and Philosophy of Science* 20:245–263.

Wilson, Andrew D. 1993. "Boltzmann's philosophical education and its bearing on his mature scientific epistemology." In *Proceedings of the International Symposium on Ludwig Boltzmann*, edited by G. Battimelli, M. G. Ianniello, and O. Kresten, 57–69. Vienna: Verlag der Österreichischen Akademie der Wissenschaften.

Wimsatt, William. 1976. "Reductive explanation: A functional account." In *PSA 1974*, edited by R. S. Cohen, C. A. Hooker, A. C. Michalos, and G. Pearce, 671–710. Dordrecht: Reidel.

Wittgenstein, Ludwig. 1953. *Philosophical Investigations.* Oxford: Basil Blackwell.

Woodward, James. 2003a. "Experimentation, causal inference, and instrumental realism." In *The Philosophy of Scientific Experimentation*, edited by H. Radder, 87–118. Pittsburgh: University of Pittsburgh Press.

Woodward, James. 2003b. *Making Things Happen: A Theory of Causal Explanation.* Oxford: Oxford University Press.

Worrall, John. 2000. "The scope, limits, and distinctiveness of the method of 'deduction from the phenomena': Some lessons from Newton's 'demonstrations' in optics." *British Journal for the Philosophy of Science* 51:45–80.

Ylikoski, Petri. 2009. "The illusion of depth of understanding in science." In *Scientific Understanding: Philosophical Perspectives*, edited by H. W. de Regt, S. Leonelli, and K. Eigner, 100–119. Pittsburgh: University of Pittsburgh Press.

Index

Printed in the USA/Agawam, MA
November 22, 2017

663201.018